ILEX FOUNDATION SERIES 7

THE LAST OF THE REPHAIM

THE LAST OF THE REPHAIM

CONQUEST AND CATACLYSM IN THE HEROIC AGES OF ANCIENT ISRAEL

Brian R. Doak

Ilex Foundation
Boston, Massachusetts

Distributed by Harvard University Press
Cambridge, Massachusetts, and London, England

The Last of the Rephaim: Conquest and Cataclysm in the Heroic Ages of Ancient Israel
By Brian R. Doak

Brian R. Doak (Ph.D., Harvard University) is Professor of Biblical Studies at George Fox University

Published by Ilex Foundation, Boston, Massachusetts, 2012
Reprinted June, 2022

Distributed by Harvard University Press, Cambridge, Massachusetts and London, England

Production editor: Christopher Dadian
Cover design: Joni Godlove
Printed in the United States of America

The cover images are original renderings adapted from ancient artwork from the Paris Psalter depicting the combat of David and Goliath (cod. gr. 139, fol. 4v; Bibliothèque Nationale, Paris; 10th cen. AD).

Library of Congress Cataloging-in-Publication Data

Doak, Brian R. author.
The last of the Rephaim : conquest and cataclysm in the heroic ages of ancient Israel / Brian R. Doak.
    pages cm. -- (Ilex Foundation series ; 7)
Includes bibliographical references and index.
ISBN 978-0-674-06673-1 (alk. paper)
1. Giants in the Bible. 2. Bible. O.T.--Criticism, interpretation, etc. 3. Giants in literature. I. Title.
BS1199.G5D63 2012
221.6--dc23
                    2012038025

for Susan

CONTENTS

Figures

All figures drawn by Christian Reed

Preface

THE FIGURE OF THE GIANT has haunted the literatures of the ancient Mediterranean world, from the Greek Gigantomachy and other Aegean epic literatures in the West to the biblical contexts of the ancient Near East. In this book, I argue that the giants of the Hebrew Bible are a politically, theologically, and historiographically generative group, and through their oversized bodies readers gain insight into central aspects of ancient Israel's symbolic universe. All that is overgrown or physically monstrous represents a connection to primeval chaos, and stands as a barrier to creation and right rule. Giants thus represent chaos-fear, and their eradication is a form of chaos maintenance by both human and divine agents. Moreover, these biblical traditions participate in a broader Mediterranean conversation regarding giants and the end of the heroic age, with profound implications for the politics of monotheism and monarchy in ancient Israel.

The initial spark of interest for this project comes from the odd note in Deut 3:11, which appears in the midst of two chapters (Deut 2–3) filled with bits of what we might call a "primitive ethnography" of certain pre-Israelite inhabitants of the land:

> Only Og, the king of Bashan, was left of the remnant of the Rephaim. Note his bed, a bed of iron—is it not in Rabbah of the sons of Ammon? Its length is nine cubits and its width is four cubits, by the forearm of a man [i.e., the "standard cubit"].

The phrase "Only Og, the king of Bashan, was left of the remnant of the Rephaim" (כי רק עוג מלך הבשן נשאר מיתר הרפאים) has captured the interest of more than a few interpreters. What does it mean for a single man, Og, the king of Bashan, to be the last of a generation of what are, apparently, giants? Is the category of "giant" confined only to physical size? Why does this generation of giants come to end? In the case of Og and the Rephaim, how are these human, indigenous residents of the land related (if at all) to other conceptions of the Rephaim—both in the Hebrew Bible and at Ugarit— viz. as shades of the dead or past monarchic heroes or warriors? And what role do these groups of giants play both in the Conquest narrative and, more broadly, in the narrative formation of early Israelite identity?

In addition to these passages in Deuteronomy 2–3, other texts come immediately to mind, in which various giants or heroic warriors are invoked and often explicitly and meaningfully conflated with one another—most prominently:

- the Nephilim (Gen 6:4; Num 13:33);
- Anaqim (Num 13:22,28,33; Deut 1:28, 2:10,11,21, 9:2; Josh 11:21,23, 14:12,15, 15:13);
- Rephaim (Gen 14:5, 15:20; Deut 2:11,20, 3:11,13; Josh 12:4, 13:12, 15:18, 17:15, 18:16; cf. 2 Sam 5:18,22, 23:13; Isa 17:5; 1 Chr 1:15, 14:9);
- certain Gibborim (e.g., Gen 6:4, 10:8–9; 1 Sam 17:51; 2 Sam 1:19–27; 2 Samuel 23 / 1 Chr 11; Ezek 32);
- the Emim (Deut 2:10);
- and Zamzummim/Zuzim (Deut 2:20; Gen 14:5).

In Amos 2:9 we discover that, in the mind of a putatively eighth-century prophet, the entire native population (subsumed under the rubric of "Amorite") destroyed by God on behalf of the Israelites was marked by one particular physical trait: spectacular height, "like the height of cedars" (כגבה ארזים גבהו). Other representatives of the native population, such as the Anaqim (ענקים), are famously described as abnormally tall (Deut 1:26–28; 9:1–2; Num 13:28–33), and they serve as the point of comparison for other groups. Deut 2:10, for example, characterizes the Emim—in their sole appearance in the Hebrew Bible—as a "great" (גדול) and "numerous" (רב) people, who are as large as the Anaqim (ורם כענקים). Certain individuals qualify as giants based on their height or status as the descendants of giants, the most obvious example being Goliath of Gath (1 Sam 17:4), but also Ishbi-benob (2 Sam 21:16), Saph (2 Sam 21:18), an Egyptian (1 Chr 11:23), and Sippai (1 Chr 20:4). Others may be considered giants by implication, such as Og (mentioned above), whose enormous bed (Deut 3:11), coupled with his status as one of the Rephaim, seems to identify him as a giant. Still others participate in the world of the preternatural and grotesque poignantly embodied by the giant in many languages and literatures, such as through transgressive primordial acts (Gen 6:1–4; cf. the Greek Giants and Titans) and malformed body parts (e.g., the anonymous six-finger and six-toed individual in 2 Sam 21:16 // 1 Chr 20:6).

One might begin to define the giant solely in terms of physical height: an individual who towers over others, even to the point of unnatural or impossible dimensions. But deeper analysis shows that these creatures represent more than bodily anomalies or enemies of great material power, whose might merely points up YHWH's own superior might in defeating them. The authors of the Hebrew Bible participated in, and meaningfully instigated, a range of interpretive options for the giant, and intentionally sought to conflate ancient warriors of old and other giants. Moreover, various biblical authors forged a specific interpretive link between the broader and widely attested concept of the giant and that of the heroic warrior as a specific individual or category of humans (e.g., Gen 6:1–4; Num 13:33; Deut 2:10–11). Indeed, the re-invocation of the giant in post-biblical sources (e.g., 1 Enoch 6–11, 15–16) indicates that ancient audiences began to explicitly endow these figures with quite a range of meanings—for which physical gigantism was only a starting point, but then spreading out into the territory of moral pollution, sexual transgressions, demonic possession, overeating, hubris, and violence.

We are thus faced with a kind of metaphysical rumination on the meaning of these figures already in the biblical corpus. Such materials raise a series of fascinating and very much under-explored questions about (a) the meaning of the conflation of these groups of giants, and (b) the role these characters play in the memory of the Conquest narrative and the early monarchy, as well as in the formation of Israelite identity broadly. The invocation of the category of hero brings us immediately into conversation with the epic materials of the Aegean world, and we find contacts between some elements of the Greek heroic tradition (not to mention the Gigantomachy-Titanomachy) and the biblical giants. Like the Greek hero, the giant represents a legendary, local, native tradition of strength and land possession; both groups embody the mounting violence and arrogance associated with their size and raw power; both groups were eradicated by the gods for this arrogance, wrongdoing, or heroic over-reaching; both act simultaneously on the battlefield of epic and in a resurrected context of cult and ongoing literary imagination; and both were fashioned by ancient authors into representatives of a heroic age, whose terminus stands on the brink of the (real, historical) collapse of the old Bronze Age civilizations of the Mediterranean (c. 1250–1100 BCE).

My argument proceeds through five chapters.

In Chapter One, I review selected examples from the history of the obsession with the figure of the giant, both in the modern and ancient world, which attempts to explain or categorize the existence of the biblical giant. Indeed, a complicated assessment of the meaning of the giant began already in antiquity, and the monstrous possibilities embodied in the biblical giant reverberated throughout Western cultural history. In this chapter, I also establish the terms necessary to draw Greek and Semitic Mediterranean materials into a productive comparative context, by appealing to the notion of a "Mediterranean *koine*" and acknowledging the long history of Greek-Semitic comparative efforts in the Classics and in biblical scholarship.

In Chapter Two I come to the primary biblical texts, translating and commenting upon the various biblical passages mentioning giants. These various groups, I will show, are connected on two basic levels: (a) they are all said (or implied, at least in later tradition) to be extraordinarily tall, i.e., giants, etc., inhabiting the land prior to the Israelites; (b) various authors in the Hebrew Bible intentionally conflate these groups with one another. Though basic, I argue that the demonstration of this conflation is by no means completely obvious, but neither is it haphazard or merely synthetic. Rather, it represents a broader attempt to identify and categorize one "larger than life" element of Israel's military and ideological foes in the land, figures that are characterized simultaneously as inhabiting past, present, and omnitemporal dimensions of Israel's history. Even when races of giants are supposed to have been eradicated from the earth—such as after the Flood or Conquest—they continually reappear in subsequent contexts, acting as human enemies in Israel's ongoing drama to define itself and carve out a place for itself in the land.

In Chapter Three I proceed to argue that the biblical presentation of giants falls into a pattern that has instructive parallels in archaic and classical Greece, as well as in other ancient Near Eastern materials. Specifically, this pattern involves a three-stage progression: (a) iniquity, violence, or pollution committed by a certain population; (b) the rising iniquity/violence/pollution reaches a critical mass and pollutes the land, or causes an outcry; (c) divine punishment or displacement follows, in the form of a cataclysm by deluge or a symbolic deluge.

Once the demise of giant races has been put into this context, in Chapter Four I address a perplexing issue regarding the dual presentation of the Nephilim and Anaqim, some Gibborim, and Rephaim as both "human" residents of Canaan, residing in a particular place and fighting battles in a particular "historical" period, and yet occurring, in other contexts, as residents of the underworld, or as figures that are somehow supra-human. To explain this dichotomy, I take up a model long propounded by classicists for Greek heroes, viz. the idea that the hero exists not only as a figure *in epic*, doing battle, etc., but also—or perhaps *primarily*—as a figure *in cult*, in the afterlife. After describing the Aegean hero cult dynamic, I use this interpretive paradigm to explore some of these biblical texts presenting giants as human figures fighting the Israelites (epic) and as residents of the underworld. Specifically, I argue that an epic pattern of thinking regarding heroes in the Greek context also underlies the dual presentation of giants in the Hebrew Bible, and that the dual presentation itself is a narrative sublimation of heroic themes that reveals aspects of ancient Israelite thought regarding giant warriors and their fate. In sharp contrast to Greek hero cult, however, the Hebrew Bible reveals nothing directly regarding the power or efficacy of the dead as such, though the fact that certain passages may be read as a polemic *against* the notion of the powerful, heroic dead is in itself evidence of countervailing theologies. This focus on the religious dynamics of hero cult, hitherto unaddressed in the recent major studies of Israelite death cult generally, opens up vistas not explored in other treatments of "heroic culture" in ancient Israel.

Finally, in Chapter Five, I broaden this discussion to address the role of these groups of heroic giants as one incarnation of a "heroic age" in ancient Israel. I do not argue that this is the only option for a heroic age in Israel as the Bible conceives it—indeed, I think others fit this label better if other criteria are used to define a heroic age—but rather that the demise of these giant groups constitutes a moment of historiographic organization for the Deuteronomist and other sources. Moreover, the presentation of these groups of giants forms an important part of Israel's own story of origins vis-à-vis the "Other," and I will explore the way this formulation of a corrupt generation of giants serves to define Israel. Along these lines, I discuss the ways in which themes of heroic might and power are recontextualized in exilic/post-exilic texts, as well as the "resurrection" of the giant in the Enochic corpus and other post-biblical materials.

Ultimately, and on the broadest level, I contend, both the strong presence and intentional diminishment of heroic themes in the Hebrew Bible display a paradoxical image of heroic existence and ideals, and this tension is poignantly and creatively displayed through the epic pattern of giant heroes and their fate. The Israelite encounter with the Anaqim, Rephaim, Emim, and others thus represents a type of suppression functioning as both straightforward and inverse analogies to the Greek view of the end of the heroic age. In Greek epic imagination it is the Trojan War and the eradication of heroes that brought about the demise of the hallowed Mycenaean civilization and thus the end of the old world of heroic action. Similarly, in ancient Israelite thought the end of the heroic age of pre-Israelite giants marks the defeat of the last representatives of a certain heroic race (Deut 3:11; but cf. 2 Sam 21:15–22). Whereas in classical Greek conceptions the aristocracy were said to have descended from the heroes and thus from divine-human miscegenation (preserving the powerful and noble aura of the heroic age in a positive manner), in the ancient Israelite view the divine-human giants are portrayed as Israel's enemy, as transgressors whose iniquitous acts culminate not only in eradication but in eternal ignominy.

What I am proposing, then, is a complete re-evaluation of the meaning and role of the biblical giant—one that strives to interpret these figures not simply as dramatic monsters who can provide some believable threat against which God's chosen agents can emerge victorious. Rather, giants are capable of introducing into the narrative all kinds of meaning and havoc, and they have been an under-utilized window through which we might gain important insight into central aspects of Israel's ancient symbolic world, of the history of its religion and the development of concepts of monarchy, order, and monotheism. In their role as embodiments of the oversized human *Chaosmacht*, giants force us to consider new questions regarding the role of oversized enemy threats and the heroes who confront these threats. Can the world of epic—rife as it is with multiple deities, multiple poles of heroic power, and continual conflict—comfortably co-exist with the ideological world of the single monarchy? Is epic as a genre compatible with monotheism?

The collision between images of the gigantic and the heroic in the Hebrew Bible takes us directly to the heart of the theological politics of genre and the poetics of power in ancient Israel. The Bible's invocation of the giant, I hope to demonstrate, constitutes a creative evaluation of Canaan's heroic past and of physical might, and stands as a forceful reminder of the place of Israel's deity among the axes of power that giants represent. Indeed, the overall biblical engagement with the category of the giant, along with the concomitant fusion of the giant with images of the heroic in ancient Aegean literature, signify a profound meditation on the category of epic in the ancient world—even a decisive, ultimate rejection of epic and heroism as controlling tropes of the biblical worldview.

The current project began as my doctoral dissertation (completed in April of 2011, under the same title) at Harvard University, in the Department of Near Eastern Languages and Civilizations, and I owe many and continuing thanks to the members of my committee: Peter Machinist, Jon Levenson, and Gregory Nagy. My primary advisor, Professor Machinist, provided encouragement at all stages of this project, and the generosity of his scholarly vision has inspired me in every way. Professor Levenson's work on both the *Chaoskampf* motif and the concept of narrative sublimation gave me two important concepts for this project, and his support during the later stages of my doctoral work was very meaningful to me. I first accessed much of the classical literature represented here through Professor Nagy's groundbreaking publications and pedagogy, and Greg's encouragement and advice were primarily responsible for bringing this project to publication in its current form. Two others at the Center for Hellenic Studies and Ilex Foundation deserve mention: Niloo Fotouhi, and Christopher Dadian, for his expert work on the manuscript, which saved me from many errors. I presented inchoate ideas from the present work at meetings of the Society of Biblical Literature, the American Academy of Religion, and the Society for Ancient Mediterranean Religions in 2008–2011, and I received valuable feedback in each of these settings. Dr. Suzanne Smith (Harvard University) provided lengthy and formative responses to earlier drafts of these chapters, and indeed it has become difficult for me to separate her ideas from my own in certain parts of the study. Other colleagues at Harvard, and beyond—such as Hilary Evans Kapfer, Jonathan Kaplan, Jonathan Kline, John Noble, and Keith Stone—provided aid in various forms. Professor Carolina López-Ruiz (Ohio State University) made incisive, hand-written comments on an early draft of the entire project, and she became a mighty ally as I endeavored to make the comparative elements of this study viable. Finally, my colleagues in the Religious Studies Department and beyond at George Fox University have been a constant source of hospitality and friendship since I joined the faculty in the fall of 2011. Paul Anderson and Roger Nam, in particular, read drafts of some of the chapters and helped me tremendously, and three other individuals contributed to the book through conversation and much needed encouragement along the way: Corey Beals, Patrick Ray, and Abigail Rine.

I hold all of the individuals named here responsible for what the reader finds good and useful in what follows.

Abbreviations

Note: Abbreviations for all scholarly works, languages, biblical books, and other ancient sources follow the conventions of the *SBL Handbook of Style* (1999), including, or with the exception of, those listed below.

A	Codex Alexandrinus
AA	*Aevum Antiquum*
ABSA	*The Annual of the British School at Athens*
Ac	*The Academy*
AcOr	*Acta Orientalia Academiae Scientiarum Hung. Tomus*
ABD	D. N. Freedman (ed.) (1992), *The Anchor Bible Dictionary*, 6 vols., New York
ACF	*Annuaire du Collège de France*
AcS	*Acta Sumerologica*
AE	*Archaiologike Ephemeris*
AES	*Archives européennes de sociologie*
AFS	*Asian Folklore Studies*
AHR	*American Historical Review*
AJA	*American Journal of Archaeology*
AJBI	*Annual of the Japanese Biblical Institute*
AJP	*American Journal of Philology*
AJSLL	*American Journal of Semitic Languages and Literatures*
AJT	*American Journal of Theology*
AmAnt	*American Antiquity*
AOASH	*Acta Orientalia Academiae Scientiarum Hungaricae*
ArHist	*Artibus et Historiae*
ASSR	*Archives de sciences sociales des religions, 21e Année*
B	Codex Vaticanus
BA	*Biblical Archaeologist*
BABESCH	*BABESCH (Annual Papers on Mediterranean Archaeology)*
BASOR	*Bulletin of the American Schools of Oriental Research*
BAR	*Biblical Archaeology Review*
BCSMS	*Bulletin of the Canadian Society for Mesopotamian Studies*
BDB	*The Brown-Driver-Briggs Hebrew and English Lexicon* (Peabody, Mass.: 2003; reprint of 1906 edition)
BibOr	*Bibliotheca Orientalis*
BJE	*British Journal of Ethnomusicology*

BJS	*The British Journal of Sociology*
BMCR	*Bryn Mawr Classical Review*
BR	*Bible Review*
BTB	*Biblical Theology Bulletin*
BZ	*Biblische Zeitschrift*
CA	*Classical Antiquity*
CAD	*The Assyrian Dictionary of the Oriental Institute of the University of Chicago* (1964–), 21 vols., E. Reiner, *et al.* (eds.), Chicago
CAE	J. M. Foley (ed.) (2007), *A Companion to Ancient Epic*, Malden, Mass.
CANE	J. M. Sasson (ed.) (2000), *Civilizations of the Ancient Near East*, 4 vols., Peabody, Mass.
CBQ	*Catholic Biblical Quarterly*
CE	*Chronique d'Egypte*
CJ	*Classical Journal*
CL	*Comparative Literature*
COS	W. H. Hallo and K. L. Younger (eds.) (2003), *The Context of Scripture: Monumental Inscriptions from the Biblical World*, 3 vols., Leiden.
CP	*Classical Philology*
CQ	*Classical Quarterly*
CR	*Classical Review*
CSCA	*California Studies in Classical Antiquity*
CSSH	*Comparative Studies in Society and History*
CT	Cuneiform texts from Babylonian tablets
CTA	*Corpus des tablettes en cuneiforms alphabétiques découvertes à Ras Shamra-Ugarit de 1929 à 1939, par Andrée Herdner* (1963), Paris
CW	*The Classical World*
DBS	*Dictionnaire de la Bible, Supplément* 10, L. Pirot (ed.) (1985), Paris
DDD	*Dictionary of Deities and Demons in the Bible* (1999), 2nd edition, Karel van der Toorn, Bob Becking, and Pieter W. van der Horst (eds.), Leiden
DJD XII	*Discoveries in the Judaean Desert XVII* (2005), F. M. Cross, D. W. Parry, R. J. Saley, and E. Ulrich (eds.), Oxford
DS	*Dante Studies, with the Annual Report of the Dante Society*
DSD	*Dead Sea Discoveries*
DTT	*Dansk teologisk tidsskrift*
EMC	*Echos du monde classique: Classical views*

ErIsr	*Eretz Israel*
FB	*Forschungen und Berichte*
GBH	P. Joüon and T. Muraoka, *A Grammar of Biblical Hebrew* (2005), 2 vols., Rome
Gen. Rab.	*Genesis Rabbah* (1985), vol. I. Parashiyyot One through Thirty-Three on Genesis 1:1 to 8:14, J. Neusner (ed.), Atlanta
Gilg.	*The Babylonian Gilgamesh Epic: Introduction, Critical Edition and Cuneiform Texts* (2003), 2 vols., A. R. George (ed.), Oxford
GKC	W. Gesenius; E. Kautzsch (ed.); A. E. Cowley (trans.), *Gesenius' Hebrew Grammar* (2006; first published 1813), Mineola, N.Y.
GolJMR	*Golem: The Journal of Monsters and Religion*
HA	*The Heroic Age*
HAR	*Hebrew Annual Review*
HJ	*The Heythrop Journal*
HR	*History of Religions*
HSCP	*Harvard Studies in Classical Philology*
HT	*History and Theory*
HTR	*Harvard Theological Review*
HUCA	*Hebrew Union College Annual*
HZAG	*Historia: Zeitschrift für Alte Geschichte*
IDB	*The Interpreter's Dictionary of the Bible* (1967–1976), 5 vols., G. A. Buttrick, et al. (eds.), Nashville
IEJ	*Israel Exploration Journal*
IJHS	*International Journal of Hindu Studies*
ILN	*Illustrated London News*
JAJ	*Journal of Ancient Judaism*
JANER	*Journal of Ancient Near Eastern Religions*
JAOS	*Journal of the American Oriental Society*
JAR	*Jahrbuch für Anthropologie und Religionsgeschichte*
JBL	*Journal of Biblical Literature*
JCS	*Journal of Cuneiform Studies*
JESHO	*Journal of the Economic and Social History of the Orient*
JETS	*Journal of the Evangelical Theological Society*
JFI	*Journal of the Folklore Institute*
JHI	*Journal of the History of Ideas*
JHS	*Journal of Hebrew Scriptures*
JHSt	*Journal of Hellenic Studies*
JNES	*Journal of Near Eastern Studies*
JNS	*The Journal of Nietzsche Studies*

JNWSL	*Journal of Northwest Semitic Languages*
JPOS	*Journal of the Palestine Oriental Society*
JR	*Journal of Religion*
JRGZ	*Jahrbuch des Römisch-Germanischen Zentralmuseums*
JRH	*Journal of Religious History*
JRS	*Journal of Roman Studies*
JSJ	*Journal for the Study of Judaism*
JSOR	*Journal of the Society of Oriental Research*
JSOT	*Journal for the Study of the Old Testament*
JSS	*Journal of Semitic Studies*
JWH	*Journal of World History*
KAI	*Kanaanäische und aramäische Inschriften* (1962–1964), 3 vols., H. Donner, W. Röllig, O. Rössler (ed.), Wiesbaden
KAR	E. Ebeling, *Keilschrifttexte aus Assur religiösen Inhalts* I/II (1915–1923), Leipzig
KTU	*Die keilalphabetischen Texte aus Ugarit* (1976–), M. Dietrich, O. Loretz, J. Sanmartin (eds.), Neukirchen-Vluyn
L&T	*Literature and Theology*
LEC	*Les études classiques*
LIMC	J. Boardman (ed.) (1981–2009), *Lexicon iconographicum mythologiae classicae*, Zürich
MLN	*Modern Language Notes*
MLR	*The Modern Language Review*
MMMD	*Mélanges offerts à M. Maurice Dunand. Mélanges de l'Université Saint-Joseph*
MT	Masoretic Text
MP	*Modern Philology*
MQ	*Milton Quarterly*
MR	*Maynooth Review / Revieú Mhá Nuad*
NEA	*Near Eastern Archaeology*
OEANE	*The Oxford Encyclopedia of Archaeology in the Near East* (1996), 5 vols., E. M. Myers (ed.), Oxford
OP	*Ordia Prima*
Or	*Orientalia*
OT	*Oral Tradition*
OTGr	A. E. Brooke, and N. McLean, *The Old Testament in Greek* (1917, 1927, 1932), 3 vols., Cambridge
PAPS	*Proceedings of the American Philosophical Society*
PCP	*Pacific Coast Philology*
PMLA	*Proceedings of Modern Language Association*

RB	*Revue Biblique*
RC	*Religion Compass*
RF	*Rivista di Filologia*
RHR	*Revue de l'Histoire des Religions*
RHA	*Revue Hittite et Asianique*
RLA	Reallexikon der Assyriologie
RMP	*Rheinisches Museum für Philologie*
RS	Field numbers of tablets excavated at Ras Shamra/Ugarit
RSI	*Rivista Storica Italiana*
SCJ	*Stone-Campbell Journal*
SEL	*Studies in English Literature, 1500–1900*
SJOT	*Scandinavian Journal of the Old Testament*
SMEA	*Studi Micenei ed Egeo-Anatolici*
SO	*Studia Orientalia*
SR	*Sociology of Religion*
ST	*Studia Theologica*
TAPA	*Transactions of the American Philological Association*
TC	*Technology and Culture*
TDOT	*Theological Dictionary of the Old Testament* (1974–2004), 5 vols., G. J. Botterweck, H. Ringgren, *et al.* (eds.), J. T. Willis, *et al.* (trans.), Grand Rapids, Mich.
TESL	*Transactions of the Ethnological Society of London*
TOGen	M. Aberbach and B. Grossfeld (eds.) (1982), *Targum Onkelos to Genesis*, New York
TPAPA	*Transactions and Proceedings of the American Philological Association*
TRIA	*The Transactions of the Royal Irish Academy*
TZ	*Theologische Zeitschrift*
UDB	*Ugaritic Data Bank: The Texts* (2003), J. -L. Cunchillos, J-. P. Vita, and J. Á. Zamora (eds.), A. Lacadena and A. Castro (trans.), Madrid
UF	*Ugarit Forschungen*
VT	*Vetus Testamentum*
VTSupp	*Supplements to Vetus Testamentum*
WJ	*Women in Judaism: A Multidisciplinary Journal*
WTJ	*Westminster Theological Journal*
ZAG	*Zeitschrift für Alte Geschichte*
ZAW	*Zeitschrift für die Alttestamentliche Wissenschaft*
ZTK	*Zeitschrift für Theologie und Kirche*
ZK	*Zeitschrift für Kunstgeschichte*

Chapter One

A Race of Big Men There Was

I. A Giant Will Come to Rescue Me

IN WHAT MAY PROVE to be one of the great epic novels of the twenty-first century, *2666*, Roberto Bolaño invokes the uncanny and monstrous power of the human giant in contradictory and even unexpected ways.[1] An accused serial killer—probably a guilty serial killer, but proclaiming his innocence—named Klaus who is described as "enormous" walks through a prison, his footsteps sounding like "the footsteps of a giant" to the terrified visitors waiting to interview him. He sings a song: "I'm a giant lost in the middle of a burned forest. But someone will come to rescue me."[2] Oddly, the giant here cryptically refers to another "giant" in the novel, an elusive author, Benno von Archimboldi, who is also persistently described as strikingly tall.[3] Archimboldi's little sister, Lotte, hears her brother's footsteps in dreams as he returns from fighting in a war, "the footsteps of a giant." As a young girl, Lotte believes that "giants never die," and that his return "from that moment on everything would change. But what exactly would change? She didn't know."[4] Much later in the novel's chronology, the accused serial killer turns out to be Lotte's son, and thus Archimboldi's nephew; as adults, both Klaus and Lotte have dreams of Archimboldi the giant, "bad dreams."[5] Lotte dreams "of a cemetery and the tomb of a giant. The gravestone split and the giant's hand rose up, then his other hand..."[6] At the very end of the book, Lotte discusses Klaus' situation with Archimboldi. "She...talked about Klaus' dreams, the dreams in which he saw a giant who would rescue him from prison, although you, she said to Archimboldi, don't look like a giant anymore." Confronted with the specter of his gigantism, Archimboldi replies: "I was never a giant."

---

1. Bolaño 2004.
2. Bolaño 2004, 349. Elsewhere in the passage at hand, the tall serial killer is explicitly called a "giant" by the narrator (twice).
3. Archimboldi's mother in the novel is "blind in one eye" (Bolaño 2004, 637), possibly a gesture toward the giant Cyclops in the *Odyssey*.
4. Bolaño 2004, 865. Cf. 873.
5. Bolaño 2004, 881.
6. Bolaño 2004, 889–90.

Another contemporary masterpiece of gigantic rhetorical excess, David Foster Wallace's *Infinite Jest* (1996), utilizes oversized bodies as terrifying representatives of all that is awful, polluted, and excessive.[7] In the novel, giant, malformed, feral infants haunt a toxic wasteland ("the Concavity") at the liminal space between the United States and Canada.[8] Dysfunctional, emotionally abusive parents are described as iconically tall: James Incandenza ("The Mad Stork"), an alcoholic filmmaker who commits suicide in a gruesome fashion, and his wife, the scholar Avril Incandenza, marked by voracious sexuality and wracked with mental disorders.[9] The moral hero of the story, a recovering drug addict named Don Gately, is himself "the size of a young dinosaur,"[10] revealing a recurrent and thus significant plot trope in stories involving gigantism: only a giant can oppose or defeat another giant. Other relatively recent works of fiction, such as Jeanette Winterson's 1996 novel *Sexing the Cherry*, draw the giant body (of the female "Dog Woman") into the world of farce, comedy, and surrealism reminiscent of the sixteenth-century Rabelaisian vision of the gigantic.[11] The possibilities seem as expansive as the oversized body itself.

Such recent depictions confirm the judgment of W. Stephens, who, in his masterful work on the cultural history of the giant, makes the following programmatic statement:

> The fact that the Giant can be not only either "mythical" or historical, but also either good or evil by definition, is highly significant. If the Giant can represent radically different, even diametrically opposed concepts in different societies, or in different social groups of the same society, then he must be a figure fundamental to the representation of both culture and authority. If he can represent either what humans most admire or their most nightmarish anxieties, then the real question he evokes is not one of scientific progress versus obscurantism and superstition, but rather one of ideology.[12]

The giant can be a giant in heroic memory, or a monstrous parent, an artist, perhaps even suspected of murder, a brother or a savior or a mother. The giant is that which disrupts the nuclear family and the domestic home, and

7. Wallace 1996. Wallace's use of the odd neologism "ascapartic" (i.e., like the giant Ascapart, defeated by the medieval hero Bevis of Hampton) at various points in the book (e.g., p. 290) demonstrates the intentionality of Wallace's invocation of the giant.

8. Wallace 1996, 1055–56. On the "feral" theme, see Ryan 2012, Ch. 7.

9. Wallace 1996, 227, 898, etc.

10. Wallace 1996, 55.

11. Winterson 1996. I thank my colleague Abigail Rine for bringing this book to my attention.

12. Stephens 1989, 5. Similar types of statements are made regarding the "wild man" (which includes giants as a subcategory) by Bernheimer (1952, 4–5, 19–20).

also the nation as "home" for its citizens; in this sense, the giant is a poignant signal of the uncanny, the *unheimlich*, i.e., the not-at-home.[13]

Looking backward through many centuries, in many contexts, one finds a complex and fascinating web of references to giants, stretching back to the ancient world and eventually back to the Mediterranean and Near Eastern materials that will take center stage throughout this book. In these texts, including most famously the Bible but also other literatures, the existence of giant humans is a straightforward historical fact. Though one is not surprised to find speculation about giants in earlier sources, one may be taken aback to find ambivalent descriptions documenting races of freakishly large humans well into the nineteenth and even twentieth centuries.[14] The well respected *Encylopaedia Britannica*, for example, contained an entry for "Giant," which, from 1878–1911, entertained a discussion concerning "the conception of giants as special races distinct from mankind" and thus seemed to display an odd insouciance about the existence of such figures. Nevertheless, the authors of the article found it necessary to declare finally that "so far as can be judged from actual remains, it does not appear that giants, in the sense of tribes of altogether superhuman stature, ever existed, or that the men of ancient times were on the whole taller than those now living."[15]

Josias Porter's late nineteenth-century *The Giant Cities of Bashan* may

---

13. Here I follow the categorization of the monster by Beal (2002, 4–5). Invoking the Freudian concept of *unheimlich*, Beal affirms monsters as "personifications of *unheimlich*. They stand for what endangers one's sense of at-homeness...one's sense of security, stability, integrity, well-being, health, and meaning...They are figures of chaos disorientation *within* order and orientation, revealing deep insecurities in one's faith in oneself, one's society, and one's world." In this conception, giants and other monsters as *unheimlich* may threaten "one's confidence in the meaning, integrity and well-being of the entire cosmos (the world ecology as 'house')." See also Beal 2002, 9–10.

14. Indeed, even contemporary scholars have succumbed to the urge to speak about giants in some quasi-historical sense, by diagnosing this or that biblical giant with a case of gigantism or hypopituitarism. For the medical interpretation of giants, see, e.g., Kellermann 1990, 350–51 and Ford 1992, 88, and even a recent attempt to establish the straightfoward historicity of the biblical giant stories by Billington (2007). These are not promising avenues of investigation. Presumably, gigantism as a physical condition was as (un)common in the ancient world as it is today, and, needless to say, there is no archaeological evidence that a populous race of giants lived in any part of the world at any time. One can certainly find scant archaeological remains that suggest gigantism, e.g., two seven-foot (female) skeletons were uncovered at Tell es-Sa'idiyeh, just east of the Jordan (twelfth century BCE); see reference in Tigay 1996, 17, 347 n. 102. Note also a famous passage from a late thirteenth-century BCE Egyptian letter describing the terrain and inhabitants of Palestine (Pritchard 1969, 477): "The narrow valley is dangerous with Bedouin, hidden under the bushes. Some of them are of four or five cubits [seven–nine feet] (from) their noses to the heel, and fierce of face. Their hearts are not mild, and they do not listen to wheedling."

15. Quoted in Stephens 1989, 2. As Stephens points out, it was the study of Luanois and Roy (1904), that first "accomplished the scientific demythification of the Giant."

serve as one example of the manner in which the popular genre of the Middle Eastern travel diary dealt with the issue of giants and the pseudo-scientific correlation between the Bible's stories and contemporary geographical and ethnographic realities.[16] In commenting upon the giants of biblical tradition, Porter finds it "strange to say" that

> traditionary memorials of these primeval giants exist even now in almost every section of Palestine, in the form of graves of enormous dimensions, —as the grave of Abel, near Damascus, *thirty* feet long; that of Seth, in Anti-Lebanon, about the same size; and that of Noah, in Lebanon, which measures no less than seventy yards!...We shall presently see...that the cities built and occupied some forty centuries ago by these old giants exist even yet. I have traversed their streets; I have opened the doors of their houses; I have slept peacefully in their long-deserted halls.[17]

Porter returns time and again throughout his travelogue to ponder the deeds of the giants; he gazes in a "pleasing reverie" on the "wild and wondrous panorama" of Argob in which giants erected monuments and committed wild and terrible acts.[18] He measures doors and walls in Kerioth, noting that "the houses of Kerioth and other towns in Bashan appear to be just such dwellings as a race of giants would build," and that "there can scarcely be a doubt...that these are the very cities erected and inhabited by the Rephaim."[19] J. Baikie, in his 1914 *Lands and Peoples of the Bible*, similarly assumed the reality of the Bible's description of giants. Commenting on the Nephilim, Rephaim, and others, Baikie asserts that they "were no fantastic dream of the early Hebrew invaders. A race of big men there was...very terrible to look at, but not of much account when you actually came to fight with [them]...And they hewed for themselves...great caves."[20]

In 1938, the archaeologist G. E. Wright confronted some of these fantastical notions, specifically the idea that Israel's aboriginal inhabitants were actually giants or that they lived in caves.[21] Indeed, Wright was able to cite Oesterly and Robinson's *A History of Israel*, an edition of which was published just six years earlier (1932), to demonstrate the prevalence of such ideas

16. J. Porter 1884.

17. J. Porter 1884, 12.

18. J. Porter 1884, 29–30.

19. J. Porter 1884, 84.

20. Baikie 1914, 60–61.

21. This latter notion was often based on the supposed etymological connection between the biblical חרי ("Horite") and חר ("cave, hole," etc.). G. Wright 1938, 305–09. E.g., Driver (1902, 38) endorses this etymology in his commentary on Deuteronomy. Cf. Farrar (1867, 117), who asserted that narrative traditions of giants or semi-divine native populations originated with historical groups of "primeval troglodytes" and "irreclaimable savages."

in (specifically) English language biblical scholarship.[22] Wright goes on to affirm the folkloristic origin of Israel's giant aboriginal inhabitants, pointing out that the skeletal remains of prehistoric peoples in the region whose genes could plausibly be found in Israel's "real" precursors show them to be of underwhelming height, somewhere between five and a half and six feet on average. Massive structures and walls from Bronze Age Ai, Shechem, Jericho, and Tell Beit Mirsim may have provided fuel for speculation on the size of the individuals needed to build such fortifications[23]—and in fact, several passages in the Hebrew Bible connect impressive structures with the Anaqim specifically (Num 13:28; Deut 1:28, 9:1; Josh 14:12).

Not all concerned scholars found themselves caught up in debates about the literal existence of Israel's enemy giants. As early as 1869, T. Nöldeke briefly suggested groups such as the Rephaim, Emim, and Zuzim were the ancient Israelite version of the German Hünen and Scandinavian Jöten, legendary creatures who play an important role in the folkloric origins of a people.[24] F. Lenormant saw stories of autochthonous, wicked giants as a "universal tradition" among ancient people, most often adopted by an incoming or conquering new society to conceive of the land's previous inhabitants as monsters or ghosts.[25] E. B. Tylor also moved beyond the realm of science into myth and folklore in his monumental *Primitive Culture*, noting that "it was not till the real world had been so thoroughly explored as to leave little room in it for the monsters."[26] For Tylor, it was the world of comparative myth that gave meaning to tales of giants, who take their place among the broader catalogue of aberrants recounted, according to Tylor, in every far-flung corner of the world.

Indeed, the pre-modern Christian imagination was obsessed with the giant in this role of the monstrous aberration. In his review of the history of the giant in Latin Europe, Stephens goes on to claim that the giant "is in fact a historical touchstone of ancient and medieval anthropological discourse. In both chronological and conceptual terms, he is the most fundamental

22. See G. Wright 1938, 305.

23. G. Wright 1938, 308. More recently, see Hendel 2009.

24. Nöldeke 1869, 161. See also the folkloric approach in Gaster 1969, 311–12, 402–03.

25. Lenormant 1899, 351–57. Lenormant attempted to argue for the ultimate origins of all giant mythology in some indistinct archaic period.

26. Tylor 1920, 1:385. Along with some other interpreters, Tylor (1920, 1:387) suggested that giant-stories might be connected to giant fossils. Cf. Lenormant 1899, 352 (and n. 10). Mayor (2000) advances the striking thesis that many curious ancient travelers engaged in a version of amateur paleontology, and drew the only conclusions they could have possibly made from their finds, viz., that there existed monstrous creatures in the distant past. Their conclusions were not so far from the truth, though obviously not in the way ancient interpreters thought.

figure of the Other..."[27] Stephens identifies an important transformation in the image of the giant in Rabelais' *Gargantua* series (beginning in 1532),[28] before which the giant was almost universally described as a monstrous threat and embodiment of pride and wickedness. The Rabelaisian giant is a "good fellow," and thus stands as the type of the modern giant, who is an attractive figure of cartoon advertisement, a positive symbol of sports greatness, or a signal of superior achievement ("a giant in their field").[29] The folk environment out of which Rabelais' depiction of giants grew, however, depicted the giant in the standard way as a symbol of fear and otherness, and thus Rabelais' treatment was a recent turn on the motif of the giant even in his own time.[30] The positive role of the gigantic appears differently in the modern era's most influential formulation of state control and the meaning of political power, Thomas Hobbes' *Leviathan* (1651). Hobbes draws directly on the image of the monstrous as the focal point for engagement with the meaning of kingship; the state must become a giant, a Leviathan, whose heroic gigantism alone can confront the monstrous gigantism of civil and international disorder.[31]

II. The Christian Giant and the Early Jewish Giant

Prior to the Enlightenment, however, interpreters imagined the giant primarily as an embodiment of the chaotic. Theologians of the medieval period

27. Stephens 1989, 58. Two other important recent theoretical works treating the category of the giant deserve mention here. J. Cohen (1999, xii) similarly points to the symbolic value of the giant qua monster: "The monster appears to be outside the human body, as the limit of its coherence; thus he threatens travelers and errant knights with dismemberment or anthropophagy, with the complete dissolution of their selfhood. But closer examination reveals that the monster is also fully within, a foundational figure; and so the giant is depicted as the builder of cities where people live and dream, the origin of the glory of empire, the base of heroism...The giant is humanity writ large, a text literally too big to ignore." Stewart (1984, 86) focuses on the way in which narratives of the miniature operate vis-à-vis the gigantic. "The gigantic is viewed as a consuming force, the antithesis of the miniature, whose objects offer themselves to the viewer in a utopia of perfect, because individual, consumption. The giant is frequently seen as a devourer, and even, as in the case of Cyclops, a cannibal."

28. Rabelais 1972.

29. Stephens 1989, 4.

30. Stephens 1989, 56–57, etc. Stephens' view here is largely in opposition to the reading of Bakhtin 1968. Bahktin's carnivalesque reading of the giant in general is not misguided, though, as images of the giant in terms of the grotesque on the one hand and as the austere embodiment of power on the other are often intermingled in the giants' literary landscape. In addition to Bahktin's reading, see Anspaugh 1995, 129–52 on the grotesque giant.

31. Hobbes (1962 [first published 1651], 3) made this explicit from the beginning of his study, where he states that the "great LEVIATHAN...or STATE...is but an artificial man; though of greater stature and strength than the natural, for whose protection and defense it was intended..."

took the giant seriously as one manifestation of the "monster" or "wild man," and as R. Bernheimer points out, the concept of "wildness"

> meant more in the Middle Ages than the shrunken significance of the term would indicate today. The word implied everything that eluded Christian norms and the established framework of Christian society, referring to what was uncanny, unruly, raw, unpredictable, foreign, uncultured, and uncultivated. It included the unfamiliar as well as the unintelligible.[32]

Exegetes were thus forced to ask uncomfortable questions regarding the status of the giant in God's salvific scheme: Where did the giant come from? Did he have a soul, or was he an animal?[33]

Two major literary embodiments of the Christian imagination significantly dealt with giants: Dante's *Commedia* and Milton's *Paradise Lost*.[34] It is well known that Milton drew on classical presentations of the Greek gigantomachy in his vivid descriptions of Christ's battle with the demons.[35] Satan and his cohort are first equated with the giants of Greek myth in *Paradise Lost* I.192–202, where we find Satan "extended long and large...in bulk as huge / As whom the Fables name of monstrous size" (e.g., the Titans).[36]

Milton's presentation follows Dante's *Commedia* (c. 1316), where in Canto 31 the biblical Nimrod and several figures from Roman/Greek myth inhabit the ninth circle of Hell. Dante mistakes their massive bodies for towers (31.31); in the deepest ring of torment (Canto 34) lies Satan, whose iniquity is symbolized, among other ways, by his massive size:

> The emperor of the despondent kingdom
> so towered—from midchest—above the ice,

32. Bernheimer 1952, 19–20.

33. See Stephens 1989, 58–138.

34. For an overview, see Butler 1998, 352–63. On the *Commedia* specifically, see Kay 2002, 17–34; on *Paradise Lost*, see Ericson 1991, 79–89; Gay 1995, 355–69; West 1952, 21–23.

35. See Butler 1998, 356–57.

36. Quote taken from Milton 1968 (first published 1667), *Paradise Lost*, I.510, 570. In VII.604–05 Jehovah is described as "...greater now in thy return / Than from the Giant Angels," and yet in XI.576–87 Milton identifies the "sons of God" with the mortal descendants of Seth. In *Paradise Regained* II.178–81, the sons of God are again considered as a wicked angelic race. The description of Satan-as-Giant in *Paradise Lost* moves seamlessly into a reference to Leviathan, connected not only by their size but also by their opposition to God. Milton continued to use the image of the giant as an important symbol in his later work; in *Samson Agonistes*, Goliath's father, Harapha, claims descent from ancient giants such as Og, Anaq, and the Emim. See Milton 2003 (first published 1671), lines 1076–82. The appearance of this giant vis-à-vis Samson likely had great significance for Milton, who cast Samson as a type of Christ—thus, the encounter between Samson and Harapha stands as a prefiguration of the David and Goliath battle, itself a type-scene of Christ's own victory. See Gay 1995, 355.

> that I match better with a giant's height
> than giants match the measure of his arms.[37]

Even in these astounding descriptions of physical gigantism in Hell, Dante did, in a sense, seek to demythologize the giants: he strips them of several grotesque physiological features (such as multiple limbs, etc.) that figure prominently in classical accounts, and instead renders these beings wholly anthropomorphically. And while classical sources focused on *physical* aspects of a giant's irregularity, Dante's austere descriptions magnify *psychological* and *moral* deformities, as if in rebuke of the misdirected pagan representations.[38]

Augustine (354–430 CE) devoted two subsections of his *City of God* (XV.9,23) to the question of the origin of giants, particularly in relation to Gen 6:1–4 and the supposed intercourse between angelic beings and human women.[39] By way of demonstrating the straightforward historical believability of such narratives, Augustine cooly reports his own personal experience with fossils, such as a giant tooth, to prove the demise of such races in the Noaic deluge.[40] Other matter-of-fact reports come from Josephus (*Ant.* XVIII.103), who recounts among the gifts sent to Herod by Artabanus a certain Jew named Eleazar, dubbed Γίγας (Giant) on account of his seven cubit (= ten feet) height.[41] In his *Historia Naturalis* (completed c. 79 CE), Pliny the Elder records several examples of giant humans (VII.73–6), and speculates that the entire human race is shrinking gradually as the result of "the fertility of the semen...being dried up by the conflagration into whose era the cycle of ages is now declining."[42] Likewise Lucretius, in his first-century BCE *De rerum natura* ("On the Nature of Things"), takes for granted the physical hugeness of individuals in previous generations, speculating that the primitive human race "was built up within with bones larger and more solid [than in the present day]" (5.925; see also 1.199; 3.984; 5.907–24).[43] Pausanias' *Guide*

37. Dante 1995 (first published 1316), *Purg.* 34.28–31; see also *Purg.* 2.25–36.

38. I draw these observations from Butler 1998, 359–60. Butler does not seem to realize, however, that even in accounts of the giant where physical deformities (aside from height) are emphasized to the exclusion of "moral" qualities, there is often a *strongly implied correlation* between states of physical and psychological deformity.

39. See Augustine 2000, esp. the examples in book XV.

40. See the fascinating discussion on the tooth in Nolan 2009, 64–69.

41. *Ant.*, 74–75.

42. Pliny 2005, 74–75.

43. As Gayle (1994, 43–45) argues, Lucretius may have a rather complicated symbolic agenda in mind in his evocation of the familiar imagery of the Gigantomachy at several points, through which Lucretius reverses the normal interpretation of the Gigantomachy (i.e., the giants representing barbarism and chaos, with the deities representing order) by evoking imagery suggesting that the Giants achieved a *victory*—and then presenting the Epicureans, of

to Greece (second century CE) also contains a reference to this apparently widespread narrative documenting the decrease of human size since archaic times in an extended section of comment on giants in Book VII.29.1–3. After noting Homer's general reticence concerning giants (except in the *Odyssey*, on which see below), Pausanias recounts the uncovering of a giant coffin, housing a giant corpse, whose size was due to his great antiquity.[44]

Eusebius' fourth-century CE *Praeparatio evangelica* stands as a bridge between the Roman era sources and earlier traditions, as Eusebius cites several authors dating back to the third century BCE regarding ancient Near Eastern giants. In *Praep. evan.* 9.17, Eusebius quotes at length from Alexander Polyhistor (first century BCE), who is himself recounting writings from a certain Samaritan, (Pseudo-) Eupolemos (c. second-third century BCE):[45]

> Eupolemus in his book *Concerning the Jews of Assyria* says that the city Babylon was first founded by those who escaped from the Deluge; and that they were giants, and built the tower renowned in history. But when this had been overthrown by the act of God, the giants were dispersed over the whole earth.[46]

Then, apparently quoting Artabanus' *Jewish History*, Eupolemus (again, via Polyhistor, via Eusebius) draws Abraham into the narrative of giants (9.18) by asserting that "Abraham traced his origin to the giants" dwelling in Babylon. We also find a plethora of materials dealing with giants in the Enochic corpus and at Qumran—specifically, in 1 Enoch 6–11 and 15, and *4QBook of Giants*[47]—among other sources, and I will return to these in greater detail later

---

whom Lucretius is a representative, as analogous to the Giants (e.g., *De rerum natura* 1.72–74, 5.117).

44. Pausanias 1913, 1: 412; see also 1: 416. This view of human physical degeneration is repeated in a number of sources, including, most famously, Hesiod's *Works and Days*, but also 4th Ezra 5:52–55, Pliny, *De opif.* 140, Cyprian, *ad Demetrianum* I.352, and various passages of rabbinic literature (*j. Demai* 3:1 // *Gen. R.* 60:8; *j. Shek.* 5:1; *b. Shabb.* 112b, etc.), as cited in Stone 1990, 142, 153–54.

45. I learned of these sources from Gmirkin 2006, 127–29. Note that there was a Jewish author Eupolemus, whom Eusebius confuses with an anonymous Samaritan author, viz., *Pseudo-Eupolemus* (Gmirkin 2006, 127 n. 281).

46. J. C. Reeves (1993, 110–15) argues that 1QapGen and 1 Enoch 106–07 attempted to refute the notion that *Noah* was a giant—a notion which was, Reeves claims, possibly upheld in the traditions recorded by Psuedo-Eupolemus. Moreover, according to Reeves, an Aramaic tradition was used as the vehicle by which characters such as Noah and various Mesopotamian figures "travelled" about the Near East and made appearances in disparate literatures and traditions. The "Prayer of Nabonidus" is one example of this phenomenon; see Steiner and Nims 1985; cf. Huggins 1995.

47. For Enoch, see the relevant passages in Nickelsburg 2001; on *4QBook of Giants*, see García Martínez 1992, 97–115 and Stuckenbruck 1997.

in this study. For the moment, suffice it to say that the "resurrection" of the giant in post-biblical materials took its creative impetus from the biblical materials themselves (especially Gen 6:1–4), and seized upon interpretive possibilities bound up in the monstrous and enigmatic features of biblical characters.

III. The Giants of Old

We now arrive at the earliest documented examples of giants that became the fixations of later audiences, from the ancient Mediterranean world. In the Archaic (c. 800–480 BCE) Aegean and Greek speaking contexts, narratives of Giants (*Gigantes*), Titans (*Titanes*), and other oversized beings played a variety of significant roles, though we do not possess an early, independent, fully-developed textual account of these beings' origins. The Titanomachy was, apparently, the first (or second) poem within the so-called "Epic Cycle," the existence of which is first vaguely attested probably by Aristotle (*Anal. Post.* I.12), but which was probably already in some written form in the sixth century BCE.[48] The status of the Cycle itself within the corpus of Greek epic and myth, and the giants' place within this Cycle, is telling: "Cycle" was a derogatory term used by both scholars both ancient (e.g., Aristotle, in the *Poetics*) and modern (J. Wackernagel), the latter echoing Aristotle's criticisms by pointing to the Homeric *Konstanz des Stils* (consistent style) as opposed to the slapdash style of the *Little Iliad*, for example. Thus, the Greek giant traditions, it would seem, were sometimes embedded within a subset of stories that were early on considered inferior to (or, at least, different from) the Homeric corpus.

Whatever the case, elements of a Titanomachy already appeared embedded within Hesiod's *Theogony* (617ff.) in the eighth century. Earlier in the *Theogony* (173ff.), Giants (along with the Erinus) are conceived and born, after an indeterminate period of incubation, as the result of blood-drops issuing from Cronus' castration of Ouranos (Gaia). Hesiod's giants are born pre-fitted with shining armor, spears in hand. As M. West points out in his commentary, these auto-armored beings recall the Sparti of the Cadmus

---

48. A very good summary of the Cycle and the history of its scholarship, from which I draw heavily here, is M. Davies 1989, 1–3. The other works in the Cycle include the *Cypria, Aethiopis, Little Iliad, Iliou Persis, Nostoi,* and *Telegony.* As Nagy (1992, 37) points out, the most ancient references to Homer credit him with composing not just the *Iliad* and *Odyssey* but also other parts of the Cycle, specifically the *Cypria* and *Little Iliad.* Further summaries can be found in Burgess 2001, 7–10; M. Davies 1989, 33–52; Burgess 1996, 2002; Finkelberg 2000; Griffin 1977. On possible references to the *Iliad* in the *Cypria,* see Tsagalis 2008. But Burgess (1996) has argued that parts of the Epic Cycle must predate Homer, and that the *Iliad* alludes to material spelled out clearly in the Cycle. On this, see Marks 2002.

legends, earth-born figures born from sown dragon teeth as a fully-armed fighting force. The Giants are born to make war, even though Hesiod barely mentions the Gigantomachy proper (see *Theog.* 954).[49] We do not know much about the Titanomachy, which should and should not be distinguished from the Gigantomachy proper.[50] The Gigantomachy is technically subsequent to the Titanomachy—even though Zeus and company had established control over the cosmos by defeating Cronus and the Titans in the deep past, further Giants (and other monstrous figures) arise and are barely defeated in an exhausting battle.[51] The two words, *Titan-* and *Gigant-omachy*, are graphically similar in the Greek writing system, and there is evidence that scribes mis-copied one word for the other; moreover, the Titanomachy and Gigantomachy were conflated already in the fifth century, if not earlier, based on the similarity of themes and basic actors.[52]

This Titanomachy-Gigantomachy sequence begins to establish a pattern: giants must be defeated by (would be) ruling authorities on multiple occasions, as their eternal banishment cannot be easily guaranteed. Indeed, this must be the impetus behind the Greek obsession with depicting the Gigantomachy, specifically, as a major artistic theme in sixth-century temple art and architecture.[53] The Siphnian treasury building (*thēsauros*) at Delphi—one among many at the site during the sixth century—was the most artistically ornate and important structure of its kind.[54] Among the striking friezes, the north side images—running through the sanctuary parallel to the "sacred way," thus providing the most conspicuous visual commentary to visitors of the Siphnian treasury—portray the Giants, decked out as Greek hoplites,

49. West 1966, 220–221. West claims that *Theog.* 954 is a post-Hesiodic "allusion" to the Gigantomachy, presumably the reference to Zeus' "great work among the immortals." The reference seems less than clear.

50. See Vian 1988; Mondi 1986; West 2002. See also the older but still authoritative works of Dörig and Gigon (1961) and Vian (1952). For later adaptation of these motifs, see, e.g., Hardie 1983.

51. Note also that Hesiod's Titanomachy (*Theog.* 617–38) ends in a draw, after a painful and inconclusive battle. For the most detailed version of the Gigantomachy, see the second-century BCE work of Apollodorus (1921, I.vi.1–3). In some of these later traditions, the Giants mount an attack on Olympus by building a "tower," as it were, up to the heavens, and still later accounts (Ovid's *Metamorphoses* 1.151–62, 262–312) involve yet a new generation, born from the blood-drops of the giants themselves, which is then exterminated via divine flood. See references in Mussies 1999, 343. Apollodorus' version may also allude to the flood in one particular fragment of the Titanomachy; see Bremmer 1998 for a more extended discussion.

52. M. Davies 1989, 14.

53. The Titanomachy, by contrast, cannot be specifically identified in any extant iconography. See Bažant 1997, 31–32. On the Gigantomachy iconography, see Moore 1995, 1979.

54. The mid-southern Aegean island of Siphnos had amassed wealth from precious metal mining on their island; see Neer 2001; Watrous 1982; R. Osborne 1998, 122–24.

fighting the gods (see Figure 1).[55] Though the ultimate meaning of the battle scene is debated, what remains clear is the ongoing relevance of the cosmic battle against the giant in contemporary, politicized contexts.

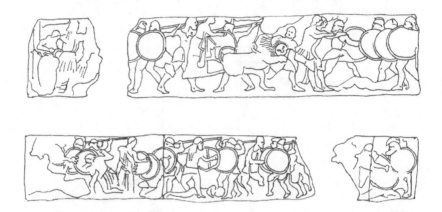

Figure 1. North side frieze, Siphnian treasury at Delphi.

Despite its popular appeal for students of the ancient Greek world, the Gigantomachy is not the lone exemplar of the gigantism motif from this era. In the archaic and classical traditions of the ancient Aegean world, we find an often explicitly stated assumption that the Greek heroes were giants.[56] Consider, for example, Herodotus' account of an anonymous ironsmith finding Orestes' bones in *Hist.* 1.68: "...as I was digging I came on a huge coffin—ten feet long! I couldn't believe that men were ever bigger than they are today, so I opened it—and there was the corpse, as big as the coffin! I measured it, and then shoveled the earth back in."[57] Though the Gigantomachy and explicit references to the typically grotesque aspects of gigantism play only a relatively minor role in Homer, a passing reference in the *Iliad* (5.302–4) reveals the superior physical status of the heroic warriors: "But the son of Tydeus grasped in his hand a stone—a great deed—one that not two men could carry, such as mortals now are; yet easily did he wield it even alone." Similarly, in describing one of his own battles of yore, Nestor recounts that "I fought as my own man; but with them no man of all mortals that now are on the earth could fight" (1.271–72)—presumably the "mortals now on the earth" continue to grow smaller and weaker, so that even the mighty deeds of Diomedes pale in comparison to yet earlier exploits.

55. Refer to the List of Illustrations on page ix for bibliographic information for all figures.
56. Indeed, the identification of heroic bones was premised upon their gigantic size. See McCauley 1999, 93; Mayor 2000, 260–81; R. Fox 2008, 319–32; Lenormant 1899, 352.
57. Quotation from *Hist.*, 30.

With such statements Homer may be suggesting the physically giant status of the Trojan War heroes, though the gulf between the heroic race and the contemporary ancient Greek audience was presumably viewed as more expansive than a simple difference in height or sheer physical strength. Explicit references to giants make several prominent appearances in the *Odyssey*, populated as the story is with fantastical creatures of various kinds. Most famous are the Cyclopes, brutish and cave-dwelling, "an insolent and lawless folk" (9.106), represented most personally by Polyphemus. Moreover, the Laestrygonians are "not like men, but like Giants" (10.120), one of whom (their queen) has a mountain-like stature (10.112-3).

Subtler identification of Greek heroes with giants may be found, moreover, in texts where the actions of particular figures are patterned after motifs and plots in the mythic Greek giant traditions, thus demonstrating an interpretive conflation not simply relegated to physical size but extending to re-enactment of mythic plots.[58] The conflation of the phenomenon of the giant as a historical curiosity and the giant status of humans in the heroic age is by no means accidental or incidental; the allusion in *Il.* 5.302-04 to a "heroic age" whose inhabitants are qualitatively different from those in the world of the "normal" human audience of the story resonates most obviously with Hesiod's famous description of a heroic age in the five-generation scheme of the *Works and Days* (106-201).

Some have claimed that second-first millennium BCE Mesopotamian literature (i.e., outside of Israel) did not fixate on the figure of the giant in any profound manner. As A. Schüle bluntly puts it, "the mixing and mingling between humans and gods as a result of sexual intercourse and also the emergence of heroes and giants—have no parallels in Mesopotamia. As a matter of fact, one might say these appear rather alien in the Ancient Near Eastern context."[59] Such a judgment is only partly justified in terms of the cuneiform cultures. One of the most prominent—if not *the* most prominent—human hero in this context, Gilgamesh, is, in fact, explicitly marked as a semi-human giant: see *Gilg.* I.53-61, where each of Gilgamesh's feet measures "a triple cubit" and each stride "six cubits," due in part to his status as two parts deity and one part human.[60]

---

58. See, e.g., Delcourt and Rankin 1965, 215-16 regarding the character of the hero Ajax (the Locrian) in the *Iliad* and the Greek giant traditions.

59. Schüle 2009, 122. For his own part, Schüle perceptively notes the basic similarities between Gen 6:1-4 and Greek heroic tropes, and Schüle assumes that the original audience of Gen 6:1-4 would have known about Greek heroic tropes and viewed the text in this light.

60. See *Gilg.* vol. 1: 540-41. Note that the text is broken at this point of describing Gilgamesh's physique, but an early Hittite paraphrase preserves this part of the epic, indicating that the physical description was in fact a part of the text's earlier recensions. Coupled with the immediately preceding (*Gilg.* I.48) description of Gilgamesh as "two-thirds" divine (*šit-*

Figure 2. Victory stele of Naram-Sin.

Indeed, the gods themselves in the ancient Near East were thought to be of great size, and thus it is no surprise to find their descendants sharing in their physical stature.[61] Gilgamesh's extraordinary height is not an anomaly in the early Mesopotamian context. Consider, for example, the Sumerian king Eannatum's five-and-a-half-cubit stature recorded in the Stele of Vultures,[62] as well as the portrayal of Naram-Sin on his victory stele of c. 2200 BCE, where the divinized king stands a full head and shoulders above his defeated

---

tin-šú ilum [dingir]-*ma šul-lul-ta-šú a-me-lu-tu*, "two-thirds of him god but one third of him human"), we have in *Gilg.* I.48–62 a skeletal ancient Near Eastern description of two key elements of the later Greek hero, viz., outstanding size and divine parentage.

61. In the Bible, note Isa 6:1, and cf. the iconography of the shield of Achilles described in *Iliad* 18, where the author has the gods towering above humans. But cf. Perlitt (1994, 208), who disassociates the iconographic motifs of gigantism from any concept of giant *humans* in the Mesopotamian and Egyptian sources.

62. See *Gilg.* 1: 447, and sources cited there.

Figure 3. Ramses II.

foes (see Figure 2).[63] Monumental depictions of the Egyptian Pharaoh similarly aggrandize the king through physical gigantism (Figure 3),[64] and various
cylinder seals from Ugarit and elsewhere are sometimes thought to depict
physical gigantism (Figure 4).[65] A thirteenth-century BCE Hittite relief from
Yazilikaya depicts a giant deity holding the human king (Figure 5), and the
courtyard entrance to the famous 'Ain Dara temple (tenth-eighth centuries
BCE) is marked by the giant deity's footprints.[66] To be sure, the physical size
of a being looms large in proportion to that being's power, status, and authority, and need not be confined to mundane gigantism (though ancient
audiences surely imagined such beings as literally huge).[67]

63. See Winter 1996, 2004. One is reminded also of the famous depiction of the giant king
on the frontispiece to Thomas Hobbes' 1651 *Leviathan*. Here too the king is integrated into the
broader scene, and yet looms above and beyond that scene into other, heavenly realms.

64. See Keel 1975, esp. 419, 421, 427, 440, 446, 448, etc.

65. Collon 1987, 182–186, esp. ill. 859–62. It is not clear whether or not these images are
actually "giants," or whether they are human giants or other monsters of some kind. Collon
1987, 183 thinks that depictions of giants are "rare, probably because it is difficult to give an
impression of immense size and, at the same time, create a balanced composition." Mesopotamian artists solved the problem, according to Collon, by "placing them sideways-on."

66. See King and Stager 2001, 338, and Thompson 2008.

67. See this same point, made in a different way and for Germanic giants by Motz (1982,
74–76).

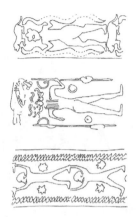

Figure 4. Cylinder seals from Ugarit.

Figure 5. Hittite relief from Yazilikaya.

IV. The Biblical Giants

Such examples could obviously be multiplied. What is important to notice here is that millennia of interpreters saw the existence of giants as a historical fact, verifiable either by esoteric appeals to the state of the world after the Deluge or by fossil remains and local folklore. Moreover, any discussion of the way giants were viewed in antiquity must acknowledge the fact that ancient audiences viewed giants as a distinct "race" of humans (even if partial-humans).[68] So too, ancient Israelite authors engaged in speculative attempts—however brief—to situate the origins of giants in a specific incident (Gen 6:1–4), and stories of giants in the land pre-Israel (Deuteronomy 2–3) and during David's era (1 Samuel 17, etc.) confirm the "reality" of the ancient speculation.

Moreover, in the Hebrew Bible various giants are explicitly drawn into an ethnographic narrative, which then places the giants within the framework of Israel's own attempt to identify itself as a legitimate people inheriting the land. However the Israelites came to occupy their place in the central hill country beginning in the late thirteenth century BCE, Israel's forerunners in the land were *not actually giants*—there is no archaeological or other evidence to suggest this—and this indicates that we are dealing with an explicitly *ideological* tradition, marked not by a disinterested catalogue of the land's aboriginal inhabitants but rather by an intentional, sustained,

68. On this, see Stephens 1989, 78–79.

interpretive program. From a historical point of view, then, these groups of giants in the land present us with the problem of *two* ethnicities and *two* geographies—the real ethnic groups that presumably lived in pre-Israelite Canaan (including the "proto-Israelites" themselves)[69] and the mythical inhabitants, the giants, and the mythical geographies they inhabit.[70]

In their invocation of giants, Israelites participated in a longstanding ancient tradition, documented briefly above, of speculation regarding giants who lived mostly in a bygone era but also sometimes persist into the contemporary world. In fact, as we have already seen via several post-biblical examples, the Bible's giants become *the* model, the exemplary, canonical presentation of the giant for Western civilization. We are thus led to the question of *why* ancient Israelites authors engaged in this tradition, and *how*, exactly, they chose to evoke it.

There are, of course, obvious and simple interpretations—which are by no means incorrect in their obviousness or simplicity—to these questions of "why" and "how," e.g., that giants-as-enemies of Israel make Israel's victories seem more miraculous, and serve to elevate the power and status of Israel's warriors, and so on. A closer consideration, however, of Israel's giants and the manner in which these figures are presented reveals a more complicated storyline. Succinctly put, it becomes quickly apparent that the category of the giant as a grotesque embodiment of the enemy becomes conflated with another concept, that of the giant as a heroic warrior;[71] we have giants in

69. These real, historical entities are studied in their own right, of course; see, recently, Killebrew 2005. The extent to which the Hebrew Bible and other *textual* materials from the Late Bronze – Iron Ages can give us accurate historical information about the pre-Israelite residents of the land has been the source of much contention. See, e.g., Na'aman 2005a. *Pace*, e.g., Lemche 1991, I do believe in the possibility that the Hebrew Bible and other ancient texts used ethnic designations with some historical precision, though each case must be investigated on its own merits.

70. I am using the word "myth" here somewhat loosely, in the more modern "functional" sense it has sometimes acquired, i.e., not only as "story about the gods" (in the formal tradition) but as a label for a story of origins that is not straightforwardly "historical." Compare with Waardenburg 1980, 55: "mythic elements derive their force precisely from the fact that they suggest rather than explain...They function as foundation stones from certain basic assumptions in the life of a community or person," as well as Dundes 1984, 1: "A myth is a sacred narrative explaining how the world and man came to be in their present form."

71. At this point, it is important to note that one may begin to define the "hero" and the historico-literary context in which he exists in two interrelated—yet also potentially isolatable—ways, each of which is significant in its own right: (1) as an *individual* whose conception, birth, flight, experience, return, etc. fall into a recognizable patterns—see, e.g., the psychoanalytic approach of Rank (1959, 3–86); Raglan (1956), who adopts a myth and ritual school approach in his famous essay; and the very well-known work of Campbell (1950); and (2) as one part of a larger group of heroes (many of whom may be individually nameless) who comprise a "heroic age," i.e., *a group* living within an epoch wherein heroic individuals (who no longer

both their familiar capacity as "freaks" (six fingers, giant beds, etc.) and also as a multitudinous indigenous population in the land of Canaan—a group the Israelites are to defeat in a sort of Israelite gigantomachy.

Studies of the ancient Israelite encounter with giants by Biblical scholars have been sporadic, though a spate of promising studies has begun to focus on the topic.[72] For example, a recent contribution by C. Lemardelé on the topic of giants, heroes, and the possibility for Greek-Semitic interaction on these topics anticipates some central assertions of the present study.[73] Lemardelé argues that that the notion of gigantic, ante-diluvian warriors mentioned in Gen 6:1–4 have their origin in West-Semitic notions of the heroic and not the Greek Gigantomachy, and briefly reviews other passages in which heroic and gigantic concepts intersect (Num 13; Deut 2–3; Isa 14; Ezek 32; 2 Sam 21, 23; Judg 5, 15). A most intriguing, but very much undeveloped, concept in Lemardelé's essay is the suggestion that these bygone heroic warriors played some role in afterlife conceptions, the strongest evidence for which occurs in Ezek 32.[74] An earlier and more comprehensive study by L. Perlitt also directly addresses the Bible's giants, though Perlitt is skeptical of any meaningful connection between the living heroic or gigantic races and the living (such as may be embodied in the living and dead Rephaim).[75] For Perlitt, the Bible's giant traditions are "ein mythologisches Spiel, das dem Alten Testament fremd ist," and the Mesopotamian and Egyptian sources so vital to the Bible's own ideological world had no direct conception of the giant as such.[76]

---

exist in the historical present of the narrator) were thought to be prevalent upon the earth (see, e.g., the famous description in Hesiod's *Works and Days* 106–201 and *Catalogue of Women*, as well as similar reflections on the rise and fall of heroic ages in Homer's *Iliad*, the *Cypria* cycle, and the Indic *Mahābhārata*). It is most poignantly in this latter sense, I will argue, that the biblical depictions of giants partake in this definition of the hero, and it is this theme of the heroic age in the Bible that is very much underexplored, especially vis-à-vis attempts to see, e.g., the Judges or David as heroes, etc.

72. Note the forthcoming work of Goff (2014), as well as three recent dissertations: Galbraith (in progress); Doak 2011; Thomas 2005. For articles, see, e.g., Goff 2010a; 2010b; 2009a; 2009b; Lemardelé 2010b; Hendel 2009.

73. Lemardelé 2010b. Unfortunately, this article—as well as Perlitt 1994—came to my attention too late for a more robust treatment; nevertheless, I have attempted to integrate them into the discussion wherever possible. See also J. Wright (2011, 145–46, 153), who draws attention to the Israelite encounter with the giant as a heroic motif.

74. See Lemardelé 2010b, 167 on the relationship between the Gibborim, Rephaim, Nephilim, and fallen heroic warriors, as well as my forthcoming article, "Ezekiel's Topography of the (Un-)Heroic Dead in Ezek 32:17–32," in the *Journal of Biblical Literature*. See also, recently (and briefly), Schüle 2009 for comments on Gen 6:1–4 in conversation with Greek heroic literature.

75. Perlitt 1994, esp. 231 on the question of the Rephaim.

76. Perlitt 1994, 208 asserts that Egyptians and Mesopotamians had no concept of the giant (*Riese*) as a word or a concept.

Other modern interpreters have, in a mostly limited and relatively isolated manner, delved into several aspects of the giants in the Hebrew Bible.
For example, the identification of Og of Bashan's עֶרֶשׂ בַּרְזֶל ("bed of iron") in
Deut 3:11 as either a literal "bed" of iron or a monument of some kind (perhaps a tomb) has spawned many comments, with interpreters lined up on
either side of the debate.[77] Such a question may seem trivial, but it is certainly the case that the figure of Og stands as an important crux in the tradition
of pre-Israelite giants, associated as he is with what appears to be a shared
tradition in the southern Levant of giants inhabiting the Transjordan (Deut
3:8; but cf. 3:11; Josh 12:4, 13:12, etc.).[78] In a highly original—if not at points
highly problematic in its rather loosely argued structure—study entitled
"The Aegean Ogygos of Boeotia and the Biblical Og of Bashan: Reflections of
the Same Myth," S. Noegel argues that the Greek hero Ogygos (as featured
in Aeschylus, *Seven Against Thebes* 3.21; Hesiod, *Theogony* 806, etc.) and the
biblical Og are either independently attested examples of the same mythic
character and accompanying plot lines, or that the story was transmitted
from East to West sometime in the Iron Age.[79] Noegel cites what he views as
the similarity of the personal names and geographic origins, a pejorative,
anti-deity tradition associated with each character, connections between
both figures with the underworld, martial exploits, and some shared accompanying symbolic imagery (snakes, necklaces, floods, and cows), and
draws the not unreasonable conclusion (though it is stated with some hesi-
tancy) that these two mythic complexes are related. To be sure, any one of
these parallel aspects on its own would hardly be worth mentioning, but as
a group, they suggest the Og-Ogyges association and its implications for the
origins of both stories in an early and widely disseminated Mediterranean
context are worth further exploration.

Another, more common point of conjecture regarding both giants and
Greek-Semitic connections involves the figure of Goliath of Gath. Besides the
issue of Goliath's Philistine origin and the putative homeland of the Philistines somewhere in the Aegean or Cyprus (see Amos 9:7), much attention has
been focused on Goliath's armor and whether its description in 1 Sam 17:5–7
preserves any historical memory of the Mycenaean style gear a warrior like
Goliath might be expected to wear.[80] Two recent—and very different—essays

77. A detailed discussion of this issue appears in Chapter 2 of this study, with further analysis of the Og tradition in Chapter 4. See Linquist 2011; Veijola 2003; Millard 1988.

78. See Bartlett 1970.

79. Noegel 1998. Wyatt (2005) has followed up on some of Noegel's suggestions, and note
also Brichto 1998, 136.

80. See, e.g., Galling (1966, 150–69), who is pessimistic about the historical reality of the
Bible's portrayal of Goliath. His views have been taken up by I. Finkelstein (2002). Cf. Zorn 2010
and King 2007.

by A. Millard and A. Yadin tackle this question anew.[81] Millard rehearses the standard arguments for the historicity of the armor's description (iconographic parallels with Mycenaean art, the motif of single combat in Greek sources, and the use of bronze instead of iron) and concludes that the Bible should be given the benefit of the doubt in such matters. Yadin offers a different approach to the question. Citing arguments both for and against the historicity of the famous duel, Yadin highlights the "turn toward the heroic past" evident in Greece and elsewhere in the Mediterranean in the seventh century BCE and afterward,[82] and then argues that the depiction of David in 1 Samuel 17 contributes significantly to Israelite "collective memory," in which the "anti-hero" David is shown shunning the entrapments of armor and defeating the Greek-style warrior. Rather than reflecting an Iron Age origin for Goliath's armor, Yadin contends that this story should be read as Israelite "national narrative," with knowing and deliberate intertextual references to the theme of single combat in the *Iliad* specifically.[83] In this way, Israelite identity is forged through a contest of competing identities involving the Philistines and specifically through the connection, found in various places in the Bible, between the Philistines and giants (e.g., 2 Sam 21:15–22 // 1 Chr 20:4–8).[84] In arguing thus, Yadin raises fascinating and underexplored questions regarding the manner in which stories of giants and heroic death intersect with the Greek world and its own presentation of heroes, and these questions should be applied not only to 1 Samuel 17 but to other texts wherein these same themes occur.

Yet a third text with great relevance for the present study wherein giants and Greek elements have often been found is the incident in Gen 6:1–4 involving divine-human miscegenation. Scholars have devoted an immense amount of attention to this short and enigmatic passage, focusing primarily on problems of syntax and translation, antecedent Mesopotamian traditions, and the identity of the various groups mentioned with such tantalizing brevity (the "sons of God" or "divine beings," Nephilim, and Gibborim).[85] The

---

81. Millard 2009; A. Yadin 2004; cf. some earlier comments by Y. Yadin (1963, 265) and MacLaurin (1965). I deal with MacLaurin's thesis in the following chapter.

82. A. Yadin 2004, 384.

83. A. Yadin 2004, 385, 393–94. While not directly suggesting that the biblical author read Homer, Yadin ambiguously states that the shared features were "spurred" by "the spread of Homeric epic" (A. Yadin 2004, 385).

84. On the issue of early Israelite identity vis-à-vis the Philistines, see also Machinist 2000, 64–65. Specifically, Machinist makes the significant argument that the Philistines—often represented by giants (Goliath, the Anaqim, and various other individuals [2 Sam 21:15–22 // 1 Chr 20:4–8])—are the primary "opponent" or "other" vis-à-vis monarchic Israel.

85. The secondary literature on Gen 6:1–4 is enormous. For an overview, see Collins 2008; Hendel 2004; Westermann 1984, 363–83.

polysemy inherent in the sparseness of Gen 6:1–4 opened up a world of interpretive possibilities in the post-exilic apocalyptic writings, which found a point of departure in the Torah in these four verses.[86] Though rarely cited in the secondary literature, one of the more significant studies to explore Gen 6:1–4 and Greek concepts of the giant and the hero is R. Bartelmus' 1979 monograph, *Heroentum in Israel und seiner Umwelt*.[87] Regarding Gen 6:1–4, Bartelmus forwards the argument that the heroes were born to confront the giants and defeat primeval monstrous beings.[88] Gen 6:1–4 then functions, in Bartelmus' view, as an etiological tale recounting the beginning of the *ongoing battle* between the hero and the giant. This conflict not only appears in Israel's own "historical" narrative in the David and Goliath battle, to which Bartelmus devotes an extended discussion,[89] but also scattered throughout the accounts of conquest in Numbers through Joshua, where the conquering Israelites must face either a selected group of giants, or, as implied in other parts of the tradition, an *entire land* populated with giants.[90] These latter examples of the appearance of giants are mostly ignored by Bartelmus, but would have served as compelling examples of the extension of the *Heroenkonzept* ("hero concept") from Gen 6:4 to later materials.[91] Bartelmus does make very brief reference to a number of literary fragments of the *Heroenkonzept*, including the Shamgar episode (Judg 3:31), various appearances of the word גבור (Gibbor), and other heroic acts surrounding the encounter between David's army and the Philistines, but he does not develop any of these at length.[92]

The mythical notion of the gigantomachy, of course, has its most explicit expression in the Greek sources,[93] but Bartelmus is able to adduce other aspects of the *Heroenkonzept* in the Homeric epic tradition, such as the motif of humans in battle against deities, the grounding of the genealogy of the landed aristocracy in the persons of the heroes of old, and the conception

86. See Stuckenbruck 2004 and Collins 2008.

87. Bartelmus 1979, 207–17. Note also Dexinger 1966, 46–53 and 67–69, where Dexinger takes up the interpretation of the Gibborim in Gen 6:4 in terms of Greek heroes.

88. Bartelmus 1979, 23.

89. Bartelmus 1979, 128–50. The other major biblical story employed as an outgrowth of the *Heroenkonzept* is the Samson cycle in Judges 13–16 (pp. 79–111).

90. E.g., Deut 9:2 and Josh 11:21 seem to allot a significant portion of the territory west of the Jordan to the Anaqim.

91. By "extension" here I mean, at least, in a literary sense following the canonical order of the materials (if not historically, i.e., source-critically). Bartelmus 1979, 28 n. 23 implies a very late dating for Gen 6:3, citing the fact that the issue of the 120-year lifespan is first alluded to in Jub 5:8.

92. Bartelmus 1979, 112–13.

93. See Hesiod's *Theogony*, lines 173, 617–88; cf. Ovid's *Metamorphoses* 1.151–62, 262–312.

of a "heroic age" in Hesiod (*Works and Days* 106–201, etc.).[94] Moreover, Bartelmus is correct to temper his comparative evidence with recognitions of difference; the Greek heroic world developed its heroes far beyond what we see on the surface of the narrative of the Hebrew Bible, into the realm of apotheosis and hero cults.[95] Bartlemus' comparative thrust is not limited to Greek materials, but also includes instances of the *Heroenkonzept* in the Near Eastern world as well. Bartelmus first finds a "spiritual homeland" for the motif of heroic origins in divine-human miscegenation in the world of Sumerian and Akkadian myth, particularly in the stories surrounding the figures of Enmerkar and Gilgamesh,[96] and he views Ugarit as the cultural mediator between the Near East and Greece for the spread of the *Heroenkonzept* in the Mediterranean.[97]

Another important study dealing with Gen 6:1–4 is R. Hendel's 1987 article "Of Demigods and the Deluge," in which Hendel directly tackles the question of the biblical episode in light of Greek epic tradition and the role of giants in the Conquest narrative.[98] Hendel's method—spelled out in his earlier study, *The Epic of the Patriarch*[99]—is explicitly comparative. In his essay on Gen 6:1–4, Hendel probes more deeply into the interrelationship between Israel's stories of beginnings and the Greek epic context. Hendel makes the not completely original argument that the boundary-crossing act

94. Bartelmus 1979, 63–74.

95. Bartelmus 1979, 78.

96. Bartelmus 1979, 36–55.

97. Bartelmus 1979, 55–59. The Ugaritic texts themselves, however, are not seriously considered by Bartelmus.

98. Hendel 1987b.

99. Hendel 1987a. Hendel draws explicitly upon the work of Lord in *The Singer of Tales* to discuss epic and oral patterns in the patriarchal narratives. Hendel views the similarities in birth accounts of prominent characters between Ugarit and Israel as "multiforms in the continuous tradition of oral narrative in the Canaanite-Israelite sphere," a tradition whose purposes ultimately lie in the bardic act of telling the story itself, with "the important moments occur[ring] at the point of an impasse or a resolution" (Hendel 1987a, 58–59). Hendel's recognition of the relationship between epic, hero, and cult is significant; Hendel points to the link between the Jacob traditions and the Bethel cult as an example of this symbiosis. Other, subtler clues appear, such as Jacob's act of dressing himself in animal hides to deceive his father, an act charged with "a ritual play on the role of the sacrificer and the sacrificed and on the nature of the ritual blessing." In the Jacob narrative, as well as in the account of conflict between Aqhat and Anat, one finds "a narrative design in which traces of ritual, death, and taboo remain" (Hendel 1987a, 70–71). Such assertions, of course, have their underpinning in the work of the so-called "myth and ritual" theorists, the pioneers of which were W. Robertson Smith and J. G. Frazer in the late nineteenth century. See Segal 1998. Furthermore, in this context of underlying myth and cult we find a tension between the hero and an "other," his adversary (e.g., Gen 32); "the hero and the other are also opposites; from their encounter comes the harmony we call epic" (Hendel 1987a, 101–02; see also 103–09).

of divine-human sexual congress is meant, within the narrative of Gen 1–11, to provide the rationale for the Flood.[100] Moreover, Hendel argues, this particular motif of an out-of-control and partially divine population as cause for a cataclysmic divine judgment is a motif found both in Mesopotamia and in Greece, and thus Gen 6:1–4 represents Israel's own "peculiar twist" on this motif as it traversed the fertile crescent and Mediterranean and back again.[101] The Mesopotamian manifestations of the Flood story are indeed well known and important, but it is Hendel's treatment of Greek parallels that is most provocative and suggestive for my interests here.[102]

Citing a tradition inscribed into various Indo-European texts, including the *Cypria*, *Iliad*, and the Indic *Mahābhārata*, in which human overpopulation (or specifically the overpopulation of raging heroes) and mounting human offenses prompts a divine extermination, Hendel suggests that the Flood and Trojan War tradition writ large represent parallel moments of epic/mythic action.[103] The biblical Nephilim, then, like the Homeric heroes, "exist in order to be wiped out"—they live in order to die.[104] Where Hendel's study falls short, in my view, is that this very notion of mounting iniquity involving the heroes, giants, and divine-human miscegenation is by no means a trope limited to Gen 6:1–4, spectacular though this text may be; this pattern is scattered throughout various texts wherein giants and other non-Israelite heroic figures are to be found. Hendel is able to point out, with some puzzlement, the connection among the Nephilim, Rephaim, and death, and the connection between these groups and the Greek heroic generation, but he

100. Hendel 1987b, 16–18.

101. Hendel 1987b, 17. Especially instructive here is the fact that Hendel has opened up the possibility that such motifs traversed through the Levant in *two* directions, from east and west and back again. Astour 1965, 361, asserted that "Semiticism was the prologue of Greek civilization." This East-West movement was surely one stream, but the exchange went both ways (and was ongoing), and a recognition of the historical origin of certain elements in the east in no way precludes the possibility of influence in the opposite direction, or of originally Semitic motifs mediated through Greece and re-asserted back on the East. Our a priori assumption, in fact, must be that the exchange was at least this complex, and probably even more so.

102. Hendel 1987b, 20. Hendel relies heavily at this point on the earlier studies of Scodel (1982); Koenen (1994); Nagy (2006). Far earlier (and not acknowledged by any modern scholar of which I am aware), Hobbes (1962 [first published 1651], 356) had conflated the identities of Greek heroes and biblical giants: "...because those mighty men of the earth, that lived in the time of Noah, before the flood, (which the Greeks call *heroes*, and the Scripture *giants*, and both were begotten by copulation of the children of God with the children of men,) were for their wicked life destroyed by the general deluge; the place of the damned, is therefore also sometimes marked out, by the company of those deceased giants..."

103. Hendel 1987b, 20–21. Hendel (1987b, 23) even suggests these motifs share a historical origin in the Late Bronze Age.

104. Hendel 1987b, 21.

is unable to take this exploration to the next level, i.e., of understanding how the exact relationship among death/afterlife, the Greek hero, and the appearance of biblical figures like the Rephaim represents a complex and shared Mediterranean matrix of religious ideas regarding aspects of both the biblical "generation" of giants and the Greek heroic *génos*.

Finally, an additional extended study attempting to integrate various elements of comparative epic and classical studies of the hero with selected biblical stories is G. Mobley's *The Empty Men: The Heroic Tradition of Ancient Israel*, a book that partly overlaps with ideas expressed earlier by Mobley in an article entitled "The Wild Man in the Bible and the Ancient Near East."[105] Though Mobley nowhere addresses the Mediterranean context from which terms like "hero" and "heroic age" are inevitably drawn—a significant drawback of the study, if not a lost opportunity, in my view[106]—he does use these categories in ways that invite further discussion in terms of my project in two areas: the "heroic age" and the function of such an age in the periodization of history, and the interface between giants and heroic action in the Hebrew Bible.

For Mobley, it is the category of the "empty men" (אנשים רקים, Judg 9:4, 11:3; 2 Chr 13:7), i.e., the propertyless adventurers of the early Iron Age, that serves as a gateway into the broader issue of Israelite heroic culture, and it is particularly the eras of the Judges and the Davidic monarchy that form, in Mobley's conception, Israel's "heroic age." More specifically, in Mobley's view, the Deuteronomistic History periodizes its narrative first in terms of the heroic age of Gibborim (גברים), followed by an age of kings (מלכים) beginning with Solomon's rise to kingship, and finally, for most of the book of Kings, it is the prophet (נביא), presumably embodied most clearly in the Elijah-Elisha cycle, who represents the third movement in this periodization.[107] This focus on the periodization of history is a compelling avenue for further investigation, though Mobley's own treatment is significantly light on substance and detail. Mobley does not devote enough attention, for example, to the complex questions of *why* one age ends and another begins, and there are, as Mobley would no doubt recognize, other, more complex movements in the Deuteronomist's (and the Pentateuchal authors') historical periodization that could be pursued.

One other aspect of Mobley's work worth mentioning for the purpose of my own interests involves the role of giants in heroic action. In his 1987 article, Mobley lists giants as one manifestation of the category of the "wild

---

105. Mobley 2005; 1997.
106. Mobley 2005, 53–54 makes one brief reference to "single combat."
107. Mobley 2005, 229–33.

man" in the Hebrew Bible, though he does not discuss them except in passing.[108] The identity of the giant as "freak" and a grotesque representation of otherness and uncontrollable wildness is often recognized, and Mobley is correct to give the giant a place on this continuum. Mobley views the biblical giants only from the perspective of the biblical hero—they are an "elite adversary" to be killed by Israelite heroes, victims of God's design in promoting his chosen agents (as in the David/Goliath duel). In this view, the giants are merely listed as footnotes in lists of the courageous exploits of Israel's military elite.[109] However, Mobely has not paid enough attention to the giants themselves and the variety of roles they play in the narratives he chooses to interpret; but he is hardly alone in this neglect, as almost no biblical interpreters have ventured to view the Bible's giants as anything more than a fantastical prop.

V. A Mediterranean *Koine*

Having given some outline of past scholarship dealing with giants, I now turn to some theoretical aspects of the task of comparing Semitic and Greek materials, such as the kind I undertake throughout this study. On what grounds have scholars compared Greece and the Near East? How have classicists and biblical scholars, respectively, gone about making these comparisons, and what are the results of these efforts? In what follows, I address these questions by reviewing previous scholarly work in order to lay a foundation for the study of Israel's giants and their connections (both historical and typological) with the Mediterranean world. My attempt to examine several important ancient texts involving Israel's giants and their relationship to the actions and fate of the Greek heroic generation is not, on its broadest terms, *de novo*; rather, such an investigation is situated in a larger and ongoing conversation regarding the correlation and disjunction between the historical, mythical, and epic traditions in Greece and the ancient Near East.

The act of comparing concepts from the archaic and classical Greek-speaking worlds with the Hebrew Bible has a long and sometimes venerable history, beginning already in antiquity itself and continuing through many prominent studies in the twentieth century and the current decade, though, recently, classicists have been more productive and responsible in this regard than biblical scholars.[110] Indeed, from the perspective of classical studies, it

108. Mobley 1997, 11–12.

109. E.g., as in the tales of David's mighty men. Mobley 2005, 50.

110. See López-Ruiz 2010; Louden 2011. Other modern works include Burkert 1992; West 1997a; Walcot 1966; Auffarth 1991; Penglase 1994; Rollinger and Ulf (eds.) 2004; Duchemin 1980.

now seems to be an unfortunate omission not to mention the relationship of Greek myth and epic to its Near Eastern and Egyptian contexts, though this has not always been the case.[111] Encouragingly, the past few decades of work in classical Greek scholarship have witnessed a significant set of studies dedicated to understanding Greek mythology and various epic motifs in terms of the ancient Near East broadly.[112] This is in stark contrast to earlier isolationist tendencies in the scholarship, which resulted in a bifurcation of the classics, on the one hand, and biblical studies (along with other fields of ancient Near Eastern studies) on the other.[113] An opposite reaction—equally unbalanced, in my own view—can be found, for example, in Martin Bernal's controversial *Black Athena*, which essentially posits an Egyptian origin (beginning in the eighteenth century BCE) for all of the essential features of Greek culture.[114]

A more balanced view of the topic must begin by simply acknowledging the historical fact that Greece and the Near East had significant contact with one another from a relatively early period, and that this contact must have meant something for the development of society, culture, and religion in each realm.[115] From the Aegean side of the equation, as thoroughly demonstrated by J. Boardman, Greek penetration into the East can be considered under four regions of influence: North Syria (including connection with the various major empires of Mesopotamia that occupied the area); Phoenicia and Palestine; Cyprus; and Anatolia. These contacts are amply borne out by archaeological discoveries (ceramics, architecture, cultic objects, etc.) in the Near East, as well as in Greece (reflecting North Syrian, Urartian, Assyrian, Phoenician, and Cypriot artistic motifs).[116] The primary facilitators of these contacts from the Greek world include immigrants to the East in the form

111. See, e.g., the prominent place given to ancient Near Eastern and Indo-European texts recently by Nagy (2006).

112. Generally, see Witte and Alkier 2003; Hoffman 1997; Wilson 1986; Braun 1982; Dunbabin 1979. For an overview of *ancient* Greek attitudes toward the East, see Kuhrt 2000. The clash between the Persians and Greeks in the fifth-fourth centuries BCE is obviously the most prominent instance of large scale (albeit hostile) relationships between *oriens* and *occidens* on a state level in antiquity, though earlier contacts of this kind are known; see, e.g., Cogan and Tadmor 1977; López-Ruiz 2010; Mondi 1990.

113. Consider, for example, a particularly strong (if not unusually strong) statement by Wilamowitz-Moellendorff (1884, 215).

114. Bernal 1987–2006.

115. See the balanced view of Liverani (1996).

116. Boardman 1999, 38–56. On Phoenician pottery in the Aegean, see Anderson 1990. Note the recent discovery of an amphora from Lesbos at the Tel Qudadi fortress (at modern Tel Aviv, dating to the eighth-seventh centuries BCE), confirming contacts between the two realms; Fantalkin and Tal 2010. Finally, see the earlier pioneering study of Schachermeyr 1967.

of craftsmen, merchants, itinerant seers, and mercenaries.[117] On the Eastern side, the Phoenicians have most often received attention for their expansion westward beginning as early as the initial flourishing of the coastal cities in the late Bronze Age (c. 1500 BCE), colonizing Cyprus around 1200 BCE and reaching as far west as Spain by at least the eleventh century.[118]

Quite a bit of literature has been devoted to either confirming or discrediting references to Phoenicians by Homer or Herodotus and other Greek authors. The German-born professor at the University of Rome, Julius Beloch, was a famous skeptic of the value of East-West comparisons, and his doubt about the value of ancient sources for relaying trustworthy information on the Phoenicians, particularly, influenced a generation of scholars.[119] In recent years, however, the tide seems to have turned in favor of taking classical Greek sources seriously, at least in their general assertions of Eastern merchants and travelers.[120] Even more elemental than the reliability of the content of the literary sources is the fact that the very alphabet by which the Greeks recorded their first epics and myths was of Semitic origin (already attested in the fifth century BCE by Herodotus[121]). The community of classicists traditionally attributes the origins of the Greek alphabet to the eighth century BCE—coinciding with the date of the earliest archaic Greek inscriptions in the new alphabet, and just in time for the *Iliad* and *Odyssey* to be recorded—though others have pushed for an even earlier period of borrowing.[122]

117. Boardman 1999, 56–57; 99–101; see also Cook 1965, 64–66; West 1997a, 586–630; Burkert 1992, 9–24, 41–42.

118. Technically, of course, the "Phoenicians" of the Bronze Age were "Canaanites." See, e.g., the essays in Dietler and López-Ruiz (eds.) 2009, esp. chs. 4 and 9, and Negbi 1992. The dating and nature of these colonies are controversial and currently the subject of much debate, though no one seriously doubts the existence of Phoenician activity in the West by ninth-eighth centuries BCE. A sampling of some recent literature includes: Aubet 2001; Niemeyer 1982; Frankenstein 1979.

119. Beloch 1894.

120. For a review of the problem, see Winter 1995; Niemeyer 1984; Gehrig and Niemeyer 1990; Muhly 1970. Albright (1972, 239–40) believed Sanchuniathon, a Phoenician priest upon whose writings Philo of Byblos purports to have relied in composing his first-century CE *Phoenician History*, was a genuinely tenth-sixth century BCE source, which, if true, would validate a conflation of Semitic and Mediterranean traditions at a very early date. On this, see Attridge and Oden (eds.) 1981; Kaldellis and López-Ruiz 2009.

121. *Hist.*, 322 (5.58).

122. See Powell 2002; 1991, where Powell argues that Greeks adopted the alphabet with the explicit intention of recording Homer's poems. Naveh 1987, 185, makes the origins of the Greek alphabet roughly contemporaneous with the advent of writing in Israel and Aram, c. 1100 BCE. Bernal 1987 argued for a very early date for the borrowing of the alphabet (in the Late Bronze Age), a suggestion that has not been broadly accepted. McCarter 1974, 68 suggests that the Greeks experimented with the Phoenician alphabet c. 1100 BCE, but did not adopt

A View from the West: Classical Scholarship and the Near East

Several examples of comparative work involving Greece and the Near East by classicists may serve as evidence of the recent acceptance of at least typological parallels, if not historical-cultural influence, between the two regions.[123] One of the more influential recent monographs is W. Burkert's *The Orientalizing Revolution*.[124] Burkert addresses the question of the Greek adaptation of Eastern materials on several fronts: physical objects with clearly Eastern derivations found in the Aegean,[125] ritual and religious practice, and the major literary traditions. Historically, these contacts fall into two major periods: the era of the "Aegean *koine*" in the thirteenth century BCE, and the "Homeric epoch" between c. 750–650 BCE.[126] Taking a suggestive passage from *Od.* 17.383–85 as his point of departure—in which Homer mentions itinerant seers, public workers, and singers—Burkert suggests that Greeks adopted not merely a few trinkets or loanwords from the Eastern context but rather "were influenced in their religion and literature...to a significant degree."[127] All of this is not, in Burkert's view, to suggest a sort of mindless and static use of foreign materials in Greek religion and literature, as compara-

it as an independent tradition until the eighth century; see also McCarter's expanded study, McCarter 1975. Cf. W. Röllig 1995, 193–214; Sass 1988. More recently, Woodard (1997, 3) argues for an "unbroken continuum of Greek literacy" which places far less emphasis on any single period for transmission. For a survey of the earlier views among classicists, see, Snodgrass 1971, 78–84 and Powell 1989.

123. I do not mean to imply that only in the past few decades have classicists engaged in this sort of comparative endeavor. Already in the first century CE, Josephus remarked in reference to Gen 6:1–4 that "the deeds that traditions ascribe to them [the giants] resemble the audacious exploits told by the Greeks of the giants" (*Ant.* I.73). The seventeenth-century British scholar Zachary Bogan attempted to compare Homer and the Bible; see Bogan 1658, and other sources in Dowden 2001, 168–69. Both Robert Brown and Otto Gruppe, to cite but two late nineteenth-century examples, worked within the comparative tradition of the nineteenth-century German orientalist and Sanskrit scholar Max Müller; see Gruppe 1887 and Brown 1898. Note also Farnell 1911, 30–32; Ungnad 1923; T. Robinson 1917; Wirth 1921; Pistor 1932; and further sources in Astour 1965, xvi–xvii n. 2.

124. Burkert 1992; see more recently Burkert 2004.

125. On East-West comparative artistic traditions, see Gunter 2009; Crowley 1989; Borell 1978; Akurgal 1968.

126. This is the period, for Burkert (1992, 5 [and bibliography on p. 157 n. 24 for the Late Bronze context]), of the "orientalizing revolution." See also Penglase 1994, 5. To these two primary moments of cultural contact, we must of course add the post-Alexander Hellenistic period, which has received the most scholarly attention. See, e.g., several of the other essays in Alkier and Witte (eds.) 2004, and Dafni 2006. For reasons that will become clear throughout this study, I do not think it is helpful to push the dating of various biblical texts (particularly the ones I will be examining in the following chapters) forward into very late periods simply to accommodate comparisons based on this latest and most noticeable point of contact after 333 BCE.

127. Burkert 1992, 6.

tive balance is everywhere to be found in the culturally bounded manner in which the Greeks adopted and adapted various traditions as their own.

Perhaps the most sustained and comprehensive attempt to understand the full impact of ancient Near Eastern materials upon Greek myth and epic has been carried out by M. West in a number of publications, the most prominent of which is *The East Face of Helicon* (1997).[128] Though the parallels West adduces often read more like a catalogue of similar-sounding stories, motifs, mythic structures, etc. than an assessment of, or interaction with, the meaning and importance of the parallels, the amount of material West is able to garner gives one a thorough appreciation for the direction further studies could take. Besides numerous examples from the Ugaritic corpus and other cuneiform literatures of Mesopotamia, West also significantly deals with the biblical texts (a task rarely attempted by classical scholars). Though some troubling indications appear demonstrating West's status as an outsider to the field of Hebrew studies—he confidently glosses the word "Hebrew" (עברי) as "People from Beyond" and classifies the Hebrews as "desert nomads," to give two cringe-inducing examples from the very first sentence of the section on ancient Israel[129]—West is nonetheless able seize upon elements of the Israelite literary tradition wherein the broader implications of Israel's position at the crossroads between Mesopotamia and the Mediterranean are manifest, e.g., early Israelite song traditions, wisdom compositions, historical cycles, and myth.[130] Overall, the primary contribution of West's work does not lie in any single interpretive move or comparison, but rather in the clear message that Greece and the Near East *should* be compared with one another, that the similarity of motifs and the certainty of historical contact calls for such comparisons.

Many other classicists have affirmed the validity of this comparative program. In a series of articles in *Ugarit Forschungen*,[131] P. Walcot explores

---

128. West 1997a. See also West 1971; 1985, esp. 11–27 for the comparative thrust. For a helpful review article on West's efforts, as well as those of Astour in *Hellenosemitica* (discussed infra), and Bernal's *Black Athena*, see Dowden 2001.

129. West 1997a, 90.

130. West 1997a, 90–98.

131. Walcot 1969; 1970; 1972; 1966. In his *Ugarit Forschungen* articles, Walcot builds upon the earlier work of Considine (1969). Rather than endorsing a one-way mode of transmission from East to West, Walcot (1972, 131–32) argues for *mutual influence* from a common, earlier source, viz., the Hurrians. Walcot's insistence on the Hurrians as a vehicle for the transmission of *Theogony*-like myth to both Greece and Ugarit seems at first to be in contradiction with his earlier claim that it was the West-Semitic *Enuma Elish* that provides the best model for the *Theogony* (and not the Kumarbi or Ullikummi texts; cf. Jacobsen 1968). Presumably the Hurrians could have transmitted the battle-for-kingship-in-heaven motif anytime beginning in the mid-third millennium and passed it on to the West Semitic world, where the Babylonians then adopted it and whence it then found its way back to Greece (!). However, if the Hurrians

thematic connections between Greek and Ugaritic literatures, and, most recently, C. López-Ruiz has again looked to the mythology represented in the Ugaritic texts as a source for Greek motifs.[132] In *Der drohende Untergang: "Schöpfung" in Mythos und Ritual im alten Orient und in Griechenland* (1991), C. Auffarth makes the central argument that the *Odyssey* represents a type of epic enthronement and initiation pattern with close parallels in the ancient Near Eastern world (from Babylonia, the New Year's festival in which the Enuma Elish was apparently used) and Ugarit (represented by the struggle between El and Baal).[133] C. Penglase's *Greek Myths and Mesopotamia* (1994) explores parallels between the ancient Near East, on the one hand, and the Homeric Hymns and Hesiod, on the other.[134] Penglase reasonably argues that the penetration of Eastern mythic motifs into the West was early and deep; not only did Greek authors possess a seemingly intimate knowledge of ancient Near Eastern plot lines, but *their audiences* also must have had an almost equal acquaintance with these ideas.[135] Most recently, Bruce Louden's *Homer's Odyssey and the Near East* (2011) explores a wide array of comparative possibilities; Louden avers that the biblical book of Genesis "shares more genres of myth in common with the *Odyssey* than does any other ancient narrative," and the particular combination of motifs in the *Odyssey* "has more in common with ancient Near Eastern sources than any Indo-European materials."[136] Louden even briefly draws the biblical giant traditions into the discussion, citing the heroic engagement with the giant as a subset of the

---

themselves maintained a wide presence in the Mediterranean, then Walcot's view would be quite justified, regardless of how it was cross-transmitted after its initial dissemination. Such a view moves us away from heavy-handed and impossibly precise theories of "borrowing" between one group and another, though it also introduces new problems involving the precision with which such a thesis could be demonstrated. See also Walcot 1969, 115.

132. López-Ruiz 2010. See López-Ruiz 2010, 8–16 for a concise and helpful review of Greek-Near East comparative efforts in the past few decades. Note already, from the perspective of a biblical scholar, Eissfeldt 1939, where Eissfeldt argued for the Semitic character of certain elements of Nonnos' *Dionysiaca* (primarily in books 40–43).

133. Auffarth 1991, 38–64.

134. Penglase 1994. The elucidation of Hesiod's *Works and Days* and *Theogony* in light of Mesopotamian and Anatolian myth is a well-established sub-stratum of classical studies; e.g., López-Ruiz 2010, passim; Penglase 1994, 159–236; Griffiths 1958, 91–93; West 1966; Walcot 1966; Solmsen 1989; Podbielski 1984.

135. Penglase 1994, 238. Who these audiences were, exactly, is an open question. Riva 2005 has argued that the spread of eastern ideas into the west was an "elite," "orientalizing" movement by which local Mediterranean elites sought to emulate eastern social and religious customs, evident, inter alia, through the archaeological record of cultic artifacts and even individual burials. Riva speculates that the eastern motifs in Hesiod were included for just such an audience, which was aware of the prestige attached to Mesopotamian myth.

136. Louden 2011, 3, 6 (respectively).

Near Eastern and Aegean *Chaoskampf* motif—a worthy comparison that deserves further exploration.[137]

A View from the East: Biblical Scholars and the Aegean World

Having reviewed some attempts at comparison between Greece and the Near
East from the perspective of classical scholarship, let us now consider the
efforts of biblical scholars in elaborating some of these same types of comparisons. It must be said at the outset that in many respects some of these
studies will bear little resemblance to the types of comparison and specific
foci I intend to pursue in the chapters that follow, and yet it is important
to acknowledge that the act of comparing Semitic and Greek spheres on
several levels has a distinguished genealogy in the field. For purposes of convenience, I divide the biblical scholarship into two areas: (1) studies that are
primarily "etymological" (or philological) attempts to compare Israel and
Greece, i.e., studies whose primary content is the listing of cognate words
that were supposedly borrowed or transferred from East to West, as well as
other sparsely argued lists of parallel customs, religious beliefs, mythical
plots, etc., and (2) studies that function on the level of comparative "epic,"
in which scholars assume Israelite authors utilized techniques of oral composition, structural techniques, and some epic motifs in parallel with other
Mediterranean sources and then proceed to compare Semitic and Greek materials on that basis. Though these two categories are admittedly *Idealtypen*,
and many assumptions are shared between them, they nonetheless provide
a convenient way of distinguishing two different approaches to this specific
comparative task.[138]

For biblical scholars and Assyriologists, comparisons of the biblical materials with the East pass with relatively less anxiety vis-à-vis the situation

137. Louden 2011, 182–83, 191–92.
138. Overlap among these two categories and other approaches that cannot adequately
be described as either "etymological" or "epic" in focus makes this division problematic, but it
is nonetheless a helpful manner of organizing past scholarship. Moreover, it is almost always
the case that proponents of the etymological methods would accept the general conclusions of
the epic school as I characterize them here (though the reverse is less true). The etymological
studies are usually accompanied by a set of observations that delve deeper into the characters,
stories, economic, or social institutions that accompany the relevant linguistic phenomenon—
and the reverse is also often true, that comparisons on the level of mythic motifs and social
institutions are fleshed out with correlations on the level of shared vocabulary. However, as I
show briefly below, it is often the case that interpreters utilizing the etymological technique
exploit a single point of correspondence and then proceed to "discover" correspondences on
other levels that are less convincing than the original parallel—which is itself often tantalizing
but extremely difficult to prove.

in the classics, possibly for the simple fact that much of the cultural and linguistic borrowing is presumed to have gone in an East to West direction, thus leaving the historical priority of the Bible and its Near Eastern world intact. But other factors must be acknowledged. Attempts at comparing biblical materials and classical sources have gained a somewhat prominent position among biblical scholars over the past few centuries and have been fueled, in some instances, by the prestige attached to Greek and Latin in the academy.[139]

The Etymological Approach. One of the most persistent, confident, and sustained modern attempts to posit comparisons between Greek materials and the ancient Near East was undertaken by Cyrus Gordon.[140] In his first sustained attempt at this comparative effort, a sixty-five page article in the *Hebrew Union College Annual* in 1955 entitled "Homer and Bible," Gordon begins to sketch out some lines of connection—many of which would be explored in his later writings on the topic and also in the work of his students—between Israelite and Greek materials.[141] In Gordon's view, the problem is framed by associations on very broad levels: bodies of water (the Mediterranean, in this case) provide inevitable commercial and social interaction between people groups;[142] both the Pentateuch and the *Iliad* served, according to Gordon, as charter documents for national festivals;[143] the *Odyssey* bears resemblance

---

139. In his important treatise on Hebrew poetry, Lowth (1839 [first published 1753]) declared that "Hebrew poetry is metrical." He did so, however, not because of the clear evidence of meter within the texts—Lowth himself admitted as much—but rather based on the perceived need to place Hebrew poetry alongside the world's other important poetic traditions, viz., Greek and Roman metered poetry (Lowth 1839, 32). Note also Cross 1983, 23: "I have often wondered if Julius Wellhausen's change of title of his great work from *Geschichte Israels I* (1878) to *Prolegomena zur Geschichte Israels* (1885) was owing less to a desire for accuracy than a subtle claim to parallel rank with Wolf's *Prolegomena ad Homerum* (1795)." Indeed, the change in titles seems hardly subtle at all, especially given the fact, as Cross notes (Cross 1983, 23 n. 29), that the completion of the *Prolegomena* (*Israelitische und jüdische Geschichte* [1894]) was dedicated to the great classicist Wilamowitz. See the more detailed comments in Machinist 2009, 499–502. Finally, consider R. H. Pfeiffer's and W. C. Pollard's idiosyncratic and revealingly titled 1957 book, *The Hebrew Iliad: The History of the Rise of Israel Under Saul and David. Written during the reign of Solomon probably by the priest Ahimaaz.* Pfeiffer and Pollard find in the Hebrew Bible a "buried epic," written "in the same way as the epics of other peoples," composed by the true "Father of History," a certain Ahimaaz (son of Zadok) (Pfeiffer and Pollard 1957, 7). Moreover, the Philistines are declared to be "of the same stock as those involved in the Trojan War around 1200 B.C." (Pfeiffer and Pollard 1957, 15) and the battle between the Achaeans and Trojans is made parallel to the battle between the Israelites and Philistines.

140. In many important ways, Gordon's work straddles both the "etymological" and "epic" approaches as I have generically categorized them here.

141. C. Gordon 1955. See also C. Gordon 1958, and the comments of Conroy (1980, 6–7).

142. C. Gordon 1955, 44–49.

143. C. Gordon 1955, 55.

to the Gilgamesh Epic;[144] and we find Semitic loan words in Greek texts.[145] This last realm of (etymological) relationships between the languages often became the focus of such comparisons from the perspective of Semiticists, and a frequent overreaching in this arena would prove to be perhaps the major downfall of the Greek-Semitic comparative effort in the latter half of the twentieth century.[146]

The rest of the essay is a series of subject areas fleshed out with rapid-fire examples and associations between Aegean and Levantine literatures (focusing mainly on Greek epic and the Hebrew Bible). For Gordon, concepts of war/battle, religion and ritual, and stylistic features between Israel and Greece share important common features,[147] and both realms show evidence of the conception of a "heroic age," marked by charismatic leadership, specific folkloric motifs, hospitality motifs and gift-giving scenes, "the epic premium on daughters" and women, and constant warfare in both settings.[148] "No longer can we assume," Gordon maintains in his conclusion, "that Greece is the hermetically sealed Olympian miracle, any more than we can consider Israel the vacuum-packed miracle from Sinai. Rather must we view Greek and Hebrew civilizations as parallel structures built upon the same East Mediterranean foundation."[149]

Gordon's views were further expressed in perhaps their most cogent form in *The Common Background of Greek and Hebrew Civilizations*.[150] Gordon's thesis, simply put and repeating the exact wording of his 1955 monograph, is that "Greek and Hebrew civilizations are parallel structures built upon the same East Mediterranean foundation."[151] These parallel structures, for Gordon, find expression not just in broadly shared mythic or epic themes, but also in law, customs, and ritual matters.[152] The "Indo-European War

144. C. Gordon 1955, 57.

145. C. Gordon 1955, 60–63.

146. C. Gordon (1966a and 1966b) even pushed the connections between East and West into the realm of the decipherment of Linear A in what is nearly universally agreed to be an unsuccessful attempt to posit the Semitic character of the language. See the review of Greenfield (1967). Note, however, a recent attempt to revive some of Gordon's thesis by Best (2000).

147. C. Gordon 1955, 82–107.

148. C. Gordon 1955, 65–81.

149. C. Gordon 1955, 108.

150. C. Gordon 1962. In his final major attempt to address the topic in *The Bible and the Ancient Near East* (Gordon and Rendsburg 1997), we find Gordon as convinced as ever regarding all of his previously expressed theses, though the Greek-Semitic connections are tempered somewhat and relegated only to limited parts of the study.

151. Italics removed; C. Gordon 1962, 9.

152. C. Gordon 1962, 12–13. Note also Gordon 1997 on Indo-Hittite and Hebrew household institutions. The notion of a shared Mediterranean legal culture has been championed recently by Raymond Westbrook; e.g., Westbrook 2003; 2009.

Epic" motif (viz., containing the abduction-of-the-bride type scene, where the hero must fight for her return) finds its first expression in the Ugaritic Kirta epic, which is of primary importance for Gordon since it "anticipates the Helen-of-Troy motif in the *Iliad* and Genesis, thus bridging the gap between the two literatures."[153] At many other points, Gordon sees parallels between Greek and Israelite literatures that bespeak historical borrowing or the common ancestry of the two cultures. For example, it is the non-hereditary aspect of Mycenaean kingship—at its apex during the time of the Judges according to Gordon—that best explains the "charismatic" and ad hoc leadership so prevalent in the Book of Judges.[154] David, too, is best understood in this broader East Mediterranean matrix, especially in his combination of warrior, king, poet, singer, and dancer aspects,[155] the book of Job is swept into the angst of Greek tragedy, and in both Greece and Israel, "historiography and drama were rooted in epic."[156]

To be sure, Gordon's work has been the subject of quite a bit of disparagement and controversy. Critics have been quick to charge that Gordon strained and distorted his primary materials in myriad ways in order to highlight certain parallels,[157] and Gordon's misguided assertions that inscriptional material from North and South America (e.g., the so-called Bat Creek inscription from Tennessee and the Paraiba inscription from Brazil) comprised evidence for a Phoenician journey across the Atlantic no doubt brought Gordon's own comparative quest into doubt (even if these miscues unfairly reflected upon Gordon's other work).[158] Indeed, this quest for the primeval unity of far-flung cultures is perhaps the stereotype or parody of the pitfalls of the comparative effort generally, to wit, that the comparativist simply knows not enough about far too much and then misapplies this information in futilely strained attempts to relate one datum to another. But this can only be the criticism of comparative efforts at the extreme, and where Gordon's work represents an overreaching, it is a learned overreaching.[159]

Either through direct pedagogical influence or other forms of support, Gordon's work influenced a generation of comparative attempts along the lines of his own project. In his *Hellenosemitica* (1965), M. Astour embarked on an ambitious project to correlate important myths and elements of the

---

153. C. Gordon 1962, 26, 284.
154. C. Gordon 1962, 297.
155. C. Gordon 1962, 299.
156. C. Gordon 1962, 299.
157. E.g., Pope 1964.
158. E.g., Gordon 1971; cf. Cross 1968; Mainfort and Kwas 2004.
159. See Marbelstone 1996.

Greek world with the Mediterranean's eastern shores.[160] The first major argument in *Hellenosemitica* is, in the author's words, "one of the corner stones of [the] entire study," namely the equation of the Danunians (*Dnnyn*) of Northern Syria / Anatolia with one element of the wave of Sea Peoples, the Danuna (= the Greek *Danaoi*, "a regular Hellenization of the Semitic ethnic name Danuna," according to Astour), who had initially migrated to Greece during the Hyksos period in Egypt.[161]

This connection between the Danunians/Danaoi had been, and to some extent continues to be, one of the holy grails of Greek-Semitic comparative studies, as its veracity would establish a concrete historical link between the two spheres. Astour pushes this connection into relatively precarious and unexplored interpretive territory. Relying on supposed correspondences among many disparate languages and literatures—several of which appear quite tenuous[162]—Astour posits the existence of "essential thematic skeletons" common to both Greek myths and the Israelite Exodus narrative.[163] These conjunctions in the realm of myth, then, serve as "proof" of the linguistic connection between the names of the Danunians and the Danaoi. Both Moses and Danaos flee Egypt after a murder, and the same number of generations separates Moses from "Leah the 'wild cow' and Danaos from the cow Io."[164] Both Danaos and Moses found springs in the desert.[165] Other conflations between Danel and Moses are adduced:

> The name of *Aqht*, the son of Danel, returns as *Qᵉhāt*, the grandfather of Moses. The name of the locality *Mrrt*, where *Aqht* was killed, figures in the gentilic form *Mᵉrarî* as the brother of *Qᵉhāt* in the Levite genealogy. The name of *Pǵt*, the daughter of *Danel* and the devoted sister of *Aqht*, is met in the Moses story as *Pûʿā*, a midwife who saved the life of the newborn Moses. The very name of Moses, in the feminine form *Mšt*, is, in the Ugaritic poem, the first half of Danel's wife's name, while the second half of her name, *Dnty*, corresponds to the name of Levi's sister Dinah.[166]

160. See Astour 1965 for many of Astour's earlier works on the topic.

161. Astour 1965, 69, 52 (respectively). Cf. Albright (1950, 172–73), who acknowledged the "clear-cut evidence for the participation of 'Danaan' Greeks in the movement of the Sea Peoples in the earth twelfth century" but denied that these movements had anything to do with the *Iliad* or the Homeric tradition generally. On this, see Y. Yadin 1991, 301–02.

162. E.g., the examples regarding the justice and agriculture themes supposedly evident in the Danaos myth are very unclear. The Semitic parallels to the Io myth (esp. Astour 1965, 84–85) seem completely uncontrolled as comparative data, and cannot possibly serve to confirm a secure correspondence with the Greek storyline.

163. Astour 1965, 69–80.

164. The ultimate significance of this parallel seems particularly murky.

165. Astour 1965, 99.

166. Astour 1965, 99–100.

I quote this list to demonstrate Astour's method here and at many other places in *Hellenosemitica*: criss-crossing between stories and languages, parallels in only suspiciously similar names (and half-names), and generally garbled plotlines. In order to find an adequate corresponding Semitic parallel for the Greek stories in question, Astour creates a dubiously and artificially conglomerate West Semitic story (including non-Semitic Near Eastern elements),[167] though in the end one is forced to admit that such parallels seem oddly numerous to be purely coincidences. Whether they should be cited as secure evidence of Astour's thesis is another question.

Astour's second major investigation in *Hellenosemitica* involves the Semitic origin of the Cadmos (Semitic *qdm*) mythology and the Dionysus cult.[168] As with so many of Astour's other claims, this one is poised somewhere between groundbreaking scholarship and unfortunate hyperbole. Astour muddies the waters considerably with an attempt to find traces of the origins of Dionysiac religion in the biblical Deborah's epithet אשת לפידות ("wife of Lappidoth," Judg 4:4). Deborah's husband's name, Lappidoth, is, in Astour's view, simply the plural of לפיד, "torch," and as such, "we are inclined to...understand [the name] as a relic of the nightly festivities with torches, so characteristic for the Greek Bacchanals."[169] The Semitic character of Bellerophon and various "healer-heroes" form the main substance of Chapter Three, and Astour piles example upon example of correspondences between numerous Semitic and Greek figures and symbols.[170] The Rephaim (רפאים), for example, are to be understood (as others have surmised) etymologically from the root רפא, "heal," and thus are remnants of chthonic healing deities as are to be found also in Greece.[171]

I have gone to some length to point out the specific examples above because they are emblematic of the etymologizing tendency that has been so often—and appropriately—viewed as the primary Achilles' heel of Astour's (and others') method. Even though language is obviously the primary vehicle

---

167. For these reasons, *Hellenosemitica* received mixed reviews, with most scholars in agreement that Astour had presented valuable data while at the same time exaggerating the evidence. See Duke 1965; Purvis 1968; McGregor 1966.

168. Astour 1965, 113–75, 147–49. To be sure, Euripides himself concedes as much (through Dionysus' opening speech) in *The Bacchae*.

169. Astour 1965, 185. Astour fails to note that לפיד is masculine in Hebrew and appears in the plural seven times in the Bible, all masculine (i.e., besides the form לפידות. See Exod 20:18 [לפידם]; Judg 7:16,20, 15:4,5; Ezek 1:13; Nah 2:5; Job 41:11; pl. cnst. Dan 10:6). לפיד is widely considered an *Aegean loanword* from λαμπάς ("lamp, torch") and is feminine in Greek (fem. pl. nom. λαμπάδες; *lampîd > lappîd). See already Sayce 1892, 366. At any rate, the connection between torch-rituals and this single name, לפידות, is hardly a decisive clue.

170. Astour 1965, 225–322.

171. Astour 1965, 233–34.

by which one might access many of these questions, there is the ever-present hazard of a type of etymological fallacy at play, i.e., by assuming a common origin for two words one falls into the trap of assuming, up front, that they *continued* to share common meanings worth comparing. Nevertheless, Astour's project represents a learned catalogue of comparative possibilities, and Astour's main argument, that "long before Hellenism imposed itself over the ancient civilizations of the East, Semiticism had exercised no less an impact upon the young civilization of Greece,"[172] cannot be seriously doubted today as a general formulation—despite the obstacles that seemingly faced such a view in the late eighteenth and early nineteenth centuries.[173]

The Epic Approach. A parallel—and, in my view, far more insightful and productive trend—among biblical scholars over the past few decades involves what I will call the "epic" approach toward Greek and Semitic literatures. The words "epic" and "hero" can, of course, be defined generically, as in the simple, colloquial English sense of hero as "a person of distinguished courage or ability, admired for his brave deeds and noble qualities" (or even "the principal character in a story") and "epic" is defined simply as "a long poem about a hero." Many studies use words and phrases like "hero" and "heroic age" rather uncritically and assume informal definitions.[174] The practice of defining epic and hero in terms of one another is not completely misguided, though to yoke the two concepts together as an unaddressed assumption would be inappropriate. As Albert Lord pointed out in his famous study of oral epic, many poems of a discernibly "epic" style are not particularly long, and "many of the songs which we include in oral narrative poetry are romantic or historical and not heroic, no matter what definition of the hero one may choose."[175]

Because of the vast diversity among arguably epic materials in many cultures and languages through thousands of years, a cross-cultural

---

172. Astour 1965, 361.

173. Though less influential and original than the studies of Astour or C. Gordon, John Pairman Brown's magnum opus, the three-volume *Israel and Hellas* (1995–2001; only the first of these volumes concerns us here), also represents a significant contribution to the topics at hand. Several of the essays from these volumes were reprinted in Brown 2003. The bulk of Brown's studies focus on the usual list of topics: shared vocabulary, religious institutions, socio-legal spheres, etc. As with some of the other studies mentioned above, Brown made himself vulnerable to the harshest criticism in regards to his philological/etymological method. See, e.g., West's appropriately derisive comment in response to Brown's attempt to equate the Heb. *mélek* ("king") with Greek *wanak ("king, ruler") by positing a w/m and l/n "interchange" (?) in the same word (West 1997b, 112).

174. See Conroy 1980, 15–22 on this question of definition.

175. Lord 2000, 6; see also Nagy 2006, §9–13.

definition of epic can, as R. P. Martin persuasively argues, only and ever be a "notional instead of normative term"; formal features such as length, meter, epithets, "typical" scenes, and so on have proven inadequate when taken in isolation, and are complicated when considered as aspects of performance.[176] Nevertheless, I generally use the word "epic" in this study to describe what commentators of the past have called "epic," i.e., sustained, extended narrations of national or tribal origins, often involving intense battle and populated by individuals whose stature and deeds greatly exceeds humans living in the present time. Isolating the "present time" from the world of the epic is not to say that epic tales do not begin with a true, historical circumstance—they often do—but rather recognizes that for most of their reception history, including our contemporary world, epic is set in the past with characters whose actions are likely no longer attainable by the audience. The heroes whose actions often form the core of epic are, however, less amenable to exact, a priori definitions, and must be analyzed as particularistic manifestations of some epics in some historical circumstances.[177]

Doubt has been expressed from several different quarters regarding the possibility of Israelite "epic" or "heroic" literature.[178] Throughout the nineteenth century, various German scholars arose to deny the notion that the Bible contained anything like a full "epic," granting at most the possibility of some scattered epic themes and vaguely epic-like passages. H. Ewald, E. Reuss, E. Sievers, and E. König all fall into this category,[179] and in Conroy's own critical discussion of the history of the question, he asserts that the "conclusion seems unavoidable that the JE [the combined Jahwist-Elohist source narrative] material does not exhibit the characteristics of heroic literature nor does it reflect a state of society that could be called a Homeric Age."[180] In his commentary on Genesis (1901), H. Gunkel expressed thanks that the Israelites "did not produce a Homer" or any "true 'Israelite national epic'," since the passages as we now read them are "left in an essentially unfused state" and thus allow us to access the various layers interwoven to form the current text.[181] Nevertheless, Gunkel did speak of an Israelite *epischer Stil* in certain

176. See Martin 2007, 10–11, with a helpful bibliography on p. 19.

177. In the field of biblical scholarship, see most recently Echols 2008, 135–64, where Echols devotes the entirety of Chapter 7 of his book to an investigation of heroic narrative poetry and epic as comparative categories in Greece and the Near East.

178. See especially Conroy 1980 and Niditch 2007; 2010.

179. Ewald 1864–1868, 58; Reuss 1881, 151–59; Sievers 1901, 377; König 1918, 26–28; Conroy 1980, 3–4.

180. Conroy 1980, 21. The reference to JE is primarily a reference in opposition to Cross's view (discussed infra) that the JE stratum does indeed reflect an epic source. Further skepticism of the Israelite epic can be found in Talmon 1991, 412–13; Talmon 1981.

181. Gunkel 1997 (first published 1901), lxxxvi.

texts (e.g., Gen 19:30–8, Judg 9:8, Job 1–2) and adduced literary and linguistic markers such as "purposeful parallelism" as indicative of this style.[182]

Despite these doubts, others affirmed the presence of epic in the Bible, thus demonstrating that the epic categories employed by some modern scholars are in no way recent innovations.[183] Already in 1783, for example, J.G. Herder spoke of "the oldest and most authentic epic of the deeds and laws of Moses" and drew a direct parallel between Homer and the Greeks and Moses and the Israelites,[184] while both W. M. L. de Wette and J. C. W. Augusti spoke of the Pentateuch, specifically, as an epic narrative.[185] In both de Wette's and Augusti's treatments, however, it is not entirely clear whether the term "epic" is being used with anything but a loose comparative sense, without specific definition and meant primarily to elevate the biblical texts to the level of other epic materials (such as Homer). For example, Augusti's own statement on the issue ends by conceding that "epic" may not be an entirely appropriate term, but at any rate, one must acknowledge that the Pentateuch is no orderinary lawbook.[186] "Epic," then, becomes a kind of honorary appellative meant to drive home the notion that the Torah is special in some literary, cultural, or religious sense.

In the twentieth century, several scholars rose to the challenge of identifying epic in the Hebrew Bible with far greater specificity than what had been attempted in the past, arguing either that certain narratives or poems in the Bible could straightforwardly be defined as epic or, alternatively, that a written or oral epic stood as the *Urtext* upon which the written sources were based.[187] One of the earlier coherent attempts to argue for an Israelite epic was made by S. Mowinckel, who in a 1935 article seized upon the ספר

182. Niditch 2007, 277. This focus on "epic style" is taken up by Polak 2006.

183. For the following material, see also Conroy 1980, 2–3.

184. Herder 1825, 72–75.

185. Augusti 1827, 149; De Wette 1822, 171–72.

186. Augusti 1827, 149. Compare Wellhausen's use of the word "epic" in his *Prolegomena*, where "his use of the adjective 'epic'…is meant to indicate that these traditions, unlike those dealing with the 'legends' of Primeval and Patriarchal history, were based upon historical facts" (as discussed in Conroy 1980, 3). Wellhausen (1878, 360) stated that "we should decline the historical standard in the case of the legend of the origins of mankind and of the legend of the patriarchs, while we employ it to a certain extent for the epic period of Moses and Joshua"; epic, as opposed to legend, has "its source…in the period it deals with." Wellhausen (1878, 314) does, however, refer to a "primitive world history" upon which J has drawn.

187. Conroy (1980, 5) classifies these two approaches as the difference between "existing epics" and "underlying epics," the former group being represented by A. Bruno, W. G. Pollard, R. A. Carlson, B. Duhm, C. Schedl, C. Gordon, L. Fisher, and S. Tengström, among others, while the latter is championed by H. Harari, R. Kittel, S. Mowinckel, U. Cassuto, I. E. Seeligmann, F. M. Cross, and D. N. Freedman, among others. Some of these views are summarized below, and for others, consult Conroy 1980, 5–15.

הישר ("Book of the Upright, or Brave Ones") mentioned in Josh 10:13 and 2 Sam 1:18 and also the ספר מלחמת יהוה ("Book of the Wars of YHWH") in Num 21:14 as evidence of a now lost Israelite epic.[188] Since this epic appears in E but is not cited in J, Mowinckel dated the original epic poetic source (of which both the "Book of the Upright" and the "Book of the Wars of YHWH" were a part) to between 750–587 BCE[189]—though, as Conroy points out, Mowinckel was forced to modify this view when in 1964 he denied the existence of E as a source altogether.[190]

In a somewhat obscure and mostly neglected article first published in Hebrew in 1943, entitled "The Israelite Epic," Umberto (Moshe David) Cassuto proposed that many enigmatic references in the Hebrew Bible could be best explained as fragmentary Israelite recensions of a "continuation of the epic tradition" of Canaan.[191] This epic tradition, according to Cassuto, existed in a greatly expanded form beyond what we now read in the canonical biblical texts, and included many different poetic accounts—the most prominent of which Cassuto identifies is some version of the *Chaoskampf* (e.g., Isa 51:9–10; Ps 74:13–5; Job 7:12, etc.), but also several other stories of combat, heroes, and creation. According to this view, these complete stories are now lost to us, and yet evidence of their presence lies scattered within the biblical texts. Indeed, the Bible itself seems to explicitly refer to just such antecedent traditions in texts such as Josh 10:13 and 2 Sam 1:18, where the "Book of the Upright" is invoked as a source for the author, as well as the reference to the "Book of the Wars of YHWH" in Num 21:14.

When one considers the references to the various groups of giants in the Hebrew Bible (Nephilim, Rephaim, Anaqim, Zamzummim, Zuzim, Emim, and some Gibborim) two questions come to mind: first, why do these materials appear so infrequently? For example, if indeed Israelite tradition had accorded such a prominent place to giants as symbolic figures and embodiments of a bygone era of battles in the land, why is their presence relegated to only brief appearances in scattered biblical texts? On the other hand, one may pose the question differently: why include these figures *at all*? The mere three passing references to the Emim (Gen 14:5; Deut 2:10–11) only seem to highlight the enigma of their identity, and the same can be said of the two references to the Nephilim (Gen 6:4 and Num 13:33) and the single note regarding the Zamzummim (Deut 2:20; cf. the Zuzim in Gen 14:5), not to mention the ill-defined Rephaim and the sparse hint in Gen 6:4 that the

188. Mowinckel 1935; Conroy 1980, 8–9; Niditch 2007, 277–78.
189. Mowinckel 1935, 143–44.
190. Conroy 1980, 9; Mowinckel 1964.
191. Cassuto 1973–1975a, 2:77.

Nephilim are to be somehow equated with הגברים מעולם אנשי השם. Cassuto's thesis, in part, offers a provocative solution to this problem: texts like Gen 6:1–4 (Nephilim), the various passages referring to Rephaim, the Flood narrative, and several other stories involving "the acts of the heroes of Israel" are all vestiges of an earlier, epic literature that presumably had cultural and at least thematic contact with other, similar traditions in the broader Mediterranean and Near Eastern worlds.[192] Cassuto's project, like others of its type, promises a glimpse behind and beyond the text as we have it, into a putatively earlier (or at least other) world of meanings.

Cassuto claims, in fact, that other "obscure sections of the Bible" can be explained in this manner; in the category of "other" lost epic poems, Cassuto places the creation story, the Eden narrative, Gen 6:1–4, references to the Rephaim, the Flood story, the reference to Enoch, the "Generation of Division" in Gen 10:25, the stories of Job and Daniel, the destruction of Sodom and Gomorrah, and the "acts of the heroes of Israel."[193] It is important to notice that, in Cassuto's argument, there are certain *counter-stories*, passages marking "signs of opposition to the stories of the ancient poems" such as the Song of the Sea in Exodus 15 (which does not mention the battle with the sea directly) and Gen 1:21 (relegating the sea monsters to the role of mundanely created animal), as well as many other locations. Pagan epic lurks in the background, sometimes still threateningly, but the biblical reinvention has stripped away its original power. This antagonism between the epic and the counter-story, then, explains the loss of "much of the writings of the previous era," even as such things were not lost entirely.[194]

The two major books by F. M. Cross, *Canaanite Myth and Hebrew Epic* (1973) and *From Epic to Canon* (1998) take up the mantle of these earlier studies of epic. Both works significantly contain the term "epic" in the title and attempt to elaborate on various aspects of Israel's own epic tradition.[195] In the preface to *Canaanite Myth and Hebrew Epic*, Cross described epic as "the constitutive genre of Israel's religious expression" and defines an "epic" narrative as one

---

192. Cassuto 1973–1975a, 2:108–09. Many others have since assumed a vast, but hitherto unrecovered (or unrecoverable) background literature that circulated in Canaan during the Iron Age. Pointing to the large number of bullae that have been recovered in ancient Israel—most or which probably sealed written documents on papyrus or animal skins—Zuckermann (2010) has referred to this background literature as the "dark matter" of biblical studies. In parallel with the role of dark matter in physics, biblical scholars must assume these materials existed in order to explain the complex literary traditions with which biblical authors interacted.

193. Cassuto 1973–1975b, 2:103–09.

194. Cassuto 1973–1975b, 2:101–02.

195. Cross 1973; 1998, esp. 22–52. Cross seems to have been influenced by Martin Noth's concept of a *Grundschrift* ("G") from the period of the Judges (as spelled out in Noth 1981b). See also Cross 2009, which supplements Cross 1983.

in which "a people and their god or gods interact in the temporal course of events." Epic, then, is contrasted with history and with myth, the latter of which "is concerned with 'primordial events' and seeks static structures of meaning behind or beyond the historical flux." Epic is that genre which, in Cross' view, embodies the "perennial and unrelaxed tension between the mythic and the historical."[196] For Cross, the epic tradition is at the basis of the Pentateuch, and is to be identified with "the so-called JE sources and the common poetic tradition that lies behind them."[197] Although Cross asserts that the "reenactment of primordial events of cosmogonic myth gave way to festivals reenacting epic events in Israel's past," there is no straightforward path from myth to epic, and "it will not do to describe the process as a progressive historicizing of myth." The dialectic is complex, and there is neither a complete rupture between "Canaanite" myth and Israelite epic nor an easy adoption of myth in Israelite epic.[198] Though certain periods saw the "recrudescence" of myth (in creation and kingship themes), viz., the Solomonic era and the Exile, in certain texts (Isaiah 40–55) "the myths were transformed and combined with historical themes in order to formulate an eschatology, or a typology of 'old things' and 'new things' in the drama of salvation."[199]

In *Epic to Canon*, Cross addresses the methodological and historical issues of epic more directly and in a more sustained fashion. In his essay "Traditional Narrative and the Reconstruction of Early Israelite Institutions," Cross distinguishes again among three types of literature in early Israel, viz., "historical narrative" (secular or "ordinary" events), "mythic narrative" ("actors are exclusively the gods, the terrain cosmic"), and *epea*, "traditional epic," which is defined with reference to Homeric epic. Like the archaic Greek literature, Canaanite epic traditions contain evidence of oral

196. Cross 1973, viii.

197. Cross 1973, 83 n. 11; see also p. 85: "...the epic order of events—Exodus, Covenant at Sinai, Conquest—is based on older historical memory..." It is also of interest to note that Cross' teacher, W. F. Albright, at first accepted the notion that both J and E relied on a national epic—a notion adopted, apparently, from R. Kittel (so Conroy 1980, 11)—but later was presumably forced to abandon this view (though it is not abandoned explicitly in print) when he embraced the Volz-Rudolph position that E was only a northern version of the J source and not an alternate to J based on a common, archaic epic. See Conroy 1980, 11–12, and Albright 1957, 241–50 vs. Albright 1963.

198. Cross 1973, 143–44.

199. Cross 1973, 135–36. It should be noted that, for Cross, the adjective "recrudescent" ("breaking out again") takes on an ambiguous tone—in fact, a *negative* one—in keeping with the etymology of word, Lat. *recrūdescō* (of wounds, "to grow raw again, to get worse"). It is the apocalyptic corpus, then, which becomes unfettered from history, turning to myth and thus becoming, as it were, like an old wound opened anew. See the comments on the "recrudescence" idea by Hutton 2007. Hutton nicely demonstrates the possibility of a more nuanced use of "myth" in Israelite literature. I will return to this significant issue of "recrudescence" and the return of genuinely early materials in later contexts in Chapter 5.

composition, such as "parallelism in bicola and tricola, parallelism on pho-
netic, morphological, and semantic levels," and "word and phrase pairs."[200]
The oral literature grew in ancient Israel, as in Greece, through oral, bardic
performance, though Cross concedes that "early Israel was not a 'heroic
society' in the Homeric pattern." "At the same time," Cross argues, "it is per-
missible to define epic as the traditional narrative cycle of an age conceived
as *normative*, the events of which gave meaning and self-understanding to a
people or nation."[201] In summary, epic is marked by (a) "oral composition in
formulae and themes of a traditional literature"; (b) "narrative in which acts
of god(s) and men form a double level of action"; (c) "a composition describing traditional events of an age conceived as normative"; and (d) "a 'national'
composition, especially one recited at pilgrimage festivals."[202] The Israelite
author "was seeking to sing of Israel's past using traditional themes, the
common stuff of generations of singers and tellers of tales."[203] Cross assumes
that Israel's old epic cycle was in fact different from the J (or JE) source, and
may well have been longer than any of the canonically preserved materials.
Briefly put, this epic form was "a prosaizing, propaganda work of the united
monarchy, and specifically the program of Solomon to constitute an Oriental monarchy in the Canaanite pattern," though the "essential shaping"
of this epic "came not from the Yahwist but from the singers of the early
Israelite league."[204]

It is worthwhile at this point to remark on the manner in which Cross
is able to achieve clarity through the associations he finds in his materials.
First, Cross finds the Greek materials most valuable for his project because
they most closely resemble the early Israelite stories in a fundamental manner not congruent with other Near Eastern materials. Whereas in so much
East and West Semitic myth the action occurs on the divine plane and concerns predominantly divine actors, Israel's early oral narratives were poised
somewhere productively between the "mythic" and the "historical" (involving humans)—in the realm of *epea*, comparable to the traditional mode of
expression in Homer.[205] Rather than comparing various elements of plot or

200. Cross 1998, 22–24.

201. Cross 1998, 27.

202. Cross 1998, 29. Note that Conroy (1980) has challenged Cross's use of the term "epic"
to describe any aspect of ancient Israelite literature; for Cross' response, see Cross 1983, 17–18,
which includes a much more detailed consideration of the implications of Israel's epic, and
which is stated again succinctly in Cross 1998.

203. Cross 1998, 28.

204. Cross 1998, 36, 50.

205. Cross 1983, 13–14. But cf. the Ugaritic Kirta and Aqhat "epics," or such Mesopotamian compositions as the "Curse of Agade." Regarding the character of archaic Greek epic and
early Israelite poetry as "oral narratives," it must be emphasized that this categorization is
not based on pure speculation; as Cross (1983, 14–15) points out, we have from Ugarit a tablet

motif between Homer and the Bible, however, for Cross the realm of Homeric epic provides a set of guiding assumptions about the function, role, and quality of the early Israelite epic cycle. For example, the Israelite epic was, according to Cross, likely sung at various local shrines by a variety of performers and yet also served to create a national identity around the events in the epic (as with Homeric bards and the Greek national recitals in Athens).[206] Homeric verse preserved very old elements of Mycenaean culture and mythology, and thus it can be expected that the biblical patriarchal narratives, though in final form the product of a long development that ended relatively late in Israel's history, contain very ancient and reliable memories.[207] Cross is then able to make use of his parallel Greek epic tradition to develop a sustained interpretation of the role of Israelite materials that is balanced in its application of Greek models and illuminates not only the Hebrew Bible but also has the potential for helping classical scholars reflect back on their own materials and methods.[208]

A Mediterranean koine. This selective review of comparative attempts from two different perspectives—classicists looking East and biblical scholars looking West—demonstrates, I believe, the continuing vitality for such studies and, at the very least, points to the potential such comparative efforts contain. Though I have been largely critical of the "etymological" attempts of Gordon, Astour, and others, these scholars did produce some striking and detailed insights into shared social religious institutions, the evidence for which sometimes lies at the most fundamental level possible, that of language. In a frenzy to pile disparate example upon example, however, two

colophon in the Baal epic that explicitly identifies the mode of storytelling as dictation and copying. See also Cross 1974, 1 n. 1.

206. Cross 1983, 16–17.

207. Cross 1983, 16; Cross (1983, 34) even entertained the notion that "much of the patriarchal lore is very old, some of it reaching back, perhaps, into the Middle Bronze Age."

208. Though less comprehensive and methodologically coherent than Cross' ongoing encounter with epic, Moshe Weinfeld's study of Israel's conquest and settlement traditions in Weinfeld 1993, 2 explicitly begins with the assumption that "Israelite literature had much in common with the Greek milieu," especially regarding the genre of the "foundation story." The focus on Greek materials (as opposed to other ancient Near Eastern texts) in comparison with Israel's own story of settlement is appropriate because, as Weinfeld explains, both Israel and Greece were founded by colonization, by individuals and groups establishing new sites. Thus, a simple but profound methodological point here is that we must look where we have relevant material to compare. Another convincing recent promoter of the idea of a pan-Israelite oral culture, Israelite epic, and the continuing importance of reading heroic concepts into the Hebrew Bible is Susan Niditch, who in several compelling books has argued for the full inclusion of the ancient Israelite traditions within the broader environment of epic and heroic cultures worldwide. See Niditch 1987; 1993; 1996; 2008.

mistakes occur. First, emending an observation made in both Ecclesiastes and Proverbs, in a multitude of examples error is not lacking. Second, the desire to produce these multitudinous examples often squelches the next—and in my view, most important—phase of comparison, to wit, providing detailed and meaningful explanations of what the parallels mean and how the parallels actually help us understand something we did not know before about either (or both) the *primum comparandum* or the *secundum comparatum*.[209]

Regarding the Israel and Hellas relationship, the most promising comparative assumption to take up, in my view, is that of a pan-Mediterranean religious *koine* on the broadest level. By "koine," I mean a common, base-level, shared language of symbol, material artifacts, custom, and religious practice. Of course, all of the scholars discussed above have openly or implicitly ascribed to such a concept, but, in contrast to some of the more ambitious comparative studies, I would suggest that this *koine* be held in strict tension with the local and the particular. This recognition of a Mediterranean *koine* does not imply homogeneous expressions between any two regions or among any particular aspects of language, culture, or society as a rule, but rather represents an invitation to explore the often under-emphasized elements that bound Mediterranean religions—including those of ancient Israel—together.[210]

VI. A Note on the Comparative Method

Before proceeding to a close textual examination of the passages in the Hebrew Bible involving giants of various kinds, I would briefly like to address the important issue of methodology in comparative religious studies, as Chapters Four, Five, and Six of my own project here depend upon direct comparisons with archaic and classical Greek materials. Though my methodological notes here are obviously not comprehensive, such concerns simply cannot be ignored altogether—as they have been too often in the past by biblical scholars. Indeed, the comparative endeavor has become such a well-entrenched part of biblical studies—not to mention ancient studies

---

209. Astour's *Hellenosemitica* (Astour 1965) in particular is a good example of this, as many of the pages of the book contain four or five discrete subheadings; relatively little space is devoted to this second, most important step of explaining the significance of the comparisons.

210. Compare this to Riva (2005, 203), who also invokes this idea of a Mediterranean *koine*, stating that "one may...define this koine as international. At the same time, the modes of its reception were geographically specific, giving rise to local interpretations and meanings that individual groups assigned to it."

and comparative literature generally—that one often feels little need to justify the invocation of parallel social institutions, shared mythology, or philological cognates. It seems eminently reasonably that in discussions of the biblical Flood story (Genesis 6–9), for example, one mention, even off-handedly, the strikingly similar story in tablet XI of the standard version of the Gilgamesh Epic; one would seem to be committing a naive error of omission if one delved too deeply into an explication of ox goring laws in Exodus' covenant code without ever invoking the legal currency this trope held in Mesopotamian, Hittite, and Mediterranean law; and passages like Ps 74:12–17 or Isa 51:9–11 seem almost nonsensical without perfunctory nods toward cognate *Chaoskampf* motifs in the Enuma Elish or Ba'al epic.

Yet the rationale for comparison is not always so self-evident; indeed, just beneath the surface of even the most natural of thematic or social correlations lurk questions that are not easily answered: Are the materials compared similar because of geographical proximity (and thus presumed contact)? If so, what is the nature of the contact (e.g., oral, scribal, administrative, etc.), and can the question of the certainty of contact be regarded with anything but insouciance if physical evidence of the contact cannot be located? If strikingly similar materials appear in regions remote from one another, does one posit something like an independent, corresponding cultural development in each milieu to account for the parallels? What if the cultural developments are too dissimilar to account for such similarities? Can one then retreat into notions of a Jungian "collective unconscious"? Can materials be compared as only typologically similar—and if so, what does this mean?—or must texts appear in the same historical and linguistic stream to warrant association?

A striking amount of comparative scholarship by Hebrew Bible scholars has proceeded with little or no acknowledgment of the major upheavals wrought upon the validity of comparative religion generally in the second half of the twentieth century.[211] Interestingly, one can find simultaneous

211. Two volumes (of a four volume series) that simultaneously stand as partial examples of this problem and partial exceptions to it are the "Scripture in Context" essay collections (Evans, Hallo and White 1980). Hallo recognizes the "frontal assault" waged upon comparative studies from some quarters (Hallo 1980, 9) and simply concludes that "comparison" and "contrast" must always remain "twin components in a contextual approach to the Bible" (Hallo 1980, 18). Almost none of the other authors represented in these volumes, however, spent very much productive space justifying the validity of their assorted comparative endeavors at a basic level, other than to implicitly show that their comparanda shared some broadly conceived, common feature—or the issue is posed only in terms of historical influence (if the authors of text A could have known about text B, or stood in its general stream of tradition, then comparison can proceed). On method and comparison in biblical scholarship, see Talmon 1991.

streams of evidence demonstrating both the continued relevance and de-cline in popularity for "comparative religion"; only a cursory search reveals well over 100 studies in the last century—either monographs, edited vol-umes, handbooks, or dictionaries—with the specific words "Comparative Religion" in the title. And yet a great number of these were published be-fore 1950, and the last few decades have witnessed a number of strident critiques of the subfield of comparative religions.[212] Comparison, it is often argued in so-called postmodernist circles, is negatively loaded with the baggage of the enlightenment project generally, i.e., it is conceived in the sin of Christian- and Western-centric models born out of the eighteenth-century European religio-intellectual context as part of the grand scheme of organizing the world's religions vis-à-vis Christianity. Moreover, an un-critical focus on typological similarity can drift far from the moorings of the historical, the political, and the local. Perhaps the culminating moment in the twentieth-century comparative religion movement was M. Eliade's stan-dard work, *Patterns in Comparative Religion* (first published in 1958).[213] Words like "every," "universal," and "always" appear frequently in Eliade's motif-based approach, which catalogued similarities in broadly shared symbols and categories such as sky, sun, moon, water, stone, earth/woman/fertil-ity, regeneration, agriculture, sacred time and renewal, and the *axis mundi*. Examples spanned time and space, though Eliade did acknowledge locality: "the most personal and transcendent mystical experiences are affected by the age in which they occur," even if "the greatest experiences are not only alike in content, but often also alike in their expression."[214] This emphasis on *sameness* and *universality* at the expense of *difference* and *history* (so goes the accusation, at least) has been the subject of a number of critical reviews.[215]

At this juncture, I would like to highlight one particular essay that influenced a generation of religious studies scholarship, J. Z. Smith's "In

212. Note that many of the studies published after 1950 are in second, third, or fourth editions, the first of which is pre-1950. Recent material on the topic includes, e.g. Gothóni 2000; M. Hamilton 1995; Smith 1995; and even Lazarus 2008.

213. Eliade 1996. In many respects, J. G. Frazer's earlier *Folk-lore in the Old Testament: Stud-ies in Comparative Religion* (Frazer 1919) represents a similar type of project in scope and impor-tance, in that it is focused around themes or tropes that Frazer thought were broadly shared geographically and historically (east to west, ancient to modern), and also focuses on similar-ity (as opposed to difference).

214. Eliade 1996, 2, 3 (respectively).

215. A standard example of this critique can be found in Lincoln 1997, 141–51. Note also J. Z. Smith 2000a, which examines the historical and intellectual milieu out of which Eliade's major work flowed and ultimately demonstrates a deep appreciation—though not without profound criticism—of Eliade's project. Dissatisfaction with the comparative method is not an invention of postmodernism; see Vernant 1976; Haydon 1922.

Comparison a Magic Dwells" (first presented in 1979);[216] indeed, I endorse and attempt, to a certain degree, to utilize Smith's methodological contributions throughout this project. Smith argued that the traditional scholarly mode of comparison had been ruled by a single concept: similarity.[217] Finding patterns is the easy part, Smith maintains; "[b]ut the 'how' and the 'why' and, above all, the 'so what' remain most refractory. These matters will not be resolved by new or increased data. In many respects, we already have too much. It is a problem to be solved by theories and reasons, of which we have had too little."[218] One pathway out of the trap of comparative sameness involves, for Smith (articulated in another essay, "Fences and Neighbors: Some Contours of Early Judaism"[219]), the concept of a "polythetic" (as opposed to "monothetic") classificatory scheme. Borrowing language from the mathematical sciences, specifically R. Sokol and P. Sneath's *Principles of Numerical Taxonomy* (1963), Smith argues for the value of *polythetic* classifications in comparative religious studies. Unlike monothetic systems of comparison, which treasured "the idea of perfect, unique, single differentia" and relied on a "definitive sine qua non," the polythetic approach opts for a flexible (but ultimately undefined) number of similarities between two exempla in comparison, thus leaving one free to argue for both difference and similarity without the fear of losing the "essential," single point of contact between two materials.[220]

The point I wish to emphasize here by way of Smith's work, then, is that comparison is not identity, nor is it a religious or ideological attempt to subordinate some culture, language, or religion to another.[221] Nor are there completely firm criteria by which one might decide which elements of which cultures or religions make "natural" or "necessary" points of mutual evaluation; inevitably, the program of comparison involves *choice*. Smith re-emphasizes this notion in a recent essay, and attempts to move the discussion of comparison away from the language of "discovery" and toward

216. J. Z. Smith 1982a.
217. J. Z. Smith 1982a, 21. Hallo (1980) made this same point specifically for ancient Near Eastern studies.
218. J. Z. Smith 1982a, 35.
219. J. Z. Smith 1982b. This delineation of monothetic and polythetic approaches is directly applied to taxonomic systems, e.g., whether a particular expression counts as a "religion" or not; but these categories can be applied, mutatis mutandis, to comparative categories, i.e., as a method of determining whether two stories or myths or motifs in different sources can or should be compared with one another.
220. J. Z. Smith 1982b, 4–5.
221. Perhaps the most infamous case of this problem in the modern field of biblical studies is the 1902–1904 "Babel und Bibel" controversy, on which see the convenient summaries in Arnold and Weisberg 2002; Larsen 2000.

"invention." "There is nothing 'given' or 'natural' in those elements selected for comparison," Smith contends.[222] Despite my sympathies with Smith's views generally, I confess to finding this notion of "invention" somewhat disconcerting and misleading. There *is* something *more "natural"* about comparing the Enuma Elish with Ps 74:14–17, for example, than with comparing Psalm 74 to a phone book. To say that specific elements of a religious system *demand* or even *invite* comparison with elements in other systems is not simply a hyperbolic rhetorical flourish, but a recognition of some central symbol, motif, or extended plotline shared between two systems, and it is this recognition which is the starting point toward showing how these shared elements illuminate each other in some compelling fashion.[223]

Moreover, Smith suggests "four moments in the comparative enterprise: description, comparison, redescription, and rectification," and these moments deserve attention insofar as I hope to use them as a loose grid for my own investigation:[224]

> Description is a double process which comprises the historical or anthropological dimensions of the work: First, the requirement that we locate a given example within the rich texture of its social, historical, and

222. J. Z. Smith 2000b, 238–39.

223. Alternatively, the criterion of "falsification," raised by Talmon at several points in his treatise on the comparative method (Talmon 1991, e.g., 413, 415), is not necessarily a helpful one in deciding which comparisons are valid, since in the humanities generally the question of falsification is typically decided by the persuasiveness of one's argument for a particular reading. Such arguments, of course, involve the accumulation of "evidence" of all kinds, but are not based on mathematical certainty or the (relative) precision of the "hard" sciences (Talmon seems to refer to "falsification" in this latter sense, though this is not made entirely clear).

224. J. Z. Smith 2000b, 239. Two other suggestions for ordering comparative studies from which I take some direction should be mentioned here. First, Talmon (1991, 415) makes the reasonable suggestion, which I follow in this study, that the "interpretation of biblical features...with the help of inner-biblical parallels should always precede the comparison with extra-biblical materials." He further asserts that comparisons should be made only among cultures within the same "historical stream," and "grand scale" comparisons should be shunned, though the meaning of these strictures is less than clear. Note also the historian of religion Bruce Lincoln's comments on the study of myth in Lincoln 1997, 151, organized in a seven-point protocol (in abbreviated form here): establish the categories and the relationships between these categories in a given text; compare these texts to related materials in the same cultural milieu and discuss the connections between these materials; attempt to situate these materials historically; specifically, this interpretation should focus on relationships of power, "the way the categories constituting the social order are redefined and recalibrated such that certain groups move up and others move down within the extant hierarchy." The possibility for comparison, it seems, comes in at stage four: "Establish any connections that exist between the categories that figure in these texts and those which condition the relations of the social groups among whom the texts circulate."

cultural environments that invest it with its local significance. The second task of description is that of reception-history, a careful account of how *our* second-order scholarly tradition has intersected with the exemplum. That is to say, we need to describe how the datum has become accepted as significant for the purpose of argument.

It is this second task that I have attempted, in at least a preliminary and admittedly incomplete fashion, to address in this review of scholarship. "Only when such a double contextualization is completed," Smith contends,

> does one move on to the description of a second example undertaken in the same double fashion. With at least two exempla in view, we are prepared to undertake their comparison both in terms of aspects and relations held to be significant, and with respect to some category, question, theory, or model of interest to us. The aim of such a comparison is the redescription of exempla (each in light of the other) and a rectification of the academic categories in relation to which they have been imagined.

As Smith's own continued commitment to the comparative task demonstrates, and the pitfalls of comparison notwithstanding, postmodern critiques have not killed the comparative endeavor. Rather, they have made it stronger and more viable for continued use in the twenty-first century and beyond by appropriately emphasizing questions of methodology and of history.[225]

225. Indeed, a reaffirmation of the comparative effort in the "postmodern" age has come from several fronts; many good responses come in a single volume, Patton and Ray 2000; see esp. D. White 2000; Paden 2000.

Chapter Two

The Flood, The Conquest, and the King

I. Introduction

IN THE PRESENT CHAPTER, I bring together passages—with text-critical, philological, literary, geographic, and historical commentary—in which giants of various kinds appear in the Hebrew Bible.[1] These figures appear in three distinct blocks of material: (1) stories recounting the *origins* of the giants; (2) the giants of the *pre-monarchic age* that occupy the land before Israel arrives and who fight with the Israelites during the Conquest; and (3) the giants of the early *monarchic age*—specifically Philistines—who do battle with David and his men. Interestingly, after each of the first two blocks, the giants should have been completely eradicated (by the flood and by the Israelite Conquest, respectively), and yet they are not; it is only David's triumph that finally brings the race of the giants to an end, thus revealing the decisive nature of the early monarchy in the formation and ongoing meaning of these stories.

Despite this periodization (or perhaps because of it), the existence of giants is also presented as something of a *continuum*—i.e., for much of the biblical narrative, these figures are not simply relics of the past, but an *ongoing presence*, with the capacity for invocation at significant points of military and ideological conflict. Statements like those in Deut 9:1–2 certainly reveal one aspect of the purpose of these descriptions of giants: Israel is entering a hostile land, and has "come to possess nations greater and more numerous than [themselves], great cities, fortified up to the heavens, a people great and tall...," and it is only with YHWH's help that such a small and weak nation can defeat such a large and strong opponent.[2] This simple explanation,

---

1. Gen 6:1–4, 10:8–9, 14:15, 15:20; Num 13:28–33, 21:33, 32:33; various references in Deuteronomy 1–3 and Joshua 11–15, 21; 1 Sam 17; 2 Sam 21:16–22 // 1 Chr 20:4–8. I present these materials in their canonical order, which is not at all to imply that the canonical order is the historical order in which these materials were produced. At some point in the ancient world, the text as it now stands became a historical artifact that can be analyzed, and, for the sake of organization at this point, I follow the canonical macro-narrative of the Pentateuch through Samuel and its story of giants.

2. Indeed, this is the exact and repeated argument of the Deuteronomist in his insistence that the people in the land are *more numerous* and *stronger* than Israel (e.g., Deut 7:1,7,17; cf.

however, does not represent the full extent of the purpose of the Bible's giants. Indeed, the giants appear as complex and frightening representatives of human chaos, and in this capacity they act as a sort of earthly parallel to the descriptions of the *Chaoskampf* ("Battle Against Chaos") which can be meaningfully evoked in various settings as a demonstration of Divine providence and creative power.[3] Likewise, the Bible's giants serve as recurring potent symbols of a chaotic peril that can rise up at different points and threaten order, but are ultimately defeated by God or God's human agents. In this chapter, I shall argue that giants appear in the Hebrew Bible particularly at moments of historical and political crisis, as a marker of all that is disorderly, overgrown, and wild. They must be eradicated from the earth (Genesis 6–9; Josh 11:21–22), cut down like a forest (Josh 14:17–18), and dismembered (1 Sam 17:51).

Two broad objectives permeate and guide my investigation here. First, on the simplest level, I hope to show that these giants, both as groups and as individuals, have a significant and meaningful place in the Bible. Such a point may seem obvious, yet the fact that interpreters have largely neglected to give biblical giants a comprehensive, sophisticated treatment suggests otherwise. Moreover, a close examination of the relevant texts will show, I contend, that at points the giants loomed so large in the biblical imagination that their presence on the eve of the Israelite invasion of the land in the books of Numbers, Deuteronomy, and Joshua was thought to be nearly ubiquitous, their territory encompassing nearly all of the land east and west of the Jordan. Thus, the chronologically extended existence of giant, non-Israelite groups is matched (or even exceeded) by their geographical pervasiveness. Second, I will show how various biblical authors attempted to conflate the "races" of giants with one another, thus revealing a storyline telling the history of these figures, who are first created (or identified) in Genesis 1–11 and who then persist into later periods. Though

---

2:10,21). The motif of a mighty, strong (עצום, רב/רבב) people, either as a blessing or as a description of what Israel will/should be, is in fact one of the most pervasive descriptions of Israel in the Bible; see, e.g., Gen 17:2,20, 22:17, 26:4,24, 28:3, 50:20; Exod 1:9, 5:5; Num 22:3; Deut 1:10, 9:14, 10:22, 28:62,63, 30:5,16; Josh 17:14,15,17; 1 Kgs 3:8, 4:20; Zech 10:8; 1 Chr 5:23, 23:17, 27:23; 2 Chr 1:9. For the moment, I am using the words "Deuteronomist(ic)" and "Deuteronomistic History" broadly, without any specific argument other than to affirm Martin Noth's (not unchallenged) insight into the cohesive character of Deuteronomy through Kings in his seminal *The Deuteronomistic History* (Noth 1981a). Regarding issues of dating for the various strata of these books, I am committed at this time only to insist that the basic form of the work dates to the mid-sixth century BCE, but drew upon earlier materials from the seventh and even eighth centuries, specifically (partly following Römer 2006, which at any rate gives the best available summary of the various schools of thought on this topic).

3. E.g., Isa 27:1, 51:9–11; Ps 74:12–17; Dan 7:1–14; Job 26:5–14. I draw on Levenson (1988) for this category of the *Chaoskampf* as a recurring drama in the biblical narrative.

explicit statements are sometimes lacking to indicate this conflation, they do appear in enough places in the Bible (e.g., Num 13:33; Deut 2:9–15) and in later, postbiblical traditions to give us some sense of the interpretive matrix in which these ancient authors were working.

Overall, this catalogue of primary texts will provide the source- and historical-critical work necessary to understand further aspects of the Bible's presentation of giants, including the meaning of their death by flood and battle in parallel with Greek models (Chapter Three), their ongoing existence as powerful figures in the afterlife (Chapter Four), and their ultimate decline as tropes of power and heroism later in the biblical storyline (Chapter Five).[4] The present chapter, however, is not only a catalogue of biblical texts. Rather, I attempt to highlight how, exactly, the giants appear in a given passage, how they function symbolically as embodiments of historical and political chaos, and how the story of the rising and falling and rising again of the giants appears throughout a wide range of biblical materials.

II. Origins: Nephilim and Gibborim

Within the so-called Primeval History of Genesis 1–11 we find two moments wherein the origins of giants are addressed: in the famous (and famously enigmatic) Gen 6:1–4, and also in the reference to Nimrod as the first Gibbor (גבור) in Gen 10:8–9 (// 1 Chr 1:10).[5] How exactly the description in Gen 6:1–4 is related to giants and other such figures is not a completely straightforward issue, and the relationship among the "divine beings" (בני אלהים), the Nephilim, and the ancient Gibborim must be demonstrated by exegesis and not assumed a priori. But whatever the case, generations of both ancient and modern interpreters are mostly in agreement—and correctly so, in my view—that the author(s) of this passage thought that giant races and other heroic figures were the product of an illicit divine-human union. Partial evidence for this intention in Gen 6:1–4 is the fact that later interpreters—even within the period of the composition of the biblical texts themselves (Num 13:33)—were quick to associate the Gen 6:1–4 scene with the origin of giants.

Although it may not be immediately clear how the very brief reference in Gen 10:8–9 to Nimrod as the first Gibbor is related to either Gen 6:1–4 or the issue of the giants generally, several lines of evidence suggest the text is

---

4. Recall the simple but appropriate methodological suggestion of Talmon (1991, 415), mentioned in the previous chapter, viz. that comparative studies involving the Hebrew Bible should first take into account the interpretation of the biblical texts on their own terms and in their own setting.

5. Although the most obvious criterion for defining the "giant" is gigantic physical size, other aspects should also be invoked (which I develop throughout this study): extreme arrogance, semi-divine origin, hubristic oppositon to God, monstrous physical features, and so on.

relevant to the discussion. The fact that Nimrod is cited as the first Gibbor on the earth immediately draws attention to Gen 6:4, where divine-human intermarriage produces "the Gibborim of old, famous men." Nimrod is presumably one cited example of this group, and the note on his very existence provides further etiological information for the existence of the Gibborim, hunting, and the founding of the Assyrian empire. Finally, it should be mentioned that the very term Gibbor (גבר/גבור) suggests, in at least some instances, a special type or class of human beyond the "warrior," "champion," or even "hero" (in the most generic sense). These two passages display a legitimate, albeit fragmentary, narrative regarding the origin of various giant races and heroic giants, a starting point that serves to frame and situate the Bible's giants and their fate.

Sons of God and Daughters of Men

Gen 6:1–4 (v. 1) When humans began to increase upon the face of the land, and daughters were born to them, (2) certain divine beings (בני האלהים)[6] saw how beautiful the human women were, and so they took wives for themselves from among them, whomever they chose. (3) YHWH said, "My spirit will not remain (ידון) with humans forever, for they are but (בשגם) flesh[7]; their lifetime will be 120 years." (4) The Nephilim (נפלים)[8] were on

6. The majority of Greek traditions have οἱ ἄγγελοι τοῦ θεοῦ here, though υἱοὶ θεοῦ is retained in v. 4. Such a move could serve to disassociate the reference in v. 2 with the reference to the נפלים/γίγαντες in v. 4, though it is unclear exactly what this would accomplish. The Targum (Onkelos), as might be expected, changes בני אלהים here to בני רברביא ("the sons of the great ones"), as well as in v. 4. Note R. Simeon bar Yohai's translation for בני אלהים in 6:1 as בני דייניא ("the sons of the judges"). The Hebrew texts cited in this chapter are those of the MT, except where noted. I have not gone to extraordinary lengths in dealing with text-critical issues that do not directly affect the presence or action of giants in the passages I treat here, and I have generally not attempted to make a critical Hebrew text in my replication of the MT (with a few notable exceptions). Greek variants in Genesis through Joshua infra are cited from OTGr I, except where stated otherwise. References to the Targ. here and infra in Genesis are from TOGen.

7. Two famous problems appear here in v. 3; first, the hapax ידון most likely means "remain" (so Westermann 1984, 375), though other possibilities, such as deriving the term from דין ("judge"), the Ugaritic *dnt* ("be oppressed"), or Akk. *danānu(m)* ("be strong," i.e., "strive") have been suggested. Hendel (2004, 15) points to a reading from 4QCommGen[a], ידר ("dwell"), reflected in Targ. Onk., the Peshitta, the Vulgate, and Jub 5:8, though this Aramaism is "best explained as a linguistic modernization of an archaic and obscure term." בשגם is also difficult; the text itself may be corrupt, or the term could be an otherwise unattested combination of the preposition ב + relative ש + גם. See Westermann 1984, 375–77. Cf. שגם in Eccl 1:17, 2:15, 8:14. Kvanig 2002 makes the argument that ידון is a reflection of the Akk. *danānu* and refers to the strength of life inherent in the beings described in these verses, while בשגם is parallel to the Akk. *šagāmu*, "roar, clamor, noise," thus infusing the text here with the idea of noise and overpopulation found in the Atrahasis epic.

8. The Greek translators here used γίγαντες, both for the Hebrew נפלים at the beginning

> the earth in those days—and also afterward (וגם אחרי כן)—when the divine beings procreated with human women. They bore children to them; they were the heroes of old, famous men (הגברים אשר מעולם אנשי השם).[9]

Gen 6:1–4 is not only the first passage of interest for our theme to appear in the canonical Hebrew Bible, but it also has a disproportionately significant place in the history of interpretation that gives it a special importance within the corpus of examples I am considering. This short episode has probably engendered as much commentary and speculation as any other in the Hebrew Bible; indeed, several points of ambiguity have consistently bedeviled interpreters. Who are the "sons of god(s)" (בני האלהים)?[10] Are they multiple "divine beings" (in a polytheistic system), "lesser deities" of some kind, angels, or even humans? What role is played by YHWH's decree of a reduction in life span for humans—and why to 120 years, specifically? Who are the Nephilim? Are they the product of the putative divine-human miscegenation described in v. 1, or a different group? And so on. Reference to the Nephilim appears only here and in Numbers 13:33,[11] though it is not clear prima facie whether Num 13:33 is a later elaboration on the reference in Gen 6:3, or whether Gen 6:3 itself is a very late insertion—perhaps based on Num 13:33?—or whether both references appeared simultaneously.

Ancient interpreters writing in the fourth century BCE – first century CE and beyond found enormous reinterpretive currency in Gen 6:1–4.[12]

---

of the verse and also for גברים. The LXX uses γίγαντες to translate various Hebrew terms over forty times. The Targ. also avoids נפלים here by using גבריא.

9. All translations of biblical passages (and any other non-English texts) in this book are my own, except where noted. At certain points, I have attempted to maintain something of the literal wording of Hebrew idioms or syntax where it seems to contribute to the overall style of the passage (placing English words which have no Hebrew equivalent, but which are nonetheless implied, in parentheses, and other explanations in square brackets), and at other places I have basically followed the conventions found in modern translations such as the NJPS or NRSV. Also, I have sometimes rendered PNs and GNs with non-standard spellings, e.g., consistently transliterating Hebrew names with ק as a "q" and with כ as a "k," with י as "y" instead of "j," etc. The tetragrammaton is rendered as "YHWH" except when spelled differently by others in quotation.

10. בני (ה)אלהים appear also in Job 1:6, 2:1, 38:7, and Deut 32:8, which reads בני ישראל in the MT. But *4QDeut*[j] and *4QDeut*[q] both suggest אלים/בני אלהים (confirmed by some Greek variants). Cf. Dan 3:25, בר אלהין, where אלהין in the mouth of a foreign monarch must be plural. See M. Smith 2008, 193–216, and Rollston, 2003, 102–04. For בני אלים, see Pss 29:1 and 89:7. Cf. Ps 82:6 (ובני עליון). The בני in the phrase בני אלהים is always plural ("sons of"), yet it is not clear if (אלהים) is plural in this construction. For plural uses of אלהים that seem to imply a polytheistic system, see Pss 82:1 and 97:7,9, and there are over 200 other clearly plural uses of אלהים (as opposed to well over 2000 wherein the word is singular). See Loretz 1968, 32–39.

11. Num 13:33: ...ושם ראינו את הנפילים בני ענק מן הנפלים; see infra.

12. See Stuckenbruck 2004, especially the helpful bibliography on p. 87 n. 1 (this essay is a revision and expansion of Stuckenbruck 2000), and the most recent survey of Collins (2008).

Probably the first source (outside of Num 13:33, or Ezekiel 32) to deal with the Nephilim tradition is the Aramaic Enoch texts, written in the late fourth century BCE and then retranslated into Greek and Ethiopic.[13] In 1 Enoch 6:1–2, the Nephilim are the grandchildren of the cohabitation of the Watchers (עירין) with human females; the Watchers and human women first bear Gibborim ("giants," in this context), and the Gibborim produce the Nephilim. This schema clearly seems to be a way of dealing with the ambiguity in Gen 6:4 regarding how the Nephilim are related to the divine-human interaction in the passage, and in fact it is not an altogether unconvincing solution. In this thinking, then, the divine beings cohabit with human women, creating some race of beings alluded to in 6:4 (the "Gibborim of Old" and the "Famous Men") with the result of this interaction being, somewhere down the line, the origin of the Nephilim. The fragmentary *4QBook of Giants* from Qumran takes up this mythology of the giants,[14] undoubtedly relying on the earlier Enoch corpus, as do several other writings from the last few centuries BCE to the first centuries CE.[15]

The Greek translation traditions, beginning probably in the third century BCE, also bear witness to the interpretation of Gen 6:1–4 as a scene involving the origins of giants. Consider, for example, the over forty instances in which the Septuagint uses "giant" or "giants" (γίγας/γίγαντες) to translate various Hebrew terms:[16] Nephilim (Gen 6:4; Num 13:33); Anaqim (ענקים; Deut 1:28[17]); Rephaim (רפאים; Gen 14:5; Josh 12:4, 13:12; Isa 14:9; Job 26:5;

13. See Nickelsburg and VanderKam 2004, 23–31; Nickelsburg 2001, 165–87; Nickelsburg 1977; Hanson 1977.

14. See Stuckenbruck 1997. The references to Gilgamesh and Humbaba in *4QBook of Giants* may indicate something of the original intention behind the references to the בני אלהים in Gen 6:1–4, viz. that the בני אלהים are famous figures known from Near Eastern myth, such as Gilgamesh, Ninurta, Keret, etc. See Goff 2009a; Coxon 1999b, 619; Jackson 2007; *Gilg*. 1: 147.

15. These passages include 3 Macc 2:4; Bar 2:26–8; Wis 14:5; Sir 16:7; and possible allusions in 2 Pet 2:4 and Jude 6.

16. See already Redpath 1905, 37–39, and, more recently, Pearson 1999. By "Septuagint" here, I refer, for the sake of convenience, to Rahlfs 1979, which relies upon Vaticanus, Sinaiticus, and Alexandrinus, though a more detailed interaction with variant Greek traditions is given as needed for individual passages below. Note that not all of the references to γιγάντες in the LXX occur in books that fall within the traditional Jewish or Protestant Christian canons.

17. Elsewhere, ענקים is simply transliterated as Ενακιμ (Deut 2:10,11,21; Josh 11:21,22, 14:12,15). ענק appears as Εναχ in Deut 9:2; Josh 15:13,14, 21:11; Judg 1:10,20; this is expected, since ענק is a personal name in these contexts. The isolated use of υἱοὺς γιγάντων for בני ענקים in Deut 1:28 can most likely be explained by the fact that the extraordinary physical status of the people is already highlighted in the verse. In three separate instances, the word Ενακιμ appears in Greek traditions where it does not appear in the MT. In 2 Sam 21:11, the Lucianic text adds καὶ ἐξελύθησαν καὶ κατέλαβεν αὐτοὺς Δαν υἱὸς Ιωα ἐκ τῶν ἀπογόνων τῶν γιγάντων (Vaticanus adds these words proceeding v. 11, and bozc₂e₂ and several other manuscripts have

Prov 21:16; 1 Chr 11:15, 14:9,13, 20:4[18]); Gibbor (גבר; Gen 10:8,9; Isa 3:2, 13:3, 49:24,25; Ezek 33:12,21,27, 39:18,20; Pss 19:6 = LXX 18:6, 33:16 = LXX 32:16[19]); and Rapha (רפה/רפא; Sam 21:22; 1 Chr 20:6,8[20]).[21] This leveling seems to presume familiarity with Greek notions of the Gigantomachy, and indeed the Greek myths dealing with the Giants and Titans seem at least superficially similar to several biblical motifs.[22] Mussies claims that the Septuagintal traditions emended Gen 6:1–4 from "the sons of God" to "the angels of God" precisely in order to avoid accusations from "opponents of Judaism" that the "God" whose sons bear giants is none other than Cronus.[23]

---

the two halves of this verse, with the addition, transposed). However, as McCarter (1984, 440, 448) points out, these words are very likely a marginal correction of the reading in vv. 15–16 of the same chapter, where various descendants of Raphah appear. Εμακιμ also appears in Jer 29:5 (= Heb. 47:5) and 30:4 (= 49:4), but here too it is likely not the original reading, but rather, in the first instance, an interpretation of the difficult Hebrew שארית עמקם, and in the second instance Εμακιμ is introduced again in a similar manner (Hebrew מה תתהללי בעמקים זב עמקך). See Lundbom 2004, 239–40, 321.

18. רפאים is transliterated as Ραπαιν in Gen 15:20; Deut 2:11,20, 3:11,13; Josh 15:8; and Ραφαιμ in 2 Sam 23:13 (note also Γεδων υἱοῦ Ραφαιν in Judith 8:1). There are some notable idiosyncrasies in the Greek translations for רפאים, however, as a toponym. In 2 Sam 5:18 and 5:22, the עמק רפאים is translated as κοιλάδι τῶν τιτάνων ("valley of the Titans")—marking the only appearance of τιτάν in the Greek Bible—and in Isaiah 17 the phrase appears as φάραγγι στερεᾶ ("firm valley"). Josh 15:8 uses γῆς Ραφαιν, while Josh 18:16 uses Εμεκραφαιν, and 1 Chr 11:15 and 14:9 both have κοιλάδι τῶν γιγάντων ("Valley of Giants"). Instances where the רפאים refer to figures in the afterlife are no more consistent. In Isa 14:9, Job 26:5, and Prov 21:16, רפאים refer to the dead and are rendered by γίγας (as noted above). In Isa 26:14, however, the Greek reads ἰατροί ("healers"), which may be the translator's intention to skew the meaning or simply the result of misunderstanding the Hebrew, though the Greek translators of Isaiah are known to diverge from, or misunderstand, the Hebrew in many places. In Ps 88:11 (= Gk. 87:11) רפאים is rendered again as ἰατροὶ, which is possibly a euphemism, or simply the translator's attempt at a literal rendering of a word which he thinks is naturally derived from the Hebrew רפא, "heal." Prov 2:18 is a bit expansive in the second half of the verse, reading "and her paths to Hades (τῷ ᾅδῃ) with the 'earth-born' (γηγενῶν)" for the Hebrew ואל רפאים מעגלתיה. The parallel Heb./Gk. portion of Prov 9:18 contains nothing unexpected in light of 2:18, and again reads γηγενής for רפאים.

19. γίγας is not the only term used to translate גבר; see, e.g., Josh 8:3 (ἀνδρῶν δυνατοὺς ἐν ἰσχύϊ; cf. Judg 6:12); Josh 10:2 (ἰσχυροί) and Judg 5:13 (ἰσχυροτέρους); 2 Sam 1:19–27, 23:8–24; 1 Chr 11:10–26 (δυνατοί); and Joel 4:11 (= Heb. 3:11) (μαχητής).

20. See infra for discussion of רפא/רפה vs. רפאים.

21. Outside of the Hebrew Bible, see Jdt 16:6 (υἱοὶ τιτάνων); 1 Macc 3:3; 3 Macc 2:4; Wis 14:6; Sir 16:7, 47:4; Bar 3:26. In the Vulgate, *gigantes* appears in Gen 6:4; Num 13:34; Deut 2:10–11, 2:20, 3:11, 3:13; 2 Sam 21:18, 23:13; Jdt 16:8; Job 16:15, 26:5; PsG 18:6, 32:16; PsH 87:11; Prov 9:18, 21:16; Wis 14:6; Sir 16:8, 47:4; Isa 14:9, 26:14,19; Bar 3:26–28; 1 Macc 3:3. See brief discussion in Travis 1999, 168, 170. Note also that the Targums level all references to רפאים, נפלים, and ענקים to a single term, גבריא.

22. On this, see especially Pearson 1999.

23. Mussies 1999, 344. Although cf. Josephus, *Ant.* I.73.

But in actuality, the very references to the Giants and Titans already suggest a world which is in some way comparable to Greek myth—indeed, the references to figures in well-known Greek stories invite such conflation.[24] Moreover, although it is customary to claim that the Greek translators used such terms only to help their audiences understand the biblical tales in terms of their inherited Hellenistic cultural milieu, the effect of the introduction of Greek mythological vocabulary in suggestive and enigmatic places can only, in effect, serve to make the Greek Giants and Titans part of the biblical story. True, such references to Giants had probably already achieved a kind of generic usage by the time the Greek translations were made, but the implications of certain formulations could not have gone unnoticed.[25]

Early Jewish and Christian interpreters produced sporadic insights on the passage. For example, rabbinic commentators (e.g., as represented in a work like *Bereshith Rabbah*) avoided the implication that the בני אלהים were "sons of God" (i.e., deities) in any sense.[26] Furthermore, the phrase ויהי כי החל האדם לרב ("when the humans began to increase") was interpreted in terms of a rebellion, by seizing upon the word חלל ("begin," but with the influence of חלל, "desecrate") in other putative contexts of rebellion, viz. Gen 10:8 (Nimrod), Gen 11:6 (the Tower of Babel builders), and even Gen 4:26 (those who "begin" [= rebel] to call upon the name of YHWH).[27] Thus, the multiplication of humans on the earth becomes a rebellious *overpopulation*. Moreover, the rabbinic commentators divided the Nephilim into seven subgroups (Nephilim, Emim, Rephaim, Gibborim, Zamzumim, Anaqim, and Avim)—an interpretive move not entirely unwarranted in terms of the conflations made in the biblical text itself (Num 13:33; Deut 2:10–11, etc.).[28]

24. This is also the conclusion of the detailed short study of this topic by Goff (2009b).

25. Specifically, I would cite LXX Prov 2:18 and 9:18 as prime examples, where the term γηγενῶν, "earth-born," refers specifically to the genealogy of the γίγαντες, i.e., that they are born from Gaia and later imprisoned in the earth. Note also the reference to the Titans in LXX 2 Sam 5:18 and 5:22 (as well as Jdt 16:6), which is completely unnecessary as a simply generic equivalent, given the fact that רפאים is unproblematically transliterated in other locations or translated with the less specific γίγαντες elsewhere (e.g., parallel passages to 2 Sam in 1 Chr 11:15 and 14:9, where γιγάντων appears). Cf. references to "Hades" (ᾅδης) in the LXX, which mark an analogous identification of a Hebrew concept (שאול) with its putative Greek counterpart (Pss 6:6, 48:15, 87:4, 93:17; Prov 2:18; Eccl 9:10; Job 14:3, 33:22; Hos 13:14; cf. Bar 2:17).

26. *Gen. Rab.* XXVI:V, 282.

27. *Gen. Rab.* XXVI:IV, 280.

28. *Gen. Rab.* XXVI:VII, 286–87. While each of the other six groups in this list is either explicitly or implicitly categorized as gigantic in the biblical texts, the Avvim (only in Deut 2:23; Josh 13:3, 18:23) are nowhere said to be of huge stature. One could argue for their giant status by a tenuous extension, in that Deut 2:23 lists the Avvim as a conquered group (by the "Caphtorim") on the parallel pattern of the Rephaim/Anaqim (whom the Israelites destroy) and the Horim (whom the sons of Esau destroy), but of these three aboriginal groups biblical authors

The "men of name/fame" in 6:4 were identified specifically with various characters in Genesis 1-11 (Irad, Mehujael, Methushael, and Lamech) and also with Eliphaz the Temanite, Bildad the Shuhite, and Zophar the Naama-thite, in accordance with the belief that Job's generation was the generation of the Flood. Early Christian voices, alternatively, seem more willing to iden-tify the "divine beings" of Gen 6:1-4 with angels or humans (e.g., in the line of Seth, as opposed to the "daughters of men" in the line of Cain).[29]

Modern scholarship has proceeded in multiple directions, but it is fair to generalize that source-critical methods have allowed scholars to isolate Gen 6:1-4 from its surrounding context and treat various elements of the passage as intrusive or additional.[30] In his *Prolegomena*, for example, Well-hausen does not give prolonged exegetical treatment to Gen 6:1-4, but the type of raw material at hand in the passage provides him an opportunity to argue further for a distinction between J and P. For Wellhausen, both J and P have expunged the "true meaning and contents" from source material rife with "primitive legend," but it is the Priestly group that carries this program further forward, to the point "where it actually comes as a surprise when some mythic element shines through."[31] In J, however, such myth can be integrated with the narrator's broader purposes:

> The mythic materials of the primitive world-history are suffused in the Jehovist with a peculiar somber earnestness, a kind of antique philosophy of history, almost bordering on pessimism: as if mankind were groaning under some dreadful weight, the pressure not so much of sin as of creaturehood (vi. 1-4). We notice a shy, timid spirit, which belongs more to heathenism. The rattling of the chains at intervals only aggravates the feeling of confinement that belongs to human nature; the gulf of alienation between man and God is not to be bridged over.[32]

In P, this mood has dissipated. Even as P's concept of sin is perceived as a new kind of "leaden weight," this sin can be dealt with, and human ruin is

---

only make comment on the giant size of the Rephaim and Anaqim. Cf. Josh 13:3, where the Avvim are related to the Philistines (some of whom are giants).

29. See, conveniently, Louth and Conti 2001, I:123-26. By identifying this stream of inter-pretation as "ancient," I do not mean to imply that no modern interpreter has ascribed to this notion; see, e.g., Cassuto, 1961, 292-94.

30. Verse 3 is most typically viewed as the interloper. See Westermann 1984, 363-83; V. Hamilton 1990, 261-72. Focused studies include: Kraeling 1947; Childs 1960, 49-57; Loretz 1968; Bartelmus 1979; Clines 1979; Eslinger 1979; Scharbert 1967; Wifall 1975; Hendel 1987b; 2004. Earlier studies include: Kurtz 1857; Scholz 1865.

31. Wellhausen 1878, 314. References to Wellhausen in German here come from *Prolegom-ena zur Geschichte Israels* (Wellhausen 1927).

32. Wellhausen 1878, 314.

not a victim of "not-to-be-averted fate" (*unabwendbaren Verhängnis*), as it apparently is at some points in J.[33]

H. Gunkel saw the Nephilim clause in v. 4a as a later addition to Gen 6:1–4, and affirmed that it is an "incidental note," without connection to the surrounding materials.[34] Moreover, Gunkel thought the author had only included the story as a means of subduing otherwise objectionable content (i.e., perhaps an extended giant/Nephilim narrative?), and thus attempted to explain the origins of giants in terms of the divine-human intercourse. This raises the question of why an author would not assuage his anxiety by *simply omitting* the reference altogether. At any rate, Gunkel considers the story as a "torso," barely worthy to be called a "story" at all, and yet acknowledges that the original story must have been more detailed ("Die ursprüngliche Erzählung muss viel reicher gewesen sein").[35] Von Rad, however, saw greater coherence in the passage. He claimed that "the original purpose of this story was…to account aetiologically for the origin of heroes from such marriages," and argues that although the giants-as-offspring of divine-human intermarriage motif was part of the *original* myth, this formulation "is not mentioned at all in the present text." Still, the author "wanted to represent the mixing of superhuman spiritual powers with man, a kind of 'demonic' invasion."[36] Westermann essentially sees the unit as comprised of two stories—one "purely etiological" (explaining the origin of giants) and the other a "mythical story" recounting the "dangerous transgression" of the divine beings.[37]

Recent analysis of Gen 1–11 as a whole has focused on the possibility of thematic parallels between Gen 6:1–4 and 11:1–9, though some have pointed out that it is not entirely clear that these two moments of apparent transgression are human encroachments into strictly divine spheres.[38] J. M. Sasson claims "the obscurity of crucial vocabulary [in Gen 6:1–4] (e.g., in v. 3) makes hopeless our task of understanding its 'original' purpose," though the broader goals of the redactors can be seen in the existence of two separate but parallel cycles, from Gen 1:1–6:8 and from 6:9–11:9. In each of these parallel structures, the movement toward increasing hubris results in divine

33. Wellhausen 1878, 315.
34. Gunkel 1901, 53.
35. Gunkel 1901, 54.
36. Von Rad 1972, 115. So too Westermann (1984, 365, 369) concludes that the final "purpose of the narrative" is to posit an origin for the גברים in v. 4—but this purpose was only a secondary stage in the tradition.
37. Westermann 1984, 368.
38. See, e.g., Clines (1994, 297), who mentions the possibility of "a sin of violence on the purely human plane," not comparable with the more severely hubristic act of the tower-builders in ch. 11. On this notion, see also Kline 1962 and Dexinger 1966, both cited by Clines (1994, 297 n. 37).

destruction, followed immediately by a decision to particularize the divine-human relation in a single individual (Noah and Abram, respectively).[39] This compositional technique suggests that the compilers viewed the transgressions in Gen 6:1–4 as thematic parallels to the sin at Babel in 11:1–9. Moreover, several *Leitworten* appear in the two passages and other biblical stories that invite comparison. Consider, for example, the appearance of the word "name" (שם) here and in the words of the tower builders in Gen 11:4 ("let us make a name for ourselves"; ונעשה לנו שם) and in the promise to Abram in Gen 12:2 ("I will bless you, and make your *name* great"), as well as the motif of "seeing and taking" (לקח...ראה) as a transgressive act in Gen 6:2, Gen 3:6, 12:15, and 2 Sam 11:2,4.[40]

Interpreters have also sought out appropriate parallels to the themes of transgression, divine-human intermarriage, and the origins of giants in Greek and ancient Near Eastern sources. Kraeling identified the origin of the Bible's Gibborim tradition as "a Western adaptation" of the Babylonian stories and lists of antediluvian kings, while the separate Nephilim tradition is derived from Greek myth; thus, Gen 6:1–4 presents a conflation of these two streams of thought.[41] In different ways, A. Kilmer and W. Winfall also derive the characters of Gen 6:1–4 from the realm of antediluvian kings, with Kilmer arguing for an identification with the *apkallu* (sages) and Wifall suggesting that the Gibborim and Nephilim references recall, on one level, the historical presence of Amorite rulers in the first half of the second millennium in Canaan, and, on another level, images of historical events from the life of King David.[42] E. A. Speiser found the closest parallel to Gen 6:1–4 in the Hittite (translation of the Hurrian) myth of Teshub's ascension to power upon defeating Ullikummi, a story which is the most likely candidate as the source for the famous Greek tales of divine castration and Zeus' ultimate battle with the Titans and Typhon.[43] Hendel gives the most comprehensive overview of Canaanite, Phoenician, Mesopotamian, and Greek traditions (including those already mentioned) bearing affinity to Gen 6:1–4.[44] I think it is very reasonable to endorse Hendel's assertion about the relationship among

39. Sasson 1994, 454, 456–57.

40. In these latter two instances specifically, as Westermann (1984, 366–67) points out, the issue involves seeing the beauty of a woman and taking her by force.

41. Kraeling 1947b, 200.

42. Kilmer 1987. Wifall (1975) argues for the connection with David on the basis of Walter Brueggemann's work relating David to Adam (see Brueggemann 1968; 1972), and offers the "saw...took" motif discussed above as evidence of an intentional literary connection between the two stories.

43. On this, see Kraeling 1947b; Speiser 1964, 45–46; West 1997a, 103–06, 285, and López-Ruiz 2010, 84–129.

44. Hendel 2004, 23–32.

these literary streams in terms of what he calls a "maximal view," to wit, that it "is not necessary to relate the surviving texts [from throughout the Mediterranean] to each other directly," but rather "each text [articulates] its distinctive discourse out of the available materials of tradition" circulating in the Late Bronze and early Iron ages.[45]

Let us return to the text of Gen 6:1–4. Regarding the role of v. 4a, the *crux interpretum* is perhaps the אשר ("which, that which"; here "when") clause: "The Nephilim were on the earth in those days—and also afterward—when (אשר) the divine beings procreated with human women." One solution would be to view the Nephilim as living *concurrently* during the time of the divine-human miscegenation; they are not the product of this intermingling, but rather the author offhandedly mentions them, which in any case is awkward. Westermann's claim that the אשר "is an afterthought" and that its translation as temporal, iterative, or causal "does not really matter," is too dismissive,[46] as one could attempt to tease some nuance out of the אשר which would help the connection between the Nephilim and the children of the union appear more organic.[47] For example, reading the אשר as a *result* clause, a *purpose* clause, or as a *causal* marker[48] could bring about a reading such as "The Nephilim were on the earth in those days, with the later result being that the divine beings…(i.e., the Nephilim somehow were involved in inciting the divine-human congress).[49] Or, as Childs has claimed, removing the intrusive phrase "and also afterward" connects the (causal) אשר to vv. 1–2, indicating straightforwardly that the product of the divine-human union is the giants (i.e., the *Nephilim* were the result of the union—the Nephilim are the heroes of old).[50] What it means for the Nephilim to live on the earth "and also afterwards" in the text as it stands is a bedeviling problem, the solution to which may be found in (or was created by) the very idea of the conflation of the Nephilim with the giant, pre-Israelite heroes of Canaan.

One solution, embraced by many a commentator,[51] introduces two

45. Hendel 2004, 32. See also Schüle (2009, 127), who assumes that the audience of Gen 6:1–4 knew of Greek traditions "more diverse and variegated than we sometimes tend to think."

46. Westermann 1984, 377.

47. Discussion of the variety of meanings for אשר can be found in Williams 2007, 163–66; Huehnergard 2006; *GBH* 2: 595–98.

48. Cf. Gen 13:16; Exod 20:26; Deut 4:40; 1 Sam 15:15; 1 Kgs 3:13; 2 Kgs 9:37, and other examples in Williams 2007, 165–66, as well as *GKC*, 165b, 166b.

49. See the conclusions based on the אשר drawn out by Bartelmus (1979, 22–23).

50. Thus, for Childs 1962, 53–54, who does not explicitly translate the text in his book, the "original" text would read something like this: "The Nephilim (= Giants) were on the earth, i.e., the result of the Sons of Gods going in to the Children of Men. These (Nephilim) were the heroes of old…"

51. E.g., Westermann 1984, 378, and sources cited therein.

sources into v. 4, with the first (earlier) description in 4a ("the Nephilim were on earth in those days") and 4c ("these were the heroes of old...") identifying the products of the intermarriage as the Gibborim, while the second layer in 4b ("when the sons of God went in...") connects the Nephilim with these Gibborim. This solution is dissatisfying on certain levels, however, since we are left with no secure method of situating such an insertion historically.[52] When, exactly, were the Nephilim identified with the Gibborim? And what, exactly, did the author or subsequent interpolators think the word "Nephilim" meant? Regarding an etymology and meaning for the word Nephilim, there seems to be little disagreement that the root here is נפל, "fall," but the exact significance of the "falling" is less than clear.[53] It is instructive to notice a cluster of passages in Isaiah and Ezekiel as well as a particular turn of phrase in 2 Sam 1:19,25,27 alongside Gen 6:4, wherein the verb נפל (*nāp̄al*) appears in the context of battle, cataclysm, and the afterlife.

For example: the taunt or "proverb" (משל) directed against Babylon in Isa 14:4–20 describes a personified Babylon's descent to Sheol with terminology that is evocative of what we will come to recognize as the intermingling of traditions regarding the Nephilim, giants, Rephaim, and the afterlife. In Isa 14:9, the Rephaim (Greek γίγαντων) are aroused in Sheol to meet the fallen leader, to wit, the fellow "leaders of the earth" (עתודי ארץ) and "kings of the nations" (מלכי גוים). In 14:12, the verb *nāp̄al* appears in its crucial context: "How you have fallen (נפלת) from heaven, Shining One, son of Dawn!"[54] One immediately also must notice the series of terms in this passage that convey cognate notions of falling down or being cast away, such as "stretch out, cast forth" (שלח), "lie down" (שכב), "descend" (ירד), "cut down" (גדע), and "lie prostrate" (חלש). These words are then powerfully opposed to the verb עלה ("ascend") in 14:13–14.

A similar juxtaposition of rising and falling in terms of life and death appears in Isa 26:14: "the dead will not live, Rephaim will not rise up" (מתים בל

---

52. This is, of course, a persistent problem in source-critical work. The simple fact is that we do not possess these supposedly earlier, fragmented traditions and we thus have no way of knowing whether this alleged two-stage redactional process occurred with long (multi-century) distances between the "layers," or whether such conflations were the result of a single hand attempting to solve several problems at one fell swoop.

53. Recent overviews are in Hendel 2004, 21–22; V. Hamilton 1990, 270; Hess 1992, 4:1072; Coxon 1999b. The best grammatical explanations for the word are given by Hendel (2004) and V. Hamilton (1990): נפלים is a *qāṭīl* for passive adj. along the lines of *pāqîd*, "appointed one," *māšiaḥ*, "one who is anointed," *'asîrīm*, "prisoners" (cf. Gen 39:20 for the passive plural participle, as noted by V. Hamilton [1990, 270]).

54. Cf. Isa 21:9, נפלה נפלה בבל, as well as Jer 51:4,8,44,47,49. I am inclined to see Isaiah 14 as earlier, though both could be drawing from a common source. Amos 5:2 interestingly uses the "X נפלה" motif for *Israel*: נפלה לא תוסיף קום בתולת ישראל. Cf. Amos 8:14.

יהיו רפאים בל יקמו). Moreover, vv. 18–19 of the same chapter seem to exploit the nuances of נפל (*nāpal*) in an enigmatic reference often thought to be part of this chapter's reference to resurrection:

> (v. 18) We conceived, we writhed, but we bore wind; we did not achieve any salvation on earth, and the inhabitants of the earth (תבל) have not fallen (יפלו). (19) Yet your dead (מתיך) will live, your corpses (MT: נבלתי)[55] will arise—wake up and sing for joy, dwellers in the dust! For your dew is a dew of lights (טל אורת) (?), and it will be cast upon (תפיל; be made to fall upon) the Land of Rephaim (ארץ ראפים).

The lament over Tyre in Ezek 26:18 is intoned "on the day of your fall" (מפלתך, also in v. 15), an event which culminates in a cataclysm by flood (v. 19).[56] In chapter 28 the king of Tyre is cast from the holy mountain down to "earth" (v. 17, על ארץ השלכתיך).[57] It is important to notice the connection in Ezek 26:20 between the fall of the arrogant ruler and the primeval inhabitants of the underworld: "I will bring you down with those who go down into the Pit (בור), to the ancient people (עם עולם), and I will settle you in the earth below among the ancient ruins (כחרבות מעולם)..."

Ezekiel 32 is often cited in discussions of Gen 6:1–4 in terms of the meaning of Nephilim.[58] Consider, for example, the confluence of נפל (*nāpal*) and Gibbor in Ezek 32:12:

> By the swords of Gibborim (גבורים) I will bring down (אפיל) your multitude, ruthless nations, all of them, and they will plunder the pride of Egypt; its entire multitude will be destroyed.

Also, in 32:27:

> And they will not lie down with the uncircumcised fallen Gibborim (את גבורים נפלים) who go down to Sheol, with their implements of war, their swords laid under their heads, and their iniquities upon their bones—for the terror of Gibborim (גבורים) is in the land of the living.

One final possibility regarding this connection occurs in the threefold refrain of David's lament for Saul and Jonathan in 2 Sam 1:19,25,27: "How the Gibborim have fallen!" (איך נפלו גבורים). Given the potentially archaic nature of this poem, its use of language with respect to the Gibborim who "fall"

---

55. Emending נבלתי to נבלתיך. See Millar (1976, 53), who also points to the connection between dew and life in Psalm 137. Cf. Wildberger 1997, 556, 567–68; Childs 2001, 187–88.

56. Cf. Ezek 26:3–6, 27:17,27,34, and the discussion in Hanson 1977, 211.

57. It should be noted that ארץ here, as elsewhere in the HB and cognate NWS and Mesopotamian literatures, may refer to the *under*world—cf. 26:20 where this is made more explicit.

58. Hendel 1987b, 21–22; Cassuto 1961, 298; Coxon 1999b, 619; V. Hamilton, 270; Hanson 1977, 209–10; Westermann 1984, 378; Kraeling 1947b, 196. See my discussion of Ezekiel 32 in Chapter 4, as well as Doak (forthcoming 2013).

(נפל) is possibly more specific than the many other references to various warriors who fall in 2 Samuel 1–3.[59]

The Gibborim in such passages, then, are not simply strong fighters (as they are elsewhere in the Hebrew Bible), but rather a *special category of human*, whose deeds on earth and fate after death are a matter of special consideration. One should also bear in mind the fact that the Gibbomr of Gen 6:4 are said to be "from ancient times" (מעולם; cf. Ezek 26:20), whereas other Gibborim are perhaps of more recent vintage, as in Ezekiel 32 (but cf. 32:27 in the LXX: τῶν γιγάντων τῶν πεπτωκότων ἀπὸ αἰῶνος, "the giants who fell in ancient times"). I will return to these passages (and others) in terms of this dual identity of the "hero" at length later in this study. I invoke them here to point out the fact that the reference to both Nephilim and Gibborim in Gen 6:4 is not as isolated or unusual as it first appears to be, but rather participates in a world of mythic tropes and epic involving heroic figures.[60]

In summary, modern scholarship has very largely abandoned the notion that the "divine beings" are "angels," so popular among early interpreters, as well as the Sethite/Cainite lineage explanations, and more appropriately sought a native understanding of Gen 6:1–4 in terms of other ancient Near Eastern and Mediterranean myth. Whether the products of the transgression of gods with humans in this passage are merely humans along the lines of the Mesopotamian antediluvian kings (who are not "merely" humans at any rate!) or baldly divine-human hybrids, in light of the Ugaritic and other Canaanite literatures, it is difficult to avoid the implication that the tale of the divine beings and the human women is a straightforwardly mythological fragment. We should therefore resist the temptation, reflected often in the tone of the secondary literature, to insist that such a story was only "borrowed" and that it was somehow entirely un-Israelite.

There still remains, however, the potent question of exactly *why* an Israelite author would tell a story like this, a question bound up further with the question of why any material which was likely derived from non-Israelite mythical sources appears in the Hebrew Bible at all. Is not such a story the very "myth" ancient Israel had supposedly rejected (under some interpretive schemes) in favor of its own demythologized, "historical" *Weltanschauung*? Many interpreters regard the actions in Gen 6:1–4 as the ultimate motive for the Flood,[61] though there remains disagreement regarding the ultimate purpose of 6:1–4 within the context of Genesis 1–11 as a whole.

59. Jer 46:12 combines נפל and גבר in a derisive manner: כי גבור בגבור כשלו יחדיו נפלו שניהם ("Gibbor stumbles over Gibbor, both of them fall together").

60. See, similarly, Schüle 2009, 123; Coxon 1999a.

61. See, e.g., Hendel 1987b, 16; Speiser 1964, 46, etc.; for a refutation of the notion that the action in Gen 6:1–4 caused the Flood, see Westermann 1984, 368–69. I discuss this question further in Chapter 3.

The cacophony of interpretive voices would seem to leave little room for yet another novel interpretation of Gen 6:1–4, and it is not my goal to offer one here. Rather, I would simply like to focus on one aspect of the passage that is relatively clear: the "heroes of old" (גברים אשר מעולם) are indeed the product of the intermingling between super-human beings and humans, and it is this union which is responsible for the heroic races of the ancient world. Here, and in other places detailed below, the Bible engages in fragmentary and yet sustained reflection on the origin and nature of ancient heroic figures, and it is this focus on the origin of the hero—including, here, races of giants—that lies at the heart, I contend, of Gen 6:1–4.[62] To call the story "merely etiological," as Westermann does,[63] is to fail to recognize the fact that the biblical texts ascribe a major role to Gibborim and the constellation of characters drawn into the orbit of the title Gibborim. One can only justly label Gen 6:1–4 "etiological" if one is willing to recognize that the etiology is quite important for subsequent interpretive traditions, evident within the Bible itself at least before the sixth century. Moreover, Childs is unjustified in calling Gen 6:1–4 "a foreign particle of pagan mythology,"[64] as if the passage can be so easily removed from the context of Genesis 1–11.[65] Of course, one can fruitfully isolate it for historical-critical purposes, but in fact the situation to which this "particle" alludes—the existence of giants in some archaic period—is to be found throughout the Hebrew Bible and is demonstrated in complex ways. A mythical narrative, like the one represented in Gen 6:1–4, seems to stand as the wellspring of these other

62. In focusing on this "heroic" aspect of Gen 6:1–4, I follow a number of previous studies that have approached the topic with a focus on heroes and heroic ages, demigods, divine-human miscegenation, and the cataclysms/battles that bring an end to these heroes. See especially Hendel 1987b; Nagy 2006; Gese 1973; Wifall 1975; Bartelmus 1979, 22–23; Dexinger 1966, 59–87.

63. For Westermann (1984, 379), the story in its current form and setting "is just a piece of information that is to be handed down; a merely etiological line is not interested in passing judgment." Cf. Childs 1962, 55, etc. Note also that Bartelmus (1979, 23) affirms the etiological view generally ("die Bezeichnung 'Mythische Ätiologie' erscheint tatsächlich sachgemäß") but does so with, I think, a far greater appreciation for the complexity of the story than either Westermann or Childs.

64. Childs 1962, 54.

65. Childs 1962, 54. The dismissal here is particularly inappropriate considering the lengths to which Childs went throughout his career to argue *against* the isolation of such texts from their context in the canon. It should be noted, however, that the comments in *Myth and Reality* were first published about a decade before Childs' breakout study *Biblical Theology in Crisis* (1970) and other later works in which Childs' concept of "canonical criticism" was fully developed. Moreover, in his *Introduction to the Old Testament as Scripture*, for example, Childs is quick to criticize Westermann for "overemphasizing" "internal divisions" in Genesis (such as separating the primeval history from chs. 12–50; Childs 1979, 146), and presumably internal divisions within Gen 1–11 have been, in Childs' view, overemphasized as well (though he does not mention Gen 6:1–4 in his discussion of Genesis in Childs 1979, 136–60).

passages.[66] Here, as elsewhere, a race of lawless, transgressive figures who were thought to be giants meets with a decisive end—as they do twice more in the Hebrew Bible: extermination.

Nimrod, The First Gibbor

Gen 10:8–12 (v. 8) Cush bore Nimrod; he was the first to become a Gibbor (גבר)[67] on the earth. (9) He was a hunter Gibbor before YHWH; thus it is said, "Like Nimrod, a hunter Gibbor before YHWH (לפני יהוה)."[68] (10) The beginning of his kingdom was Babel, Erech, Akkad, and Kalneh in the land of Shinar. (11) From that land he went out to Assur[69] and built Nineveh, Rehoboth-'Ir, Kalach, (12) and Resen between Nineveh and Kalach—it is the great city.

The reference to Nimrod as the first Gibbor immediately brings to mind the earlier invocation of the "Gibborim of old" in Gen 6:4, and it is noteworthy that the Bible provides here a prototype of all Gibborim in the figure of Nimrod. Though it is not clear that Nimrod is a "giant," two possible lines of interpretation suggest that Nimrod was thought to be something greater than an ordinary human. Van der Toorn and van der Horst make the interesting suggestion that the biblical authors have intentionally given a précis of Mesopotamian history through the cities mentioned in vv. 10–12, thus suggesting that the lifetime of Nimrod as founder of these cities spanned several hundred years (i.e., from Akkad in the Sargonic period through Kalach in the first millennium).[70] Of course, it may well have been that the biblical authors simply condensed the origin of these cities into one brief period and schematically attributed them to a single founder. Kraeling proposed that לפני יהוה in v. 9 referred to Nimrod's great physical stature ("measuring up to great size"), though he was able to offer scant evidence for such a reading.[71]

Finally, it should be noted that postbiblical lore credited Nimrod with giant status and associated him with the building of the Tower of Babel in Gen

---

66. On the Gen 6:1–4 scene as the source of biblical thinking regarding giants and the _Heroenkonzept_ in the Bible, see also Bartelmus 1979, 31–35.

67. The majority of Greek witnesses here translate גבר as γίγας; Sym. has βίαιος ("mighty") as do other mss. for v. 9. Targ. Onk. reads גבר תקיף, "a mighty potentate."

68. The exact nuance of לפני יהוה here is unknown. Speiser (1964, 64) suggested a translation of "by the will of Yahweh," citing לפני as a marker of judgment, will, or approval in Gen 6:11, 7:1, 17:18, 27:7, and 43:33, as well as the Akk. idiom _pānušūma_, "if he chooses."

69. Assur could be read either as the subject of the sentence (as in the majority of Greek witnesses, ἐκ τῆς γῆς ἐκείνης ἐξῆλθεν Ασσουρ καὶ ᾠκοδόμησεν τὴν Νινε…; see also Targ. Onk.) or, as in my translation here, as an accusative of direction, "_to_ Assur."

70. See van der Toorn and van der Horst 1990, 7–8, and souces cited therein for the putative historical founding of these cities.

71. Kraeling 1922, 217. Kraeling cited Jonah 3:3 as evidence of this meaning for לפני יהוה, where the text reads, in part, ונינוה היתה עיר גדולה לאלהים (Kraeling clearly thought the preposition ל here stood as an equivalent to לפני).

11:1–5 (probably due to Nimrod's association with Shinar).[72] Furthermore, the Greek translation of Gibbor as "Giant" (γίγας) in Gen 10:8–9 attests to what may have been a popular, and not altogether illogical, interpretation that Nimrod's stock as a giant somehow was passed through Noah, thus manifesting the hubris with which giants are often associated in his act of founding several cities (cf. Gen 4:17) and inciting the Tower of Babel project.[73] These suggestions are perhaps not particularly compelling beyond their value as remarkable yet unsubstantiated ideas in the history of interpretation. Outside of the narratives devoted to major characters in Genesis 1–11, Nimrod is one of only a few individuals singled out for special, parenthetical comment (see also Enoch in 5:24 and Peleg in 10:25). The brevity of the comment here suggests a deeper background story. We must assume, therefore, that the authors of this pericope knew something more expansive about the character of Nimrod than what appears in the biblical text and that Nimrod held some extraordinary status—possibly as a giant—in the minds of the ancient audience.

Two interrelated issues have dominated the relatively voluminous literature on this short passage, viz. the question of an identification of Nimrod with a deity (e.g., Marduk or Ninurta) or human figure from the cuneiform literatures (e.g., Sargon, Naram-Sin, or Tukulti-Ninurta), and the identification of the locales mentioned in vv. 10–12.[74] Though solutions to all of these various problems cannot be adequately pursued here, I would tentatively propose a broad two-stage historical development for the biblical Nimrod reference.[75]

(1) The earliest layer possibly belongs to memories stemming from the late third millennium context of the Sargonic dynasty; a figure like Naram-Sin was famous throughout the region for a long time period (i.e., well into later periods) and could very well have served as the inspiration for a primeval Gibbor and founder of cities.[76]

---

72. See van der Toorn and van der Horst 1990, 16–29, for a full review of this interpretive trajectory.

73. On this, see Stuckenbruck 2000, "The 'Angels' and 'Giants' of Genesis 6:1–4," 356–57. Cf. the classical Greek concept of "thinking big" (μέγα φρονεῖν) and its connection to hubris, discussed by Cairns (1996).

74. Essay length treatments not mentioned above include, e.g.: Levin 2002; Lipinski 1966; Speiser 1994; Poplicha 1929. See also the helpful summaries in Machinist 1992; Uehlinger 1999; Vlaardingerbroeck 2004. For commentaries, see especially Westermann 1984, 495–97, 514–17; Speiser 1964, 64–67. In particular, see Machinist 1983a, 720 n. 2 for significant problems with the Tukulti-Ninurta identification (most cogently proposed in Speiser 1994).

75. Traditional source-critical theory suggests that 10:1b–15, 21, 24–30 are attributed to J, while the rest of the "Table of Nations" belongs to P. Note, e.g., the use of ילד, which is characteristic of J. See the division in von Rad 1972, 145–46.

76. Machinist (1992, 1117) suggests either this third-millennium context or the late

(2) References to Assyrian locations and motifs suggest a later expansion in the Neo-Assyrian period particularly. For example, Aššurnasirpal II only recovered the city of Kalach in the ninth century BCE and made it a noteworthy capital, and the reference to Nimrod as a hunter must have its origin in reference to reliefs of royal hunting scenes in the Neo-Assyrian period.[77]

The potentially secondary character of v. 9 with its reference to hunting is revealed by the parallel passage in 1 Chr 1:10 (i.e., without reference to hunting, suggesting that the original identification of Nimrod as the first Gibbor was either misunderstood (and thus clarified) or intentionally obscured and qualified by the hunting reference at a later date.[78] It is also very possible that v. 9 is, in fact, a primary tradition. If we accept the apparently established saying[79] as authentic to the context, then it would be the case that the saying "Like Nimrod, a mighty hunter before YHWH" had always been a part of the Nimrod legend, or that two independent Nimrod traditions were joined with one another in this text.[80] At any rate, the conclusion that the passage represents a mélange of figures and traditions seems quite reasonable, and thus overconfident equations of Nimrod with any one personage are bound to falter.

What, then, is the significance of Nimrod's status as the first Gibbor on the earth? And how is the word "Gibbor" to be translated in Gen 10:8 // 1

---

seventh–sixth centuries BCE as appropriate ones for the references to Babylon, Erech (Uruk), and Akkad (Agade), and to Babylonian superiority and expansion westward to Assyria. The Naram-Sin legends were very well known in the ancient Near East, and Naram-Sin's famous hubris in promoting himself to the sphere of divinity sparked negative reactions from several quarters (perhaps even reflected as a wordplay in the name נמרד, which could be derived from מרד, "rebel"; see Hess 1993, 144. As Levin (2002, 361–62) notes, contact through cuneiform literature is attested, e.g., the Gilgamesh tablet from Megiddo (which we now know originated in southern Palestine and not Mesopotamia; Goren, Mommsen, Finkelstein, and Na'aman 2009), as well as portions of the Sargon epic among the Amarna letters.

77. See Machinist 1992, 1117. Note that the activity of hunting (ציד) only appears one other time, in Lev 17:13, outside of these references to Nimrod and the multiple references to Esau hunting game in Gen chs. 25–27. Neither Nimrod nor Esau enjoys a particularly positive status in the biblical narrative, thus slandering (at least implicitly) the activity of hunting itself.

78. Cf., e.g., R. Klein 2006, who in commenting on 1 Chr 1:10 assumes, along with the majority of other commentators, that the passage in Chronicles *omits* the material in Gen 10:9–12. This is only an (unargued) assumption, and the growing appreciation for the Chronicler's use of independent sources might militate against such assumptions. See Gunkel 1997 (first published 1901), 90, who, I think, appropriately highlights the independent nature of the hunting proverb in v. 9.

79. I.e., marked by the *niphal* verb יאמר. See also, e.g., Gen 22:14; Num 21:14 (a reference to the "Book of the Wars of YHWH"); 1 Sam 19:24; 2 Sam 5:8; Eccl 1:10.

80. The only other mention of Nimrod in the Hebrew Bible comes in Mic 5:5, where נמרוד seems to be another title for Assyria.

Chr 1:10? As I have suggested briefly above, it may well be that the reference to Nimrod as a Gibbor was a freestanding tradition apart from his association with the hunting motif, and if so, the etiological notice may serve to connect future Gibborim as a special class of heroic warriors to this archaic origin in the post-diluvian period.[81] Whether those who first composed Genesis 1–11 meant for the reference to the "Gibborim of old" in Gen 6:4 to be connected to Nimrod's status as the first Gibbor in 10:8 is unclear, and yet the canonical position of these chapters invites such a reading.

III. Pre-Israelite Giants in the Land of Canaan

If Gen 6:1–4 and, to a lesser extent, Gen 10:8–12, provide an explanation or justification for the existence of giant beings of the remote past, how do the giants in later periods stand in continuity or discontinuity with these ancient figures? We seem to have an awkward interpretive dilemma, in that the products of the divine-human miscegenation, whether they are the ancient Gibborim or Nephilim (or both), are supposed to have been *completely eradicated* from the earth via the Flood in Genesis 6. All flesh had corrupted its ways, and all flesh must die, and only Noah and his immediate family would survive—as clearly affirmed by Gen 7:21–23. This dilemma could lead to the view that Noah himself was of giant stock.[82] If indeed giants were thought of as discrete "races" in antiquity, then it is reasonable to deduce that the genes of the race of giants survived via Noah and his family on

---

81. גבר as a noun is used in variety of ways in the Bible; see *BDB* 150; Kosmala 1975. E.g.: (1) as generic term for "mighty one," "strong one," etc., and/or used with another qualifying term (note the particularly common idiom, גבור חיל): Judg 6:12(?), 11:1; 1 Sam 9:1; 1 Kgs 11:28; 2 Kgs 15:20; Isa 5:22(?), 13:3(?); Amos 2:14,16; Pss 89:20(?), 112:2; Prov 30:30 ("a lion is a גבור among the beasts"); Ruth 2:1; Dan 3:20; Neh 11:14; 1 Chr 5:24, 7:2,5,7,9,11,40, 8:40, 9:13, 9:26, 26:6,31; (2) a divine title, YHWH compared to a גבור, or divine agents as גבורים: Deut 10:17; Isa 9:5, 10:21, 13:3(?), 42:13; Jer 14:9, 20:11, 32:18; Zeph 3:17; Pss 78:65, 103:20; Job 16:14; (3) a generic term for any participants enlisted for battle, e.g., soldiers under a king or national leadership, or the type of person one must be to be conscripted for such service: Josh 1:14, 6:2, 8:3, 10:2; Judg 5:13,23(?); 1 Sam 2:4, 14:52, 16:18; 2 Sam 1:19,21,22,25,27(?), 10:7, 16:6, 20:7; Isa 21:17, 49:24,25; Jer 5:16, 9:22, 26:21, 46:5,6,9,12, 48:14,41, 49:22, 50:9,36, 51:30,56; Ezek 32:12,21,27, 39:18(?),20; Hos 10:13; Joel 2:7, 4:9,10,11; Obad 9; Nah 2:4; Zeph 1:14; Zech 9:13, 10:5,7; Pss 33:16, 45:4, 52:3; Prov 16:32, 21:22; Song 3:7, 4:4; Eccl 9:11; Dan 11:3; 1 Chr 19:8, 29:24; 2 Chr 13:3, 17:13,14,16,17, 25:6, 28:7(?); (4) a special class of individuals, i.e., different from a "common" soldier or generically strong/valiant individual: Gen 6:4, 10:8–9; Josh 8:3, 10:7 (?); Judg 5:13,23(?); 1 Sam 17:51(?); 2 Sam 1:19,21,22,25,27(?); 17:8,10, 22:26(?), 23:8,9,16,17,22; 1 Kgs 1:8,10(?); 2 Kgs 24:14,16; Isa 3:2; Jer 51:57; Ezr 7:28; Neh 3:16; 1 Chr 1:10, 11:10,11,12,19,24,26, 12:1,4,9,22,26,29,31, 27:6, 28:1; 2 Chr 26:12, 32:3.

82. See Stuckenbruck 2004, 96–98; Peters 2008, 46–47; J. C. Reeves 1993, but cf. Huggins 1995.

the ark.[83] Gen 6:4 has thrown in an escape clause, which seems to partially address the problem without really explaining it or solving it: the Nephilim were on the earth "in those days" (i.e., the primordial days of the cohabitation of human women with divine beings), but also *afterward* (וגם אחרי כן), in later times. Thus it seems that the problem was noticed and acknowledged within the biblical text itself—and it apparently had to be, for the conquest traditions in Numbers, Deuteronomy, and Joshua all record significant encounters with giant beings who are connected with the very Nephilim who were to be killed in the Flood (Num 13:33; note also Deut 2:10–12, discussed in detail below).

At various points, tradition would look back on the conquest of Canaan and see a land filled with giants. The prophet Amos, for example, putatively writing in the eighth century BCE, makes a tantalizing reference (Amos 2:9–10):

> (v. 9) But I destroyed the Amorite from before them, whose height was like the height of cedars (אשר כגבה ארזים גבהו), and he was strong like the oaks—but I destroyed his fruit above and his roots below. (10) And I brought you up from the land of Egypt, and I led you in the wilderness forty years, to possess the land of the Amorite.

Though no other passage in the Hebrew Bible directly asserts that the *Amorites* were of large stature, Deut 4:47 and Josh 2:10 associate Og, who is classified as a giant elsewhere (i.e., at least by implication in Deut 2:10–12 and 3:11,13), with the Amorites. Maximally, Amos 2:9–10 could suggest that this prophet viewed all of the native inhabitants of the land—subsumed here under the title "Amorites"—as giants, and not just one or another group (such as the Rephaim or the Anaqim).[84] Whatever the case, the specific pattern embodied in this passage is one found throughout the books of Numbers, Deuteronomy, and Joshua:[85] before the saving act of the deliverance from Egypt can take effect, the land must be cleared of its residents,

---

83. Note that Ber. Rab. 31:13, Bav. San. 108b, Targ. Ps. Jon. Deut 2:11, 3:10, and several other Jewish sources recount Og's existence before, and through, the Flood; he escaped the deluge by riding Noah's ark.

84. The biblical picture of the Amorites is inconsistent. In Gen 15:16, "Amorite" refers to all of the people in pre-Israelite Canaan. In other places, the Amorites appear in lists of groups inhabiting the land, e.g., around Hebron (Josh 10:5) or south of Judah's territory (Deut 1:19,27,44), or the Amorites are a Transjordan contingent divided into two kingdoms (Heshbon and Bashan; see Josh 2:10, 9:10, 24:8; Judg 10:8, 11:19–23). See van Seters 1972; Andersen and Freedman 1989, 329; Perlitt 1994, 221–22.

85. Andersen and Freedman (1989, 325–26), consider Amos 2:9–11 to be a "ritual recitation" used at the Bethel cult shrine and see similarities with this passage in various covenant prologue formularies.

which includes, minimally, pockets of giants (e.g., Josh 15:12–14), or maximally, an entire land filled with giant beings (Josh 11:21; Deut 9:1–2).

The following discussion considers the pre-Israelite giants in the land
in two parts: first, the Anaqim (Num 13:22,28–32; Deut 2:9–15; Josh 11:19–
22, 14:12–15, 15:12–14, 21:11–12; Judg 1:20), followed by the Rephaim (Gen
14:5–7, 15:18–21; Deut 2:19–23, 3:8–13; Josh 13:12, 17:14–18) and, briefly,
other groups associated with the Rephaim such as the Emim and Zuzim/
Zamzummim (Gen 14:5; Deut 2:10–11,20–21).

The Sons of Anaq are from the Nephilim

Num 13:22, 28–33 (v. 22) They went up to the Negev and came to Hebron;
Ahiman, Sheshai, and Talmai, descendants of Anaq (ילידי הענק),[86] were
there. Hebron was built seven years before Zoan in Egypt…(28) But the
people who live in the land are strong (עז), and the cities are heavily
fortified and very large. Also, we saw the descendants of Anaq (ילדי הענק)[87]
there. (29) Amaleq dwells in the land of the Negev, and the Hittites, the
Yebusites, and the Amorites dwell in the hill country, while the Canaanites
live by the sea and alongside the Jordan. (30) Kaleb silenced the people
before Moses, and said, "We will certainly go up and possess it—for we are
able to overcome it!" (31) But the men who went up with him said, "We are
not able to go up against the people, because they are stronger than us."
(32) So they brought a bad report of the land that they had spied out to
the sons of Israel, saying, "The land that we have gone through as spies—it
is a land that eats up (אכלת)[88] its inhabitants! And the people we saw in
its midst are huge (אנשי מדות).[89] (33) We also saw the Nephilim (הנפילים)[90]
there—the sons of Anaq are from the Nephilim (בני ענק מן הנפלים)[91]—and we
seemed like grasshoppers in our eyes and likewise we were in their eyes!"

86. The presence of the definite article with the singular ענק is unique here and in v. 28,
though the significance of this is unclear (i.e., it is possibly tied up with the etymology of ענק,
see infra). Noth (1968, 105) believes the article is a sign that we are "dealing here not with a
proper name but with an appellative" which is tied to ענק = "necklace," though he is rightfully
skeptical of what might be meant by the phrase "necklace descendants."

87. Targ. Onk. reads בני גיברא (also in v. 22); see Drazin 1998, 154–55.

88. Targ. Onk. לאללא יתה ארע מקטלא יתבהא היא. As Drazin 1998, 155 n. 24 points out, only
Targs. Onk. and Ps-Jon explicitly interpret the MT's "eating" as "killing" (cf. Lev 26:38 and Ezek
36:13).

89. Lit. "men of [notable] measure." See also איש מדה in Isa 45:14; 1 Chr 11:23, 20:6.

90. Targ. Onk. גיבריא. This is the noun used in all of the Targums for נפלים, ענקים, and רפאים
(Drazin 1998, 156 n. 27). Greek τοὺς γίγαντας.

91. It seems that only one Greek tradition (Codex Colberto-Sarravianus) reflects the MT
here by adding υἱοὺς Ενακ ἐκ τῶν γιγάντων after γίγαντας, and all other Greek mss. lack the
explanatory note in the MT about the Anaqim being from the Nephilim (see *OTGr* I, 457 n.
34). Unfortunately, Num 13:33 does not appear in the materials from Qumran. The Targ. here,
however, does seem to represent the MT.

The result of the spying expedition in Numbers 13 is mostly despair. The Israelites, poised to enter the Promised Land, find large, unassailable cities in the space they are to inhabit; the land itself takes on a monstrous quality— capable of eating its citizens alive (v. 32)—and the country is populated with the "descendants of Anaq," a people of great physical stature who certainly seem stronger than the Israelites.[92] A total of eighteen references to Anaq/Anaqim appear in the Bible, concentrated in the books of Numbers (13:22,28,33), Deuteronomy (1:28, 2:10,11,21, 9:2), and Joshua (11:21,2, 14:12,15, 15:13,14[2x], 21:11[93]), with a sole reference in Judg 1:20, suggesting that the biblical authors exclusively saw the Anaqim as a phenomenon of the conquest and settlement traditions.[94]

Where do the Anaqim live? One immediate problem involves the territory occupied by the Anaqim. Num 13:22, Josh 14:15, 15:13–4, and Judg 1:20 represent a tradition in which the Anaqim are located specifically (or just primarily?) in *Hebron*, whereas Deut 9:1–2 seems to make the *entire territory* west of the Jordan a land of Anaqim:[95]

92. Aside from passing references in commentaries and scattered short treatments, including Mattingly 1992a, I:222 and Schnell 1962, I: 123–2424, there is no sustained study (to my knowledge) of the Anaqim. Indeed, there would seem to be little that can be said. The older study most often cited in discussions of the Anaqim is Albright 1928, but note also Karge 1917, 641–44, which anticipates many of the problems discussed below.

93. Only in Josh 21:11 do we have הָעֲנוֹק, whereas all other references have הָעֲנָק. Anaqim appear twice in the Greek versions where they do not appear in the MT: Jer 29:5 [Heb. 47:5]: ἥκει φαλάκρωμα ἐπὶ Γάζαν ἀπερρίφη Ἀσκαλὼν καί οἱ κατάλοιποι Ενακιμ...("Baldness has come upon Gaza, Ascalon was cast away, and the remnant of the Enakim...."). This reference suggests that the translator—and possibly the Hebrew text with which he was working—thought the Anaqim were a contingent of Philistines along with Gaza and Ashkelon (Machinist [2000a, 74 n. 67] sees Anaqim here as the more natural reference). At least one Greek tradition in Jer 39:4 [v. 20 in some Greek mss.; Heb. ch. 49] reads מה תתהללי בעמקים ("Why do you boast in the valleys...") as τί ἀγαλλιάσῃ ἐν τοῖς πεδίοις Ενακιμ ("Why will you exult in the plains of the Enakim..."). See Lundbom (2004, 239–40, 321), who argues for the reading עמק in both instances.

94. The exception to this trend comes in Josh 11:22, on which see infra.

95. The ubiquity of the Anaqim implied in this passage vis-à-vis the other references seems to have gone unnoticed in the secondary literature. Of course, Deut 9:1–4 offers a potentially alternative view of the conquest tradition as a whole. In vv. 3–4, the narrator asserts that YHWH is about to go before the people into the land as a "devouring fire" (אש אכלה), and that he will personally drive out the inhabitants, suggesting a supernatural eradication of the Anaqim's descendants. As von Rad (1966, 73–74) points out, the emphasis here may not point to a variant tradition but rather is an attempt to emphasize that Israel's righteousness is not the cause for their inheritance. The significance of Hebron is highlighted in the patriarchal narratives and in the stories of David; the most extensive treatment is in Noth 1968, 105–06, and cf. Milgrom 1990, 103. See also Hammond 1997; Ashley 1993, 237–38; Noth 1968, 105–07; Levine 1993, 354–55; Mattingly 1992a; Schnell 1962.

(v. 1) Hear, O Israel! You are crossing the Jordan today, to come to possess nations greater and more numerous than you, great cities, fortified up to the heavens, (2) a people great and tall (עם גדול ורם), the sons of the Anaqim (בני ענקים), whom you know (all too well)—you have heard (the saying), "Who can stand up before the sons of Anaq (בני ענק)?"

So too Josh 11:21 assigns much of the Cisjordan to the Anaqim, when it is asserted that Joshua "cut off" (ויכרת) the Anaqim from the hill country, Hebron, Debir, Anab and from the *entire hill country* of Judah and Israel, enacting the *ḥerem* (חרם), i.e., total destruction of all life, on essentially the whole territory.[96] Through the lens of this reference in Joshua 11, then, Hebron is indeed a noteworthy center of the Anaqim but only alongside other specific locales and only in light of the fact that the author seems to describe *the entire land*, metonymically, as a land of Anaqim.[97] The entire episode stands as one specific example of YHWH's plan to eradicate Canaan's residents—a plan made clear in Josh 11:19–20:

(v. 19) There was no city that made peace with the sons of Israel, except the Hivvites, inhabitants of Gibeon. All were taken in battle. (20) For it was YHWH's doing to harden their hearts, so that they would come out to meet Israel in battle and thus he would utterly destroy them (החרימם); there would be no mercy for them, but rather he would exterminate them just as YHWH commanded Moses.

The announcement of the completed task follows in Josh 11:22, which adds yet another piece of geographical data:

None of the Anaqim remained (לא נותר ענקים) in the land of the sons of Israel—only in Gaza, in Gath, and Ashdod did they remain.

At this point, then, the giants are driven outside the land of Israel, to Philistia.[98]

We thus have two descriptions of where the Anaqim dwell *pre*-Conquest, viz. around Hebron specifically (Num 13:22; Josh 14:15, 15:13–4; Judg 1:20) and also spread throughout in the entire land (Josh 11:21; Deut 9:2), and

96. Debir and Anab are fifteen and twenty kilometers south of Hebron, respectively. This verse, along with the list of conquered kings in Joshua 12, is the closest any biblical narrator comes to asserting the Israelites *completely eradicated everyone* previously living in the promised land—a narrative line belied by the opening chapters of Judges (e.g., 1:21–35) and even the book of Joshua itself (in 13:2–6).

97. One observes a similar phenomenon in the various places where any particular ethnogram, e.g., "Canaanite," "Amorite," etc. is used broadly as a description of every group in the land. If these examples are truly comparable, then Josh 11:21 would be the only place where the Anaqim fill this role.

98. See infra for discussion of Philistine giants.

these locations give way to the *post*-Conquest existence of the Anaqim in three of five cities of the Philistine pentapolis (the others, not listed, being Ashkelon and Eqron). The significance of Hebron is highlighted throughout the ancestral narratives and Joshua through 2 Samuel. Abram builds an altar in Hebron (Gen 13:18) and Sarah is buried there (Gen 23:2).[99] Hebron appears to be an important military center with its own king (Hohan) in Joshua 10, and later becomes the land grant (נחלה) of Kaleb in Josh 14:13.[100] David makes Hebron his impromptu capital (1 Sam 30:31; 2 Sam 2) and is anointed king over Israel there (2 Sam 5:5), and Absalom later stages his coup from Hebron in 2 Sam 15:10.[101] Noth assumed that the giant Anaqim with specific names residing in Hebron in Josh 13:22, 15:14, and Judg 1:10 are "figures of a legendary period, of whom a local tradition from Hebron purported to tell, powerful 'giant-like' figures." This is difficult to substantiate in a satisfactory manner, but is intriguing nonetheless.[102]

Who defeated the Anaqim? If there is some cloudiness in the biblical record regarding the location of the Anaqim, it also pertains to the identity of their conquerors. As already noted in Josh 11:21–22, Joshua completely eradicated the Anaqim living in the hill country of Israel and Judah, though v. 22 is quick to point out the continued existence of Anaqim in three Philistine cities.[103] On the other hand, it is Kaleb who, in Josh 14:12–15, 15:13–14, and Judg 1:20 enacts the victory. Two factors further complicate this delineation.

99. The narrators note that Hebron is to be equated with Kiriath-Arba here and in Gen 35:27; Josh 15:13, 21:11; Judg 1:10; and also with Mamre in Gen 23:19.

100. This is complicated by the fact that, as Milgrom (1990, 391–92) correctly notices, three different individuals/groups are said to have conquered Hebron: Kaleb, Joshua (Josh 10:37, 11:21), and the entire tribe of Judah (Judg 1:10,19–20). Apparently, the prestige of the site prompted several competing traditions of its conquest. See Beltz 1974 for a full consideration of the Kaleb narratives.

101. The association of Hebron with Zoan (Tanis) in Egypt in Num 13:22 is confusing. Some attribute the relationship between the two cities to a vague desire to root Hebron in the prestigious antiquity of an Egyptian site (Levine 1993, 354–55; Noth 1968, 105; Milgrom 1990, 103), while Na'aman (1981) has suggested that the synchronism of the two locations is an attempt to correlate events in the career of David already with the Conquest tradition (see David's seven-year reign in Hebron in 1 Kgs 2:11; cf. 2 Sam 2:11, 5:4–5; 1 Chr 29:27).

102. Noth 1968, 105. See also this same conclusion, based on the names of the Anaqim listed in Num 13:22 and elsewhere, by Kempinski (1982; cited in Levine 1993, 355).

103. Presumably, the dual mention of "Judah" and "Israel" encompasses the entire inheritable land; the division into these two regions would already seem to anachronistically presuppose the later national division into north and south narrated in 1 Kgs 12 (see also 1 Sam 17:52; 2 Sam 18:16, 5:5, 11:11, 21:2, 24:1, etc.). The tension here between vv. 21 and 22, i.e., between a total eradication of all Anaqim in "Israel" and "Judah" (= the whole land, from Jordan River to Mediterranean coast?) vis-à-vis the continued existence of Anaqim in Philistia, may well be the result of source divisions in the text itself. V. 22, then, would be secondary.

First, the note in Joshua 11 may be intended only as a broad summary of the Conquest as a whole, thus crediting Joshua as the primary military and political leader for the entirety of the victory. Second, Kaleb is only specifically said to have battled with the three sons of Anaq (Sheshai, Ahiman, and Talmai—named specifically in Josh 15:13-14 as well as Num 13:22). Are these three individuals, then, supposed to comprise the totality of the "Anaqim"?[104] Moreover, in Josh 14:12-15, we read of Kaleb asking Joshua for Hebron as an inheritance, as though it were already available for the taking. This situation casts Kaleb's battle with the Anaqim as a limited struggle with only three strong men, which nonetheless stands in tension with the relatively comprehensive nature of the reference in Josh 11:21.[105]

The "necklace" people? Greek rulers? The etymology of Anaq/Anaqim (ענק/ ענקים) is not entirely clear, either. Rabbinic sources exploited the nuance of the word Anaqim as "chains" (i.e., that which lies upon the ענק, "neck"; cf. Ps 73:6),106 while most modern commentators default to an explanation involving long necks or necklaces—a solution which is not particularly convincing or illuminating.[107] In 1928, Albright identified a certain Yʿnq (Yaʿnuq) mentioned in the Egyptian "execration texts" from c. 2000 BCE with the biblical Anaq on a philological level, but denied that the connection could be taken any further based solely on geographic factors; Yʿnq was located in the north, while Albright assumed that the biblical Anaqim were to be found only in the south and along the coast.[108] As I have shown above, however, the biblical tradition itself does not speak univocally regarding the location of

104. Driver (1902, 24) suggests that these are families or clans of Anaqim, not individuals.

105. See Josh 21:11 for another complicating factor: Aaronid/Kohathite Levites receive Hebron—but, the narrator hastens to add, Kaleb had already received the fields of the city and its villages.

106. Ber. Rab. 16:7, 26:7; b. Sotah 35a; Num Rab. 16:11; Deut Rab. 1:24; b. Yoma 10a; b. Shab. 85a; etc. See references in Drazin 1998, 153 n. 14 and Milgrom 1990, 103.

107. E.g., Mattingly 1992a, I: 222; Schnell 1962, 123; Noth 1968, 105; G. Gray 1920, 141; see also definitions in BDB, 778; E. Klein 1987, 478, including postbiblical derivatives, e.g., ענקיות, "huge, enormous," etc.; Clines 2007, 510. See also Lipinski 1974, 43. For ענק as neck(lace), see Judg 8:26; Ps 73:6; Prov 1:9; Song 4:9. Cf. Akk. *unqu/uqqu*, which seems to cover a similar semantic range; the root is not attested in Ugaritic as far as I can tell. The verbal use of ענק in Deut 15:14 (העניק תעניק לו), which seems to mean "provide liberally to him," is likely derived from the necklace meaning: "necklace [i.e., a rich gift] upon him…"

108. Albright 1928, 237-39. Albright convincingly shows that the names of Yʿnq's three chieftains, ʾ3m, ʿbymmw, and ʿk3m, are clearly Semitic, but does not venture a guess as to the meaning or etymology of ʿnq. Cf. the brief comment in ANET3, 328 n. 2. Rainey and Notley (2006, 58, 70) vocalize the execration text GN as Yaʿnuqa; note also an Egyptian town called Yanqa (= ʾU-nù-qa in a list of Thutmose III), but the linguistic or historical connections between this fact and the appearance of Yʿnq here are unclear. See also the discussion of the possibility for the equivalence of Yá- in the execration text with a Hebrew ע in Lipinski 1974, 41–42, 47.

the Anaqim, and if the locale in the execration text and the Anaqim of the biblical tradition are, as many assume, to be equated on the level of the language, then it is not so implausible to think that they are connected in other ways as well, including geography, though exactly how is unclear.

Finding "no satisfactory Semitic etymology," E. C. B. MacLaurin attempted to equate the biblical ענקים with the Greek *(w)anax*, a title of rank used of gods and heroes in *Il.* 1.442, *Od.* 11.144, 151, etc.[109] More specifically, MacLaurin argues that the Anaqim and the סרנים were members of a broader Mycenaean system among the Philistines, where the "Seranim" ("lords," סרנים) were "military and civil governors" and the "position of the Anakim seem[s] to have been hereditary and deriving from remote antiquity."[110] The relationship of the Anaqim to the Philistines or Sea Peoples more broadly is a somewhat natural one in terms of Josh 11:22, where the Anaqim are relegated to Gaza, Gath, and Ashdod, and it has been suggested, most recently by M. Dothan, that the Anaqim may have been a contingent of Sea Peoples distinct from (but later conflated with) the Philistines.[111] One other significant problem in this formulation involves the antiquity of the *Y'nq* of the Egyptian texts—if *Y'nq* was a known term in the twentieth century BCE, and if indeed this word is etymologically connected to the biblical Anaq, then MacLaurin's suggestion may only be, at best, evidence of a conflation or loose association of a Greek word with a much older Semitic term.[112]

109. MacLaurin 1965, 471–72. MacLaurin suggests that "Anak" may have been a Philistine word (borrowed from Greek, or a Canaanite word borrowed into Philistine and conflated with *wanax*?). *wanax- itself has no Indo-European parallels or etymology, and it is unclear whether this would have been adapted with an initial ע in Hebrew. On the correspondence of Hebrew and Greek letters, see Brønno 1943. I thank John Huehnergard (personal communication, Nov. 2009) for his help in sorting out this issue. MacLaurin continues to push the issue of the Greek etymologies into the realm of the three names of the Anaqim at Hebron. See MacLaurin 1965, 468 n. 4, as well as Mazar 1981; Lipinski 1974, 45–47; Tigay 1996, 347 n. 101, and sources cited there; Na'aman 2005b, 337, 360–61.

110. MacLaurin 1965, 473–74.

111. See the discussion on this issue in Machinist 2000a, 66–67, which points to the argument of Dothan (1993, 53–55), viz. that the Anaqim were a separate Sea People who arrived in the land before the Philistines and settled in Ashdod. The argument is based on extremely speculative biblical references and an inconclusive archaeological argument.

112. Shai (2009, 21–22, 22 n. 19), argues that there is no evidence of connection between the Bronze Age *Y'nq* and any biblical group. Rather, in Shai's view, the Philistine newcomers were linked with a Canaanite group, the ענקים. This forms a small part of Shai's broader argument about Philistine immigration and integration with the local population, an integration that, for Shai, was apparently so complete that "the Philistines were considered a native group in the Bible." Since 1 Chr 20:4 suggests that the Sippites are descended from the Rephaim, a native Semitic group, this correlation can be connected, Shai argues, with the Anaqim-Philistine link and serves as evidence of a process by which the Philistines were merged with Canaanite groups by the biblical authors.

The Anaqim are from the Nephilim. What are we to make of the assertion in
Num 13:33 that "the sons of Anaq are from the Nephilim" (בני ענק מן הנפלים)?
This reference obviously draws us back to the previous discussion of the Nephilim in Gen 6:1–4, as the invocation of the Nephilim here is the only one
outside of Gen 6:4. Moreover, the "and also afterward" (וגם אחרי כן) clause in
Gen 6:4 may be somehow related to the reference to Nephilim in Numbers
13, though several different (and equally plausible) lines of literary development present themselves. For example, it could be that the idea of Anaqim
as progeny of the Nephilim was an innovation of Num 13:33, after which the
words "and also afterward" were added to Gen 6:4. Or, approaching the question from the opposite direction, some had assumed the Gen 6:4 notice was
added specifically in *anticipation* of the already known reference to the Nephilim represented by the Num 13:33 tradition.[113] It is also possible that Num
13:33 and Gen 6:4 developed independently, and relied on a broader Neph-
ilim-Anaqim tradition. Source-critically, both references belong to J (with
Num 13:33 attributed to JE).[114] Whatever the relationship is between these
two sparse references, Num 13:33 clearly seeks to form a bridge between
the Nephilim and some pre-Israelite inhabitants of the land.[115] Of course,
it is quite possible that Gen 6:1–4 generally—and the "and also afterward"
clause specifically—make reference to any number of traditions regarding
Nephilim in the land at later periods that are no longer contained within the

113. So Budde 1883, 43. See also Kraeling 1947b, 195, which argues for the secondary
nature of Num 13:33, as well as the brief general discussion of these two passages and the
ambiguity they embody in Stuckenbruck 2000, 356–58; 2004, 89–93.

114. Levine 1993, 359. Notice also the different phrasing to describe the descendants/
sons of Anaq in vv. 28 and 33, ילדי הענק vs. בני ענק, respectively. ילד is the hallmark of J's description of descendants, while the בני designation is presumably E (for those who think these
verses are JE) or P. Elsewhere, ילד is used only in Num 13:22 and Josh 15:14 (where ילד and בני
are used in the same verse), while בני appears in Deut 1:28, 9:2; Judg 1:20 (ענק/ענקים appears
alone without בני or ילדי in Deut 2:10,11,21; Josh 11:21, 14:12, 15:13). P also presumably uses בני
in describing people groups (Gen 10:20), but never mentions the Anaqim (cf. Noth 1968, 107,
who thinks the giants and Nephilim tradition in Num 13:33 is P).

115. One oddity of the narrative insertion of בני ענק מן הנפלים in Num 13:33 is that the
clarification comes in the midst of a quote, whereas in other instances it is primarily the anonymous, third-person narrative voice offering a clarification in the midst of its own, anonymous narration. Such explanatory notes are not uncommon. See the following minimal list of
passages, where, e.g., הוא/היא marks an explanatory aside, often translated "(that is, X)": Gen
14:3,7,8,17, 23:2,19, 35:6,27, 36:1,19,43, 48:7; Num 33:26; Deut 4:48; Josh 15:8,9,10,13,25,49,54,60,
18:13,14,28, 20:7, 21:11; Judg 7:1, 8:35, 19:10; Dan 10:4; Ezra 10:23; Esth 2:7; 1 Chr 1:27, 8:7, 11:4;
2 Chr 20:2. These statements usually fit organically within the narrative or character's speech,
unlike in Num 13:33. As this list shows, the technique is primarily used in the Pentateuch,
Joshua, and Judges (though it is by no means confined to only these places), and is most often
(though not exclusively) utilized in reference to geographic locales, e.g., to identify Jebus with
Jerusalem. Whether the Num 13:33 reference can be considered with the others listed here is
less than clear, since the specific הוא/היא element is absent in Num 13:33.

biblical text as we now have it. In fact, these two brief references to Nephilim in Gen 6:4 and Num 13:33 are nonsensical without such an assumption.

Various attempts have been made to deny any actual genealogical intention behind the reference to the Nephilim in Num 13:33. For example, Speiser asserts that "the people found by the spies *were like* the very Nephilim of old" (italics mine).[116] Likewise, Sarna argues that, since the Nephilim cannot have survived the Flood, Num 13:33 cannot refer to *actual* Nephilim; rather, "it is used simply for oratorical effect, much as 'Huns' was used to designate Germans during the two world wars."[117] These assertions, in my view, are not quite correct. Admittedly, Num 13:33 does not explicitly say that the Anaqim are *descendants of* (ילידי, etc.) the Nephilim specifically, only that the "sons of Anaq" (בני ענק) are *from* (מן) the Nephilim.

But what can this mean? The use of the preposition "from" (מן) with the nuance of "being like," "resembling," etc. is not attested in the Hebrew Bible. מן does, however, signify birth or genealogical derivation (and often physical/geographical derivation broadly), making the physical/geographical connection of the Anaqim with the Nephilim here more likely.[118] It is also quite possible that Num 13:33 makes the Nephilim a superordinate category—much like the term "Rephaim" in Deut 2:11 (on which see below)—under which the Anaqim are classed as a subordinate unit. Whatever the case, the Anaqim here are most certainly thought to be the physical (and thus "moral" or "spiritual") descendants of the Nephilim—origins that bode ominously for the future of these giants. Kraeling thus moved toward an important realization when he stated: "Perhaps one may...assert that in Num 13:33 the *Urzeitmotif* of the primeval 'giants' has simply been transferred into another area which, in a way, is also *Urzeit*, so far as the history of the Hebrew people is concerned."[119]

Kaleb and the Three Anaqim. One final set of references to the Anaqim must be discussed here. In Num 13:22, Josh 15:13,14, 21:11, as well as Judg 1:20, we are told of specific "sons" or "descendants" of Anaq inhabiting a city called Qiryat 'Arba' (equated with Hebron).[120] Josh 14:15 in particular informs us of a certain Arba, the greatest man of all the Anaqim:

---

116. Speiser 1964, 44.

117. Sarna 1989, 46. See also Ashley (1993, 243), who asserts that the connection here with the Nephilim "is an exaggeration for rhetorical effect."

118. See *BDB* 577–83; *GKC*, 101a, 102b, 103i,m, 119v–z, 133a–e, etc.; Williams 2007, 120–25. Note, e.g., the use of מן in terms of genealogical derivation in Gen 15:4, 35:11; 1 Sam 2:20; cf. Num 3:12; Josh 12:4, etc.

119. Kraeling 1947b, 195.

120. For fuller commentary on these passages, see, e.g., Nelson 1997, 167–89, 232–235; Boling 1982, 373–76; Soggin 1972, 170–83, 199–206.

Josh 14:12–15 (v. 12) "And now, give me this hill country about which YHWH commanded on that day—for you heard on that day that the Anaqim (עֲנָקִים) were there, and great fortified cities. Perhaps YHWH will be with me, and I will drive them out just as YHWH commanded." (13) So Joshua blessed him and gave Hebron to Kaleb son of Yephunneh as an inheritance. (14) Thus Hebron became an inheritance for Kaleb son of Yephunneh the Qenizzite until this day, because he completely followed (מִלֵּא אַחֲרֵי)[121] YHWH, God of Israel. (15) The name of Hebron previously was "City of Arba" (קִרְיַת אַרְבַּע)[122]—this Arba was the greatest man of the Anaqim (הָאָדָם הַגָּדוֹל בָּעֲנָקִים הוּא).[123] Then the land had rest from warfare.

In Josh 15:13–14, we see spelled out a crude genealogy of four named Anaqim:

Josh 15:13–14 (v. 13) And to Kaleb son of Yephunneh he gave a portion in the midst of the sons of Judah, according to the command of YHWH to Joshua, (viz.) the City of Arba (קִרְיַת אַרְבַּע), father of Anaq (אֲבִי הָעֲנָק)[124]— that is, Hebron [i.e,. the City of Arba = Hebron]). (14) Kaleb drove out from there the three sons of Anaq (בְּנֵי הָעֲנָק), Sheshai, Ahiman, and Talmai, descendants of Anaq (יְלִידֵי הָעֲנָק).

Here we have Arba, the "greatest" of the Anaqim, and his three sons, Sheshai, Ahiman, and Talmai. Anaq would presumably be a discrete individual—the eponym of the Anaqim?—while Arba lived in some past period (the alternation between בְּנֵי ["sons of"] and יְלִידֵי ["descendants of"] in Josh 15:14 may indicate confusion on this point).[125] As noted above, the potentially non-

---

121. The idiom מִלֵּא אַחֲרֵי (lit. "to fill after") denotes wholehearted obedience and fidelity through correct actions, and is used of Kaleb elsewhere in Num 14:24, 32:12; Deut 1:36; Josh 14:9, and by Kaleb (of himself) in Num 14:8. Other than Kaleb, individuals or groups are only said *not to* מִלֵּא אַחֲרֵי YHWH (Num 32:11; 1 Kgs 11:6).

122. Some Greek witnesses here have πόλις Αργοβ (= אַרְגֹּב; elsewhere in the MT in Deut 3:14,13,14; 1 Kgs 4:13; 2 Kgs 15:25), while others have Αρβωκ, αρκωβ, αρβε, etc.

123. In place of this aside regarding Arba's status among the Anaqim, the Greek has a different explanatory note: the aforementioned Αργοβ (see note infra) is μητρόπολις τῶν Ενακιμ αὕτη ("the capital city of the Enakim"). Thus, Arba is construed as a locale, Argob, etc., as also in Josh 15:13, 21:11.

124. As in Josh 14:15, the Greek reads this phrase, אֲבִי הָעֲנָק, as a *geographical idiom*, i.e., Arba (Αρβοκ) is a city that is the capital (μητρόπολις) of the Anaqim. Such familial language for cities can be found, e.g., in 2 Sam 20:19 (עִיר וָאֵם בְּיִשְׂרָאֵל); Num 32:42; Josh 15:45,47, etc. (וּבְנֹתֶיהָ, "and its daughters [= villages]"). But the language is always feminine—daughters and mothers—and not the masculine terminology of fathers and sons.

125. It is unclear with the use of the definite article ה bears any special meaning in the expressions בְּנֵי/יְלִידֵי הָעֲנָק (Num 13:22,28; Josh 15:14; Judg 1:20; versus בְּנֵי עֲנָק in Num 13:33; Deut 9:2). Both may express the same thing, with or without the article: the Anaqim (i.e., in parallel with the בְּנֵי יִשְׂרָאֵל [but never בְּנֵי הַיִּשְׂרָאֵל], the Israelites; cf. בְּנֵי חֵת [Gen 23:10], etc.).

Semitic nature of the names Sheshai, Ahiman, and Talmai may in fact be a method for the biblical author to signal some kind of foreignness for these persons and their origins.

In Josh 21:11–12, it is the entire tribe of Levites who inherit Hebron, though 21:12 is careful to affirm that "the fields of the city and its villages were given to Kaleb" as his own possession. Alternatively, Judg 1:19–20 brings the entire tribe of Judah into the mix when we are told that Judah, specifically, dispossessed all of the hill country inhabitants and then gave Hebron to Kaleb in return for his acts of giant slaying.[126] Kaleb's status as a somewhat minor character in the biblical narrative (at least vis-à-vis Joshua and Moses) probably determined that his victories were to be partially overwritten and credited to others in various places, but his status as the Bible's first (human) giant slayer remains strongly entrenched in several locations.[127]

Og the King of Bashan, Last of the Rephaim

The biblical traditions of the Rephaim as a living, pre-Israelite people group in the land appear scattered throughout several blocks of material:[128] Gen 14:5, 15:20; Deut 2:11,20[2x], 3:11,13; Josh 12:4, 13:12, 15:18, 17:15 (not to mention the ילידי הרפא/הרפה as monarchic enemies of Israel in 2 Sam 21:16,18,20,22; 1 Chr 20:6,8 [cf. 1 Chr 8:2 and 1 Chr 8:37], all treated below).[129] The most famous (and only individually named) of the Rephaim is a certain Og (עוג), king of the region of the Bashan—indeed, this Og is identified as the last remaining survivor of the Rephaim (Deut 3:11; cf. Josh 12:4, 13:12), and

126. Na'aman (2005b, 360) argues that although Kaleb is presumably not originally a Judahite, he is "'Judahized' by implication" in Judg 1:20 (see also Num 13:6, 34:19; 1 Chr 4:13–15). I am inclinded to agree with those who see the tradition of Kaleb's conquest of Hebron as primary; see also Driver 1902, 24.

127. See, e.g., Milgrom 1990, 391.

128. On the Rephaim as aboriginal inhabitants of the land, see, e.g., Liwak 2004 XIII: 611–14; M. Smith 1992, V: 674–76; Rouillard 1999, 697–99; Caquot 1985, X: 344–47. I am foregoing a discussion of the etymology of the word רפאים until ch. 4, where the issue is taken up in detail. For the time being, it is enough to note that the word seems to be used in places as though it had a clear meaning (e.g., Deut 2:11, רפאים יחשבו).

129. Note also the עמק רפאים as a geographical locale in Josh 15:8, 18:16; 2 Sam 5:18,22, 23:13; 1 Chr 11:15, 14:9; Isa 17:5 (discussed infra). Entities called רפאים also appear in contexts where they must be shades of the dead in the underworld (Isa 14:9, 26:14,19; Ps 88:11; Job 26:5; Prov 2:18, 9:18, 21:16; possibly 2 Chr 16:12). So much attention has been devoted to the Rephaim at Ugarit and as denizens of the underworld in the Hebrew Bible that very few scholars have considered the role of the Rephaim as *human enemies* of Israel, and thus my focus here will be on these human Rephaim. The relationship between the dead Rephaim and the living ones is an intriguing question and will be taken up in detail in ch. 4 of this book. For the moment, see the suggestive comments in Weinfeld 1991, 184, as well as Noegel 1998.

his line is presumably eradicated with the Israelite conquest (Num 21:35).[130] Og is always mentioned in tandem with Sihon,[131] a neighboring king over the region of Heshbon, and the two are thrice identified as "the two kings of the Amorites across the Jordan to the east" (Deut 4:47; Josh 2:10, 9:10).[132] The territory ruled by Og—and thus presumably the territory inhabited by the Rephaim—is variously recorded, but the available geographical traditions all place Og and the Rephaim in the northern Transjordan in and around the region of Bashan, where the cities of Ashtaroth and Edrei feature prominently.[133] However, references to Og's territory, including Mahanaim (Josh 13:30) and Salekah (Deut 3:10) much farther south and east, may suggest an ancient Israelite imagination that saw a huge swath of land—nearly the entirety of the Transjordan between the Dead Sea and the Sea of Galilee?—as inhabited by giants. In other words, the geographical range of Og and his compatriots may not be an accidental result of ancient biblical editors

130. See del Olmo Lete 1999b, Bartlett 1970; McMillion 1992, 9. See further bibliography below under the discussion of Deut 3:11, as well as Coats 1976, 183–84, 189 and Sumner 1968, 220–26.

131. Num 21:26–35, 32:33; Deut 1:4, 3:1–3, 4:47; Deut 29:7, 31:4; Josh 2:10, 9:10, 12:2–5, 13:10–12,27–31; 1 Kgs 4:19; Pss 135:11, 136:19–20; Neh 9:22.

132. See map in Rainey and Notley 2006, 133. Sihon, however, is mentioned without Og—but only in Judg 11:19–21 and Jer 48:45. Though this fact may indicate Sihon's status was better known than Og's in the Transjordanian tradition, the fact that the two are mentioned together probably indicates their equal status as powerful enemies in Israelite memory. The descriptions in Deut 2:24–37 of Sihon and 3:1–11 of Og are particularly good examples of the parallel space given to each king.

133. The multiple references to Og's location are somewhat daunting, but can be summarized as follows: Og's army comes to battle at Edrei in Num 21:33; Deut 3:1. Og is said to have reigned in both Ashtaroth and Edrei in Deut 1:4 (יושב) and Josh 13:12 (ממלכות עוג); he is said to have ruled (יושב) in both Ashtaroth and Edrei in Josh 12:4, and he "ruled as king" (מלך) in both Ashtaroth and Edrei in Josh 13:12. The territory ruled by Og is twice (Deut 3:4; Josh 13:28–31) said to include sixty towns (cf. 1 Kgs 4:13), located throughout the "entire region of Argob" (Deut 3:4; Argob = Bashan, "a land of Rephaim," in Deut 3:13) and also including "all the towns of the plain (המישר)," all of Gilead and Bashan as far as Salekah and Edrei (Deut 3:10). Josh 13:28–31 includes the region of Mahanaim as Og's territory (see Gen 32:2; 2 Sam 2, 17, 19, etc.), as well as Bashan, including "all the settlements of Ya'ir." 1 Kgs 4:13,19 is confusing, in that 4:13 seems to be describing one of Solomon's administrative districts east of the Jordan in terms of the exact location of Og's territory, and yet 4:19 lists yet a *separate district* which is said to encompass the old territory of Og and Sihon. All of this amounts to a multiplicity of traditions filtered through various literary sources over time.

For further discussion of the geography, see Aharoni 1979, 34–35, 191, 235; Rainey and Notley 2006, e.g. 41, 114, 133. Note also de Vaux 1941; Glueck 1946; Sauer 1986. Bartlett 1970, 276 argues that part of the confusion and overlap between Og's and Sihon's territories (and within the descriptions of these territories individually) is the result of a desire by the Deuteronomist to create a simple division of the Transjordan into two parts, when in fact at least three regions—the plain, Gilead, and Bashan—existed in reality. Thus, Gilead is arbitrarily given either to one or the other "half." On the geography of Num 21 specifically, see Noth 1940–1941. On the symbolism of the Transjordan, see Hutton 2009, 1–7, 29–31, 61–76.

heedlessly combining contradictory source materials, but rather the result of a series of genuine and intentional combinations, evoking a terrifying space bordering the promised land.

War with Og. The Israelite battle with Og occurs for the first time in the biblical narrative in Numbers 21, and is recorded with striking brevity:

Num 21:33–35 (v. 33) They turned and went up the road of Bashan, and Og king of Bashan (הבשן)[134] marched out to meet them, he and all his people, for war at Edrei. (34) But YHWH said to Moses, "Do not fear him, for I have given him, with all his people and his land, into your hand; and you will do to him just as you did to Sihon king of the Amorites who dwelt in Heshbon." (35) So they struck him down, along with all his sons and all his people, until there was no survivor (בלתי השאיר לו)—and they possessed his land.

YHWH uses Moses' and the peoples' earlier victory over Sihon as encouragement for the next encounter, and the fate of Og and his army consequently follows that of Sihon: total annihilation.[135] The narrator, however, records no divine mandate to take the territory of Sihon around Heshbon in Num 21:21–32, while the battle against Og is the result of YHWH's command (21:34), and Deut 2:24 inserts YHWH's divine order for the conquest of both territories. One explanation for the differing treatments, given by J. Milgrom, is that the omission regarding Sihon of Heshbon in Numbers 21 comes as the result of the Priestly authors' conception of the boundaries of the promised land. Since P saw the Jordan River as the limit of Israel's inheritance on the eastern side (Num 34:12; cf. Josh 22:19; Ezek 48:17), the Transjordanian territories were not included.[136] This view does not completely comport with the biblical data, however, since the promised land including Bashan described in Num 34:10–11 does, in fact, include land east of the Jordan (all or most of the Bashan was clearly Transjordanian), and thus it is not clear what is to be gained by attributing Num 21:33–35 to P (as Milgrom does).[137] On the other

134. Targ. Onk. here has מתנן (Mathnan) in both places where בשן appears in the MT; see also the Targ. in Deut 1:4, 3:1–14 (עוג מלכא דמתנן), and many other passages. All other relevant ancient witnesses reflect the MT.

135. See the classic study of von Rad (1991), as well as Stern 1991; Y. Hoffman 1999, 202; Malul 1999. Cf. the East Semitic concept of *asakkum* (*CAD* A/2, 326–27), and the reference in the Mesha stele, *KAI* I.33:14–18; II.176–77.

136. This in contrast to Deut 2:24 and all "later" traditions, which combine Og and Sihon (Num 32:33; Deut 1:4, 4:47, 29:6, 31:4; Josh 2:10, 9:10; Neh 9:22; Pss 135:11, 136:20). Milgrom (1990, 183–84, 319 n. 58), however, holds to the not uncontroversial view here that P is prior to D.

137. Noth (1968, 166) thinks vv. 33–35 are Deuteronomistic and thus copied from Deuteronomy 3. Though this is not the place for a full description of the problems relating to the historical priority of either D over P or P over D, I tentatively side with the traditional source-critical scheme (reflected by Noth). Admittedly, however, there is something more natural in assuming the author of Deuteronomy transformed a pre-existing third-person narrative into

hand, the fertile area known as the Bashan may have mostly (or entirely?) covered a space so far north of Gilead so as to be north of the Sea of Galilee, and thus not included in territories exactly "east" of the Jordan. If the Bashan was located north of the Yarmuk, however, as most assume, then in fact the Bashan is directly east (and not just northeast) of the Jordan.[138]

Cast as Moses' speech in retrospect, the material in Deuteronomy 1–4 presents us with a number of important additional passages wherein the Rephaim and Og traditions appear.[139] Though certain aspects of this presentation seem to be summaries of earlier material (e.g., Numbers 13, 21, etc.), at other points the author adds new information that takes us more deeply into the problem of the giants' identity. First, we have the recapitulation of the spies' negative report in Numbers 13 given in altered form in Deut 1:26–28, taking us back to the Anaqim:

Deut 1:26–28 (v. 26) You were not willing to go up, and you rebelled against the word of YHWH your God. (27) You complained in your tents and said, "With hatred YHWH brought us out from the land of Egypt, to give us into the hands of the Amorites, to exterminate us! (28) Where are we going? Our brothers have melted our hearts, saying 'A people greater and taller than us (עם גדול ורם ממנו),[140] with great cities, fortified to the heavens (בצורת בשמים), and we even saw the sons of the Anaqim (בני עֲנקים)[141] there!'"

Added to the description in Numbers 13 are a few flourishes (besides the second-person narrative voice):[142] the people accuse YHWH of being

a first-person narrative in Deuteronomy 3—but one still need not assume Deuteronomy 3 belonged to the seventh-century (or earlier) version of the book, and therefore exilic redactions of D may well have been later than, or nearly contemporary with, P. On this, see Levenson (1975), who sees elements of Deuteronomy 3 specifically as an exilic product. It is perhaps best to say that the issue is far from being settled, and likely never will be. On the question of dating P to long before the exilic period, see, e.g., the seminal study of Hurvitz 1982.

138. This seems to be the understanding of Levine (1993, 109).

139. For commentaries on these passages, see, e.g.: Driver 1902, 23–25, 36–41, 51–55; Von Rad 1966, 43–45; Weinfeld 1991, 142–45, 154–67, 180–85; Tigay 1996, 16–17, 26–30, 34–35; Nelson 2002, 21–52.

140. The Greek and other witnesses here add another adjective to these two in the MT: ἔθνος μέγα καὶ πολὺ καὶ δυνατώτερον ἡμῶν ("a people great, many, and much more powerful than us"). This is possibly to match the formula in Deut 2:21; see Nelson 2002, 22. In these two instances, at least, the Greek eschews an emphasis on physical stature.

141. Greek υἱοὺς γιγάντων; Targ. Onk. בני גיברא ("sons of the גיבר" [sing.]). As Drazin (1982, 66 n. 28) explains, it may be that the singular is meant "to inform us that all were children of one man," a move in line with the other Targums (e.g., Targ. Nef. has "sons of Anaq, the warrior"; Ps-Jon has "sons of Ephron, the warrior"; cf. Josh 11:21 and 12:4 in the Targums).

142. Weinfeld (1991, 144–45) points to other differences, such as the purpose of the

motivated with hatred toward them, and the cities are "fortified to the heavens" (בצורת בשמים; see also Deut 9:1).[143] The designation "Amorites" appears here, as elsewhere in the Hebrew Bible as well as other ancient Near Eastern sources, as a blanket term for those living west of the Euphrates.[144] Perhaps most frightening of all, for the people, are specific giants in the land, the "sons of Anaqim," whose stature alone would obviously present a military problem—not to mention their giant cities, walled up to dizzying heights.[145]

Conflation: Rephaim, Emim, Anaqim, Zamzummim. In describing the peoples' journey through the Transjordan, the narrator Moses proceeds to describe the interactions between the Israelites and various Transjordanian groups. In Deuteronomy 2 the conflation of aboriginal giants appears most directly:

Deut 2:9–13 (v. 9) YHWH said to me: "Do not harass Moab and do not provoke them (בם)[146] to battle (תתגר),[147] for I have not given their land to

---

spying mission, e.g., to search out the exact nature of the land and its features in Num 13:18–20, vs. a "merely strategic" purpose here in Deuteronomy. Weinfeld attributes this divergence to a "profound theological reflection" of the author, i.e., the narrator in Deuteronomy does not dare have Moses doubt the goodness of the land and thus has no need to spy it out for those purposes (as in Numbers 13).

143. Cf. בצורת in Num 13:28 and Josh 14:12 (specifically relating to the cities of the Anaqim), as well as Deut 3:5, Isa 2:15, 27:10, 37:26; Jer 15:20, etc. Weinfeld (1991, 144) points to a parallel phrase used in the Assyrian annals of a Judean fortress: "the city of Azekah...located on a mountain ridge...reaching high into heaven (*ana šamê šaqû*)."

144. See also Deut 1:44. The appellative "Hittite" appears to be used this way at times as well.

145. See Sifre Deut., *Pisḳa* 3 (Hammer 1986, 30–31): "Had Og not been mighty but dwelt in Ashtaroth, it still would have been difficult (to conquer them); and had the city not been so mighty but had Og dwelt in it, it would have been difficult (to conquer them) because the king was mighty. How much more difficult was it with both a mighty king and a mighty city!"

Stepping back for a moment from observations rooted only in the textual material at hand, we should ask whether such a description of the heavily fortified cities is simply an invention of the narrator, i.e., the cities that are בצורת בשמים are a literary prop accompanying the individuals who live in the land (the giant people need giant cities in which to live). In fact, remains of the great LB urban centers were probably visible in many locations, as attested, for example, in the very name of 'Ai (עי), "ruins," and such ruins would have been clearly visible throughout the entire biblical period. See Joshua 7–8. Hendel 2009 suggests that the giant architectural remains the Israelites found abandoned in the land must have belonged to equally giant inhabitants, thus inspiring stories of giants. This "fossil theory" for the origins of stories of giants is too reductionistic to be taken *tout court*, and yet it may have provided imaginative fodder for the amplification of such stories. (On this, see Mayor 2000, which cites the fact that a fossilized mastodon skeleton, whose bones are arranged in a certain way in the ground, must have certainly looked like a giant human to ancient observers.) The reality of some of these heavily fortified pre-Israelite cities has been documented in Burke 2008.

146. The Sam. Pent. has בו, "against him" (Moab).

147. The Greek here has second plural verbs here, ἐχθραίνετε and συνάψητε (for the MT's second sing. תצר and תתגר, respectively).

you as a possession; rather, to the sons of Lot I have given Ar (ער)[148] as a possession. (10) Previously, the Emim (העמים)[149] lived in it [Ar], a great and numerous and tall (גדול ורב ורם) people like the Anaqim (כענקים).[150] (11) They are also thought to be Rephaim (רפאים יחשבו),[151] like the Anaqim (כענקים), but the Moabites call them "Emim" (עמים). (12) The Horites previously lived in Seir, and the sons of Esau dispossessed them and exterminated them from their presence and settled in their place—just as Israel did in the land it possessed, which YHWH gave to them. (13) Now, rise up and cross over to the Wadi Zered..."

Deut 2:19–22 (v. 19) And you will draw near to the sons of Ammon—do not harass them and do not provoke them, since I did not give the land of the sons of Ammon to you as an inheritance; rather, I gave it as an inheritance to the sons of Lot. (20) It (the territory of Ammon) is reckoned as a land of Rephaim (ארץ רפאים תחשב)[152]—indeed Rephaim formerly lived in it (ישבו בה לפנים), but the Ammonites call them "Zamzummim" (זמזמים).[153] (21) (They are) a great and numerous and tall (גדול ורב ורם) people, like the Anaqim (כענקים), but YHWH exterminated them from before them (the Ammonites), so that they could dispossess them and live in their place. (22) He (YHWH) did the same thing for the sons of Esau who live in Seir when he exterminated the Horites before them so that they could dispossess them and live in their place until this very day. (23) (As for) the Avvim, who live in the settlements around Gaza, Caphtorim who came out from Caphtor exterminated them and lived in their place.

In these fascinating passages, which have received very little interpretive attention in the secondary literature, we find the most self-conscious reflection in the Hebrew Bible on the identity of the giants and their relationship to one another. To be sure, on the surface this reflection is not particularly revealing, and it is not entirely clear *why* the narrator—whom

148. Targ. Onk. has לחית (Lehayath), which is always used for ער in the Targ.; Greek Σηειρ (Seir).

149. Greek Ομμειν (here and below also); alternate spellings in the mss. include ομμειμ, ομμιειν, ομιην, εμμειν, etc.

150. Targ. Onk. here has כגבריא, in accordance with its typical method of rendering this name; also twice in v. 11.

151. Greek Ραφαειν (throughout these passages); alternatively spelled Ραφαειμ, Ραφαειρ, Ραφαην, etc.; one manuscript, a2, (erroneously) omits the entire phrase רפאים יחשבו אף הם כענקים.

152. Targ. Onk., again, has גיבריא for MT רפאים, here and throughout this verse and in v. 21.

153. Targ. Onk. here has חשבני ("Heshbani," i.e., residents of Heshbon). Greek (B) has Ζοχομειμ, spelled variously in the mss., but also Ζοζομειμ, Ζοομειν, Ζομζομμειν, etc. The relationship of this group to the זוזים in Gen 14:5 is unclear (discussed infra).

most think to be a later interpolator, and some see as the Deuteronomist himself[154]—even bothers to tell us these things.

Moreover, the names "Emim" (אמים) and "Zamzummim" (זמזמים) are mysterious. The moniker Emim is usually thought to be a play on the Hebrew (and presumably also Moabite[155]) אימה, "terror, dread," thus, the *Terrifying Ones*, but this is far from certain.[156] The plural form of אימה (אימים) is used derisively in Jer 50:38 as a euphemism for "idols" (פסלים), opening up the possibility that the "terror" of the Emim here is to be read as a double entendre.[157] Zamzummim is even more enigmatic. Driver, citing W. R. Smith and Wellhausen, suggests the Arabic *zamzamah*, a "distant, confused sound," or the "eerie sound of the Jinn in the wilderness."[158] Thus, the name may be onomatopoetic, comparable to the Greek βάρβαρος ("Barbarian") or the (possible) mimicking of foreign speech in Isa 18:2,7 and 28:10,13 (קו קו, or קו לקו קו לקו).[159]

Von Rad assumed that the antiquarian notes were only the result of Israel's ever increasing historical consciousness and had nothing to do with

154. E.g., the narration turns in 2:12 to the third-person, as opposed to Moses' characteristic second-person narration—and the verse also speaks of the conquest in the past tense. See Tigay 1996, 26.

155. Albrecht Alt thought that the erectors of the twelfth-century Bālûʿah Stele were "Emites," who had migrated from Western Palestine; see reference and brief discussion of Van Zyl (1960, 31–32), who endorses Alt's view. If this presumption were accurate (and we have no real reason to believe it is accurate), then at least one of the figures depicted on the bottom of the Bālûʿah Stele could be one of the Emim. To be sure, due either to artistic style or demands of the material at hand, the three individuals on the stele appear to be quite tall and long limbed (!). See Horsfield and Vincent 1932, pls. XI–XII, as well as the drawing of the figures' proportions, 423 fig. 4. Van Zyl treats the אמים as though they are a clearly historical group, antecedents to the Moabites east of the Jordan. For Van Zyl (1960, 107–08, 113), the Emim were a sedentary population who perhaps arrived in the seventeenth century BCE. Van Zyl's entire reconstruction is overwhelmingly based on the biblical texts in Deuteronomy 2 and Gen 14:5, with the inclusion of sparse archaeological conjectures and the undeciphered Bālûʿah Stele.

156. See Nelson 2002, 39; Weinfeld 1991, 161; Tigay 1996, 27; and Mattingly 1992b, II: 497, all of whom briefly endorse the אימה/terror etymology.

157. Cf. the only other masc. pl. form of this root (outside of Deut 2:10–11 and Gen 14:5) in Job 20:25 (יהלך עליו אמים, "terrors come upon him"). Otherwise, see Ps 55:5, where אימות (fem.) are a personified force (cf. Exod 23:27, את אימתי אשלח לפניך, "I will send out my terror before you").

158. Driver 1902, 40; W. R. Smith explained the meaning of the *zamzumim* sound this way: "I take it that the old giants were still thought to haunt the ruins and deserts of East Canaan" (quoted in Driver 1902, 40 from an un-cited source). The suggestion about the sound of Jinn in the wilderness is drawn from Wellhausen 1887, 136.

159. See Tigay 1996, 349 n. 32. Nelson (2002, 41) translates Zamzummim as "the 'buzz-buzz people,' perhaps a reference to their unintelligible speech or eerie and supernatural sounds." Cf. Strong and M'Clintock 1894, X: 1060, which cites meanings derived from Arabic such as "long necked" (*zamzam*); they also note זמים, "obstinate" (so Luther) and זמזם, "noisy."

Israel itself.[160] I would suggest, however, a quite specific reason for these historical asides, and a complex theological and historiographic reason at that.[161] Indeed, these brief notices fill an important place in Deuteronomy's presentation of the Conquest, and can be revealingly compared with other texts that bear a similar type of land ideology—most notably Deut 32:8–9 and Judg 11:24. Four examples in Deut 2:10–11,20 present YHWH as the divine realtor par excellence: (1) Moab received Ar by dispossessing the Emim; (2) the progeny of Esau inhabit Seir by exterminating the Horites; (3) Ammonites destroy Rephaim (whom they call "Zamzummim") so they can live in Ammon; (4) and the Caphtorim, biblical progenitors of the Philistines, conquer the Avvim around Gath and inhabit the territory (cf. Amos 9:7). Thus, not only have other nations received their territory as a gift from YHWH in the same way that Israel is to receive its land, but some of them have even done so by defeating groups of giants (in the form of the Rephaim-Emim-Zamzummim).

This pattern of extermination and divine placement in the land suggests a straightforward theological point: Israel's own actions and inheritance are not sui generis, but rather are part of larger, macro-regional plan to situate people in their place. With the exile in view—as it surely is in Genesis through Kings[162]—YHWH's actions in the past take on added significance, since Israel can be shown to fall under the purview of YHWH's established norms of possession and exile. One can only assume, on analogy, that nations may not inhabit their original land forever. Nevertheless, the understanding of Deut 2:9–23 is rooted in a theory of flux—and presumably this change of inhabitants is not willy-nilly, but based on divine decisions which are in turn responses to human behavior.[163]

The conflation of these groups in Deuteronomy 2 is unique in the biblical corpus. These groups are presumably all giants, a point made both explicitly (they are "tall" [רם], and one of the Rephaim, Og, has a giant bed) and implicitly (they are like, or equated with, the Anaqim, who are elsewhere said to be fearsomely tall). Deut 2:10–11 and 2:20 drive home the string of con-

---

160. Von Rad 1966, 43. For a similar conclusion, see Perlitt 1994, 246, and 223–32 on the question of the Rephaim generally.

161. Similar views to what I express below can be found in brief form in Sumner 1968, 220 and Nelson 2002, 35.

162. See, e.g., Lev 18:24–30, 20:22–24; Deut 29:27, 30:1–10; Josh 24:19–20; 1 Sam 12:25; 1 Kgs 8:33–4,46–53.

163. Gen 15:16 is perhaps most suggestive toward this end, not to mention the terms of the covenant in Deuteronomy 29–31. But in Deut 32:8–9, we are given no indication of why YHWH receives Israel as his portion; likewise, Jephthah gives no moral rationale for Kemosh's land grant for the Moabites in Judg 11:24, etc.

nections: the Emim are Rephaim, and Anaqim are also Rephaim (thus Emim = Rephaim = Anaqim[164]); and the Rephaim through Ammonite eyes, the Zamzummim, are also like the Anaqim. The Rephaim seem to be the point of reference here, though regarding the physical aspects of size, the Anaqim are the example; the Emim (Moabite for "Rephaim," according to the narrator[165]) are physically tall, like the Anaqim (כענקים), and are reckoned (חשב), or (merely?) thought to be Rephaim.[166]

Regarding the scope of this conflation, however, we must be clear: the equation of Rephaim = Emim = Anaqim = Zamzummim seems to be, in terms of the canonical biblical corpus, an innovation of the Deuteronomist. In other words, it is not clear that all biblical authors who speak of the Rephaim (much less the Anaqim) would have accepted this conflation—though I suspect they would have approved of it in much the same way as early interpreters and translators did. The blending of these groups of giants, then, must have been particularly meaningful to the Deuteronomist, and probably not only as a geographical curiosity. The fate of these aboriginal inhabitants forms part of the pattern of possession and exile in which Israel partakes; but it is also the case that the Moabites and Ammonites, at least, defeated giants to inhabit their own lands. Israel's gigantomachy, like its exodus and its reception of land, is part of a regional pattern involving many people—and, apparently, many giants.

Og's Bed. In Deuteronomy 3, we find yet another archaeological notice, this time applying specifically to Og:

> **Deut 3:8–14** (v. 8) At that time we took the land from the hand of the two kings of the Amorites beyond the Jordan, from the Wadi Arnon up to Mount Hermon—(9) Sidonians call Hermon "Sirion" and the Amorites call it "Senir"—(10) (including) all the cities of the plain, all Gilead, and all of the Bashan, as far as Salekah and Edrei, cities of the kingdom of Og in Bashan. (11) Only Og, the king of Bashan (מלך הבשן),[167] was left of the

---

164. Recall, of course, the fact that Num 13:33 makes the Anaqim = Nephilim; this connection would then synthetically bring the Nephilim into the string of equated giants, though we can only be certain that this connection is the result of the biblical text as we now have it and not an idea directly addressed in Deuteronomy. If Num 13:33 is from P, as Noth (1968, 107) suggests, and if P is later than D, then P must have been aware of the circle of associations into which the Nephilim were drawn in Num 13:33.

165. Or, to be less specific, the author is forging a link—and perhaps an artificial one—between a native Moabite understanding of a group, the Emim, and a group known by Israelites, the Rephaim.

166. See Stuckenbruck 2004, 92.

167. Targ. Onk. מתנן ("Mathnan"), as in Num 21:33 and elsewhere in the Targums; Targ. Nef. here has "Botniin."

remnant of the Rephaim (נשאר מיתר הרפאים).[168] Note his bed, a bed of iron (ערש ברזל)[169]—is it not in Rabah of the sons of Ammon? Its length is nine cubits and its width is four cubits, by the forearm of a man [i.e., the "normal cubit"].[170] (12) This land that we possessed at that time, from Aroer which is next to the Wadi Arnon, and half the hill country of Gilead and its cities, I gave (it) to the Reubenites and to the Gadites. (13) And the remainder of Gilead and all of Bashan, the kingdom of Og, I gave it to the half-tribe of Manasseh, all the territory of Argob. All of (that) part of Bashan was called a land of Rephaim (ארץ רפאים). (14) Ya'ir son of Manasseh took all the territory of Argob, up to the boundary of the Geshurites and the Maacathites, and he named them, that is Bashan, after his own name, Havvoth-Ya'ir, as it is to this day.

Like other materials in Deuteronomy 1–2, the notice leading up to this passage in Deut 3:1–3 echoes accounts in the book of Numbers, specifically Num 21:33–35.[171] Deut 3:11 seems to be the intrusive element here, with the notice of Og's "bed" representing an attempt at expansion. Rarely in the Hebrew Bible is such energy spent describing the personal effects of any individual—comparable, perhaps, is the description of Goliath—and these archaeological "footnotes" indicate, again, an author concerned with making some use of apparently arcane knowledge at his disposal concerning giants.[172] In three specific instances biblical authors situate Og within the tradition of Rephaim: in Deut 3:11, Og is called the "only one" (רק) "who remained of the Rephaim" (הנשאר מיתר הרפאים), while in Josh 12:4 Og is

---

168. For רפאים, Targ. Onk. גיבריא. This is one of the few instances where the Greek simply transliterates the Hebrew רפאים as Ραφαειν (also at the end of v. 13). It is possible that the Greek translators wanted to avoid the contradictory implication that Og was the last of the γίγαντες, since the LXX mentions several γίγαντες later in Samuel and Chronicles. This interpretation of the LXX's motives is confirmed by the rendering of רפאים as γίγας in Josh 12:4 and 13:12 where again Og is said to be of the remnant of the Rephaim, but it is not explicitly said in Josh that Og was the *very last* of his kind (as it is in Deut 3:11).

169. The Greek traditions here all have κλίνη, "bed/couch."

170. Targ. Onk. has באמת מלך, "by the royal cubit." Assuming a 17–½ inch // 45 cm cubit, the author is claiming that Og's ערש is over 13 feet long and nearly six feet wide (approx. 4.05 meters x 1.8 meters). Drazin (1982, 79–80 n. 2) explains Nachmanides' interpretation here of the phrase in the Targum: the cubit is that of "*the* man" (with "the" implied as it frequently is in the Targ.), an important man, to wit, Og himself—Targ. Ps-Jon seems to follow this line of thinking with the translation, "in his own cubit," making the ערש all the more imposing.

171. See Lindquist 2011 for comments on these two passages vis-à-vis one another.

172. Og's association with the Rephaim draws him into the constellation of giants (based on Deut 2:9–23), and the size of his bed in Deut 3:11 only serves to confirm this fact. Postbiblical interpreters speak in near unison on Og's status as a giant; see, e.g., b.Niddah 61a; Targ. Ps-Jon to Deut 2:2 and 3:11; b.Zebahim 113; b.Rub. 30a, 48a; b.Yoma 80b (for further discussion and sources, see Stuckenbruck 2004, 93 n. 11).

simply said to be "from the remnant/remaining contingent of the Rephaim" (מיתר הרפאים) and Josh 13:12 reports that Og was "[the only?] one who re-mained from the contingent of the Rephaim" (הוא נשאר מיתר הרפאים).[173]

The exact nature and purpose of the appearance of Og's "bed of iron" (ערש ברזל) in 3:11 is a matter of longstanding and seemingly intractable debate. Every few years another essay appears endorsing one of the two main proposals for understanding the meaning of "bed" in the verse, viz. that the object is a bed/couch or that it is a funerary object of some kind (either a coffin or a monument).[174] The most straightforward interpretation of the "bed of iron" is to take each of these two words in their most straightforward meanings: "a bed of iron."[175] Many scholars take the phrase in just this way.[176] A. Millard, for example, argues that a native Israelite living in the seventh century BCE would have understood ערש ברזל simply as a(n ordinary) "bed of iron," and that the prestige and scarcity of iron in the Late Bronze Age indicates the wealth of Og in the mind of the narrator.[177] U. Hübner also argues that the ערש is a bed and that this ערש evokes the bed located in the *bīt erši* ("house of the bed") of the ziggurat Etemenanki in Babylon.[178] Not coincidentally, Hübner contends, the Esagil Tablet records the dimensions of this bed as "...nine cubits [its long] side, four cubits [its] front, the bed; the throne in front of the bed."[179] Thus the correspondence drawn by the biblical author has a polemical thrust; since the Etemenanki bed served as the site of ritual sex between Marduk and Zarpanitu, the author of Deut 3:11 is implicitly comparing Og to a cultic prostitute.[180]

Though the cultic prostitution polemic seems far-fetched, the cor-

---

173. It is not clear whether there is support for a translation such as "one of the last of the Rephaim" or "he alone was left of the survivors of the Rephaim" (so NRSV for Josh 12:4 and 13:12, respectively).

174. The two most thorough and recent treatments of the history of research here are Veijola 2003 and Millard 1988. It is not clear what the ערש is doing in Rabbah of the Ammonites; it may have been carried there as plunder (so Lindquist 2011, but with no evidence), or there may have been two traditions about Og, one situating him in the north and one in Rabbah (so Bartlett 1970, 268).

175. For ערש, see Amos 3:12 (used in parallel with מטה, "bed"), 6:4; Pss 6:7, 41:4, 132:3; Job 7:13 (in parallel with משכב); Prov 7:16; Song 1:16. ברזל appears 76x in the MT with the meaning "iron" or a related substance.

176. See, e.g., Weinfeld 1991, 183–85; Nelson 2002, 52; Tigay 1996, 35.

177. Millard (1988, 486–89) makes the assumption here that the text passes along to us genuine information from the Bronze Age.

178. Hübner 1993, with further discussion in Veijola 2003, 63–64.

179. GIŠ.NÁ 9 KÙŠ UŠ 4 KÙŠ SAG *eršu u giš* [*ku*]*ssû tar-ṣi eršu*. See Matshushima 1988, 109 for the text; cf. Herodotus, *Hist.* 1.181.

180. Hübner 1993, 92.

responding dimensions of the beds are difficult to dismiss.[181] The actual polemic in play—if indeed there is one at all—may rather have to do with the implicit correspondence between Marduk as a deity and Og as an ambiguously divine figure, the idea being that YHWH is victorious over all kings and all gods.[182] On the daringly imaginative end of the spectrum of those who interpret the ערש as a "bed" is J. C. de Moor, who supposes that the bed bore an inscription which the Israelites somehow misunderstood due to their ignorance of Canaanite religion.[183]

Dissatisfied with the bed interpretation, many others read ערש as either a straightforward or euphemistic reference to a tomb (dolmen) or a megalithic funerary monument.[184] The earliest scholarly attempt to argue for this connection was apparently that of Johann David Michaelis,[185] as noted by S. R. Driver; Driver himself affirmed the translation of ערש as "bed" but questioned whether by "bed" the author meant to imply a *funeral* bed (i.e., a coffin of black basalt, supposedly common east of the Jordan).[186] There are, in fact, several lines of thought that suggest this view is plausible, though its proponents have not, in my view, overcome the plain meaning of ערש ברזל as an "iron bed." T. Veijola has recently argued that the ערש ברזל was a basalt dolmen, comparing the Phoenician term *mškb* as a resting place for the dead (*KAI* 3.15, 9 A:1,3,9, etc.) as well as the Aramaic translation of ערש, ערסא, which can denote a "bier" (cf. Greek σορός).[187] Regarding the ברזל ("iron"), Veijola thinks this is best explained as basalt (a type of stone with iron in it; note Deut 8:9; Job 28:2), and since we have no evidence of basalt tombs of

---

181. Neo-Assyrian plunder lists contain references to this plundered bed of Marduk after the victory in 689 BCE of Sennacherib over Babylon, and the bed traveled from Babylon to Assyria and back to Babylon again in 654 BCE (in an effort to appease the Babylonians). Assurbanipal devoted references in two of his annals to the capture of this bed, thereby highlighting its political significance. See Lindquist 2011; B. Porter 2002, 523–35.

182. This is the argument of Lindquist 2011, though she does not make sufficiently clear whether Og could truly be considered semi-divine, or clarify what this would mean in the Israelite imagination. This argument deserves exploration, however, and is taken up in ch. 4.

183. De Moor (1976, 338) reconstructs this imaginary inscription as follows: "This is the bed of Og, king of Bashan, the Saviour [hrp'], who thrones with Astarte and with Adda (Adad), his Shepherd." Moreover, de Moor argues that the bed is a funerary couch offered by Og's relatives on analogy with the bed given by Enkidu to Gilgamesh in *Gilg.* VIII.iii.1.

184. Aside from the other sources cited below, see, e.g., Von Rad 1966, 44–45; Craigie 1976, 120; Mayes 1979, 144, and the other bibliography in Veijola 2003, 60 n. 1.

185. Driver (1902, 53) parenthetically cites Michaelis (along with several other sources) without indicating where Michaelis presents the view. Note also Karge 1917, 638–40, who thought the ערש ברזל was a megalithic dolmen.

186. Driver 1902, 53–54.

187. Veijola 2003, 66, with reference to Millard 1988, "King Og's Bed," 482. Veijola also points to 2 Sam 3:31, where Abner is laid out on a מטה ("bier"). Cf. 2 Kgs 4:21,32, and משכב with the meaning of a tomb or final resting place in 2 Chr 16:14; Isa 57:2; Ezek 32:25.

the enormous size described in Deut 3:11, the basalt "bed"/עֶרֶשׂ must be a dolmen of the type attested in the Transjordan and Galilee regions.[188] The tomb structure is comprised of this בַּרְזֶל, in Veijola's conjecture, because this impenetrable material would be needed to lock the vengeful spirit of Og in the netherworld.[189] Though I think the interpretation of the עֶרֶשׂ בַּרְזֶל here as an "iron bed" is probably most appropriate, Veijola's notion of the עֶרֶשׂ as a powerful ritual object comes closer than most theories to identifying something of the *tone* of the notice in Deut 3:11: awe and reverence, not polemic.

The references to Sihon and Og in Deut 1:4 and 4:47 form an inclusio around the conquest account in Deuteronomy 1–4, suggesting that these two individuals and all they represent form an important ordering device in the opening chapters of Deuteronomy. Furthermore, the Israelite encounter with Og marks a highly significant symbolic moment for Israel's engagement with the aboriginal giants of Palestine more generally. Though the wilderness generation was initially repelled by frightening reports of the giant Anaqim in Numbers 13 (repeated in Deut 1:28), and was thus forced to wander about in the southern wilderness and the Transjordan (Deut 1:46–2:1,14), their second encounter with the giants in the form of Og proved decisive.[190] Thus, the defeat of the giants marks both the moment of Israel's own military prowess coming to fruition and, more importantly for the narrator of Deuteronomy, the fulfillment of YHWH's own promise to carry the people "as a father carries a son" (Deut 1:31) so that, finally, they will cross the threshold of the Jordan to receive the land given to Abraham. The giant Anaqim and Rephaim guard the land, standing as monstrous reminders of the past (Gen 6:1–4) and of the entire cycle of wrong territorial possession, now rectified in Israel's victory.[191]

The Rephaim and history. As opposed to the materials in Genesis 6 and 10 and, to some extent, the Anaqim, the place of Og in the biblical narrative has drawn serious historical attention. For example, in his study of the emergence of Israel from autochthonous populations, G. Mendenhall supposed Israel's military and religious revolution began in the Transjordan, specifi-

188. Veijola 2003, 72–73. Prominent dolmens from the Early Bronze are still visible today in Jordan and elsewhere in the Transjordan regions; see the recent overviews by Savage 2010 and Al-Shorman 2010.

189. Veijola 2003, 75.

190. Lindquist (2011) makes this same point.

191. Besides functioning as images of the grotesque, the ominous, and the dangerous, giants are also known in a variety of literatures to act as "gate-keepers," marking important points of communal transition and rituals of inversion. Here, too, the giants as a monstrous inversion of human physicality mark the most significant transition point in the desert-wandering narrative, guarding the border between Transjordan and The Land. See Stewart 1993, 106–07.

cally in battles to control the fertile agricultural land of the Bashan.[192] If the historical repopulation of the Transjordan occurred just on the eve (or during) the Late Bronze collapse in the Mediterranean and Near East generally, i.e., around the thirteenth century, as (now defunct) older archaeological surveys generally suggested it did,[193] then we would have a situation wherein Og and Sihon were relatively new rulers of kingdoms in their infancy—a fact which might explain the willing participation of local Transjordanian groups in the overthrow of their hated overlords.[194] There is nothing particularly miraculous about the accounts of Og and the Rephaim, and certain elements seem so incidental (such as the linguistic notes in Deuteronomy 2 and the location of Og's ערש ברזל in Deut 3:11) that historically minded readers would have no choice but to acknowledge that the author was passing down information that he thought was reliable.[195]

Rephaim in the forests with chariots of iron. Outside of these materials in Numbers and Deuteronomy relating to the Rephaim and Og traditions, three other references deserve brief comment. The first, in Joshua 17, mentions the ארץ רפאים as a forested area somewhere in the hill country:

> **Josh 17:14–18** (v. 14) The sons of Joseph spoke to Joshua, saying, "Why did you give me (only) one inheritance (by) lot and (only) one portion—yet I am a numerous people, and up until now YHWH has blessed me!" (15) So Joshua said to them, "If you are indeed a numerous people, go up to the forest and cut out (ובראת) for yourselves there (a spot) in the land of the Perizzites and the Rephaim (הרפאים)[196]—if the hill country of Ephraim is (too) narrow for you." (16) The sons of Joseph then said, "The hill country is not sufficient for us [lit. it is not found for us], and all the Canaanites who dwell in the valley-land have chariots of iron (רכב ברזל), all of those in

---

192. Mendenhall 1962, 79–80.

193. See Glueck 1970 and Weippert 1971, 60–61 n. 21. The older reconstructions, however, are thrown into grave doubt by newer discoveries showing continuous occupation throughout the Bronze and Iron ages; see Sauer 1986 and sources cited therein.

194. See Mendenhall 1962, 81–83.

195. This, of course, does not mean that the information *is* actually reliable. But, as Brettler (2007, 322) points out, the standard practice in historical reconstruction is to assume extraneous points are *not* likely to have been invented. Bartlett (1970, 270) suggests that Judahites first encountered stories about Og during the time of David, when Joab made incursions into Ammon in 2 Sam 12:26–31.

196. The Greek traditions omit the clause שם בארץ הפרזי והרפאים. Nelson (2002, 200) suggests this phrase in Hebrew is an "expansion" that "could have originated as a dittography for 'hill country in Ephraim,' hrp'ym from hr'prym"—but this does not explain the reference to the Perizzites (unless הפרזי appeared as yet another expansion after the original expansion was made). Rather, we should read the omission in the Greek as a mistake of haplography (so Boling 1975, 417): ש[ם בארץ הפרזי והרפאי]ם.

Beth-Shean and its villages and in the valley of Jezreel." (17) So Joshua said to the house of Joseph, to Ephraim and to Manasseh, "You are a numerous people, and have great strength—you will not have (only) one lot. (18) Rather, the hill country will be yours. Although it is forested, you will clear it (ובראתו), and even its furthest borders will be yours, for you will dispossess the Canaanites—even though they have chariots of iron, even though they are strong."

This passage suggests that the Rephaim *still* live in the forested hill country (along with the Perizzites[197]), which appears to be in contradiction with Num 21:35 (cf. also Josh 13:12), where all of Og's army was destroyed by Moses' army.[198] It could be that the author here is merely using the "land of the Rephaim" (ארץ רפאים) as a geographical designation without any implication of inhabitants, but the way v. 15 is combined with vv. 16–18 seems to conflate the forested area of the Rephaim with the territory of the plain-dwelling Canaanites, insofar as the sons of Joseph respond to Joshua's request to clear out forest land with the rebuttal that the inhabitants (nearby?) have iron chariots. Thus, presumably, besides their natural strength the situation is made worse by the inhabitants' superior weaponry. Indeed, these super-chariots appear again in Judg 1:19, where it is claimed that Judah "did not drive out the inhabitants of the plain, because they had chariots of iron."[199]

Two conjectures might be made at this point regarding Josh 17:15–16. First, the reference to iron here reminds us of Og's iron bed (ערש ברזל) in Deut 3:11. The fact that the Canaanites—possibly here conflated with the Rephaim—possess this precious and superior metal, which is rhetorically symbolic of raw strength and aggression in the biblical texts, may indicate that some of the land's aboriginal inhabitants were thought to possess rare or brutal technologies in addition to their physical gigantism.[200] Second, in the description of the land of the Rephaim as an untamed and uninhabitable forest land (יער) in v. 15, we have a symbolic image of the threat of the giant as a wild and untamed being; the clearing out (ברא) of the forest is the symbolic equivalent of clearing out giants.[201]

197. This is the only location where Rephaim are paired with another group in this manner; note the pairing of "Canaanites and Perizzites" in Gen. 13:7, 34:30.

198. Not to mention the fact that Og is said to be the only remaining member of the Rephaim in Deut 3:11 (but notably not in Josh 12:4, 13:12).

199. רכב ברזל also appears in Judg 4:3,13, again as a mark of non-Israelite (specifically Canaanite) armies.

200. This vision of the iron-wielding natives is questionable as a historical reality (whether giants are involved or not). See the comments toward this end in Nelson 2002, 204 n. 8, with reference to Sawyer 1983. Cf. Drews 1989.

201. See Bernheimer 1952, 25 on the relationship of the giant to that which is

The Rephaim of Genesis 14 and 15. Two additional appearances of the Rephaim as native inhabitants of the land in the biblical narrative happen also to be the first two times the designation Rephaim appears in the canonical biblical narrative: Gen 14:5 and 15:19. Genesis 14 is unique in the Pentateuch in a number of ways that have been long noticed by commentators.[202] Common opinion had been—and remains to some extent—that the material here belongs to none of the four classical source documents, but rather stands as an independent addition to these sources.[203] Problems of theme and content generally also abound. As von Rad aptly put it, Genesis 14 "contains some of the most difficult and most debated material...in the entire historical part of the Old Testament," and "nowhere in the patriarchal stories do we find such a mass of historical and geographical data."[204]

Albright's early articles on the chapter brought the issue of historicity to the forefront of discussion, with Albright himself characteristically arguing that the passage utilized early Mesopotamian sources and also accurately represented a series of events in the early second millennium BCE.[205] Perhaps the most involved attempt to understand the context and symbolism of the passage as a whole was that of M. Astour, who found in Genesis 14 a complex and subtle—at times, overly subtle—web of symbolic connections with the "Chedorlaomer texts,"[206] including, most prominently, a veiled reference to the destruction of Babylon in the Persian period via the name of the "Valley of Siddim" (עמק השדים; see the references to the kings of Sodom and Gomorrah in v. 2).[207] Moreover, Astour attributed Genesis 14 to the

---

"uncultivated." Elsewhere in the Hebrew Bible the יער can evoke a sort of mysterious wildness, as in 2 Sam 18:8 (ויֶרֶב היער לאכל בעם מאשר אכלה החרב ביום ההוא; "the forest ate up more people that day than the sword").

202. For comments and further bibliography, see: Gunkel 1997, 273–84; Von Rad 1972, 174–81; Speiser 1964, 99–109; Westermann 1995, 182–208; Schatz 1972.

203. See, e.g., Gunkel 1997 (first published 1901), 282; Von Rad 1972, 175. The status of Genesis 14 as a ringer in the Pentateuch is not without its own problems of logic in terms of source-critical theory. Who inserted the source? If it were J, for example, then is not J the "source" (on parallel with arguments often made about J inserting the "pagan" reference in Gen 6:1–4 from some extraneous text)? See Westermann 1995, 190.

204. Von Rad 1972, 175.

205. Albright 1926. In a somewhat similar spirit, see Speiser 1964, 101, 106, and Gunkel 1997 (first published 1901), 273. Cf. Emerton (1971), who takes a relatively balanced view, finding problems with the maximal historical reconstruction but still acknowledging the reliance upon (Mesopotamian) sources of some kind.

206. Astour 1966; the views in this long essay are summarized in four short articles Astour wrote for the *Anchor Bible Dictionary*, viz. Astour 1992a; 1992b; 1992c; 1992d.

207. Astour 1966, 106. In Astour's reasoning, שדים "is an exact translation of Akkadian *ikû,* 'acre,' the name of the constellation *mulIkû,* the celestial counterpart of Babylon, transferred...to the terrestrial Babylon as well."

Deuteronomist, who, in his position of exile in Babylon, would have had access to the requisite cuneiform texts and would have "with burning hatred predicted the imminent destruction of their captor's capital."[208] Astour's argument for D as the appropriate source does have some compelling points, such as parallel phraseology and theme in other biblical texts (e.g., 2 Kgs 18:7–13, 24:1–13,20–25, etc.), but that issue remains inconclusive.[209]

The most specific passage of interest to us here occurs in vv. 5–7, where at least two—and quite possibly three—of the groups of aboriginal giants mentioned in Deuteronomy 2–3 appear in conjunction with one another yet again:

Gen 14:5–7 (v. 5) In the fourteenth year Chedorlaomer and the kings who were with him came and struck down Rephaim (רפאים) in Ashtaroth-Qarnaim, the Zuzim (הזוזים)[210] in Ham, the Emim (האימים) in Shaveh-Qiryathaim, (6) and the Horites in the hill country of Seir as far as Eyl-Pa'ran which borders the wilderness. (7) They turned back and came to Ein-Mishpat—that is, Qadesh—and they struck down all of the country of the Amaleqites and also the Amorites who lived in Hasson-Tamar.

Abram enters the narrative relatively late in the action, in v. 12, after Chedorlaomer kidnaps his nephew Lot. The listing of the Rephaim, Zuzim, and Emim in v. 5 appears to be only incidental geographical information in this passage, as these peoples and regions naturally belong in the Transjordanian context the author is describing. Deut 2:10–11,20 records the three groups in a different overall order—Emim - Rephaim - Zamzummim, with additional reference to the Anaqim—and scattered throughout several verses, as opposed to the rapid-fire mention of all three groups at the end of a single verse in Genesis 14. But the correspondence of the three groups is nonetheless striking, especially when one also considers the reference to the "Horites" (חרי) in Gen 14:6 and Deut 2:12.

Over a century ago, A. H. Sayce assumed that "Zuzim and Ham are merely faulty transcriptions from a cuneiform text of the Hebrew Zamzummim

---

208. Astour 1966, 106. One additional point of contact between Genesis 14 and the Deuteronomist not spelled out by Astour occurs when Genesis 14 gestures "forward" in the biblical narrative toward David and his own encounter with giants, specifically in the reference to the enigmatic Melchizedek, priest of (Jeru)Salem. For Bartelmus (1979, 141–45), this scene in Genesis 14 represents, along with 1 Samuel 17, a "secular" twist on the *Heroenkonzept*, and is therefore especially fitted for consideration in a monarchic milieu.

209. Astour 1966, 70–71.

210. The Greek here reads ἔθνη ἰσχυρά ("strong nations"); cf. Targ. Onk., תקיפיא ("strong ones"), Nef. קיותניה ("awesome ones"). These readings seem to presuppose a Hebrew text that read גוים גדלים (as in Josh 23:9) or גוים עצמים (Mic 4:3; Zech 8:22), or they are an interpretation of the unique word זוזים.

and Ammon," and commentators of the past century have more or less affirmed the probable equivalence of Zuzim and Zamzummim (Deut 2:20).[211] The broader list of "ethnic groups" in Gen 14:5-7 also provides a rare reference in such lists to the Rephaim as a people group alongside others (only here and in Gen 15:20) and the only reference in such lists in the Hebrew Bible to the Zuzim, Emim, and Horites.[212] At the very least, then, Gen 14:5-6 demonstrates that these groups (minus the Horites)—which are explicitly categorized as giants in Deuteronomy 2, but not in Genesis 14—could be viewed in a "list of nations" format akin to other such registries in the Hebrew Bible. Furthermore, the patriarch Abram's role in battle is a rather unique type of narrative action within Genesis 12-50, though it is not completely unparalleled.[213]

Finally, we must make note of the reference to the Rephaim in the list of ten nations whose land will be given to Abram in Genesis 15:[214]

> **Gen 15:18-21** (v. 18) On that day YHWH made a covenant with Abram, saying, "To your seed I give this land, from the River of Egypt to the Great River, the River Euphrates; (19) [the land of] the Qenites, the Qenizzites,

211. Sayce 1895, 38. By "equivalence," I only mean that the original authors of Gen 14:5 and Deut 2:20, if not the same person, would have agreed that they were talking about the same individuals and region. See also Von Rad 1972, 177; Gunkel 1997 (first published 1901), 275; Speiser 1964, 102; and Westermann (1995, 196), who sees Deut 2:10-12,20 as the source of the reference to the Rephaim here.

212. Indeed, the list in Gen 14:5-6 is very different from the others spread throughout the Bible. The most comprehensive "standard" list of groups shared throughout the most locations occurs in Exod 3:8,17, 23:23, 33:2, 34:11, Josh 9:1, 11:3, 12:8, and 1 Kgs 9:20, and contains the Hittites, Yebusites, Canaanites, Amorites, Perizzites, and Hivvites. Additionally, the Girgashites appear along with this core list of six nations in Deut 7:1 and Josh 24:11 (and the Girgashites appear elsewhere with an "incomplete" list in Josh 3:10 and Neh 9:8), while Exod 13:5, 23:28, Num 13:29, Deut 20:17, Josh 3:10, Ezra 9:1, Neh 9:8, 2 Chr 8:7 contain seemingly idiosyncratic permutations of some of the above mentioned groups (but never with all seven groups at once). Gen 15:18-21 (see infra) is the most comprehensive of such lists of indigenous nations, also mentioning the Rephaim, as well as the Qenites, Qenezzites, and Qadmonites (listed nowhere else). The point here, then, is that the Hebrew Bible contains many different kinds of registries of pre-Israelite inhabitants, and Gen 14:5-6 constitutes only one of these registries.

213. In Gen 48:22, there is an enigmatic reference to a battle Jacob fought against the Amorites: "And I give to you one portion (שכם) beyond your brother, [viz. the portion] which I took from the hand of the Amorites with my sword and my bow." The שכם may refer to the incident involving Shechem the Hivvite in Genesis 34. However, Jacob is not active in the razing of the city (Gen 34:25)—on the contrary, he disapproves of the action (34:30). The opponents in some of these battles may even have been comprised of giants or divine/semi-divine beings; note the enigmatic battle in Gen 32:25-32 wherein Jacob battles a "man" (איש), whom he later identifies as (an) אלהים. Such references may indicate that a larger cycle of stories once existed in which the patriarchs fought in battles—but as it stands, these stories are lost to us except in Genesis 14 and these other brief allusions.

214. See Gunkel 1997 (first published 1901), 182; Westermann 1995, 229-30.

the Qadmonites, (20) the Hittites, the Perizzites, the Rephaim (הרפאים),
(20) the Amorites, the Canaanites, the Girgashites, and the Yebusites."

Not much can be added here to our discussion above, except to note
that in this passage we have the most comprehensive biblical list of "ethnographic" entities—including the Rephaim—inhabiting the land that Abram
and his progeny are to receive.[215] While the Hittites, Yebusites, Canaanites,
Amorites, and Perizzites all commonly appear in the stock lists of Exod
3:8,17, 13:5, 23:23, 33:2, 34:11, Deut 7:1, etc., the Rephaim are not included in
such lists anywhere except here and in Gen 14:5—not to mention the Qenites, Qenizzites, and Qadmonites, who appear only here in Gen 15:19 as part
of an ethnographic registry. The addition of the "extra" groups in this pivotal chapter may be intended to magnify the enormity and special status of
the promise to Abram, but the inclusion of the Rephaim in 14:5 makes this
group an integral component of the land's pre-Israelite inhabitants.

IV. Giants in the Early Monarchy

The Israelite Conquest of Palestine—initiated in the book of Numbers, an-
ticipated in Deuteronomy, and completed in Joshua—should have, at least
in terms of the logic of the biblical narrative, completely eliminated the giants from the face of the earth. Indeed, as previously discussed, no giant
beings should have survived the Noahide Flood in Genesis 6–9, and yet we
find putative descendants of the Nephilim, viz. the Anaqim, inhabiting the
land in Num 13:33. However, in 1–2 Samuel we discover that neither total
annihilation via Flood nor the institution of the חרם ("ban") in the Conquest
was enough to eradicate these races of beings: Goliath of Gath (1 Samuel 17),
various "descendants of (the) Rapha'" (רפא/רפה) and Rephaim (2 Sam 21:15–
22 // 1 Chr 20:4–8), and other individuals who seem to be genealogically
connected to the archaic giants as recorded in the Pentateuch and Joshua
still exist. Recall the "escape clause" in Josh 11:21–22, which informs us that
the Anaqim lived to fight another day in three Philistine cities (Gaza, Gath,
and Ashdod).[216] On the one hand, Josh 11:21 has Joshua clearing out all of
the Israelite territory the people are to inhabit, but on the other, Josh 11:22
has the Anaqim still living along the coast. The narrator here apparently
does not see Philistine territory as Israelite territory, despite the fact that
land promised to the patriarchs certainly included *all* land up to the Medi-

215. That is, this passage gives a very clear picture of the geographical extent of the ten
nations as understood by the biblical author—covering all of the Levant. It is not at all clear,
a priori, whether the length of the list would make it a candidate for being the oldest or most
recent of such lists. See Westermann 1995, 230.

216. Also toward this end, note again Josh 17:15, where it is quite possibly implied that
Rephaim still inhabit forested country and other areas that need to be weeded out.

terranean Sea—a feat not accomplished, according to the Bible (e.g., 2 Sam 8:1–15; 1 Kgs 4:24), until the reigns of David and Solomon.

One possible explanation for such incongruities is that some glossator, working at a time during or after the compilation of the Pentateuch, Joshua, and 1–2 Samuel, noticed the contradiction of the presence of giants in these three "eras" (pre-Flood, pre-conquest, and during the early monarchy), and, while he apparently did not want to delete their presence from any particular scene, he did provide adequate textual notices to explain/recognize their existence twice after they should have perished (Gen 6:4, וגם אחרי כן; Josh 11:22). In fact, we do find concrete evidence of the awareness of this problem in the Greek translation traditions. For example, Rephaim (רפאים) is simply transliterated as Ραπαιν (*Rapain*) in several passages (Gen 15:20; Deut 2:11,20, 3:11,13; Josh 15:8; Ραπαιμ [*Rapaim*] in 2 Sam 23:13; cf. "Gideon son of Rapain" [Γεδεων υἱοῦ Ραφαϊν] in Judith 8:1), whereas in others the term is interpreted and translated as γίγας ("giant"; Gen 14:5; Josh 12:4, 13:12; 1 Chr 11:15, etc.) or even Τίταν ("Titan"; 2 Sam 5:18,22).

Deut 3:11 is an instructive case in point regarding the differences in translation technique: the Hebrew clearly informs us that Og was the *last of a generation*, the *only one* remaining of the Rephaim (כי רק עוג מלך הבשן נשאר מיתר הרפאים). The Greek translator of Deut 3:11, by rendering Rephaim as Ραπαιν (*Rapain*), shrewdly avoided the use of γιγάντων ("giants") for Rephaim, precisely because we find giants such as Goliath and others later in the chronology of the narrative. This sleight of translation is highlighted by the way the Greek translators of Joshua rendered two *nearly* parallel statements in Josh 12:4 and 13:12, where Og is said to be *one of* the Rephaim but *not the last one*: here, Rephaim is freely rendered as γιγάντων ("giants").[217] Ergo, Og was a giant—but not the world's *last* giant.

The point here, then, is that authors within the biblical period itself and soon afterward acknowledged the problems posed by giants who are repeatedly wiped out completely and yet survive anyway, and they solved these problems though a series of "escape clauses" and also by altering translations. The final "historical" generation of these giant figures, however, appears to encounter David and his mighty men in various passages,

---

217. It is important to note here that Josh 13:12 in the MT is at least ambiguous on this point: הוא נשאר מיתר הרפאים, which the NRSV, for example, translates as "He alone was left of the survivors of the Rephaim," apparently taking the הוא as the indicator of exclusivity (cf. NJPS: "He was the last of the remaining Rephaim"). This use of הוא, however, would seem to be anomalous; it is better to read the pronoun here as emphatic, marking Og as the chief referent. See Waltke and O'Conner 1990, 292–97. Note that Josh 12:4 only states that Og was מיתר הרפאים, which further reinforces the topicalizing purpose of the הוא in 13:12. Targ. Onk., at least, has not attempted to avoid the problem, since it affirms Og was indeed the last of the "Gibborim" (גיברין), but the Targums then have other גיברין at later periods, e.g., 1 Chr 11:15.

including the iconic David and Goliath battle and other struggles involving David's troops and certain Philistines in 2 Samuel (with parallels in 1 Chronicles).[218] In what follows, I address three specific texts wherein these figures occur, in 1 Samuel 17, 2 Sam 21:15–22, and 1 Chr 20:4–8, thus concluding the Bible's own story of its giants.[219]

David and Goliath

1 Sam 17:1–11 (v. 1) The Philistines assembled their encampments for war, and they were assembled at Sokoh, which belongs to Judah. They camped between Sokoh and 'Azeqah, in Ephes-Dammim (באפס דמים).[220] (2) Saul and the Israelites were assembled as well, and they camped in the Valley of Elah, where they arrayed for war to encounter the Philistines. (3) The Philistines were standing on one mountain, and Israel was standing upon the other, with the valley between them. (4) And the "man between" (איש הבנים)[221] came out from the camps of the Philistines, Goliath (גלית) his name, from Gath. His height was six cubits and a span (גבהו שש אמות וזרת).[222] (5) A helmet of bronze was on us head, and he was clothed in scaled armor; the weight of the armor was five thousand shekels of bronze.[223] (6) Greaves of bronze were upon his legs [lit. "feet"], and a javelin of bronze (hung, or was strapped) between his shoulders, (7) and the shaft

218. See now Garsiel 2011.

219. Besides the passages listed here, a note should be made regarding the parallel descriptions of David's גברים in 2 Sam 23:8–39 // 1 Chr 11:11–47. Here we find heroic tropes and other references with strong connections to our main texts of interest here. E.g., Elhanan appears as one the "thirty" (שלשים) in 2 Sam 23:24 and also as part of David's warriors in 1 Chr 11:26. There is an obvious wordplay between Elhanan's patronymic, בן יערי ארגים, and the description of Goliath's weapon, which is כמנור ארגים, perhaps suggesting that the association between these two characters—the son of a weaver and the giant with a spear like a weaver's beam—represents an older tradition. At the very least, 2 Sam 23:8–39 // 1 Chr 11:11–47 are likely evidence that the stories of heroes and their deeds in the biblical texts are only a fragment of available material extant at the time of the various stages of the composition of the Bible. See infra on 2 Sam 23:20–23 // 1 Chr 11:22–25. For further discussion, see McCarter 1984, 489–94, and also Driver 1890, 362–72. For other issues, including general discussion of David's גבורים, see also Kosmala 1975, II: 374–75; Mazar 1963; Elliger 1935; De Vaux 1997, 123, 220; Knoppers 2004, 532–55; R. Klein, 292–310; Japhet 1993, 231–52.

220. Vaticanus here has Εφερμεμ; other Greek traditions vary.

221. Greek supposes the Hebrew here means a "powerful man" or warrior, ἀνὴρ δυνατός.

222. I have maintained the MT here with Goliath's iconic 9′6″ height, though this is probably not the original reading. Almost all of the major Greek witnesses (B and L; but cf. A) as well as Josephus (*Ant.* VI.171) and, perhaps most importantly, 4QSamª all have *four* cubits and a span, i.e., a comparatively mediocre 6′9″ (assuming an 18″ cubit and a 9″ span). If some alteration is in play here and not a simple scribal error (in anticipation of the שש in v. 7; see comment in McCarter 1980, 286), then obviously the change would have been in the direction of inflating Goliath's height.

223. I.e., over 125 pounds (i.e., assuming a .025-pound shekel).

(וְעֵץ)[224] of his spear was like a weaver's beam used for weaving. The tip of his spear was 600 shekels of iron,[225] and a shield-bearer went before him. (8) He stood and called out to the ranks of Israel and said to them, "Why do you come out to arrange (yourselves) for war—am I not a Philistine, and you are servants of Saul? Choose (בְּרוּ)[226] for yourselves a man and let him come down to me! (9) If he is able to fight me and strike me down, we will be your servants—but if I am able (to prevail) against him, and I strike him down, then you will become our servants, and you will serve us!" (10) Moreover, the Philistine said: "I challenge the ranks of Israel this day—give me a man so that we can fight each other!" (11) Saul and all Israel heard these words of the Philistine, and they were dismayed and very afraid.

In 1 Samuel 17 we find one of the most famous scenes in the Bible, beginning here with the arrogant war taunts of a giant and culminating with David's memorable victory in vv. 49–51 (translated and discussed below).[227] Of several issues pertaining to Goliath's status as a giant in this passage, we may begin with the question of height, as 2 Sam 17:4 gives us a rare piece of data in the biblical corpus, viz., the exact height of an individual (see also 1 Chr 11:23. As is well known (and noted above), the Masoretic Text records Goliath's height שֵׁשׁ אַמּוֹת וָזָרֶת, "six cubits and a span" (roughly nine and a half feet), whereas the Greek traditions—supported by perhaps the oldest scroll from Qumran, 4QSam[a]—give us *four* cubits and a span, reducing the height by some three feet. One is tempted to say that, either way, Goliath is a "giant," and yet the difference between these two heights is enormous. The Masoretic Text's Goliath is an unhuman monster, a freak beyond any actual dimensions known for any person of any period, while the Greek Goliath would be a tall but realistic human.[228]

---

224. Following the *qere* here; *kethib* is וחץ ("arrow").

225. Around 15 pounds.

226. The root is ברר "select" (see *BDB*, 140), and is vocalized as such here (as opposed to MT's בְּרוּ; so also McCarter 1980, 287; Driver (1890, 140) unnecessarily emends to בחרו).

227. I have chosen to reproduce and translate only the portions of the long scene in 1 Samuel 17 in which Goliath himself speaks and in which David directly engages with Goliath (vv. 1–11 and 40–54), with the exception of vv. 16 and 23, which refer to previous action in vv. 1–11. For more detailed text-critical treatment on the 1 Samuel 17 text, see especially *DJD* XII; Driver 1890, 137–48; McCarter 1980, 284–98; and Hutton 2009, 245–69, dealing particularly with the source-critical problems. 17:12–31 and 17:55–18:5 are absent in Vaticanus, and thus possibly absent in the earliest Greek and Hebrew editions. On this problem, see the brief but clear comments in Hertzberg 1964, 146–47.

228. Put another way, the issue might be framed like this: in the Greek tradition, David would certainly have been noticeably shorter than Goliath—to the point where there would have been a significant power differential—but their respective heights would be comparable to the difference in size between a large and a small fully grown person in any society. In the MT, David's head would only reach to Goliath's stomach. In a 1958 letter exchange between F.

Is Goliath a "giant" in the MT? The question, then, is whether Goliath qualifies for the title "giant" at all, especially if one does defend the title with the commonly made statement that a six-foot-nine Goliath would have seemed extremely tall to an Israelite measuring five and a half feet in height and weighing around 150 pounds.[229] But the issue of Goliath's height is not merely a text-critical issue to be decided on the basis of competing textual witnesses, but also a rare window into ancient Israelite thinking regarding the actual physical height of giants. Let us recall that we have no indication (from the biblical period itself) on how tall the Israelite authors of Numbers or Deuteronomy thought the Anaqim or Rephaim actually were. I would argue, however, that Goliath does fit into the category of the giant as I am using it throughout this study, in that he is clearly marked as an individual of extraordinary height who takes on political, psychological, moral, and theological characteristics of otherness, depravity, and the grotesque. Moreover, the clearly attested way the Masoretic Text (and other textual traditions) dealt with Goliath's height in exaggerating it was probably *not* due to a situation wherein the authors thought four cubits and a span was not tall enough for David to appear as a "giant" killer. Rather, the inflation is from one generically magnificent height to another—analogous perhaps to saying that one warrior killed many thousands of enemies but another killed many tens of thousands (when, in fact, to kill even one thousand enemies is an unrealistic feat for a single warrior in any era). Thus, the likely original height of "four cubits and a span" perhaps becomes inadvertently underwhelming when one translates it into an exact feet-and-inches measurement and then considers that measurement in terms either of modern or of ancient humans. Rather, the description is simply meant to convey utter enormity, and this is the effect in the Masoretic, Greek, and Qumran traditions.

The name Goliath and the armor of the giant. Another striking issue involves the very name "Goliath" (גלית), which is not of Semitic origin; indeed, there are a series of terms in this pericope that may betray some difference in language

---

M. Cross and P. W. Skehan involving the base text of Samuel to be used for the *New American Bible*, Skehan said: "...if I chose MT's 'nine and a half feet', it would be because on that reading every hearer would know the kind of story he was dealing with; now the villain couldn't even play [professional] basketball'" (quoted in *DJD* XII, 79). Skehan's point is revealing: an audience, whether ancient or modern, must know the "kind of story" it is hearing or reading, and those who elevated Goliath's height in the textual traditions followed by the MT perhaps wanted to drive this point home more obviously. Of course, it should also be conceded that we are not dealing with exact measurements when speaking in cubits and spans, and any translation of an ancient measurement of this kind into modern terms is speculative. As Halpern (2000, 8 n. 4) points out, a different cubit measurement (the "long cubit") would still result in an eight-foot Goliath in the MT.

229. E.g., Kellermann 1990.

between the Israelites and Philistines.[230] The name Goliath seems to have an Anatolian etymology, the evidence of which appears in the terminative -*yat* element (Hittite -*wattaš*; cf. Lydian -*uattes*).[231] Repeatedly throughout these first eleven verses in the chapter, however, and again in vv. 40–54, David's opponent is not called Goliath—in fact, the name is only mentioned in vv. 4 and 23, whereas fifteen times he is called הפלשתי, "the Philistine."[232] This fact led a number of interpreters to the conclusion that the name Goliath was added to the account in order to attribute to David a victory that had originally belonged to another, lesser known figure (Elhanan; discussed below). This explanation is a likely one, though it is not unreasonable to assume that the name Goliath was inserted into an existing tradition recording David's victory in some duel.[233]

The narrator's detailed description of Goliath moves beyond the giant's height and name and into the realm of his weaponry and strategic place in the Philistine military system. First, we find the giant proposing a strategy for which he would presumably be well suited, single combat of the type known elsewhere in the Hebrew Bible and especially in the Mycenaean world (e.g., as represented most vividly in the *Iliad*, but also in Anatolia and the ancient Near East).[234] Goliath is described as the איש הבנים (17:4,23), literally "the man in between," a unique designation to this story that most likely refers to Goliath's status as a champion in one-on-one battles (note v. 51: גבורם, "their Gibbor/champion")—i.e., he is literally the man who comes out from his camp and goes in between the ranks to face an opponent who will do the same.[235] Very much effort has been expended in either defending or deny-

---

230. As in the *Iliad* and *Odyssey*, or many modern movies, opponents from far-flung regions in the Bible always seem to understand one another's language. Nevertheless, the narrator may have encoded something of the difference in language in the 1 Samuel 17 encounter via the accurate transcription of names or other technical terms (e.g., the rare or otherwise unattested words for Goliath's armament). See Machinist 2000a, 63–64 on this point, with examples. Some of the terminology in vv. 5–7 seems to be non-Semitic (קובע, שרין קשקשים); see McCarter 1980, 291–93.

231. McCarter 1980, 291. The presumed Lydian name would be *Aluattes* < Greek **Walweiattes* (Machinist 2000a, 63). The excavators of Gath (Tell eṣ-Ṣâfî) believe they have found an ostracon with the possible PN *ʾlwt*, though they caution against identifying the name with the biblical Goliath. See Maeir, Wimmer, Zukerman, and Demsky 2008, but cf. the criticism of Cross and Stager 2006, 151–52.

232. See vv. 10, 11, 16, 23, 40, 41, 42, 43 (2x), 44, 45, 48, 49, 50, 51; הפלשתי הזה in vv. 26, 32, 33, 36, 37.

233. So McCarter 1980, 291.

234. E.g., 2 Samuel 2:12–17, where a small group of warriors engages in one-on-one war games. See Machinist 2000a, 59 and 72 n. 34.

235. In fact, this meaning is alluded to at the end of v. 3, where a valley stood "between them" (והגיא ביניהם). Cf. McCarter (1980, 290–91), who translates the phrase as "a certain infantryman," citing its meaning at Qumran as a term for one involved in battle.

ing—mostly in defending—the historical realism encoded in the description of Goliath's gear as an authentic set of early Iron Age weaponry, and perhaps the best one can say is that the odd terminology in vv. 5–7 is unlikely to have been invented by someone living at an extreme distance from Iron Age contexts when such equipment could have been plausibly described.[236]

The nature of Goliath's weaponry may reveal real historical memories of Philistine warriors in the early Iron Age, but this is of course accidental to the purpose of the narrator.[237] The description of armor is about *otherness*, about power, and the frightening quality of the monster. His gear, in addition to his size, is meant to invoke an aura of overconfidence that comes as the result of reliance on brute force alone. Perhaps the most poignant example of this comes in vv. 5 and 7, were specific weights for the scaled body armor and the spearhead are given. As with Goliath's height, the measurements here are less than exact, but the 5,000-shekel (= 125 pounds?) armor and the 600-shekel (15 pounds?) spearhead invoke nothing less than terrifying strength. The giant is essentially wearing and carrying a weight of metals that is heavier than his ruddy young opponent; indeed, the contrast between the two men could hardly be greater than it appears in 17:38–39, when David finds himself ill-suited to wear the armor (שריון) of Saul,[238] and chooses to face Goliath with no bodily protection whatsoever and armed only with a sling.

> **1 Sam 17:40–54** (v. 40) He took his staff in his hand and he chose
> for himself five smooth stones from the wadi, and he put them in
> his shepherd's bag, into the pouch. His sling was in his hand, and he
> approached the Philistine. (41) The Philistine went and approached David,

236. Assuming, of course, that the weaponry is, in fact, normal for an early Iron Age context and not normal for later periods. None of this would necessarily mean that the account is historically accurate—but it may rule out a very late (Persian or Hellenistic) context for the composition of the text. The same argument is made for the biblical descriptions of the Philistines generally by Stager (2006). The most recent reviews of the arguments for and against the historicity of the David and Goliath battle on the basis of the description of Goliath's armor can be found in A. Yadin 2004 and Millard 2009 (Yadin himself opts against historicity, while Millard is for it).

237. See Zorn (2010) and King (2007), both of whom argue in some way for accurate historical recollection in the description of Goliath.

238. Though Saul would seem not to qualify as a giant, he is famously distinguished by his stature. In 1 Sam 9:2, his distinction as being a man like no other among the Israelites is immediately qualified by a comment about his height (i.e., he is a head taller than everyone else). Saul's engagement in ecstatic speech and other tormented mental states (1 Sam 10:10, 18:10, 19:23–24), combined with the issue of his physical status, at least gestures toward the presentation of cultural oddity or otherness often embodied in the giant. At least one interpreter (Mobley 2006, 81) has appropriately pointed to the issue of Saul's stature as a heroic attribute, marked in contrast to David's status as הקטן ("the youngest," or possibly also, by implication, "smallest/shortest") in 1 Sam 17:14.

with the man bearing the shield before him.[239] (42) The Philistine looked
and saw David, and he disdained him, for he was only a boy, ruddy and
attractive in appearance. (43) Then the Philistine said to David, "Am I a
dog, that you come at me with sticks?"[240] And the Philistine cursed David
by his gods. (44) The Philistine said to David, "Come to me, and I will give
your flesh to the birds of the heavens and to the beasts of the field!" (45)
But David said to the Philistine: "You come at me with sword and spear
and javelin, but I come at you in the name of YHWH of Hosts, God of the
ranks of Israel—whom you challenge. (46) This day YHWH will deliver you
over to my hand and I will strike you down and I will cut off your head
from upon you, and I will give the corpses of the camp of the Philistines
this day to the birds of the air and the beasts of the land, and all the land
will know that there is a God in Israel. (47) And all this assembly will know
that YHWH does not save by sword or spear—but the battle is YHWH's,
and he will give you into our hand." (48) When the Philistine rose up and
went and drew near to meet David, David rushed quickly toward the battle
line to meet the Philistine. (49) David put his hand into the bag and he
took from there a stone, and he slung and struck the Philistine on the
forehead.[241] The stone sank into his forehead and he fell upon his face to
the ground. (50) David was stronger than the Philistine with just a sling
and a stone, and he struck the Philistine and killed him—there was no
sword in David's hand.[242] (51) Then David ran and stood over the Philistine
and took his sword and drew it out from its sheath and killed him, and
then cut off his head with it. (52) When the Philistines saw that their
champion was dead, they fled. The men of Israel and Judah rose up with
a shout and they pursued the Philistines until you come into the valley,[243]
as far as the gates of 'Eqron. The slain Philistines fell on the road from
Sha'araim all the way to Gath and 'Eqron. (53) The sons of Israel returned
from pursuing after the Philistines, and they plundered their camp. (54)

239. This entire verse is missing in Vaticanus.

240. The Greek (B) here has an extra phrase spoken by David: ...ἐν ῥάβδῳ καί λίθοις καὶ
εἶπεν Δαυιδ οὐχί ἀλλ' ἢ χείρω κυνός ("'...with a stick and stones?' And David said, 'No—actually
worse than a dog.'"), a reading also attested in Josephus (Ant. VI.186). McCarter (1980, 289)
finds the shorter reading preferable, and Driver (1890, 146) seems to agree that this "singu-
larly vapid reply" of David is an addition. It is difficult, however, to imagine why the Greek
would expand here if the phrase was not in its Vorlage.

241. The Greek is very likely expansive here in its addition of διέδυ ὁ λίθος διὰ τῆς
περικεφαλαίας εἰς τὸ μέτωπον αὐτοῦ ("the stone slipped through the helmet into his forehead"), recalling the fact that Goliath was wearing a helmet earlier in v. 5 and assuming this
helmet would have covered his forehead.

242. This entire verse is missing in Vaticanus.

243. Greek has Γεθ ("Gath"), which is followed by most commentators (e.g., McCarter
1980, 290; Driver 1890, 147; Hertzberg 1964, 145).

Then David took the head of the Philistine and brought it to Jerusalem, but he placed his (Goliath's) gear in his (David's) tent.

Goliath is the only giant who speaks in the Hebrew Bible. The notorious hubris of the giant as a cultural type is used here toward presenting the Philistine in a state of full-blown arrogance;[244] in vv. 8–10, Goliath begins the war taunt (חרף) with the challenge to a duel, the intimidating nature of which provokes only fear in the Israelite hearers (v. 11). When David accepts the challenge, Goliath responds with derision and even humor (vv. 43–44). David's long prologue speech to the fight itself emphasizes the supremacy of YHWH over all enemies, and he proves the point with a well-slung stone.

A fair fight? B. Halpern's reading of the battle in terms of military strategy is that David's actions represent "a blow below the belt, a sucker punch, a man with a howitzer mowing down a peasant with a pitchfork." In this view, Goliath is essentially immobilized by the massive weight of his armor, and expects David to draw near (v. 44) where the giant can crush him. Instead, David "declines to abide by the rules, and fights from outside the ring," flinging a stone at the defenseless ogre.[245] This reading, however clever it may be, runs against the grain of the story, as the author clearly revels in the fact that David defeated the giant with *inferior* weapons and tactics (v. 50). Perhaps it is only the weapons that are inferior, but the point of the narrative is that it is YHWH who delivers over the giant—even as David himself benefits immensely in terms of the personal prestige his victory brings.

Goliath and cult. One additional issue bears mentioning for our purposes here. In. v. 47, David declares that "all this assembly (קהל) will know that YHWH does not save by sword or spear." The Hebrew קהל, as a noun or a verb, could certainly indicate a mundane gathering of people (e.g., Gen 28:3; Ezek 26:7), but the word more often connotes a *sacred* assembly, i.e., the people assembled as a religio-political body for covenant renewal, religious action, and sacred instruction.[246] In fact, the presence of קהל in v. 47, along with the styl-

---

244. The gigantism of Goliath made him a symbol of pride in the early church as well, e.g., for Paulus Orosius (*Defense Against the Pelagians*): "Yet there stands Goliath, monstrous in his pride, swollen with earthly power, confident that he can do everything by himself..." Quote taken from Franke 2005, 4:266.

245. Halpern 2001, 12–13. Halpern goes on to say that "This is the pattern that will persist throughout his [David's] history. He is not just Yahweh's elect: he is Yahweh's avenger. He is not just destined for greatness: he shapes his greatness by a complete disregard for orthodoxy."

246. E.g., Exod 12:6, 35:1; Lev 4:21; Num 8:9; Deut 5:22, 31:12; Judg 20:1; 1 Kgs 8:55; Neh 5:13, etc. Military gatherings, as in 1 Sam 17:47, are another instance where an assembly is called a קהל (Num 22:4; Ezek 16:40, 38:15), but this is not the most common use of the term. See Fabry, Hossfeld, and Kindl 2003, XII: 546–61.

ized and symbolic nature of the scene and David's speech mentioning "all the earth" (כל הארץ; v. 46), may indicate that this particular story was retold in community settings or at local cult sites.[247] Hertzberg endorsed this view, and a more radical formulation of the cultic nature of the story was made by J. Grønbaek, who drew the Goliath battle into a Mowinckelian concept of a New Year's drama, with the figure of Goliath serving as a historical, human representative of the forces of chaos that must be defeated in the annual drama.[248]

This notion of Goliath in connection to some cult recital or ritual is not entirely speculative, since there are several clues in this story and elsewhere that suggest just such a context.[249] After the plundering of the camp at the end of the present story, David returns to the battle scene to gather up the head of the giant, which is brought to Jerusalem, and Goliath's gear (כלי, i.e., armor, sword, etc.), which is placed in David's own tent. One can only speculate as to the role the skull and weaponry might have played in these respective settings beyond mere "symbolic" trophies of the encounter, but it is certainly possible that such relics could have been preserved as charged cultic items utilized in some fashion.[250] Indeed, we learn only a few chapters later in 1 Sam 21:2-10 that Goliath's sword made its way to the Nob sanctuary—either by action not narrated in the book of Samuel, or, more likely, in an alternative tradition placing the object at that site instead of Jerusalem.[251] Furthermore, in 1 Sam 21:10 the Nob priest reveals that the sword is "wrapped in a cloth, behind the ephod" (לוטה בשמלה אחרי האפוד), apparently a place of special importance behind the sanctuary's central cultic object.[252] Thus, we see a tantalizing glimpse of the giant's potential role

247. I came to this line of interpretation via the brief reference in Hertzberg 1964, 152, and more fully via McCarter 1980, 296-97. See also Hertzberg 1929.

248. Grønbaek 1971, 94-95. Grønbaek specifically assets that Goliath is "Verkörperung und Historifikation der Chaosmacht." The New Year's festival thesis is spelled out in detail in Grønbaek 1957 and mentioned in Grønbaek 1971, 95. Though the specific relevance for a hypothetical New Year's festival is highly speculative, the notion that the figure of Goliath could act as a *Chaosmacht* is compelling and comports nicely with my assertion that the giants acted as embodiments of recurring chaos.

249. Recall also the argument of Andersen and Freedman (1989, 325-26) regarding the status of Amos 2:9-11, which mentions a defeat of indigenous giants as part of a "ritual recitation" at the Bethel cult shrine. Such an interpretation lacks any firm evidence, however interesting it may be.

250. On the significance of heroic relics in such contexts in the Greek world, see McCauley 1999.

251. Note that in 1 Sam 21:10, David's battle with Goliath is integrated into the narrative about the sanctuary, as the priest refers to Goliath as "the one whom you [David] struck down in the Valley of Elah" (אשר הכית בעמק האלה).

252. The אפוד here is most certainly a solid object, such as a divine statue or the ark (and not a cloth, e.g., Exod 25:7; 1 Sam 2:18). See Van Der Toorn and Houtman 1994, 217, 219 n. 35.

in cult, perhaps acting as a counter-figure to YHWH in some dramatic role or providing charged objects that may have been invested with numinous power.

David's Men Battle the Descendants of Raphah

Apart from the Goliath episode we find a short résumé at the end of 2 Samuel containing several specific battles fought by David's men with certain "descendants of the Raphah" in Gath:

> **2 Sam 21:15–22** (15) The Philistines again made war with Israel. So David went down, his servants with him, and they made war with the Philistines. David grew weary. (16) Ishbi (ישבי)[253]-Benob—who was of the descendants of Raphah (בילידי הרפה),[254] whose spear weighed three hundred shekels of bronze, and he was also girded with new (weapons)[255]—said he would kill David. (17) But Abishai son of Seruyah came to rescue him, and he struck down the Philistine and he killed him. Then the men of David swore to him, saying, "You should not go out anymore with us to fight, lest you snuff out the lamp of Israel." (18) Afterwards there was another battle at Gob with the Philistines; then Sibbekai the Hushathite struck down Saph (סף),[256] who is of the descendants of the Raphah (בילידי הרפה). (19) Then there was another battle at Gob with the Philistines, and Elhanan son of Ya'are-Oregim the Beth-Lehemite struck down Goliath the Gittite (גלית הגתי)—the shaft of his spear was like a weaver's beam. (20) There was then another battle, at Gath, and there was a violent individual (איש מדון)[257] (with) six fingers and six toes on (each of) his hands and feet, twenty–four

253. Reading with the *qere*, instead of the *kethib* (ישבו). Note that McCarter (1984, 448) attempts to repair this verse by inserting a "displaced marginal plus" in the Greek (placed before v. 11 in L, and after v. 11 in B and A) into v. 15: καὶ ἐξελύθησαν καὶ κατέλαβεν αὐτοὺς Δαν υἱὸς Ιωα ἐκ τῶν ἀπογόνων τῶν γιγάντων ("…and they were released, and Dan, son of Ioa from the descendants of the giants, took them down"). The context in v. 11 refers to the sons of Saul that had been hung on a mountain to avenge Saul's earlier crimes. I am ambivalent about McCarter's suggestion here and thus leave the text as it stands in the MT. Driver (1890, 353) thinks the correct reading is וישבו בגב ("and lived in Gob") is the correct reading. This passage, like so many others in Samuel, bristles with textual problems that cannot be solved here. See the brief portion of the text in 4QSamᵃ in *DJD* XII, 179–80 (but with no major solutions for our passage).

254. The Greek translates ילידי הרפה, here and in v. 18, as ἐκγόνοις τοῦ Ραφα.

255. See McCarter 1984, 448, which cites a vast number of variants here, all apparently an attempt to interpret what "new" (חדשה) means here. I take the word to refer to newly made weaponry, as opposed to older (and thus less effective?) gear.

256. The name סף may refer to a "threshold" (e.g., Judg 19:27; 2 Kgs 23:4) as a sturdy or prominent architectural feature—i.e., "Saph" is a huge man.

257. Lit. "a man of strife" (*qere*). *Kethib* is מדין ("Midian"), which makes no sense here. Cf. איש מדון in Jer 15:10; Prov 26:21; cf. Ps 80:7. See also infra in 1 Chr 20:5. Greek has ἀνὴρ Μαδων.

(total) in number, and he was also descended from the Raphah (ילד להרפה).[258] (21) When he taunted Israel, Yehonatan son of Shimei brother of David struck him down. (22) These four were descended from the Rapha (ילדו להרפה)[259] in Gath, and they fell by the hand of David and the hand of his servants.

Are the "descendants of Raphah" giants? One initial question here of importance is whether these "the descendants of Rapha" (ילידי הרפה) or the "violent individual" (איש מדון) can be properly considered "giants." The issue is not conclusive, but we might first point out that already within the period of the composition of the biblical texts authors saw them this way. In 1 Chr 20:4–8,[260] which reproduces elements of 2 Sam 21:15–22, we find the author attempting in two specific instances to tie these descendants of Rapha into the biblical network of giants:

1 Chr 20:4–8 (v. 4) After this war broke out in Gezer[261] with the Philistines; then Sibbekai the Hushathite struck down Sippai (ספי),[262] one of the descendants of the Rephaim (מילדי הרפאים),[263] and they [the Philistines] were subdued. (5) And there was again war with the Philistines, and Elhanan son of Ya'ir struck down Lahmi, brother of Goliath the Gittite (לחמי אחי גלית הגתי)—the shaft of his spear was like a weaver's beam. (6) Again there was war in Gath, and there was a giant man (איש מדה)[264] (with) six digits (on each of his hands and feet),[265] twenty-four (total), and he was also descended from the Raphah (נולד להרפא).[266] (7) When he taunted Israel, Yehonatan son of Shim'a brother of David struck him down. (8)

258. Greek ἐτέχθη τῷ Ραφα ("he was born to Rapha").

259. Greek ἀπόγονοι τῶν γιγάντων ("offspring of the giants"). The Greek translation here is idiosyncratic, since the rendering had been Ραφα (and not γίγας) in every case up to this point in this section. The translation of "giants" here seems to summarize the group as giants.

260. For commentary, see R. Klein 2006, 409–13; Knoppers 2004, 728–42; Japhet 1993, 366–69; and Myers 1965a, 134–35, 141–42. Note also the text-critical and other comments on this passage and 2 Sam 21:15–22 in Ehrlich 1996, 126–32.

261. Cf. 2 Sam 21:18, בגוב.

262. Probably a variant spelling of the name סף in 2 Sam 21:18 (so Knoppers 2003, 731). Greek has variants such as Σαφουτ (S), Σαφου (B), Ζαφι, etc.

263. This is the only location in this passage and 2 Samuel 21 where רפאים is written out as a plural, as opposed to the singular רפה/רפא (which may be related to רפאים). Greek τῶν υἱῶν τῶν γιγάντων. Knoppers (2004, 731) notes that several Hebrew mss. have הרפא here (in anticipation of vv. 6 and 8; 2 Sam 21:18 הרפה). See also R. Klein 2006, 409–13 here and for the following verses.

264. Cf. with 2 Sam 21:20, איש מדין (*kethib*), איש מדון (*qere*). See note on 2 Sam 21:20 supra. Greek here in 1 Chr 20:6 has ἀνὴρ ὑπερμεγέθης ("a gigantic man").

265. The passage here does not mention hands or feet specifically, as does 2 Sam 21:20, only the "fingers" that are "six and six."

266. Greek ἀπόγονος γιγάντων.

These were descended from the Raphah (נולדו להרפא)[267] in Gath, and they fell by the hand of David and by the hand of his servants.

Here the Chronicler makes two major interpretive moves of note:[268] (1) Sippai/Saph (סף/ספי) is said to be from the "descendants of the Rephaim" (ילידי הרפאים), instead of the "descendants of Rapha" (ילידי הרפה); by inserting the term Rephaim here in 1 Chr 20:4, the Chronicler assumes that these figures are connected with the giant Rephaim, and also that the term "Rapha" (הרפה) is etymologically related to the Rephaim. (2) The איש מדון ("violent individual") of 2 Sam 21:20 is transformed into an איש מדה, "a giant man," in 1 Chr 20:6.[269] Neither of these interpretations proves that the authors of the 2 Samuel 21 pericope as it was first written viewed any of the Philistine opponents as giants specifically, but the Chronicler's treatment does suggest that, for ancient readers as early as the sixth–fifth centuries BCE, these figures were considered giants. It must also be remembered that in Josh 11:22, the Anaqim are relegated to three Philistine cities, Gath being one of them, and thus the existence of giant beings in Gath—including, of course, Goliath—makes sense in coordination with the descendants of Rapha in 2 Samuel 21 // 1 Chronicles 20.[270]

Considered apart from the interpretive matrix of 1 Chr 20:4–8, however, the identity of the enemies from Gath in 2 Sam 21:15–22 is far more ambiguous. Until the mid-twentieth century, scholars generally assumed "Rapha" was connected with the ethnic designation Rephaim, and that the

267. Greek ἐγένοντο Ραφα. It is not clear why the Greek translators transliterate the term here instead of rendering it as γίγας as in v. 6. Note also that the Greek here has an expansion in most mss. after οὗτοι ἐγένοντο Ραφα ἐν Γεθ, adding, πάντες ἦσαν τέσσαρες γίγαντες ("all these four were giants")—though there are only three individuals mentioned in 1 Chr 20:4–8 (2 Sam 21, on the other hand, mentions four). Perhaps the summary was meant to assimilate the passage here to the 2 Samuel 21 account, while also interpreting the enigmatic references to הרפא as being essentially equal to רפאים (= γίγαντες). See the suggestions in Knoppers 2004, 732–33.

268. Moreover, there are other, subtler indicators that the Chronicler sought to "correct" the 2 Samuel 21 passage: the ב preposition in 2 Sam 21:16 (בילידי) has been changed to מ (i.e., מילידי) in 1 Chr 20:4, perhaps better indicating genealogical derivation (compare with Num 13:33); the qal passive ילד of 2 Sam 21:20 has been turned into a niphal perfect, יולדו, in 1 Chr 20:8; and the form הרפה, used in 2 Samuel 21, is changed to הרפא in 1 Chr 20:6,8 (presumably to align this word with the spelling רפאים in 1 Chr 20:4). Given the fact that all three of these changes involve the רפה/רפא designation, one may well suspect that the Chronicler wanted so solidify the identity of these individuals as giants.

269. Cf. Num 13:32, אנשי מדות; based on this reference and 1 Chr 20:6, one is tempted to emend 2 Sam 21:20 to איש מדה also, though the fact that איש מדון is an attested phrase elsewhere with a relatively clear meaning prevents this.

270. On this point, see also Na'aman (2005b, 361), who notes a potential conflation between the ילידי הרפא and the בני/ילידי הענק based on Josh 11:21–22, since the Anaqim driven out of the hill country found a home in Gaza, Gath, and Ashdod.

phrase "the descendants of Rapha" indicated genealogical derivation from
the Rephaim. However, two articles by F. Willesen in 1958 challenged this
view.[271] Citing what he saw as parallel instances of the noun יְלִיד (*yālîd*) as a
term for adoption in the Abraham narratives (e.g., Gen 14:14, 17:12,23, etc.)
and elsewhere, Willesen asserted that the construct ילידי ("descendants of")
is "a quite exceptional way of expressing a family relationship." Instead, he
argued, the phrase "the descendants of Rapha" (ילידי הרפה)—as well as "the
descendants of Anaq," (ילידי הענק; Num 13:28; Josh 15:14)—denoted "members
of a special band of well trained, presumably professional warriors of slave
status."[272] Willeson went on to argue more specifically that הרפה (*hā-rāpāh*)
was a specific symbol of an elite fighting force in Gath whose symbol was the
scimitar (equivalent to the Greek ἅρπη, which Willesen thought was cognate to *hprh*).[273] Nearly twenty years later, C. L'Heureux tackled the problem
and correctly pointed out the tendentious nature of Willeson's arguments,
though he agreed that *hā-rāpāh* did not signify an ethnic identity. Rather,
L'Heureux argued for the identity of רפה/רפא as a divine epithet, similar to
rp', the patron of warriors from Ugarit.[274]

In fact, Willesen's argument is faulty for reasons beyond the speculative
Greek ἅρπη etymology. Willeson gives little weight to the fairly regular use
of the *qal* passive of ילד ("be bear") in many instances to denote genealogical derivation, and thus the use of ילד in this way in 2 Sam 21:20 would not
be unexpected or odd.[275] The form ילידי as a construct noun, "those born
of/descended from...," utilizing the root ילד, would admittedly be peculiar
but is not incomprehensible. The contrast Willeson draws between "sons
of" (בני) and "descendants of" (ילידי), moreover, is disrupted somewhat in
Numbers 13, where ילידי הענק (vv. 22 and 28) appears alongside בני ענק. The
form ילידי does appear here in Numbers 13, as elsewhere, followed by the
definite article, though this may have been some fixed formulation wherein
the ה indicates a class of individuals or some unusual way of rendering a
proper name. Thus I do not follow Willesen's arguments, but rather suggest

271. Willesen 1958a; 1958b.
272. Willesen 1958b, 195, 198.
273. Willeson 1958a, 331. The initial ה in הרפה, then, is part of the root, not the definite
article (note 2 Sam 21:20,22, להרפה). Along these lines, note the solution of Japhet 1993, 367,
who reads הרפה as a *matronym*, the name of a mother named הרפה.
274. L'Heureux 1976, 83–85. McCarter (1984, 450) follows L'Heureux. Becking (1999),
along with L'Heurex (1976) and McCarter (1984), sees הרפה as a simple variant of הרפא. Becking also points to the Greek of Amos 5:26, which has Ραιφαν (reflecting רפא?) instead of כיון.
275. Cf. Gen 4:26, 6:1, 10:21,25, 24:15, 41:50, 46:22; 2 Sam 3:5; Isa 9:5; Jer 20:14; Pss 87:5,6,
90:2; Job 5:7; Ruth 4:17; 1 Chr 1:10. Willesen (1958a; 1958b) downplays some of these examples,
and fails to mention others.

"Rapha" should be read as an equivalent designation for Rephaim (i.e., as an "ethnic" indicator).[276] But the problem is a difficult one.

Two Goliaths. The most notorious problem in 2 Samuel 21 // 1 Chronicles 20 involves a variant tradition for the killing of Goliath the "Gittite" in 2 Sam 21:19. In 2 Sam 21:19, Elhanan kills "Goliath the Gittite," whereas in 1 Samuel 17, it is David who kills "Goliath from Gath." Presumably, a "Gittite" is a resident of Gath in Philistia (cf. 2 Sam 6:10,11, 15:19,22, 18:2; 1 Chr 13:13, 20:5), and this is the same Goliath as the Goliath from Gath (גלית שמו מגת) in 1 Samuel 17. If so, the tradition in 1 Samuel 17 attributes a heroic deed to David, which, in fact, had earlier been achieved by Elhanan. This problem was recognized by the Chronicler, who wrought a simple solution: Elhanan killed a certain Lahmi, *brother* of Goliath.[277] The Chronicler apparently enacted his alteration with full knowledge that his readers had access to the version in Samuel where David kills Goliath; otherwise there is no point in asserting Elhanan killed the brother of Goliath at all (i.e., there is no reason to deal with Goliath in any way, since the David and Goliath duel is not recorded in Chronicles).[278] There is a venerable history to the harmonizing explanation that David and Elhanan were one and the same, i.e., that David was a throne name and Elhanan a personal name for the same shepherd boy king, but this solution cannot be accepted.[279]

The prestige associated with the slaying of a giant was apparently too great to waste on a relatively anonymous individual like Elhanan, even though he is given brief credit for two (different) heroic acts in 2 Samuel 21 and 1 Chronicles 20. On the most basic level, the movement we have witnessed here from the conquest narratives and other material in Numbers,

276. So also Knoppers 2004, 732, 735; Driver 1890, 353–54.

277. I.e., in 2 Sam 21:19, it is Elhanan, "Son of Ya'are Oregim, the Bethlehemite (= the Lahamite house)," and the Chronicler straightens this out to "Elhanan" killing "Lahmi." The Targ. to 2 Sam 21:19 (as well as 1 Chr 20:5) conflates Elhanan and David. On the problem generally, see, e.g., McCarter 1984, 450; Knoppers 2004, 736–37. As Knoppers (2004, 736) correctly argues, there is no reason to assume the Chronicler made this statement on the basis of his *Vorlage*—it is a straightforward harmonization, along the lines of the treatment of Josiah's Passover celebration in 2 Chr 35:13.

278. One wonders why the David and Goliath story was not included in Chronicles, as it might have nicely supplemented the Chronicler's overarching theological and historiographic program. Then again, it may not have; note the statements in 1 Chronicles (22:8 and 28:3) regarding David's status as warrior, whereby David is disqualified from building the Temple. Perhaps the Chronicler sought to suppress what he saw as gratuitous references to these exploits in order to elevate David's priestly role.

279. See Böttcher (1863, 235), who is often credited as the first critic of the modern era to propose the David = Elhanan solution. Other twentieth-century scholars took up this solution as well, e.g., Honeyman 1948.

Deuteronomy, and Joshua, to the exploits of David and his mighty men is an important one: giant enemies in the land continually re-appear, and the vanquishing of these giants continues to serve, at least on the surface, as a narrative device validating the status of the Israelite warrior and his deity, YHWH.

But in the case of David, the prominence of the Goliath episode takes on a richer tone. The growth of the Goliath tradition, first attributed to the unknown Elhanan and later applied to Israel's greatest king, demonstrates the important symbolic capital attached to the act of giant killing. David's ascension to the throne of Israel must, on all symbolic levels, involve a defeat of unruly forces, of chaos, and of all disorder. Along these lines, the giants in 1 Samuel 17 and 2 Samuel 21 // 1 Chronicles 20 are graphic representations of the monster of disorder, in sum, the embodiment of everything uncontrollable that a nation and king cannot tolerate alive in its midst.[280] At each stage in which we have had occasion to encounter him, the giant appears at points of significant cosmic and political change: at the end of the antediluvian world and the beginning of a new covenant culminating with Noah's descendant, Abram; at the end of the occupation of the land by the Canaanites and the beginning of Israel's possession; and at the end of a leaderless—or inadequately led—nation in its infancy, on the brink of acquiring its ideal king.

The Lion and the Egyptian Giant. Another explicit reference to a giant in the notices regarding David's mighty men occurs in 1 Chr 11:22–25.[281] A heroic individual named Benaiah son of Jehoiada slays a lion and then a large man:

1 Chr 11:22–23 (v. 22) Benaiah son of Jehoiada (בניה בן יהוירע) was a man of valor (בן איש חיל) (and) a worker of great deeds (רב פעלים) from Qabzeel. He struck down two (sons?) of Ariel of Moab.[282] And he went down into a

---

280. The identity between the giants and the Philistines (either directly or via the cities they are said to inhabit) further serves to reinforce the fact that, during the monarchy, the Philistines are the quintessential "giant," the foreign monster that must be resisted and elimated to secure a prosperous nation. This point comports well with Machinist's conclusion that "the Philistines emerge in their biblical conception as a major symbol of that which Israel is not, or at least should not be; and while this is most impressive in the treatment of the Iron I period, it reverberates through the other periods as well" (Machinist 2000a, 67). See also the brief comments in R. Gordon (2006, 165) on the conflation between the Philistines, Anaqim, and giants, and the symbolic meaning of this association (along the lines of what I am suggesting here).

281. See the brief note by Lemardelé (2010a) on the connection between warriors and lions in this passage.

282. The name "Ariel" (אריאל) seems to contain within it one of the Hebrew words for "lion" (אריה/ארי), perhaps indicating some kind of wordplay with the defeat of the lion in the pit. Note the King James Version: "...he slew two lionlike men of Moab..." See Japhet 1993, 247–48; R. Klein 2006, 305–06.

pit and struck down a lion on a snowy day. (v. 23) And he struck down an Egyptian man (המצרי את האיש), a giant man (איש מרה), five cubits tall.[283] In the hand of the Egyptian was a weaver's beam (כמנור ארגים); he went against (וירד) him with a staff, and snatched the spear from the hand of the Egyptian and killed him with his own spear.

There is, as we might expect, a parallel passage in 2 Sam 23:20–23, but here the Egyptian is not explicitly marked as a giant. Rather, 2 Sam 23:21 characterizes the Egyptian as being "of (notable) appearance," or "a hand-some man" (איש מצרי אשר מראה). Quite possibly a word is missing in the 2 Samuel description; where מראה is used elsewhere to denote physical beauty, it is preceded by some adjective (יפה מראה, "beautiful in appearence" [Gen 39:6; 1 Sam 17:42], or טובי מראה, "pleasant in appearance" [Dan 1:4]).[284] The Chronicler's move here parallels the transformation we observed earlier, where an איש מדון ("violent individual") in 2 Sam 21:20 becomes an איש מדה ("giant man") in 1 Chr 20:6. Another addition or innovation in the Chronicler's acount involves the giant's weaponry: in 2 Sam 23:21 the giant has only a spear in his hand, with no further qualification, while in 1 Chr 11:23 the spear is "like a weaver's beam" (see also the giant's weaver's-beam-like spear in 1 Sam 17:7; 2 Sam 21:19 // 1 Chr 20:5). What both the 2 Sam 23 and 1 Chr 11 texts share, however, is the noteworthy parallel between the killing of an elite animal (a lion) and the defeat of an elite enemy—even though that enemy is a seven-and-a-half foot giant only in Chronicles.[285] To be sure, for the Chronicler, the giant thus becomes a type of animal curiosity, and Benaiah's victory is an act of name-making through the extermination of exotic threats.[286]

David fighting in the Valley of Rephaim. Before leaving our discussion of the appearance of the word Rephaim in the Hebrew Bible as it relates to living, non-Israelite residents of the land, we must pause here to notice a geo-graphical designation, "Valley of Rephaim" (עמק רפאים), and the problems associated with it.[287] The Valley of Rephaim appears nine times (Josh 15:8,

---

283. That is, around seven-and-a-half feet (2.3 meters).

284. Alternatively, the phrase in 2 Sam 23:21 could have been איש מצרי אשר איש מראה, "an Egyptian man of (notable) appearance." McCarter (1984, 491) translates a "a giant Egyptian" in 2 Sam 23:21, assuming the copyist misread an original מדה (as in 1 Chr 11:23) as מרה, and then corrected the spelling to מראה (reflected also in the LXX).

285. Note also the parallel verbal cue, ירד ("go down, descend") used to describe Benaiah's descent into the lion pit and his "going down" (= against) the Egyptian giant.

286. Cf. Wright 2011: 145–46.

287. See, e.g., Hauer 1970; Tidwell 1979. Ancient geographers confirmed this location of the עמק רפאים in the vicinity of Jerusalem, e.g., Josephus, *Ant.* VII.312; Eusebius, *Onomasticon* 288, 22, etc. See other references in Rouillard 1999, 688.

18:16; 2 Sam 5:18,22, 23:13; 1 Chr 11:15, 14:9,13; Isa 17:5), and in each instance (with the exception of Isa 17:5) the valley is clearly located to the southwest and adjacent to Jerusalem, running southwest to northwest and ending just short of the slopes of the city.[288] In Josh 15:9 and 18:16 we learn that the valley of Hinnom is at the northern end of the Valley of Rephaim, and the Valley of Rephaim serves as a boundary marker for the tribal territory of Judah and Benjamin, respectively. Isa 17:5 preserves a tradition of harvesting plentiful ears of grain in the Valley of Rephaim, but the meaning of the reference is ambiguous (as is the location of the valley to which the author is referring).[289] What should strike us as odd about a location for the Valley of Rephaim adjacent to Jerusalem is the fact that the living, ethnic Rephaim are never said to live anywhere near Jerusalem, which raises the question of whether we have two independent traditions involving Rephaim—one location/people in the Transjordan, and one near Jerusalem—or whether one of the images was extended to form the other.

Though there is no clear answer to this question, it is important to note that in several instances we read of Philistine incursions into the Valley of Rephaim during the time of David (2 Sam 5:18,22, 23:13; 1 Chr 11:15, 14:9,13). In 2 Sam 5:17-25 // 1 Chr 14:9, the Philistines find themselves in a state of alarm when David secures the throne, as Israel enters a strong(er) position of territorial and cultural antagonism vis-à-vis Philistia. David quickly repels the attack, and in chapter 6 David secures the ark and brings it into the newly formed capital city of Jerusalem. The symbolism here of victory against an enemy known for its giants (Josh 11:22; 1 Sam 17; 2 Samuel 21 // 1 Chronicles 20), combined with a battle fought in a valley seemingly named after a group of autochthonous giants, the Rephaim, might be significant and point to David's supremacy over giants and the adversarial forces they represent.

Admittedly, these connections, if present at all, are very muted. But the juxtaposition between David (as symbol of monarchic order) seen here also finds a parallel in 2 Sam 23:13 // 1 Chr 11:15, where we encounter David and his mighty men camped at the cave of Adullam (1 Samuel 22), facing a Philistine threat stationed in the Valley of Rephaim. The position of the valley may have offered a strategic advantage to invaders, i.e., as a position from which to launch a siege or draw out Jerusalem's inhabitants into the open field,[290] but the associations invoked by the word Rephaim itself should be

288. See the detailed map in Rainey and Notley 2006, 183.

289. See comments in Wildberger 1997, 171-72, which suggest that "archaeological remains" of an unspecified kind in the valley may have caused local ancient residents to connect the region with the Rephaim.

290. See Hauer 1970, 576.

enough to alert us to the symbolic possibilities of the Valley of Rephaim.[291] David's military exploits at this location, against an enemy conflated with the giants of the Conquest era, draw David's own victories into a direct parallel with the deeds of Moses, Joshua, and Kaleb at the Conquest, and even, by extension, into parallel with YHWH's own divine extermination by deluge of the first generation of giants born in Gen 6:1–4.[292]

V. Conclusion

Like a popular or colorful villain in a film with many sequels, the biblical giants seem to have been too interesting and too powerful a symbol to do away with in a final stroke. Rather, authors resurrected them, as we have seen, at significant moments of cosmic, political, and historical upheaval: in Gen 6:1–4, the primeval race of Nephilim and the Gibborim of the ancient world stand at the break between creation and a new realm of divine violence marked by the Flood; on the eve of the Israelite conquest, the Rephaim and Anaqim guard the land at the Transjordan and within the hill country, respectively, and their defeat signals the fulfillment of the longstanding promise to Abram for the inheritance of the land; and, finally, during the early monarchy, when the struggling nation first sought to carve out for itself a permanent place in the land alongside the constant threat of the Philistines, giants stood in the way. In each case, the establishment of a new order is forged after a violent assault on giants (alongside other forms of opposition), and in each case the various authors show YHWH and his human agents as victorious.

Though these giants populate the antediluvian world and pre-Israelite Canaan, it is their existence in the time of David that proves decisive, as David and his men overcome—for the last time—the chaotic threat posed by (specifically Philistine) giants.[293] The imposition of law, both literally via specific monarchic decree and figuratively in terms of the divine order and image of law as a world in balance, circumscribes what is overgrown; the presence of the opposing giants, then, signifies not simply the absence of law but an active, threatening *anti-law*. Ultimately, it is the inception of the

291. Karge (1917, 633–36) also sees the association with giants as the background of the עמק רפאים designation.

292. Note David's own exclamation in 2 Sam 5:20 (cf. 1 Chr 14:11): פרץ יהוה את איבי לפני כפרץ מים.

293. Of course, the giants do rise again—as resurrected symbols of hubris, chaos, and wickedness at Qumran and in other postbiblical materials. But they are mostly invoked in these later texts as ghosts from the past, and do not figure into any "contemporary" historical narrative in the way they are presented in the Hebrew Bible itself. See 1 Enoch 6–11, 15; *4QBook of Giants*, etc.

monarchy that serves to curb this threat with finality, demonstrating a type of control that no pre-monarchic hero could achieve. Giants could be, and indeed were, defeated in repeated engagements through individuals like Moses, Kaleb, and Joshua, but in such eras, when there was no king in Israel, everyone did what was right in his own eyes. The establishment of justice in the form of monarchic law is the solution to "giants" of all kinds, and solves the crisis of authority the giant poignantly represents.[294]

In this sense, from a canonical perspective, the Noahide covenant in Gen 9:1–17 is the exact antithesis to the boundary-breaking acts of the divine beings and what they produce in Gen 6:1–4, just as Joshua's acts of partitioning the Promised Land in Joshua 13–24 and David's ultimate subjugation of the Philistines and housing of both the ark and himself in Jerusalem in 2 Samuel 6–7 stand just on the other side of their respective encounters with monstrous human threats. The Deuteronomistic Historian thus finds himself accordingly preoccupied with re-writing existing laws (e.g., the "covenant code" of Exodus 20–23) and inventing new ones in Deuteronomy 14–26, even as he is involved in making linguistic notes and describing other geographical curiosities as they pertain to giants (Deut 2:9–13,19–23, 3:11), not to mention the full-scale battles against these figures scattered throughout Deuteronomy through Samuel. And though the Deuteronomistic History cannot have taken its current form any early than the exilic period, there can be no doubt about the presence of older strata in this corpus—and of course in other sources (Gen 6:1–4, Numbers 13, etc.)—that were adopted and adapted to meet a variety of needs throughout a very long period of time.

---

294. I was first alerted to the symbolic possibilities inherent in the encounter between law/king and giant by Suzanne Smith (Harvard University; personal communication) in the summer of 2010, and I owe her many thanks for stimulating my thought on this topic.

Chapter Three

Flattening the Overgrown:
Conquest and Cataclysm in the Aegean
World and the Hebrew Bible

Then Og came, the one who had escaped from among the giants who died in the flood—he rode upon the ark, and there was a cover over his head, and he was sustained from Noah's food. Not on account of any of his own merit did he escape, but rather that the inhabitants of the world would see the power of the Lord and say, "Did not the giants from the ancient times rebel against the Lord of the world, and he destroyed them from the earth?" When these kings waged war, Og was with them...

Targ. Ps-Jon, Gen 14:13

I. Introduction

IN THE LAST CHAPTER, I observed that giants constitute a significant presence in the Hebrew Bible, and that the threats they represent in their oversized bodies—of crises of authority, of precarious change, of political and religious chaos—must be dealt with through acts of violence. In this chapter, I return to the two main methods employed to destroy the giants— flood and war—and make a series of more detailed observations regarding the giants and their demise. In doing so, we will begin to observe the ways in which the generations of giants in the Hebrew Bible stand in thematic parallel to the heroic generation as conceived by archaic and classical Greek authors. In the present chapter, more particularly, I argue that the biblical giants, along with the Greek heroic generation, represent a moment of transgression and hubris that can be addressed only through cataclysm, specifically in the form of flood and totalizing military conquest (or a mix of the two).[1] Early rabbinic interpreters even saw connections between specific

---

1. In developing these comparisons, I rely on the concept of a Mediterranean *koine* adopted in Chapter One. Even though the comparative thrust in this chapter could be considered on only a typological level, without reference to historical dissemination or modes of cultural and literary exchange, I continue to assume that texts from Israel and the Aegean were the products of earlier, pan-Mediterranean traditions.

giant figures linked with both flood and conquest. Consider, for example, the odd but striking image, found throughout the Targums and early rabbinic literature, of Og surviving the flood by riding on the ark.[2] Of course, Og's survival is, in part, an apologetic solution to the problem of how giant races survived the deluge in Genesis 6–9.[3] But, I contend, there are deeper connections here between the flood and conquest that these early interpreters may have noticed, and that deserve elaboration.

Even though the biblical Flood and conquest seemed to curb the threat of giants temporarily, it is the advent of legitimate monarchy—through David—that deals giants the ultimate blow (insofar as they appear as "historical" opponents of Israel in the biblical narrative). What is the meaning of the giants' threat, and why is kingship, apparently, the final answer to the problem of giants? The giant is indeed a difficult menace, but kingship—rightly administered—is a guarantor of right order. This guarantor invites challenge, chaos, and all sources of disorder, which must then be "leveled" back to the pristine state of order, of flatness and straightness—i.e., a return to the primordial state of the newly created world.[4] In his most basic, physical representation, the giant is that which is overgrown, excessive, and disorderly; he is simply *too much*, and thus represents a chaotic threat against ordered norms of human size.[5] The giant is a human embodiment of nature gone awry, of over-nature, and could be compared to a forest or garden growing beyond maintainable limits. Indeed, as discussed in the previous

2. See Clarke 1998, 57 n. 26 for a list of references to the trope of Og surviving the flood on the ark in early Jewish sources, including, e.g., Gen. Rab. 42,8; Num. Rab. 19,32; Deut. Rab. 1,25; Targ. Ps-Jon Deut 3:11; b. Zebah. 113b (560), etc. See also the list in Noegel 1998, 414 n. 21.

3. See Stuckenbruck 2000, 358.

4. This is not to say that creation always "begins" with a pristine world. In the *Enuma eliš*, for example, the period preceding Marduk's victory-creation is rife with chaos. However, this chaos itself emerges from a prior, ordered state of relative peace. And the *Enuma eliš* ends with what is arguably an incantation against Tiamat's future *return* (even though she has been defeated and dismembered!). In conceptualizing the giant in terms of creation and chaos maintenance, I draw on Mircea Eliade's famous description of all religious systems as "cosmogonic," that is to say, as bound up in the attempt to create an ordered cosmos against all threats of disorder. See Eliade 1959, 20–48.

5. By "size" here, I refer not only to literal, physically measurements, but also to other aspects of the human expression that can be categorized as overgrown, untamed, or unruly, such as violence, arrogance, sexual conquests, consumption of food and drink, and so on. Indeed, these secondary categories of excess are stock features of the giant in many languages and literatures. See Thomas 2005, 138–69. The making of implicit and explicit correlations between body shape/size and moral or intellectual qualities—i.e., physiognomy—was a known (and apparently well-organized) part of ancient Near Eastern religious speculation; see Popovic 2006 and literature cited there.

chapter, allusions to this motif of "cutting down" the giant like a forest appear in the biblical texts, though this is by no means the only image used.[6] By conceptualizing giants in terms of order and chaos, I find inspiration in the work of the great twentieth-century political philosopher Eric Voegelin, who focused on the symbolic presentation of order vis-à-vis disorder as "the most characteristic feature" of any "world-picture."[7] In Voegelin's conception of ancient Mesopotamia, specifically, the political is at every point a cosmological affair, just as the cosmos is itself a mirror image of the political.[8] Whenever the biblical giant, king, or the Greek hero comes to embody conflict or change in his own body, we see the interplay between disorder and order in both the cosmos and the polis. This relationship can begin with a founding act of chaos maintenance in the primeval period, but the story never ends there.

How might we go about framing some of the issues raised here? In order to draw the archaic Greek materials into fruitful dialogue with the Mesopotamian sources, what is needed is some conceptual framework that can govern these materials and help us appreciate what binds them together, while at the same time leading toward a deeper understanding of the specific impact of each text.[9] As a unifying concept for my investigation here, then, I would like to invoke a very specific concept of divine justice in the service of maintaining chaos, embodied in the Greek terms *díkē* (δίκη) and *húbris* (ὕβρις).[10] One particular method of conceptualizing *díkē* and *húbris* is in regard to vegetation: the pruned, trimmed, and manicured, that which

6. See, e.g., the suggestive use of כרת with reference to the Anaqim in Josh 11:21, and the parallel between clearing out a forest and the land of the Rephaim and Perizzites in Josh 17:15. Also, כרת is a common verb to describe various violent acts, but the primary reference seems to be to literally "cutting" things down, like vegetation (e.g., Deut 19:5; Isa 44:14; 1 Kgs 5:20, among numerous other examples). See *BDB*, 503–04. On the giant as representation of "wildness" generally, recall the comments of Bernheimer (1952, 4–5, 19–20; discussed in Ch. 1) and Mobley (1997, 11–12).

7. Voegelin 2003, 32:186. For ancient Israel specifically, see the opening volume to Voegelin's monumental *Order and History* series, Voegelin 1956, e.g., 1:21–37, on the symbols of political and cosmic order, and I:273–81 on David and Jerusalem. For a recent analysis of the maturation of Voegelin's thought throughout these volumes in relation to the ancient Near East, see Machinist 2001.

8. See Machinist 2001, 10–14, for the secondary sources upon which Voegelin relied for this concept.

9. To be sure, the limited previous attempts by at least one biblical scholar (Hendel 1987b) and some classicists (e.g., Scodel 1982; West 1997) have mostly lacked just such a framework.

10. On these terms, see the overview by Dickie (1978), as well as the comments in Nagy 1990a, 64–69 with reference to Hesiod. On *húbris* specifically, see Nikolaev 2004; note also Beekes and van Beek 2010, I:334–35 and II:1524.

is in a straight line (*díkē*), as opposed to the image of the crooked line, that which is overgrown, excessive, and uncontrolled (*húbris*).[11] *Díkē* describes that which remains within boundaries, what is "righteous," while *húbris* connotes willful disrule and injustice, the antithesis of *díkē*.

The applicability of this imagery to the Greek context may seem obvious,[12] and the prominence of the mythic Gigantomachy/Titanomanchy motif—at least in the surviving iconography—graphically illustrates the value of cutting down the gigantic in the maintenance of cultic and political order.[13] But if such concepts seem at first alien to the biblical texts, closer study suggests otherwise. Besides the characterization of the giant as that which is overgrown and needs to be cut down, one is immediately reminded of similar conceptions of straightening, leveling, and flatness, associated with the root ישׁר ("straight, right") used to speak of YHWH's justice and the facilitation of right rule most famously in Second Isaiah (45:2; see also 40:4, 42:16, etc.).[14] In Isaiah 2:12–14, the prophet speaks of YHWH's wrath against all that is "lifted up" (רם), and calls for the leveling (שׁפל) of every "elevated" thing (כל נשא)— viz. the "lofty and elevated cedars of Lebanon" (ארזי הלבנון הרמים והנשאים), the "oaks of Bashan," "lofty mountains" (ההרים הרמים), and "elevated hills" (הגבעות הנשאות). Such images draw upon the implied correlation between the shape or health of the physical world and the ability of the divine or human king to effectively maintain a bounded, ordered kingdom. Mountains that spike up and block the path must be leveled, for in God's perfect world the way is straight; that which grows up too high as an affront to the divine must be beaten down, leveled, or washed away.

The task of leveling sometimes falls to God directly, but the tangible representation of God's rule on earth is the human king, the counterpart to the divine king. As R. Simkins notes, the royal enactment of law in the Near East is a triumph of "world ordering," which draws monarchic legal decree into parallel with all of the created order.[15] To be sure, the natural world itself responds to the moral order of its inhabitants and their leaders.[16] For example,

---

11. See Nagy 1990a, 64–69, 73–77 for references and sources.

12. On the *díkē*/*húbris* alternation with relation to the heroic age, see Hesiod's *Works and Days*, 143–73, 202–13, and on flood and battle as a "flattening" technique, see *Iliad* 12, which I discuss below.

13. See discussion in Ch. 1, and also the review of prominent artistic motifs in *LIME* IV:191–270; Moore 1995; 1979; Watrous 1982.

14. Cf. the Mesopotamian concept of *mīšaru* (*CAD* 10.2, 116–18). For the applicability of the *díkē*/*húbris* concept in the Hebrew Bible—specifically Gen 6:1–4; Numbers 13, 33; and Ezekiel 32—see Humbert 1960, 69–71.

15. Simkins 1991, 167. On the role of the king vis-à-vis the cultic and political order of the cosmos, see, e.g., Mowinckel 2004, 50–61, and Seow 1989, 145–203.

16. See Simkins 1991, 167–72; Schmid 1984; 1974; Murphy 2002, 111–32.

Psalm 72:1–7,12–17 demonstrates this relationship in a very straightforward manner:[17] judging the poor with righteousness (v. 2) stands in parallel with the hills yielding plenty for the people (v. 3); the king's advocacy for the needy (v. 12) is connected to the ability of the fields to produce abundant grain (v. 16); the flourishing of people in the city and the flourishing grass in the field are discussed in the same breath (v. 16). Viewed through this lens, the giant is one of the more striking methods to represent physical existence gone wild; the giant's body is a response to something gone awry, something uncontrolled. It must be fixed and cut down to size—that is, killed and leveled. In both Greek and Mesopotamian sources, we find suggestive passages detailing the effects of "flattening"—through both flood and totalizing warfare—as a solution to what has grown excessively "upward" (whether literally or symbolically). In what follows, therefore, I delineate notions of flattening and eradication in terms of the biblical giants and also the Greek heroic traditions, and demonstrate that these sources participate in a deeply shared conceptual universe.

II. Conquest and Cataclysm in Archaic and Classical Greece

In ancient Greek texts, we find this theme of "flattening" as a response to human over-reaching or chaos management—through flood, warfare, or a mix of the two—in several different texts. Though the texts I review here (*Cypria, Iliad 12, Works and Days, Catalogue*) are by no means identical in terms of the meaning of the cataclysm motifs present in each, they offer glimpses into the broader Mediterranean context of oversized, heroic warriors and their fate.

Zeus' βουλή and the Cypria's Overburdened Earth

Though quite possibly composed after the time of Homer and Hesiod, the *Cypria* is a convenient place to begin an investigation into the themes of cataclysm and flattening in Greek epic literature.[18] The traditional origin of the *Cypria* in Cyprus is most obviously reflected in the title of the work, and, together with several other now fragmentary works describing the events preceding the Trojan War (and/or summarizing the Trojan War and its

---

17. See Mowinckel 2004, 67–71. See also, e.g., the relationship between human behavior and the response of the land in Deuteronomy 28.

18. Further summaries can be found in Burgess 2001, 7–10; M. Davies 1989, 33–52. See also Burgess 2002; 1996; Finkelberg 2000; Griffin 1977.

aftermath), forms part of the so-called "Epic Cycle."[19] The origins of some traditions in the *Cypria* may very well date back to the archaic period, and thus be contemporaneous with Homer in the late eighth century, and few scholars are willing to date the full composition—which exists now only in excerpts and fragments—to later than the sixth century.[20]

The surviving contents of the *Cypria* apparently begin with the appearance of Strife (Ἔρις) at the wedding of Peleus, leading into the familiar storyline. It is important to notice the enigmatic first line of the episode: "Zeus plotted (βουλεύεται[21]) with Themis concerning the Trojan War."[22] The reference here reaffirms the status of the conflict in terms of its origin in Zeus' ultimate design (βουλή/*boulē*), mentioned briefly at the beginning of the *Iliad* (1.5).[23] Troops are rounded up for the siege, Agamemnon (nearly) sacrifices Iphigeneia, and the war begins. The particular aspects of the *Cypria* of interest to us here involve this βουλή of Zeus by which the Trojan War is initiated. The theme of divine extermination of heroes and the end of the heroic age is a conspicuous preoccupation of the scholia on the *Iliad,* which cite the *Cypria* at a critical point. In two decisive locations, these scholia present a counter-tradition to the origins of the Trojan War, of which the *Cypria* is the only witness in its time period. On the one hand, we have the wedding of Peleus and Helen episode (*Cypria* 1–2), and on the other, we have references to a prior and premeditated plan by Zeus to destroy the heroic race:[24]

> Others have said that Homer was referring to a myth (ἱστορίας). For they say that Earth, being weighed down by the multitude of people, there being no piety among humankind, asked Zeus to be relieved of the burden. Zeus firstly and at once brought about the Theban War,[25] by means of

19. Some of the background of the Epic Cycle has already been discussed in Ch. 1.

20. See, e.g., Burgess 2001, 7–10. On possible references to the *Iliad* in the *Cypria*, see Tsagalis 2008. But Burgess (1996) has argued that parts of the Epic Cycle must predate Homer, and that the *Iliad* alludes to material spelled out clearly in the Cycle. On this, see also J. Marks 2002.

21. Though one could translate βουλεύεται neutrally as "consulted with," the sense here is likely a negative one—even punitive.

22. The most recent critical editions are those of M. Davies (1988) and Bernabé (1987); see also West 2003.

23. Note the second-century Oxyrhynchus papyrus' more explicit formulation: "Zeus, finding the race of heroes guilty of impiety, conferred with Themis about destroying them completely" (West 2003, 81).

24. Text and translation here and below from West 2003. See the discussion in Nagy 2006, §58; Bethe 1966, esp. the foreword; Finkelberg 2004, 12–15; Mayer 1996; de Jong 1985; J. D. Reeves 1966.

25. Aside from the cluster of stories surrounding the Trojan War, the Theban War represents a second, major event in which heroes perished.

which he destroyed very large numbers, and afterwards the Trojan one...this being what Homer calls the plan (βουλήν) of Zeus,[26] seeing that he was capable of destroying everyone with thunderbolts or floods... (Schol. [D] *Il.* 1.5).

Then, claiming to quote the *Cypria*:

There was a time when the countless races <of men> roaming <constantly> over the land were weighing down the <deep> breasted earth's expanse. Zeus took pity when he saw it, and in his complex mind he resolved to relieve the all-nurturing earth of mankind's weight by fanning the great conflict of the Trojan War, to void the burden through death. So the warriors of Troy kept being killed, and Zeus' plan (βουλή) was being fulfilled.

The blunt nature of the *Cypria*'s explanation for the Trojan War is striking, but possibly reflects a much broader and well-known theme at the time, viz. the overpopulation of the earth during the heroic age, and, more specifically, overpopulation combined with impiety.[27] The heroic race is apparently out of control and has exceeded its bounds, and thus it must undergo a cataclysm that will reset the clock and erase the burden they have perpetrated.[28] Moreover, Achilles' role in the *Cypria* specifically takes on a different quality from the *Iliad*; in the former, Achilles' falling out with his Greek comrades is only the result of Zeus' premeditated plan for destruction.[29]

Flood and Cosmic Destruction in the Iliad

The importance of these references in the *Cypria* become clearer when we acknowledge the full extent to which the *Iliad* engages with similar notions of totalizing cataclysm initiated in the divine world as a response to human actions. I have already mentioned the allusion to the βουλή of Zeus in *Il.* 1.5, which the *Cypria* and *Iliad* scholia identify as the ultimate plan to wipe out the heroic race. Some have argued that Homer deliberately refused to mention a cataclysmic end for his heroes with any more specificity than this, citing the Panhellenic goals of the *Iliad* and the implied continuity to

26. See Nagy 1999b, 219–20 on the "will" or "plan" of Zeus in this regard, as well as Heiden 2008, passim.

27. Similar themes appear, e.g., in the Atrahasis epic (discussed infra), as well as the Sanskrit *Mahābhārata* (11.8.26). On the latter, with comparison to Greek themes, see Katz 2007, 20–21, 23, 27; Nagy 1990a, 12–17; Dumézil 1986, 195–96; de Jong 1985, 397–400; Allen 2004. Note also the pioneering work of Jamison 1994; 1997.

28. But cf. Mayer 1996, 9–14. *Pace* Mayer, see Nagy 1999b, 219–20.

29. See J. Marks 2002, 12 and Heiden 2008, passim.

be found in Homer with the heroes of old and the classical world itself.[30] Thus, while Hesiod and the Cycle display antiquarian interests, Homer is concerned most directly with the present. This interplay between the contemporary and antiquity, however, should be cast in more nuanced light, by recognizing the appearance of several passages that suggest Homer preserved fragments of an early Greek flood narrative which was marshaled at specific, strategic moments to describe the Trojan War itself.[31]

The building and destruction of the Achaean wall in the *Iliad* (7.433–66 and 12.1–35, respectively) have always been something of an enigma. Nestor first proposes the idea for a wall in 7.336–43, as a precaution against the Trojans drawing too near to the camp,[32] and in 7.433–63, a funeral pyre and mound for the Achaean dead are built along with the wall. Poseidon stands up in immediate protest, insisting on the destruction of the wall, lest humans think they can forget about the gods and do whatever they want (seemingly an irrational fear) and lest this new and hastily built wall rival the walls of Troy (seemingly impossible) (7.448–51).[33] Scodel calls the citation of the heroes' failure to provide adequate hecatombs in (7.450) to be "motive hunting," i.e., a rhetorical pretext with no real justification in the narrative itself,[34] but it is premature to make such judgments solely on the basis of how illogical Poseidon's concern may sound when taken in isolation.[35] Indeed, Poseidon's insecurity in a very similar manner is woven into the *Odyssey* (8.564–70; 13.125–87), where again it does not clearly advance the plot of the story,[36] and the trope of seemingly inscrutable divine jealousy resulting in destruction is a stock part of ancient literature.

30. I.e., the Homeric vision has the surviving heroes participating in their respective *nostoi*, and the homes to which they return become the centers of hero cult, etc.

31. I owe many insights in this section to Scodel 1982, 33–50, as well as the summary in Nagy 2006, §§44, 58–65 and Boyd 1995. The flood themes in the *Iliad*, as well as their connection to Near Eastern myth, have received much attention in the past few decades; see, e.g., West 1997, 377–80; Singor 1992; Maitland 1999. On water imagery in the *Iliad*, see Fenno 2005.

32. Note that the threat of the Trojans reaching the Achaean camp recalls Zeus' promise at the beginning of the *Iliad* to allow them to accomplish this exact feat.

33. The lines recording Poseidon's objection (443–64) are omitted as inauthentic by several ancient commentators, and some have argued more recently for the non-Homeric nature of the passage, e.g., the relevant commentary in Kirk 1990, as well as Page 1959, 315–24. Page (1959, 319) cites Thucydides, who seems to refer to a version of the *Iliad* in which the wall is built in the *first* year of the siege (cf. *Il.* 24.30), as opposed to the tenth year. Cf. Tsagarakis (1969), who disputes Page's claim, and Scodel 1982, 33 n. 1 for additional bibliography on this problem.

34. Scodel 1982, 34. The fact that it is venerable Nestor who suggests the wall's construction is awkward, as is the fact that the Achaeans do make a sacrifice for Zeus just a few lines earlier in 7.311–15.

35. Note also that in 12.6, the neglect of offerings is repeated and takes on a more serious tone (on this, see the note in Kirk 1990, 2:289).

36. See Kirk 1990, 2:35, 48–50, but more extensively, Maitland 1999.

In *Il.* 12.1–35 we learn of the rampart's demise. Strangely, in 12.17–19, the destruction is accomplished via the diverting of several rivers—two of which are nowhere to be found elsewhere in the *Iliad*, thus providing a strong hint of the external origins of this motif (on which see below).[37] The destruction of the Achaean wall in this passage obviously serves to raise the specter of the breach of the Trojan wall, thereby giving the flooding of the wall a significant thematic purpose and drawing the scene into the *Iliad's* broader narrative and world of symbol. The flood here in book 12 turns out to be an extended affair (nine days), designed to return the beach to its original state: Poseidon

> swept out on the waves all the foundations of beams and stones that the Achaeans had toiled to set up, and made all smooth (λεῖα δ'ἐποίησεν) along the strong stream of the Hellespont, and again covered the great beach with sand when he had swept away the wall; and the rivers he turned back to flow in the channel where they had earlier poured their fair-flowing streams (12.28–33).

The flood takes on the characteristics of a cleansing event that restores the world of humans and the physical geography back to its primeval state of silence and flatness (see also 15.261–63, 21.300–04).[38] Moreover, only in this passage in Homer, viz. *Il.* 12.23, are heroes as a group called ἡμίθεοι (*hēmitheoi*), i.e., partially divine, and not regular humans. Indeed, the phrase ἡμιθέων γένος ἀνδρῶν ("race of semi-divine men") is evocative of Hesiod's characterization of a Heroic Race (on which see below), as it is the Trojan War—here represented by a flood—that stands as a dividing line between the heroes of the mythic past and later, "historical" time.[39]

The pervasive nature of this flood imagery in the *Iliad*, combined as it also is with themes of totalizing destruction, confirms the views of those who

37. The rivers not mentioned elsewhere are the Rhodios and Grenikos, but cf. Hesiod, *Theog.* 338–45, where the same list of rivers appears, as pointed out by Hainsworth 1993, 319. I follow Boyd 1995, 191 in my analysis below.

38. See also 15.261–63, where Apollo is described as destroying the wall "just as a child scatters the sand by the sea..." (15.361–63). In the ensuing scene (15.674–78), Ajax (son of Telamon) strides atop the beached ships, as if escaping the flood of both the Trojan attack and Apollo's wall-wrecking anger. See Boyd 1995, 202. The image of the flood and battle finds expression yet again, but in a markedly different way, in 21.300–04, in Achilles' battle with the river Scamander, where the flood/river threatens to obliterate the entire Achaean struggle and Achilles' own heroic quest by killing Achilles. Water imagery in the *Iliad* is pervasive as a metaphor for battle, and may also be connected with the association of the Greeks with the sea and the Trojans with rivers. The Greek invasion is repeatedly compared to a flood when Achaeans "pour forth" (ἐχέοντο) like water from ships, etc. See, e.g., *Il.* 16.267,384–93, 19.356, 21.6, etc., and many more such references catalogued in Fenno 2005, 478–90.

39. The status of the heroes here as ἡμίθεοι is highly significant, and will be discussed further below by way of Hesiod. See Nagy 1999b, 159–61 and Scodel 1982, 35.

see early vestiges of a Greek cosmic flood theme already at play in this early literature.[40] The conflation of flood imagery with sequences of intense battle at the exact point in which the heroic generation is characterized as ἡμίθεοι suggests something of the power these images could have in describing the end of the particular era of heroic action the Trojan War represents.[41] The trope of flattening, which appears specifically in *Il.* 12.25–34, 15.361–63, and 21.300–04, is an apt image to describe the return of the beach to its natural, un-molested state. Poseidon's fear about the building of the Achaean wall in *Il.* 7.437–51 is not irrational, petty jealousy, but rather signals the moment of heroic over-reach, and the transgression of building that which is an affront to the divine. The specific allusion to the ἡμίθεοι at only this location thus foreshadows the end of the heroic action in the past; the heroes, like the beach on whose sands the Achaean wall was built, are the victims of cosmic change. Their cycle had come to an end.

As Nagy points out, we see the language of flood in the *Iliad* intermixed with tropes of ecpyrosis (i.e., total destruction by conflagration) and battle at critical junctures.[42] In *Il.* 21.345–76, for example, Hephaestus' burning fire threatens to boil up the river, and later in 21.520–25 the martial acts of Achilles against the Trojans are framed in terms of a fire burning up to the heavens. In fact, Zeus' onslaught against the Titans in *Theog.* 687–710 utilizes thunderbolts of burning fire, which come dangerously close to burning up the entire earth.[43] Moreover, Zeus' destructive βουλή as a totalizing calamity that would destroy humans en masse is also reflected in Aeschylus' *Promethus Bound* (228–36), where Prometheus accuses Zeus of conspiring to annihilate the current brood of mortals.[44]

40. See Hendel 1987b, 19–20, who suggests that the flood reference in the *Iliad* is an indication of a "variant pre-Homeric flood tradition," the evidence for which can be partly found in Poseidon's anti-Achaean position here (as opposed his pro-Achaean orientation at all other points in the *Iliad*; cf. *Il.* 20:288–339, where again Poseidon is anti-Achaean and where again a variant tradition may be found).

41. Additionally, the reference to the demigods points beyond the world of the epic to the present of the audience, and the ongoing reality of the hero as a figure in cult (on which see the following chapter). See discussion in Nagy 1999b, 159–60.

42. Nagy 2006, §§58, 63–64; 1999b, 333–38.

43. "All around, the life-giving earth roared as it burned, and all around the great immense forest crackled; the whole earth boiled, and the streams of Ocean and the barren sea..." (*Hes.* I, *Theog.* 693–96). See Nagy 1999b, 322–23, 333. Hector's quest to burn the Achaean ships with fire resonates with this same language in *Il.* 9.76–77, 11.666–67, 12.198, 13.628–29, 15.597–98, 718–25, and other locations (Nagy 1999b, 335).

44. See also the βούλευμα τὸ Δῖον (619); cf. τὰν Διὸς...ἁρμονίαν (551) and τὰν Διὸς... μῆτιν (906), with discussion in S. White 2001, 109–11. Obviously, the Greek story of the flood itself also embodies this theme of total destruction.

Hesiod's Cataclysm at the End of the Heroic Age

Any discussion of the end of an era of heroic figures and cataclysm in ancient Greece must inevitably encounter Hesiod's famous five-generation scheme in the *Works and Days* (106–201).[45] The questions regarding Hesiod's own historical background, and the historical and social setting of the *Works and Days* and the *Catalogue of Women* (the two works that contain the themes of interest to us here)—not to mention the relationship between Hesiod and Homer[46] and the possibility that Hesiod relied on Near Eastern models for his cosmogony and elsewhere[47]—have all been a matter of lively discussion for many decades.[48] The vast majority of commentators see a genuinely historical Hesiodic tradition from very early in the seventh century BCE, perhaps a generation after Homer in the late eighth century.[49] Many detailed attempts have been offered by way of analyzing Hesiod's story of the Five Generations, and there is little consensus regarding key features of the story.[50] After the Pandora myth (42–105), Hesiod offers another tale, viz., the famous description of five "generations" or "races" (γένεα)[51] in terms of four metallic ages. In the Golden Race mortals lived as gods (109–26), but the vastly inferior

45. For the text that follows, I refer to Hesiod 2006 (tr. G. W. Most); For text-critical issues, see West 1978.

46. See Neitzel 1975; Edwards 1971, 166–208; Blusch 1970, 25–39; Notopoulos 1960; Østerud 1976.

47. See López-Ruiz 2010; Koenen 1994.

48. E.g., Lamberton 1988, 1–37; Walcot 1966, 104–30; Hesiod 2006 (tr. G. W. Most), xi–lxxxii; Solmsen 1982; Peabody 1975.

49. One notable exception to this view is West (1966, 40), who thinks Hesiod is earlier. Others, e.g., Sellschopp 1934, claimed to have pinpointed the writing of the Hesiodic materials to a time period between the *Iliad* and *Odyssey*, though such speculation is beyond the scope of this study. See also Edwards 1971, 166. Others simply sidestep the issue and claim both Hesiod and Homer draw on traditional oral motifs, so that none can claim chronological priority (Caldwell 1987, 2–3). Cf. Nagy 1995; 1992; Finkelberg 2000; Blümer 2001.

50. See West 1978, 172–204; Verdenius 1985, 75–118; Tandy and Neale 1996, 67–75; Wilamowitz-Moellendorff 1928; Nagy 1999b, 151–61; Mirgeler 1958; Vernant 1983, 1–72. Other essays include: A. Brown 1998; Koenen 1994, 2–6, 24–26; Falkner 1989; Querbach 1985; P. Smith 1980; Fontenrose 1974; Griffiths 1956; 1958.

51. The term "race" is perhaps an unfortunate translation of γένος, loaded as it is with modern notions of racial identity and so on. See Donlan 1985; Koenen 1994, 2 n. 3; Vernant 1983, 79. Fontenrose (1974 1 n. 1) strongly rejects the word "race" but affirms that γένος means "stock" or "breed." "Age" or "Generation" is not a wholly satisfactory alternative to "race," however, since, as Koenen (1994, 2 n. 3) points out, Hesiod "does not talk about the creation of periods of time, but about the human beings who lived in specific periods of their own." Each γένος is bound up inextricably with its place through the progression of time, and thus I use the terms "race" and "generation" or "age" interchangeably here to denote this interplay.

Silver Race (127–42) is filled with individuals who are unable to mature correctly because of various iniquities. Next comes the Bronze Race (143–55), comprised of brutish figures carrying bronze weaponry by which they destroyed one another. Interrupting the progression of metals is the age of the "divine race of men heroes" (ἀνδρῶν ἡρώων θεῖον γένος), the ἡμίθεοι ("demigods") (156–73), who are identified as the epic warriors who fought at Thebes and Troy—some of these demigods experienced death, while others, the "blessed heroes" (ὄλβιοι ἥρωες), Zeus whisked away to the Islands of the Blessed.[52] Finally, Hesiod identifies the fifth generation, the Iron Race (174–201), comprised of the workaday sufferers with whom Hesiod himself was apparently all too familiar.

Of the many points of ambiguity and interest in the myth of the Five Generations, two may be singled out in terms of our focus here, viz. the exact status of the Bronze Race and of the demigods in lines 143–73, and the issue of the direction or cyclicality of the progression of ages generally. First, it is almost universally recognized that the heroic age interrupts the four-metal schema.[53] The reasons for this interruption, however, are less than clear, especially in light of the fact that the blessedness of the ἡμίθεοι contradicts the pattern of degeneration in the progression of one metal and one age to the next. As it stands, Hesiod's men-heroes represent a spike in the graph, a temporary upsurge in the apparently sloping trend. A. S. Brown, for example, thinks that Hesiod was simply out to prove his ability as a poet, and, in an act of cosmopolitan genius, sought to adapt the Oriental scheme of decline through metallic ages and combine it with the native Greek idea that a righteous, powerful heroic race had lived just a generation previously.[54] Others cite the *húbris-díkē* scheme as guiding the insertion of the *díkē*-filled heroes after the corrupt, *húbris*-filled Bronze Race.[55]

Despite the obvious dissimilarities between the Bronze and Heroic Generations, the description of the Bronze Race seems to be very close—minus any ultra-positive moral assessments—to how one might have expected Hesiod or any other author of the period to have described the heroic age, i.e., large, armed individuals killing each other en masse (though perhaps not to the point of extinction). Indeed, the language used to describe all four

52. West (1978, 192) seems skeptical of this tradition; Verdenius (1985, 102) assumes that although Hesiod imagines a large number of heroes entering this state, he does not highlight the seeming contradiction in the fact that a number of worthy heroes die (e.g., Patroklos). See also Nagy 1999b, 159–61 on the "half gods."

53. See, e.g., Walcott 1966, 81–86; Querbach 1985, 1–2; A. Brown 1998, 386, etc.

54. A. Brown 1998, 386–87.

55. E.g., Nagy 1999b, 155; Querbach 1985, 4–5; Dickie 1978, 96–98, etc. Cf. Tandy and Neale 1996, 70.

Generations is replete with heroic imagery.[56] Like the Bronze warriors, the men-heroes wield great power, and they are similarly destroyed by acts of aggression at the hands of their fellows. The important differences lie in the fact that the race of demigods is δικαιότερον, "more just," than the Bronze Race, and some of the demigods—but notably not all—receive a special place at the Isles of the Blessed. The *húbris* (146) exhibited in the Bronze Generation is the exact opposite of the *díkē* of the demigods, and so prefigures Hesiod's admonishment in 213: "give heed to Dike and do not foster Hubris."[57] Thus, what may at first appear to be superficial similarities between the Bronze Race and the men-heroes turn out to be a deeper dissimilarity in the moral makeup of the two groups.[58]

The nature of Hesiod's description of the ages raises the very difficult question of whether we have here a "cyclical" view of the rise and fall of generations, or whether Hesiod envisions an essentially unidirectional decline on which he and his contemporaries are rapidly slipping and in the last phase. Though the majority of interpreters have affirmed this storyline, others deny it.[59] I am of the opinion that Hesiod ultimately has something more hopeful in mind than the unidirectional downward view, insofar as the fate of various races/ages is predicated on their status as filled with either *díkē* or *húbris*.[60] These races are not simply antiquities on the shelf; rather, as Vernant rightly asserts, "these races make up the 'ancient times', but that does not stop them from continuing to exist, and, in the case of some [e.g., heroes in hero-cult], to be much more real than present-day life and the contemporary race of humans."[61]

In addition to the *Works and Days*, we should note that Hesiod's most widely known composition through the fourth century CE, the *Catalogue of Women* (or *Ehoiai*), contains a broad description of the genealogies of heroes whose origins lie in the cohabitation of human women and the gods.[62] The

56. See the comments on this in Nagy 1999b, 151–55.

57. See, e.g., Querbach 1985, 7.

58. The appearance of these two sets of warriors side by side preserves a phenomenon similar to what Nagy (2006, §67) has identified as dual themes regarding the ἡμίθεοι in Hesiod and in the *Iliad* (12.17–33), to wit, destruction followed by preservation (Hesiod, i.e., the ὄλβιοι ἥρωες who are whisked away) as compared with destruction followed by no preservation (Homer, i.e., the heroic race perishes in battle).

59. Fontenrose (1980, 8) and (Querbach 1985, 5–6) reject the progressive degeneration view. See West 1978, 173 and also Fontenrose 1980, 8 n. 16 for a long list of those who affirm the degeneration scheme, including Wilamowitz-Moellendorff (1928, 139–40) and Griffiths (1956, 109).

60. Cf. Teggert 1947, 77; Koenen 1994, 10.

61. Vernant 1983, 79.

62. Attributing the work to Hesiod does not imply a naïveté about Hesiodic authorship,

proem to the *Catalogue* exalts the heroes in terms reminiscent of the Golden Age of the *Works and Days*, and descriptions of cataclysm permeate the entire document.[63] At the very end of the Catalogue, the Trojan War appears as the climactic terminus of the heroic age.[64] After Helen bears Hermione in 155.94(56)–106(68),[65]

> All the gods were divided in spirit in strife. For high-thundering Zeus was devising wonderous deeds then, to stir up trouble on the boundless earth; for he was already eager to annihilate most of the race of speech-endowed human beings, a pretext (προφάσις)[66] to destroy the lives of the semi-gods (ἡμιθέων), [   ] to mortals children of the gods (τέκνα θεῶν) [   ] seeing with eyes, but that the ones blessed [   ] as before apart from human beings should have [life and] habitations. Hence he established] for immortals and for mortal human beings difficult warfare: for the ones he made] pain upon pain, Zeus [   ] he destroyed...)[67]

An conjectural reading of this fragmentary passage by Wilamowitz had become canonical for generations of scholars:

> For at that time high-thundering Zeus planned grandiose things, stirring up <quarrel> throughout boundless earth. Already he was eager to make away with the copious race of mortals, all the while pretending to destroy the lives of the demigods, *lest the children of the gods, seeing the earthly people (?)] with their eyes, [would mix (?)] with them,* but the blest [and...], as formerly, would have their life and seats apart from men" [italics mine].[68]

---

but rather follows the most ancient Hesiodic interpretive traditions that persisted in assigning the work to him. See West 1985, 127. Many are still willing to ascribe authorship to Hesiod; see the discussion in Clay 2003 (164–66, and 165 n. 52), and Hesiod 2006 (tr. Most), xlvii–lix. See also Hesiod 1967 (ed. Merkelbach and West) and the earlier edition of Hesiod 1902 (ed. Rzach).

63. Koenen 1994, 27; Clay 2003, 167.

64. The reference to Deucalion invokes the flood myth, and the destruction of Deucalion's own generation apparently destroys the race of semi-divine heroic figures of Olympian/Titanic origin. West (1985, 55) states that "there is no reason to suppose that the myth of the great flood which Deukalion and Pyrrha alone survived was alluded to in the Catalogue," and asserts that the flood story is first attested in Epicharmus and Pindar. For West (1985, 55–56), the existence of this earlier race of semi-divine figures "would imply an earlier race of men before the heroes," an idea that appears in the *Works and Days* but not in the *Catalogue*. Cf. Merkelbach (1968, 144) and Nagy (2006, §63), who affirm the antiquity of the Flood tradition. Whatever the case, the reference to Deucalion in light of the later, more explicit stories ensures that readers after the fifth century BCE understood cataclysmic themes in the *Catalogue*.

65. In Hesiod 2007 (tr. Most), 232–35.

66. See the commentary and sources on the term προφάσις in Clay 2003, 170–72.

67. Translation from Hesiod 2007 (tr. Most), 234–35.

68. Koenen 1994, 28.

Though the notion of a divine destruction on account of the threat of human-divine intermingling is indeed tantalizingly known from other literature,[69] this reconstruction is admittedly not clear.[70] According to Koenen and West, among others, it is quite possible that the τέκνα θεῶν are not semi-divine figures as opposed to the "earthly people," but are to be identified with the fourth generation of heroes of the *Works and Days*.[71] If the standard (i.e., Wilamowitz's) reading is in fact correct, then we have yet another reference to an intentional divine plan to annihilate the ἡμίθεοι, standing in parallel to the *Cypria*'s reference to the end of the race of heroes and to the *Iliad*'s flooding of the Achaean wall in which the death of the ἡμίθεοι is prefigured. Given the fragmentary state of the critical passage here in the *Catalogue*, however, caution is obviously warranted.

As these examples plainly demonstrate, themes of a divine plan to put an end to the heroic age via the totalizing catastrophe of the Trojan War are deeply embedded in at least three separate and early Greek traditions. Though the *Cypria* and Hesiod are most explicit concerning this divine plan, conceived as either a response to a burdened and overpopulated earth or as part of a predetermined plan to advance the cycle of world ages past the age of the heroes/demigods, the *Iliad* too at critical moments hints of such a plan.[72] Though Hesiod does not go into detail about the method of destruction beyond stating that the Bronze Age came to an end through martial aggression, the *Cypria* and *Iliad* are more explicit in their themes and use of imagery; in the *Cypria*, Zeus is credited with the capability of destroying by (Theban and Trojan) wars, thunderbolts, or deluge, while in the *Iliad* battle is of course the foremost trope. But we have had occasion to observe the blatant reference to flood in the *Iliad*, invoked at the exact location (*Il.* 12.22–34) where Homer most clearly identifies the status of the heroic race (i.e., as ἡμίθεοι) as separate from humans living in later, post heroic times.

Notions of periodic cataclysm and the rising and falling of ages were apparently not limited to these allusions in the epic sources I have been describing here, however. Two examples come to mind, one from a fragment of Anaximander's *On Nature* (early sixth century) and the other from

69. See, e.g., Hendel 1987b, 18–21.

70. See Koenen 1994, 28–31, and sources cited therein.

71. Koenen 1994, 28–30. Even so, the passage still rings with the tones of ancient Near Eastern mythology and displays obvious points of contact with the Oriental literature, as still duly recognized by West, Koenen, and others.

72. As Scodel (1982, 46–47) points out, the theme of total destruction may have been muted intentionally in the *Iliad*. But others, e.g., Kullmann (1955; 1956 as cited in Scodel 1982, 46 n. 34) saw explicit references in the *Iliad* to Zeus' plot to destroy all of the heroes. See, more recently, Kullmann 1992, 11–35, 36–37.

the later writings of Plato (mid-fifth century) in *Timaeus* and elsewhere. The pre-Socratic Anaximander seems to have taken up a view of periodic, mechanical, time-bound retributive justice, enacted as a matter of the natural course of things insofar as boundaries are transgressed and retribution for the invasion of space itself must be meted out:

> ἐξ ὧν δὲ ἡ γένεσίς ἐστι τοῖς οὖσι καὶ τὴν φθορὰν εἰς ταῦτα γίνεσθαι κατὰ τὸ χρεών· διδόναι γὰρ αὐτὰ δίκην καὶ τίσιν ἀλλήλοις τῆς ἀδικίας κατὰ τὴν τοῦ χρόνου τάξιν

> The things that are perish into the things out of which they come to be, according to necessity, for they pay penalty and retribution to each other for their injustice in accordance with the ordering of time.[73]

Here, Anaximander affirms the idea that the continuing maintenance of cosmic justice is enacted through destructions that mirror the initial ordering event, i.e., out of and back into the initial stasis of the substance itself. What is made must be unmade, and the mere act of existing guarantees eventual undoing in a continuing cycle of give and take. A related idea comes in the form of Plato's myth of periodic cataclysm (expressed most famously in *Timaeus* 22–25, *Critias* 19–112, *Laws* 677–80, etc.), where again we find the impression that the existing order is overturned (and even specifically by floods), though in Plato's view these cataclysms are episodic and serve to define specific periods of human history.[74] The references discussed above could be regarded as variations on this theme of periodic cataclysm, even as they are more broadly a part of the widely attested pattern of the totalizing deluge that washes away injustice and levels that which is irregular and ascendant.

III. Conquest and Cataclysm in Mesopotamia

Overpopulation and Destruction in Atrahasis

Turning to the Semitic-speaking world, we find some of these same threads: human overpopulation, or at least a human burden on the earth; divine displeasure with humans in this regard; cataclysm by flood and/or battle.

---

73. Quote here taken from Kirk, Raven, and Schofield 1983, 117–18. For further discussion, see Kahn 1994, 166–98 and Vlastos 1947. I thank Suzanne Smith (personal communication, May 2010) for pointing me in the direction of the Anaximander fragment and the sources cited here.

74. Cambiano 2002 is often recognized as the best treatment of the topic in Plato. See also Sedley 2007, 119–20. Aristotle took up Plato's views in this regard (see references in Sedley 2007, 119 n. 58), and compare also the theory of *anacyclosis* developed by the second-century Greek historian Polybius, on which see Trompf 1979, 4–115.

Indeed, the progression of human burden and overpopulation followed by cataclysm seems to have originated in Mesopotamian literature, with perhaps its clearest manifestation in the Atrahasis epic. Once humans are created to do the hard labor originally carried out by the gods, the human population becomes unruly, multiplying to the point of noise pollution.[75] As the repeated refrain has it:[76]

> *ú-ul il-li-ik ma 600.600 mu.ḫi.a*
> *ma-tum ir-ta-pí-íš ni-šu im-ti-da*
> *ma-tum ki-ma li-i i-ša-ab-bu*
> *i-na ḫu-bu-ri-ši-na i-lu it-ta-a'-da-ar*

> Twelve hundred years had not yet passed
> When the land extended and the peoples multiplied
> The land was bellowing like a bull
> The god got disturbed with their uproar

As in the *Cypria* epic, where flood, thunderbolts, and ultimately a totalizing war are options for population reduction, in Atrahasis we read of plague, disease, starvation, and so on that are attempted without permanent success before the flood.[77] The discrete problem of noise is ambiguous. Enlil's displeasure with human loudness could be interpreted as a cynical comment on divine impatience, but the reference might indicate something like an increase in violence, or the burgeoning "noise" is representative of some other inappropriate burden humans place upon the earth or represent to the divine world, such as the work necessary to perpetrate a human over-reaching into the divine sphere.[78]

The Flood Levels Babylon in Assyrian Inscriptions

Not only do we find this pattern of overpopulation leading to cataclysm, but we also have the conflation of battle and flood—or, more specifically, diverted rivers as a re-creation of the cosmic flood used as a weapon of

75. As Scodel (1982, 40–42) points out, not everyone affirms the overpopulation interpretation of this passage; see Oden 1981, 200–207, as well as Moran 1987, which endorses the overpopulation view. Von Soden (1973) disagrees with the overpopulation interpretation, as does Pettinato 1968 and Albertz 1999, 14.

76. Text from Lambert and Millard 1969, 66–67, lines 352–55 (following their reconstructions).

77. In *Gilg.* XI.181–95, Ea chastises Enlil after the deluge, suggesting that the god should have employed more limited techniques of population reduction (e.g., ravenous lions and wolves, famine, and Erra/plague, i.e., some of the exact techniques that apparently failed in Atrahasis). In *Gilg.* XI.14, the gods decided on a deluge with no ulterior motive.

78. On the noise motif as it appears in the Erra poem, with reference to other Mesopotamian myths, see Machinist 1983b, 224–25.

literal and symbolic annihilation.[79] Several inscriptions of Sennacherib and Esarhaddon describing the destruction of Babylon (in 689 and 678 BCE, respectively) attest to the use of flooding as a means of returning the doomed locale back to its primeval state during the ancient flood.[80] There is reason to doubt the historical occurrence of such a complete destruction of the site, though incomplete archaeological investigation hinders a comprehensive assessment.[81] The motif is expressed most explicitly in an inscription of Sennacherib:[82]

> *ad-di ina ki-rib ali šú-a-tu ḫi-ra-a-ti aḫ-ri-e-ma er-ṣi-is-su-nu i-na mê*[meš] *as-pu-un ši-kin uš-še-šu ú-ḫal-liq-ma eli šá a-bu-bu na-al-ban-ta-šu ú-ša-tir aš-šú aḫ-rat û-mi kak-kar ali šú-a-tu ù bîtâti*[meš] *ilâni*[meš] *la muš-ši i-na ma-a-mi uš-ḫar-mit-su-ma ag-da-mar ú-šal-liš*

> As far as the midst of that city I dug canals, laid flat its (lit. their) earth with water; the very structure of its foundations I destroyed. I made its destruction more complete than (in) the Flood. So that, in days to come, the site of that city and (its) temples and deities would not be remembered, I completely blotted it out with water and made it like a plain.

The phrase *eli ša abūbu* should not be translated as "more complete *than by a flood*" (so Luckenbill, et al.), as in the typical flooding of a city space, and thus without reference to the primeval deluge.[83] Rather, *eli ša* here must mean "more than" or "in excess of" a particular *abūbu*,[84] and indeed the attested range of meanings for *abūbu* strongly suggests the reference must be to *the* Flood as a "cosmic event."[85] Other points of contact with the flood

---

79. See Machinist 1983a, 726–28, 735; 1997, 190–95. Machinist (1997, 194) is correct to assume, in my view, that the flooding in at least some instances (e.g., of Nineveh in 612 BCE) was a symbolic measure, a "ritual flooding," and not a technique of active warfare. For further treatment of these sources, and others, see West 1997, 377–80; Van De Mieroop 2004; Scurlock 1990, 382–84; Huddlestun 2003.

80. See Galter 1984, 164, 169, as well as Kuhrt 2000, I/II: 499–505, 582–86. For other sources on flooding, see Machinist 1997, 191 n. 49.

81. See, e.g., Kuhrt 2000, I/II: 585; Galter 1984; Landsberger 1965.

82. The following text and translation, which I have emended somewhat, is from Luckenbill 1924, 84 (lines 52–54).

83. Luckenbill 1924, 84; this translation is followed without question by Van De Mieroop 2004, 1.

84. For *eli ša* as "more than, in excess," see *CAD* IV: 89.

85. *CAD* I: 77–81. With this resonance, *abūbu* can be appropriated and personified in a variety of ways, e.g., referring to monsters, weapons, and powerful mannerisms (e.g., Esarhaddon is characterized as one "whose gait is the Flood" [*ša tallaktašu abūbumma*]; Borger 1956, 97). The *abūbu* also marks a specific division of time, as in the description of Gilgamesh as one who *ub-la ṭè-e-ma šá la-am a-bu-bi* ("brought back a message from before the Flood"), *Gilg.* vol. 1, I.8.

of the city and the primeval cosmic flood can be found. The use of the verb *sapānu* evokes a specific result of the power of the deluge in *Gilg.* XI.129, where we read of the storm "laying flat the land" (*i-sap-pan māta*), with the result in line 136 that "the flood plain was level like a roof" (*ki-ma ú-ri mit-ḫu-rat ú-šal-lu*).

The motif of flattening the city like the ancient flood conjures up the judgment associated with the flood in the broader Gilgamesh and Atrahasis traditions, and this judgment results in a complete destruction not akin to mundane local flooding. Moreover, in *Gilg.* I.8, reference to the *abūbu* is used to mark a specific, "pre-modern" period in the distant past, the time "before the flood" (*la-am a-bu-bi*), much like Sennacherib's destruction marks an end to Babylon's era and to the very memory of its physical location. A specific reference to flattening also appears, we will recall, in the leveling of the Achaean wall in *Il.* 12.30 (λεῖα δ' ἐποίησεν παρ' ἀγάρροον Ἑλλήσποντον, "he made [the beach] all smooth along the strong stream of the Hellespont"), an event marking a division between the ἡμίθεοι of the heroic era and post-Trojan-War time.

The status of the *abūbu* in Sennacherib's inscription receives further illumination through an account of Esarhaddon, who described the flood-ed fate of Babylon by comparing the inundation of the city to the ancient deluge:[86]

> *i-gu-ug-ma* ᵈ*en-líl-la₅ ilâni*ᵐᵉˢ ᵈ*Marduk a-na sa-pan mâti ḫul-lu-qu nišê*ᵐᵉˢ*-šá ik-ta-pu-ud lemuttim* ⁱᵈ*A-ra-aḫ-ti nâr ḫegalli a-gu-ú ez-zi e-du-ú šam-ru mīlu kaš-šu tam-šil a-bu-bu ib-bab-lam-ma âlu šu-bat-su eš-re-e-ti-šu mê*ᵐᵉˢ *uš-bi-'-ma ú-še-me kar-meš ilâni*ᵐᵉˢ ᵈ*ištarâti*ᵐᵉˢ *a-šib lìb-bi-šú iṣ-ṣu-riš ip-par-šú-ma e-lu-ú šá-ma-meš*

> Then Marduk, chief ("Enlil") of the gods, grew furious and plotted evil (*lemuttim*), (viz.) to lay flat the land, to destroy its people. The Arahtu was carried forth, a raging river,[87] a furious inundating wave, a wild swell, a powerful tide, a replica of the Flood (*tamšīl abūbu*).[88] He sent the waters through the city, its dwellings, its cult places—he changed them into a mound of ruins. The gods and goddesses dwelling in its midst flew away like birds and went up to the heavens.

Several points of interest arise from this passage. *Lemuttim* here is

---

86. The text here, which I have emended at points, is from Borger 1956, 13–14 (Fassung a: A, Episodes 5, 7, 8; lines 34–46); the translation is my own, sometimes following Borger and also *EFH*, 379.

87. Lit. "a river of plenty/fertility" (*ḫe[n]galli*); see *CAD* VI: 167–68.

88. *Tamšīl* here may also mean "likeness, equivalent, same as," i.e., the flood is the equivalent in power and size to the ancient *abūbu*; see *CAD* XVIII: 147–50.

typically translated as "evil," which is inevitably misleading because of the implications the word "evil" has come to have in English. Nevertheless, *lemuttum* routinely refers to that which is "bad," whether by morally perverse intention, bad luck, or disastrous consequences.[89] In this passage, the *lemuttim* must refer to the destruction specifically as an endorsement of the conquering Assyrians, which is to say, Marduk planned *lemuttim* against Babylon. However, it is certainly the case that Esarhaddon is specifically avoiding the implication that his father, Sennacherib, enacted the destruction: since Esarhaddon wanted to rebuild the city, he also sought to circumvent the obvious suggestion that his own empire had just destroyed it.[90] Ergo, the flood is attributed to the *lemuttim* of Marduk.[91]

The phrase *tamšīl abūbu* ("replica of the Flood") here is also intriguing, and is undoubtedly meant to evoke the primeval *abūbu* ("Flood") of Utnapishtim's era. The first flood is the model, and the classification of the present deluge as a *tamšīl abūbu* indicates that the flood sent upon the city was a cosmic duplicate, in form and also in purpose, of the ancient *abūbu*. The result of the deluge of Sennacherib's devising has two specific points of reference in the canonical Mesopotamian flood traditions. First, on a general level, the acts of flood and warfare are conflated insofar as their destructive effects are concerned. In the Neo-Assyrian royal inscriptions these effects are ubiquitous, and in *Gilg.* XII.111 the flood is compared directly to an act of warfare (XII.111): *ki-ma qab-li eli niši*[meš] *ú-ba-'-ú ka-šú-šú* ("like a battle the cataclysm passed over the people"). More specific is the correspondence of divine reaction in each case: the deities flee the drowned territory and retreat into the heavens. In Esarhaddon's inscription, "the gods and goddesses dwelling in its midst flew away like birds and went up to the heavens"; and in *Gilg.* XII.115, "they withdrew; they went up to the heaven of Anu" (*it-te-eḫ-su i-te-lu-ú ana šamê ša* [d]*a-nim*). In both cases, the flight of the deities is emblematic of the terrifying nature of the deluge, but the reference to the Babylonian gods flying away is more directly political, implying divine abandonment and the deities' unwillingness to protect the city.

As several classical scholars have shown, the Greek Iliadic scene of the diverting of rivers to flood the Achaean wall has its historical roots (and not merely typological correspondence) in earlier Mesopotamian military and

---

89. See *CAD* IX: 127–30.

90. As noted in West 1997, 379.

91. Diodorus records the destruction of Nineveh by flood by citing an anonymous prophecy that the city would only be taken when the river turned against it (*Bib. hist.* II.26.9), with the flooding and destruction of the walls occurring as the "natural" result of flood and not intentional diversion (II.27.1).

mythological imagery.[92] West, for example, cites no less than eight categories of similarity,[93] but perhaps the most specific indication of borrowing is the notion of diverted rivers for the purpose of destructive flooding, a technique that is most unnatural to the geography of the *Iliad*. Moreover, the notion of a flood that would divide between eras of human existence exists in both settings—encoded in the reference to the ἡμίθεοι in *Il.* 12.23 and marked by the reference to the *abūbu* in the Neo-Assyrian inscriptions and *Gilg.* I.8—probably originates with the Mesopotamian concept. It is not only the fact of historical dependency on the broadest levels of plot that deserves attention, but also the motif of flattening and the return to a primeval, pristine state caused by the leveling power of the flood and military conquest. Though giants or violent heroes are not mentioned in the Mesopotamian sources here, one still discerns notes of divine justice shot through the Mesopotamian accounts—those who rear their heads up against the Assyrian power will be flattened; the image of walls and buildings reduced to a sediment filled plain could hardly be more clear.

IV. Conquest and Cataclysm in the Hebrew Bible

Though others who have compared Gen 6:1-4 and other biblical giant traditions with the Greek texts outlined above have claimed the affinity among these literatures is "obvious,"[94] there are still several lines of investigation that deserve extended attention. How, exactly, does the varied biblical picture of the giants fit into this exchange of motifs?[95] First, summarizing elements of my discussion in Chapter Three, we have good (though not conclusive) reasons to believe that the Gen 6:1-4 tradition was intended as an etiology for the origin of giant beings. The status of the Nephilim and the ancient Gibborim as products of divine-human sexual congress is at least clear enough, leading us to believe that the products of the union were thought to be monstrous, powerful, semi-human notables of the ancient world. The reference in Num 13:33 (where the spies declare that the Anaqim

92. E.g., Scodel 1982; West 1997, 380.
93. The categories are (in West 1997, 380): destruction because of divine displeasure; rivers channeled into site; flood washed away everything; foundations torn up and turned into water; debris washed out to sea; site left level; purpose: to deny posterity knowledge of the place; river(s) returned (by gods) to original bed.
94. So Scodel 1982, 42; see also Koenen 1994, 29.
95. As I have already noted, there are several opportunities for comparison between the events in Gen 6:1-4 and ancient Greek sources. See already Gruppe 1887; 1889a; 1889b; Kraeling 1947b, 195 n. 10, 201-07; Hendel 1987b. Comparing the Israelite conquest battles with Greek materials is less explored territory, though see Weinfeld 1993, 1-51 for a comparison of the Israelite settlement narratives with those from Rome and Greece.

are "from the Nephilim" [מן הנפלים]), brief though it is, demonstrates that already within the period of the Bible's composition some author directly connected Canaan's giant inhabitants to the Nephilim.[96] The juxtaposition of the Nephilim and the Gibborim traditions in Gen 6:4 may in fact represent a conflation of two originally distinct, yet compatible, traditions, viz. giants (Nephilim) and famous ancient warriors (Gibborim).[97]

Nevertheless, we must be impressed by the truncated and enigmatic nature of Gen 6:1–4, and by the relatively suppressed nature of other biblical giant traditions (particularly the Rephaim, Emim, Zamzummim, etc.), even as other aspects of the tradition are so prominent (particularly the Og tradition, and David's encounter with giants).[98] The destruction of the giants in both flood and battle, however, provides a compelling starting point for comparison with the Greek traditions outlined above.[99] In light of these materials, we must consider how the biblical giants fit into the mythic and epic patterns of the establishment of *díkē* over *húbris* by way of a process of pruning, of cutting down and leveling off the violently overgrown.[100]

The Flood Levels the Giants

First, consider the role of the giants in the cosmic flood of Genesis 6–9, which I have already discussed from several angles in the previous chapter. Though it is not possible conclusively to show that the presence of giants is the sole or primary motivation for the flood, there is good reason to believe that the Gen 6:1–4 episode holds something of the key to understanding the divine response in Gen 6:5–7 and following in the flood narrative generally.[101] C. Westermann provides perhaps the most cogent argument against

96. As discussed in Ch. 2, it is not clear whether this reference relies upon Gen 6:1–4 as an earlier segment of the tradition, or upon some other unrecorded source that inspired both Gen 6:1–4 and Num 13:33. Post-biblical traditions overwhelmingly considered the Gen 6:1–4 story in terms of giants.

97. See this same suggestion in Scodel 1982, 49 n. 40, and references there. Indeed, such a conflation would further demonstrate the natural interplay between notions of the gigantic and the heroic, and holds well for the Greek traditions, where both heroes and giants meet their demise by divine decree in response to heroic/gigantic overreach.

98. Regarding the truncated nature of the motifs, recall the discussion of biblical "epic" in Ch. 1, in which I suggested, following Cassuto (1973–1975, 108–09), that the sparse yet meaningfully loaded appearance of certain biblical materials can only be explained by a detailed background "literature" (whether written or oral) which is now lost to us.

99. See also Hendel 1987b, 18, 20, on the dual cataclysmic motifs of flood and warfare (and the Trojan War, specifically).

100. Obviously, this image of leveling or flattening is not the only image one could use. E.g., Hendel (1987b, 23) speaks of the rectification by Flood in Genesis 6–9 as a restoration of "balance."

101. The strongest case for this relationship has been made by Hendel (1987b, 22–25) and Kvanvig (2002), whose views I follow here.

any special damning power of the Gen 6:1–4 incident. He claims that we see in Genesis 1–11 the "snowballing" of more or less equal types of sins leading to destruction.[102] This is not particularly convincing, though, since two of the three or four obvious pre-deluge infractions—Adam and Eve's illicit fruit and Cain's act of murder—have a sort of ambiguous status: each of these crimes has a specific punishment by which the deity hedges against totalizing destruction and preserves human-divine relationship (through the making of clothes and a protective mark, respectively).[103] This is not the case in the forbidden comingling in Gen 6:1–4, and, in fact, Gen 6:1–8 should really be read as a single unit, documenting the infraction of "the sons of God" (בני האלהים) and the subsequent vow by YHWH in 6:5–8:

> (v. 5) YHWH saw that the wickedness of humans on the earth was great, and every intention of even his deepest thoughts was only wicked, all the time. (6) YHWH regretted that he had made humans on the earth, and it pained his heart. (7) So YHWH said, "I will wipe out the humans that I have made from upon the face of the ground, from humans to beasts and creeping things and birds of the sky, for I regret that I made them." (8) But Noah found favor in the eyes of YHWH.

At any rate, if in fact one wants to use the image of the snowball, then it would still be appropriate to see the action in Gen 6:1–4 as the precipitator of the flood, since it pushes the burden of human wickedness over the previously acceptable bounds and forces the deity's hand into cataclysm. The nascent world could bear the knowledge that comes from eating of the tree, and individual murderers could be punished in various ways (both before and after the flood, Gen 4:11–12, 9:5), but the offspring of divine-human miscegenation proved to be an over-reaching of a different, more disastrous kind.

Whether overpopulation can be seen as the exact cause within Gen 6:1–4 for the deluge (on parallel, possibly, with the Atrahasis epic) is genuinely debatable, but I would contend that it is the specific product of the sexual union—the Nephilim and the Gibborim—that prompts the cataclysm, not a mundane increase in human numbers.[104] Kvanvig, for example, argues that it is a combination of the overpopulation motif (marked by "noise"[105]) with

102. Westermann 1984, 368–69.

103. To use the language above applied to Hesiod versus Homer on the aspect of the preservation of the heroic race, we might say here that, in response to the transgressions of Adam/Eve and Cain, YHWH opts for preservation, whereas in the case of Gen 6:1–4 there is no preservation (or, more specifically, no preservation for the transgressors).

104. Cf. Kilmer (1972) and Kikawada (1975), who argue for the overpopulation motif in Genesis 6.

105. Kvanvig (2002, 109) derives this interpretation from the odd construction בשגם in Gen 6:3, which he takes as a borrowing from the Akk. *šagāmu*, "roar, clamor, noise." But

a specific kind of antediluvian race that brings about the flood, and this may well be the case, even as a direct reference to overpopulation in the story is frankly lacking. One may find an allusion to this problem in the opening phrase of Gen 6:1, "When humans began to increase upon the face of the land…" (ויהי כי החל האדם לרב על פני האדמה), but we have no clear reason to believe that לרב ("to increase") refers to a disproportionate or otherwise unacceptable manner of growth.

D. Pedersen has offered a striking interpretation of the problem, in that he claims there is simply no reason or purposeful result of the flood whatsoever insofar as the Yahwist was concerned. Taking Gen 6:5 versus 8:21 (both of which affirm the utter wickedness of humans, both before and after the deluge), Pedersen argues that J has made an oblique comment on the flood story, which he felt compelled to record even if "with ironic detachment": the flood was for nothing, and nothing has changed (except YHWH, who now sees that humanity cannot be reformed).[106] One major reason for this incongruence in J, according to Pedersen, is the monotheistic nature of the biblical flood story—specifically over and against the Mesopotamian accounts. The author cannot easily blame YHWH for the flood and also have YHWH as the solution—which he nevertheless does—in the same way that the authors of Gilgamesh, for example, can blame Enlil for the problem and credit Ea with the solution. Pedersen's view here, however, does not take into account other Mesopotamian texts wherein the deity displays similarly bifurcated actions. One might take the presentation of Marduk in *Ludlul Bēl Nēmeqi* ("I Will Praise the Lord of Wisdom") as instructive: a cruelly powerful Marduk rains down suffering on humans, and yet this same Marduk brings merciful relief from suffering. Even though human wrongdoing plays some (ambiguous) role in the cycle of suffering, Marduk's dual role as destroyer and healer is clear.[107]

Whatever the case, it is the Priestly author who employs a blatant motif of un-creation and re-creation before and after the flood by way of linking the deluge with the order of the initial (Priestly) creative event in Genesis 1.[108] These connections appear most clearly where the language and imagery of un-creation and re-creation in the Flood story directly mirrors elements of

---

Kvanvig fails to offer a translation of Gen 6:3 (or Gen 6:1–4 as a unit) that makes sense of this correlation between בשגם and *šagāmu*.

106. Pedersen 1976, 441–46.

107. This same duality (for YHWH) also appears in the book of Job, where interpreters often assume the dual presentation of destroyer and healer results from separate editorial layers. For *Ludlul Bēl Nēmeqi*, see Annus and Lenzi 2010 and *COS* I: 486–92.

108. On the literary and thematic connections between creation and flood, see Tsumura 1994, 44–49; Clark 1971; Kikawada 1975; Kraeling 1947a, 283–84; and Pedersen 1976, 440–41. The observations here are my own, though others have noticed similar correspondences.

the primordial creation in Gen 1:1–2:4. In the reversal of creation, all that has the breath (רוח) of life will be exterminated, except for the two representatives of every species of animal, male and female, on the ark (Gen 6:17,19; 1:2,27, 2:7); all creeping things (רמש) will be exterminated (Gen 6:20; 1:24–30); on the seventh day of the flood, the earth is completely undone in a reverse Sabbath (Gen 7:10; 2:1–3), and the "deep" (תהום) erupts again (Gen 7:11; 1:2); the earth returns to a state of landless, water-filled void (Gen 7:17–23; 1:2). After the critical turning point in the narrative at 8:1, a wind (רוח) blows across the earth and the waters are divided again to allow for dry land (Gen 8:1–5; 1:2,9–10), the command to be fertile and multiply is reissued (Gen 8:17, 9:1,7; 1:28), and the deity instructs humans regarding what can be consumed (Gen 9:3–4; 1:30).[109]

Thus we see the interaction between the processes of *establishing* order and *maintaining* that order. The law must be set down and continually enforced, and the law needs both muscle and symbolic currency; one way to achieve this balance is to maintain order through acts and punishments that mimic the initial establishment of order. Read this way, the Noahic flood of Genesis 6–9 reasserts the created order of the world by first disassembling the existing cosmos back to its pre-creation state (Gen 7:10–24) and then by re-creating the world in the same way it was first established (Gen 8:1–8, 9:1–7). In this regard, it seems that the flood account in Genesis, when compared to the destructive flooding in the Greek and Mesopotamian accounts described above, is most explicit regarding the status of the flood as an agent of literal and figurative flattening, a movement that returns the earth back to its primeval status. It is this very re-creation motif that invests the flood narrative with a redemptive meaning: humanity is remade, and the world begins again with God's chosen family, Noah—just as it will begin again in Gen 12:1 with Abram.[110]

We would be stretching our material too far, I think, to assert that the *only* purpose for the flood is to destroy the monstrous creations of Gen 6:1–4. But it is fair to say that the *húbris* represented by the violations that result in the birth of giant, semi-divine beings, is at the center of the problem, and it is this imbalance that needs to be addressed in the narrative by the flood. Moreover, we are not told what, beyond the illicit sexual union, the Nephilim or Gibborim did to deserve destruction. The tradition has apparently muted this point, though we must presume a larger matrix of oral or written

---

109. See now Blenkinsopp 2011, 131–54.

110. All of this still does not answer the question of why there ever had to be a flood in the first place, a question which Pedersen thinks vexed the Yahwist, but, in this reasoning, P takes existing source material from which he cannot subtract, and adds a redemptive veneer.

material in which Gen 6:1–4 and other stories of giants made sense.[111] Thus, the solution to the problem in Genesis 6 can only be annihilation. Giants represent a primal anxiety; they cannot help but over-occupy, over-reach, and over-grow, and these infractions of physical and moral space are repeatedly not tolerated in each cycle of existence in which the giants play their monstrous role. There are multiple ways to talk about the dichotomy between *húbris* and *díkē*: overpopulation and stasis; noise and silence; violence and rest; overgrown and pruned; ascendant and flat. Thus, even the first post-Noah event in the narrative, the Tower of Babel incident (Gen 11:1–9), stands as another reflex or mirror image of the scene in Genesis 6–9.[112] Just as the flood levels the antediluvian giants, YHWH levels the tower and scatters the inhabitants; the human movement in Gen 11:1–4 is frantically and excessively *vertical*, and the divine solution is to spread humans abroad (11:8–9), a decidedly *horizontal* resolution.

Flood and Battle in the Hebrew Bible

Though the great deluge functions as the initial, primordial event of destruction, the ensuing state of tranquility can only be maintained by a continual process of "flattening." David's flattening of the Philistine giants, or example, is a visceral act of chaos maintenance that mimics the flattening of the hubristic Nephilim and Gibborim destroyed in the flood. So too the military conquests of Moses, Kaleb, and Joshua in the books of Numbers and Joshua represent the same movement and the same goal, and should be considered as continuations or repetitions of the flood in terms of the ongoing need to control the threat of the monstrous and to cut down that which has grown up too high. The chosen method for this maintenance is that of warfare, specifically enacted either via the totalizing effects of "the ban" (חרם) by Moses and Joshua, or in single combat by Kaleb, David, and David's mighty men. As a bridge between the images of flood and battle, we may begin by noting that the conflation of flood and battle imagery in the Hebrew Bible appears in several locations and thus attests to the natural affinity between these two acts of violence.

---

111. I am inclined here to agree again with Cassuto 1961, 300–01: "...the Torah's intention is to *counteract* the pagan legends and to reduce to a minimum the content of the ancient traditions concerning the giants. Of that content only so much was retained as was innocuous to Israel's monotheistic faith, and did not in the least detract from the glory of God..." Moreover, any interpreter who sees Gen 6:1–4 as a "fragment" or detached mythological element of some kind must also be implying that this story originally had a much richer, extended context.

112. See Kraeling 1947a on Genesis 11 and creation motifs vis-à-vis parallel Mesopotamian accounts.

For example, in Exodus 14–15, the water of the Reed Sea is used as a weapon. In Judg 5:4, the pouring down of rain in a storm forms part of the theophany of YHWH as divine warrior, a motif found in 2 Sam 22:12; Hab 3:9–10,15, and elsewhere.[113] In 2 Sam 5:20 // 1 Chr 14:11, David directly compares his victory in battle to the power of bursting floodwaters ("YHWH has broken out against my enemies before me like the bursting of flood waters!" [פרץ יהוה את איבי לפני כפרץ מים]), and the onslaught of Israel's enemies is compared to roaring water in Isa 17:12–13 and Ps 124:4–5.[114] Egypt's rise is compared to the rising and surging of flooding rivers in Jer 46:7–8, and a chapter later in Jer 47:2 we find a striking image of the Babylonians storming in from the north to destroy the Philistines as an overflowing torrent (לנחל שוטף) whose waters of destruction cover the land (וישטפו ארץ). In Ezekiel 26 we find what seems to be a close typological parallel to the flooding of the Achaean wall in the *Iliad*: a flood destroys city walls, because of the arrogance of a people (Tyre) dwelling on a seashore. In Ezek 26:3, YHWH compares the nations coming against Tyre with the waves of the sea. Though this image begins with the quite straightforward water-as-military-force analogy, in 26:19–20 the imagery is reintroduced with a cosmic flair reminiscent of the flood/creation complex with implications for the afterlife of the citizens of Tyre:[115]

(v. 19)...when I cast up upon you (בהעלות עליך) the great deep (תהום), and the mighty waters cover you (וכסוך המים הרבים)...

(20)...and I will bring you down (והורדתיך) with those who go down into the Pit (יורדי בור), to the ancient people (עם עולם), and I will cast you down into the earth below (בארץ תחתיות, i.e., the Underworld), like ancient ruins (כחרבות מעולם)...

Other examples of this kind could be adduced.[116] Further investigation,

---

113. See also Pss 77:17, 147:18; Isa 28:2; Jer 10:13 // 51:16; Ezek 1:24, 43:2. The image of YHWH as a storm god who marshals the power of the flood, clouds, lightning, and stormy weather has its roots in earlier Canaanite expressions involving Ba'al and Marduk; see, e.g., the discussion of the storm theophany in Syria-Palestine and ancient Israel in Miller 2006, 27, 37, 41, 50, 60, 114–15, etc. Nah 1:8, combined with Nah 2:7–9, seems to combine the water image as it relates to the Divine Warrior with a historically accurate reference to a (literal) military flood tradition; see discussion infra.

114. Cf. Pss 32:6, 144:7.

115. Note also the so-called "Jeremian apocalypse" in Jer 4:23–27, in which Frymer-Kensky 1983, 410–11 sees an allusion to flood themes to describe military conquest, and specifically to the cosmic flood of Genesis (i.e., the reference to the תהו ובהו, as in Gen 1:2). Jeremiah's imagery seems more akin to a desert, actually, as indicated in 4:26 with mention of a מדבר, but the effect is nevertheless the same.

116. E.g., the literal rising of waters makes an odd appearance in the context of battle in

moreover, reveals a series of passages wherein the destructive power of water and human martial action are combined in such a way that evokes the specific Assyrian traditions of flooding Babylon—and also a tradition that Nineveh, capital of the Assyrian empire, was itself flooded at the sack of that city in 612 BCE.[117] In Isa 8:7–8, the prophet speaks of the Assyrian threat as "the waters of the swarming and mighty River" (את מי הנהר העצומים והרבים), viz. the Assyrian king, whose flood-like attack will "spread out over Judah, flooding and overflowing until it reaches the neck" (חלף ביהודה שטף ועבר עד צואר יגיע). This description seems to be drawing on some knowledge of Assyria's acts of flooding cities, though admittedly the image is commonplace enough to be a cliché in this context.[118] In Nah 2:7–9, however, the reference is clearer. Assyria will be paid back for its actions by a flood: "the gates of the Rivers are opened" (שערי הנהרות נפתחו), "and Nineveh will be like a pool of water, whose waters are unleashed (?)" (ונינוה כברכת מים מימי היא והמה נסים).[119]

I highlight these passages demonstrating the conflation of water/flood and battle imagery in order to establish that the affinity between these two methods of destruction is widespread in the Hebrew Bible, and also by way of showing the Bible's own deep participation in what is a broader and Mediterranean and Near Eastern tradition that uses flood and battle motifs to describe a totalizing destruction of a particular group (e.g., the heroic race in the *Cypria*, *Iliad*, and *Catalogue*) or a city, an annihilation that levels what has grown upward—people or a city, or both—back to its "natural" state.

Let us turn from the flood imagery to the other method of leveling the giants: warfare. The movement here as I am describing it is more abstract; the cutting down of giants in battle is an act, I would argue, that we have to conceptualize visually as an extension of the flood. To be sure, the flood trope was both powerful enough and general enough to be used a paradigm for other situations. Consider, for example, the only explicit invocation of the flood in Isa 54:7–10, where both the punishing nature of the flood and YHWH's concession afterward are used by Second Isaiah as a model for the harsh nature of the exile and the forthcoming compassion that will be

---

2 Kgs 3:13–27. Dan 9:26 is enigmatic, but the author seems to be imagining destruction by flood (וקצו בשטף), and Dan 11:10,40 has the king of the North passing through the land like a flood of waters, using a key verb for flooding and overflowing, שטף.

117. See the treatment of these passages with reference to Mesopotamian flood imagery in Machinist 1983a, 726–27, 735–36; 1997, 190–95.

118. I.e., the author may invoke flooding as a literary motif—the Assyrians did not, in fact, flood out Judah.

119. As pointed in the MT, מימי should be translated "from the days of...," but the reading מימי היא does not make sense and is not attested anywhere else; I have assumed מימי is some form of) מי/מים so too, e.g., Roberts 1991, 61.

shown to the exilic community.[120] A different illustration comes in Ps 29:10, where we find the only reference to the specific term for "flood," מבול, out-side of Genesis 6–9. If מבול here is in fact an allusion to the deluge, then the context of Psalm 29 as a possibly archaic Canaanite hymn may indicate that the great flood held some place in the early cult, where YHWH's place as "enthroned above the Flood" (למבול ישב, v. 10), along with the immediate subsequent affirmation of YHWH's kingship (יהוה מלך לעולם), confirmed the *Chaoskampf* pattern of the victorious divine king reigning over the unruly waters.[121]

Cutting Down the Giants through Battle

If the giants represent nature reacting badly, that is, nature reacting to in-justice or hubris, then it is the job of the divine warrior and the righteous human community to resolve the situation appropriately and restore or-der. Moreover, wherever they appear, biblical giants represent an affront to harmonious human community, and to YHWH's divine plan for his chosen group. Indeed, as Simkins has shown, *within* a community, the paradigm of speaking about nature is that of *harmony*, representing the harmony within the "ingroup." When the community faces an external threat, the relation-ship with nature changes from harmony to subjugation and warfare—nature must now be *overcome*.[122] In this sense, giants are obviously a hostile threat, the ultimate "outgroup," and must, like any other aspect of nature out-of-balance, be corrected. Thus, the diverse uses of the flood motif I have outlined above, along with the conflation between flood and battle images, suggest that it is appropriate to look for analogues to the flood in its role as leveler of the giants in other contexts where giants are defeated.[123] In fact,

120. The flood motif in Isa 40–55 is not confined to this one passage, however; see Gunn 1975 and Frymer-Kensky 1983, 409–12, who draws out the implications of the exile-as-flood motif in a particularly illuminating manner.

121. If this is in fact the correct association here in Ps 29:10, then the meaning of the Flood is somewhat different from what we find in Genesis 6–9, where YHWH's control of the Flood is never a matter of question (and there is no hint of a battle to be won or any opposi-tion whatsoever). But Ps 29:10 may still function as an affirmation of YHWH's control over the situation, which is basically the view of Pardee (2005, 170–72). Others, e.g., Freedman and Hyland 1973, 254, have viewed the ל here temporally, "from the time of." It is not clear to me what this would mean, however, if the concept of the מבול as some chaotic or opposing force is absent from the context—unless למבול is simply an idiom for "from time immemorial," etc. On Ugaritic forerunners of this imagery, see Cross 1997, 147–63, as well as Day 2002, 95–98.

122. Simkins 1991, 170–72. Thomas (2005) also employs Simkins' paradigm to interpret giants.

123. Recall that both flooding and totalizing war were used to destroy the Greek heroic generation. See also Hendel 1987b, 18, 20, on the justification for speaking of both flood and warfare as parallel moments. See also Nagy (2006, §67), who compares the biblical giants and

given the image of overgrowth and flattening which I have been invoking throughout this chapter, the associations appear most natural: the giant and his world can be drowned, as all structures and all that is excessively upright are washed away, or he can be cut down by the sword.

Perhaps the most iconic moment of flattening by warfare occurs in the killing of Goliath, the giant with an explicitly detailed height, in 1 Samuel 17. When Goliath crashes to the ground, something special is initiated in David's career, and indeed for the entire young nation of Israel. David has committed his first violently political act, and, as a bookend to David's rule in 2 Sam 21:15–22 // 1 Chr 20:4–8, we yet again find David and his men battling that familiarly frightening race, struggling to cut them down like weeds that grow perpetually upward. In like manner, Kaleb's leveling of the three giants occupying Hebron (Josh 15:13–14; Num 13:22) represents a similar movement at a similarly charged moment of political and historical crisis, where the giant again stands as the symbol of disorder, of wrong ownership, of lawless possession.

The most extreme image of this cutting down is the חרם ("dedicate to complete destruction," "ban," "dedicate to holy use"), a religio-military institution brought into play in the conquest and other scenarios. The term חרם is found in a number of contexts (about eighty times overall, including non-military settings), mostly describing an action of complete annihilation carried out by Israel against their enemies and directed by God.[124] Though the חרם is not specifically invoked in most of the texts wherein giants are slain, there are two explicit references linking the חרם and giants, both in the book of Joshua. In Josh 2:10, Rahab the prostitute mentions that she has heard of the חרם enacted on both Sihon and Og (the latter being a conspicuous member of the giant Rephaim; see, e.g., Deut 3:11,13; Josh 12:4, 13:12, etc.), this being a source of fear for the residents of Jericho. In Josh 11:21 it

---

the flood concept with totalizing war and flood motifs in the *Iliad* and *Cypria*, as well as the comments on flood and battle in Frymer-Kensky 1983, 410–11.

124. Sometimes the term is used to describe what God will do to Israel (Isa 42:28, Jer 25:9, Zech 14:11, Mal 4:6, cited below), or to denote things devoted to holy use for priests (Lev 27:21; Num 18:14; Ezek 44:29; Mic 4:13; Ezr 10:8). For the conquest in particular, see Deut 2:34, 3:6, 7:2,26, 13:15,17, 20:17; Josh 2:10, 6:17–8,21, 7:1,11,15, 8:26, 10:1,28,35,37,39,40, 11:11,12,20,21, 22:20; Judg 1:17. Other references include Exod 22:19; Lev 27:28–29; Num 21:2–3; Judg 21:11; 1 Sam 15:3,8,9,15,18,20–21; 1 Kgs 9:21, 20:42; 2 Kgs 19:11; Isa 34:2,5, 37:11; Jer 25:9, 50:21,26, 51:3; Zech 14:11; Dan 11:44; 1 Chr 2:7, 4:41; 2 Chr 20:23, 32:14. For an overview, see Stern 1991; Malul 1999; Brekelmans 1959. The concept of חרם was apparently widely held in the Northwest Semitic speaking world; closest to Israel, king Mesha of Moab reports in his stele that Nebo was conquered, with its inhabitants "consecrated" (החרמת) to Athtar-Chemosh (*KAI* I.33:14–18; II.176–77). See Mattingly 1989 and Monroe 2007. Cf. the Akkadian concept of *asakkum* (CAD A/ II: 326–27) and Malamat 1966.

seems that a special point is made of the Anaqim being the victims of the totalizing method of the חרם:

> And Joshua came at that time and cut off (ויכרת) the Anaqim from the hill country, from Hebron, from Debir, from 'Anab, and from all the hill country of Judah, and from all the hill country of Israel, along with their cities: Joshua completely annihilated them (החרימם). None of the Anaqim remained in the land of the sons of Israel...

Moreover, a somewhat oblique—but valid at least on a symbolic level—connection between the flood and the חרם involves the explicitly stated role of both in cutting off the breath (רוח, נשמה) of all living things. Note the repeated phraseology in Gen 6:17, 7:15,22, in comparison with Deut 20:16, and also Josh 10:40, 11:11,14, where Joshua is repeatedly said to kill "all that breathed" (כל נשמה). Specifically, the phrase כל...נשמה in Gen 7:22 can be viewed, along with the other examples given above, as a signal marking the reversal of the created order, since in Gen 2:7 YHWH breathes the "breath" of life into the nostrils of the first humans (ויפח באפיו נשמת חיים). In a similar fashion, then, the חרם undoes the created order by also eliminating כל נשמה. The חרם as an image of complete and utter annihilation is therefore a very appropriate analogy to what the flood does to its world of monstrous and iniquitous opponents.

V. Conclusion

The similarities between the Greek heroic generation and the biblical giants run deeper than the fact that both were destroyed through similar means.[125] As I have attempted to demonstrate, the impact of the flood as that which flattens or straightens the land—language used explicitly of the power of a totalizing deluge in both Greek and Mesopotamian sources—comports naturally with the language of *díkē* and *húbris*. The visual image of flattening, then, has functioned as my ruling image in this chapter for what must continually happen to the giants, as well as to the Greek heroes and other representatives of opposition to the divine will in the ancient Near East. The biblical giants, specifically, are the victims of flood and warfare (in Genesis 6–9, the Conquest, and by David and his men), and thus it is likely the case

---

125. It is worthwhile to mention—but only briefly and tentatively at this point (see Ch. 5 for further discussion)—that the violent ends for both the biblical giants and the Greek heroes are epic and mythical reflexes of the same historical upheaval, viz. the collapse of the Late Bronze Age civilizations of the Mediterranean and Near East. On this level, the comparison between the two groups is a comparison between those who, in each case, must be destroyed before a new epoch of world history can begin. On this, see, e.g., Finkelberg 2005, 169.

that the biblical authors saw the races of giants as a special target of the totalizing, cataclysmic violence of flood and the extreme warfare represented by the חרם.

I have tried to demonstrate here, as others have before me, that there are indeed important parallels between the demise of the Greek heroic generation and the destruction of biblical giants. More than that, however, I have argued that we should extend the horizons of the investigation on the biblical end of the equation to include not just the parallel between flood motifs but also the biblical gigantomachy detailed in the conquest narrative and the monarchy. Kingship is the ultimate solution to giants because the exemplary king—David—is the only one who can ensure lawfulness and stability. The Flood narrative, viewed through this lens, is about kingship and the right administration of human justice, and therefore the flood and conquest are prefigurations of what could be made permanently real on the human plane through monarchic rule. The destruction of the giants that occurs in the flood, conquest, and in David's time represents a sustained, implicit reflection on the need to continually reassert the order brought about by cutting down that which grows too high.

But it is not only the efficacy of the king which is at stake. So too, YHWH's own singular rule is put to the test when competing sources of divine (or partly divine) power threaten the centrality of YHWH's place in the system. In this sense, Israel's gigantomachy is a variation on the mythic battle between order and chaos. This battle, like the *Chaoskampf* motifs involving mythic and recurring battles with the sea, is an ongoing drama, and indeed the battle against the giants is one form of the *Chaoskampf*.[126] Under such a system, the monstrous continually reappears, even when he is putatively crushed with finality (as demonstrated in the previous chapter); the giant grows too high, and will be cut down again. In its heavenly expression, the *Chaoskampf* is a victory of the Divine Warrior against other divine (or personified) forces; on the human plane, YHWH's chosen agents mimic the divine pattern and enact victory in battle over human enemies. In both of these spheres, one act of violence is never enough. To the extent that these powerful opponents keep springing up, we have truly *epic* conflict, i.e., a conflict between more or less equally matched powers—a kind of functional polytheism.[127] The primordial flood turns out to be an incomplete solution

126. I borrow this conception of the *Chaoskampf* as an ongoing, partly finished drama from Levenson (1988). Though Levenson's focus is the creation-chaos alternation specifically (as in the *Enuma eliš*, with reflections in Ps 74:12–17; Isa 51:9–10, etc.), the overall pattern he evokes is very pertinent to the giants as *Chaosmacht* (i.e., as I have described them here and in the previous chapter).

127. Despite the many difficulties involved with precisely circumscribing the category of

to the problem of giants, and Israel's military leaders are left to hack them down in stages, even one by one, in order to reign in the chaos. King David's decisive place in this scheme points up the extreme value of the monarchy as an institution in promoting justice and right order; the problem of giants that could once only be accomplished by God in Genesis 6–9 became the project of humans in conquest and monarchy (even if under divine decree).[128] These are issues that deserve further exploration, and we will return to them again later in this study.

On the historical and comparative levels, I have suggested that the combination of flood and battle themes in the destruction of the Bible's giants has a compelling parallel in the presence of these same cataclysmic forces in Greek epic literature, and the affinity between these literatures in this respect suggests that the Bible's story of the destruction of its giants has significant parallels in the Greek Trojan War traditions. The parallel of course reveals key differences as well, to which I have alluded throughout this chapter. One difference—and it is no small difference—between the Greek heroes and the biblical giants is the fact that the Greek heroes are objects of extreme reverence and (positive) awe (as in the *Iliad* and Hesiod's myth of the metallic ages), while the biblical giants are denigrated as a monstrous exhibition of what is unjust and out of control. There is a marked hostility toward the past in the biblical narrative at key junctures, i.e., specifically a hostility toward an era of corruption or wickedness that immediately precedes the establishment of divine order.[129] Though not explicitly characterized as such in the Bible, the giants could even be imagined as a sort of corrupt image of despotism or rule by mundane force preceding the establishment of true monarchy in Israel, analogous perhaps to the development in Greece between rulership in the era of heroes and the democracy of classical Athens.

Having therefore begun to explore aspects of comparison between some Greek texts and the biblical giants, in the final two chapters of this study I will continue to investigate the often overlooked and sometimes subtle ways that the biblical giants are caught up in an extensive ancient Mediterranean conversation regarding the existence and fate of the "hero," as a figure both

---

epic in all historical periods (as discussed in Ch. 1), many have noted epic's seemingly inevitable association with polytheism in both the Aegean and the Levant. On epic's association with polytheism in the Hebrew Bible, see M. Smith 2001, 174, and sources cited there. See also Louden 2007, 90–95, on the polytheistic nature of epic, as well as Olender 1987, 339–41 and Gregory 2006, 1–30.

128. Similarly, in the cuneiform texts discussed above, it is the king who artificially recreates the flood in service of his military goals.

129. This same pattern, however, is clearly present in the Greek Gigantomachy/Titanomachy, where the giants represent an older, corrupt order of power.

in epic and in cult (Chapter Four) and as a participant in a "heroic age" that flourishes and then dies out of historical existence (Chapter Five). In doing so, we will find that the comparative project underway here is not only a matter of finding matching textual descriptions or specific, event-oriented motifs, but also a question of deep and underlying assumptions about the shared power of broader cultural and religious ideas.

Chapter Four

Hero in Epic, Hero in Cult: The Narrative Sublimation of Heroic Dualities in Biblical Giants

How many sub-rosa twins are there, out there, really?...What if in fact there were ever only like two really distinct individual people walking around back there in history's mist? That all difference descends from this difference? The whole and the partial. The damaged and the intact. The deformed and the paralyzingly beautiful. The insane and the attendant. The hidden and the blindingly open. The performer and the audience. No Zen-type One, always rather Two, one upside-down in a convex lens.[1]

> denk: es erhält sich der Held, selbst der Untergang war ihm
> nur ein Vorwand, zu sein: seine letzte Geburt.
>
> (remember: the hero lives on; even his downfall was
> merely a pretext for achieving his final birth.)[2]

WE HAVE THUS FAR BEGUN TO SEE the manner in which some of the characteristics apparent in the Greek heroic age have been "transferred" to, and negativized in, the figures of non-Israelite giants.[3] In the Bible, the deeds of the giants are rather muted, their activities subsumed under mysterious labels such as Rephaim and Anaqim and Nephilim, and their transgressions are sometimes only the topic of the briefest of allusions. In attempting to understand the texts in question, one often labors under the suspicion that we, as modern readers, are not getting the complete picture that ancient Israel's oral and written traditions had to offer. Part of my emerging argument has been, therefore, that Israel's giants represent fragments of local memory and tradition, not all of which have been preserved, and that these giants played an even larger role for ancient audiences than we find in the Hebrew Bible—where their function is often large enough.

1. Wallace 1996, 220.
2. Rilke 1989, 152–53.
3. I use the term "transferred" here without any hard or fast judgment about whence the transfer came. Indeed, as I noted in several instances in the last chapter, some of the patterns utilized in the Greek materials likely had Near Eastern origins. Thus, finding these patterns in biblical texts may represent something of a homecoming.

In the present chapter, I narrow the focus and take up a second avenue of comparison between our giants and various figures in Aegean materials, and this comparison will take us more deeply into the identity shared between some of the giants and the fate and function of the Greek heroic generation. One significant issue, as yet unaddressed in a satisfactory manner, involves the dual identity of certain groups of giants as both "semi-divine" figures or inhabitants of the shadowy netherworld, on the one hand, and, on the other, as mundane (even if giant) mortal inhabitants of the land of Canaan before, during, and after the arrival of the Israelites. The Nephilim are apparently meant to be conflated with the divine/human miscegenation in Gen 6:1–4, and yet, via one quick stroke in Num 13:33, they are human inhabitants of a particular land, the progenitors of a very real flesh-and-blood people group that Israel is commanded to annihilate. The Rephaim appear in several biblical passages as shades of the dead, and yet the Rephaim are also a "historical" entity of pre-Israelite inhabitants, whose race dies out with the passing of Og king of Bashan.[4] The Gibborim are a class of human warriors, named and in the service of various living, human figures (most prominently David), and yet there are strong hints that other kinds of Gibborim exist, those whose origins are "of old" (מעולם) with the Nephilim (Gen 6:4; cf. Gen 10:8) and who appear, like the Rephaim, as residents of a mythical topography in the afterlife (Ezek 32:27).

How does one explain such phenomena, all involving the groups of giants I have been examining throughout this study? M. S. Smith claims that the question of reconciling the differing pictures of the Rephaim in the Hebrew Bible "has been the subject of much scholarly discussion," but in fact nearly all of the now voluminous literature on the Rephaim deals with essentially only *one side* of the phenomenon, viz. the issue of the Rephaim as shades of the dead, along with the possibly cognate depictions of beings called *rāpi'ūma* at Ugarit.[5] Some commentators have attempted to deal with the complex problem these two-sided depictions present, but few comprehensive solutions are offered.[6] To be sure, the idea that the biblical materials

---

4. Noteworthy here is the fact that the Rephaim as shades of the dead never appear in the Pentateuch or Joshua through Kings, while their status as a living people group is attested nowhere outside of Genesis through Joshua and a sole reference in 1 Chr 20:4 (but note that allusion to the Rephaim as a [perhaps long past] people comes indirectly through the geographical references in the Hebrew Bible to the עמק רפאים outside Genesis through Joshua).

5. M. S. Smith 1992, V: 674. E.g., regarding the Nephilim, Hendel (2004, 21) observes that "this dual significance...is odd" (with no ensuing discussion), and of the Rephaim, Grabbe (2007, 87) only states that "it appears that myth has been historicized, and the shades of the dead have been turned into ethnographical entities." Along these lines, see also Schmidt 1996, 267–68; Healey 1989, 35; Ford 1992, passim; Shipp 2002, 114–27; J. Day 2002, 221–25; Talmon 1983.

6. The most relevant and developed attempts are by Spronk (1986, esp. 45–48, 60–61,

under discussion here may be reflexes of Mediterranean presentations of hero cult is by no means a new one.[7]

What I shall argue here is that this oddly bifurcated presentation of various groups is not so unexpected. Rather, these seemingly disparate portrayals of the Gibborim, Rephaim, Nephilim, Anaqim, etc. can be best read in a holistic manner as heroic, epic phenomena in ancient Israel that correspond to the treatment of heroic culture elsewhere in the Mediterranean world, specifically in archaic and classical Greece. Though individual hero cults were, at least in the Greek world, a predominantly localized phenomenon (and attested archaeologically), I will argue that the power of dead heroic warriors and other significant figures of the past was a broader Mediterranean *koine* that manifested itself in ancient Israel through these ambiguous textual presentations in the Hebrew Bible. In contrast to Greek hero cult, however, the Hebrew Bible reveals relatively little regarding the power or efficacy of the dead as such,[8] though the fact that certain passages may be read as a polemic against the notion of powerful heroic dead is in itself evidence of countervailing theologies.

To make this argument, I invoke and develop an interpretive paradigm that views heroic figures in two simultaneous spheres of existence: the hero in *epic*, and the hero in *cult*.[9] Classicists have long propounded this model for Greek heroes, and it bears investigating in some detail in order to appropriately apply it to other texts. After describing this dynamic in some Greek materials, as well as Near Eastern sources (most notably from Ugarit[10]), the "hero in cult and epic" paradigm can be used to explore some of these texts presenting giants as human figures fighting the Israelites (epic), and as resi-

---

227–31, and 279–80), and Stavrakopoulou (2010, 64–70). At several points, Spronk (1986) asserts (but does not argue at length for) the equivalency of biblical giant traditions involving the Rephaim, Nephilim, and Gibborim with Greek heroic concepts. Stavrakopoulou (2010, 68) views the Transjordan as a "netherworld dwelling," and argues that "it is the dead of the land [i.e., the Rephaim], and not simply the living, who must be disempowered and supplanted. See also Dietrich, Loretz, and Sanmartín 1976; Gese 1973, 197; Loretz 1978, 176 n. 74; de Moor 1976, 336, and n. 82; Horwitz 1979, 39–40; Weinfeld 1991, 162; Liwak 2004, XIII: 605, 609, 613; F. Graf 1999.

7. See already the brief comments in: Gunkel 1997 (first published 1901), 275; Lods 1906, 92. Albright's (1957, 253–54) controversial interpretation of the biblical במות ("high places") in terms of hero cults (further discussion below) was preceded by Karge (1917, 527–623), whom he does not cite.

8. With some important exceptions, which I discuss below.

9. This view of hero in epic and cult has been cogently articulated by the classicist Greg Nagy, and I borrow the succinct categorization of the epic/cult dichotomy here and throughout this chapter from him. See, e.g., Nagy 1999b, passim; 1990a, 202–22; 2009b, I§§132–36; 2001, xv–xxxv; 2006, §§80–115.

10. Besides the Ugaritic materials, note also, e.g., the figure of Gilgamesh (see Jacobsen 1976, 209–12, as well as my discussion infra).

dents of the underworld (cult). Specifically, I reexamine materials related to the Og and Rephaim traditions, as well as some aspects of the Nephilim and Anaqim question, and, additionally, I will argue that some aspects of Ezekiel 32 can be read as a commentary on heroic afterlife concerns and on Gen 6:1–4. Through analysis of these traditions and others, I argue that the more developed pattern of epic formulation of heroes in the Greek context also underlies the dual presentation in the Hebrew Bible, and that the dual presentation itself is a narrative sublimation of more generalized heroic themes revealing aspects of Israelite thought regarding giant warriors and their fate.[11]

I am not offering a comprehensive answer to question of the identity of the Rephaim in any given period, nor am I choosing sides amongst the many and competing attempts to view the Rephaim or any other group as *either* human or divine, as *either* living or dead. Rather, I argue that the dual identity as *both* human and divine, *both* living and dead, is grounded in a duality of heroic existence that had a broad currency in the Mediterranean world and which found expression in ancient Israel as well as in the well known Aegean settings.

I. Hero Cult in the Ancient Aegean

In archaic and classical Greek materials, we find the identity of the hero representing something of a duality. The hero acts on the stage of epic as warrior, performing great deeds in battle, but he proceeds to play a role *after death*, in cult, for blessing and benefit, thus embodying what would seem at first to be contradictory roles, i.e., as killer and as healer.[12] The hero dies, as does his entire "historical" generation in the epic past, but death releases the hero into a new era of existence in the cultic present of the audience. This dichotomy is partly revealed through archaeological discovery, which

11. I use the phrase "narrative sublimation" with reference to Levenson 1993, e.g., 52. Compare the use of this term, e.g., in Greer 2006, 285, as well as Gemes 2009. As Levenson (1993, ix) states regarding his topic of child sacrifice, "[b]oth the rituals and the narratives that articulate this theme suggest that though the *practice* was at some point eradicated, the *religious idea* associated with one particular form of it—the donation of the first-born son—remained potent and productive." Similarly, I contend, ancient Israelites inherited native, Canaanite concepts of the powerful heroic dead, and even if the ongoing practice of such cults may have subsided, its underlying ideology and symbolism survived in textual forms. See Hendel 1987a, 84–86 for the use of a similar interpretive strategy.

12. See also Speyer 1988, XIV: 870. The heroic ability to ensure fertility (of land and humans) is easily transferred into the realm of healing; the Asklepius cult, in particular, combined healer and hero ideologies, but there were many others as well, such as Herakles, Achilles, and Amphiaraus. See Farnell 1921, 150–51, 234–79. Cf. the heroic epithet "healer of the world" in *Bhagavadgītā* 6 (63) 15.35–40, in van Buitenen 1981, 43.

has confirmed the reality of such cults as early as the eighth century BCE (and perhaps much earlier), and also through texts, wherein a complex and symbolic vocabulary invoking both elements of the hero's life in epic and the "hidden agendas" of heroic after-life are present. The manifestations of hero cult in ancient Greece have been the subject of enormous scholarly interest,[13] not to mention the wide variety of historical and geographical contexts in which hero cults of various kinds appear outside of the ancient Mediterranean.[14] At this point, I limit myself to describing some of the important factors involved with the hero cult development in the Aegean setting by way of laying the groundwork for the epic/cult dichotomy I wish to posit for the biblical and other Near Eastern materials.

Definitions and History of Scholarship

By way of definition, we should distinguish tomb cult generically from hero cult specifically;[15] hero cults may be thought of as a subset or extension of ancestor cults, and clearly the two are interrelated yet distinct phenomena.[16] Both involve burials and visits with offerings to the cult site, but unlike tomb cults, which are short-lived (one–two visits for offerings), hero cults are a long-term affair, stretching even over centuries at a single location.[17] Even though most of the tomb cult sites classified as examples of "hero cult" cannot be decisively identified with named heroes, long-term usage, evidence of repeated acts of ritual meals at the site, and local tradition recorded in texts can all help to confirm the heroic identity of a cult. The earliest written attestations to hero cult come from Hesiod and Homer, both presumably in the eighth century, as well as Athens' putative first lawmaker, Drakon, writing in the seventh century, and it may be reasonably assumed that these

13. For a concise and recent overview, see Ekroth 2007, 100–14, and Antonaccio, 1994; 1995; Hägg 1999; Schmitz and Bettenworth, 2009; Nagy 1999b; 2001; 2009b; 2010. These works, in addition to the specific studies cited infra in the body of the chapter, are the primary treatments through which I have accessed the question at hand. To give some sense of the energy that has been devoted to this topic by classicists, note these other modern treatments: Albersmeier 2009; Currie 2005; Ekroth 2002; Damon and Wuellner 1974; Delcourt 1992; Larson 1995; Pirenne-Delforge and de la Torre 2000. Older works on the topic, aside from those cited infra, are also plentiful: see Carlyle 1902; Foucart 1918; Wassner 1883; Paton 1921, esp. 60–151; Seemann 1869.

14. See, e.g., Brunk and Fallaw 2006; Chambert-Loir and Reid 2002; Schömbucher 1999; Chandrasekhara Reddy 1994; Forcey 1998.

15. See Antonaccio 1994; Whitley 1994, 214, 218–22.

16. I.e., a hero cult is a type of tomb cult, but a tomb cult need not involve a hero. Here I follow the views of Nagy 1999b, 115–16, who explicitly follows Rohde on the development of hero cults out of ancestor cults.

17. Antonaccio 1994, 402.

texts are not merely fictions.[18] We also have at least four major hero cult sites that can be reasonably identified as such for the eighth century—Helen and Menelaos at Laconia; Agamemnon and either Kassandra or Alexandra, also at Laconia; Agamemnon at Mycenae; and Odysseus at Ithaca.[19] From these examples, we can deduce the presence of many other smaller-scale, local, and anonymous (to us) hero cults at tomb sites.

The modern study of hero cult in Greece began with the studies of E. Rohde and L. R. Farnell,[20] and the pivotal question—which still occupies interpreters to a large degree in contemporary discussions—involved the role of Homeric epic in the development or perpetuation of hero cult.[21] Rohde had basically denied that Homer made any reference to cults of heroes, but still believed such cults were widely attested in the eighth century, while twenty years later Farnell posited that hero cult was essentially derived from, or at least heavily fueled by, Homeric verse. Over half a century later, T. H. Price reviewed crucial passages from the *Iliad* and *Odyssey* and clearly demonstrated Homer's awareness of cultic matters involving heroes.[22] Coldstream attacked the problem from the perspective of newer archaeological discoveries,[23] and indeed it is the archaeological data that have added so much insight and so many problems to the questions at hand. The earliest major archaeological study of the issue, conducted at the Argive Heraion by C. Blegen, found votive offerings at Late Helladic burial sites,[24] and subsequent studies confirmed the material reality of some type of ancestor cult—often presumed to be a cult of heroes—practiced at the Bronze Age tombs beginning in the eighth century.[25]

The meaning of the "gap" in attested heroic veneration at various

18. Antonaccio 1994, 390–91. Later sources, of course, include materials of all kinds; see infra.

19. Antonaccio 1994, 398, and notes 50–51 for bibliography. On the Odysseus cult at the Polis cave in Ithaca, see Petrakis 2006, 380–81, 391–92; cf. Waterhouse 1996. Other studies of specific sites (some in later periods) include, e.g., Whitley 1994; 1979; Broneer 1942. Many of these interpreters recognize the problems inherent in identifying archaeological remains with any particular cult (e.g., Broneer 1942, 128), but nevertheless affirm the heroic character of the cult remains and votive offerings in question. Iconographic evidence can also be effectively used, as by Kingsley (1979).

20. Rohde 1950 (first published 1898); Farnell 1921, 1–18.

21. See, e.g., Carter 1995.

22. Price 1973, 133–40; see, e.g., references to cultic rites offered to heroes, tombs, etc. in *Il.* 2.243–44, 546–51; 10.414–17; 11.166–69, 298–304; 16.604–05; *Od.* 7.80–81; 11.38, 166–69, 570, 601. Another dissenter from Rohde's thesis was Hack (1929). But see now Nagy 2012.

23. Coldstream 1976.

24. Blegen 1937.

25. But note that (non-heroic) tomb cults are attested from at least the tenth century BCE, as discussed by Antonaccio (1994, 402).

sites between the establishment of the tombs in the Late Helladic period and the eighth century is not completely clear.[26] The vast majority of these eighth-century votive offerings are anonymous, i.e., not accompanied by inscriptions designating the name of the offerings' recipient(s), which raises the question of why anyone in antiquity associated these sites with heroes. Snodgrass had made the proposal that the eighth-century cults were the result of peasants who inhabited long unoccupied land and felt the need to propitiate the local (dead, heroic) powers that be, thus forging a link of legitimacy with the past.[27] Whitley finds this too limiting, and instead argues that previously landed elites instituted the local hero cults (i.e., by adopting the local Mycenaean burial sites, regardless of whether these were "heroic" burials in origin) as a claim not just to the "title" of the land in which they were living, but by way of making a claim to worthy succession to a heroic past.[28] Whatever the case—and Whitley's proposal seems more reasonable here[29]—it seems clear that the hero cults were a *local* phenomenon, which is not to say that a particular hero could not be venerated at multiple sites, but rather that a hero and his or her cult were identified with a local piece of land, as heroic ancestors in that land. The presence of the body would thus guarantee fertility and prosperity for the local inhabitants, as dramatized very pointedly in Sophocles' *Oedipus at Colonus*, where the final resting place of the hero's body is of the utmost concern.

One is still left with the question of why these proto-hero cults first (re-) flourished in the eighth century as opposed to some other period. S. Hiller argues persuasively that Homer is not primarily responsible for the renewed interest in the past in his eighth century context (*pace* Farnell and his congeners), but rather he is responding to a broader contemporary revival.[30] The basis of this revival, for Hiller, is not entirely clear; Hiller suggests that it has something to do with the onset of Mediterranean colonization (in both the East and the West) from the tenth–eighth centuries BCE and the prosperity resulting from this colonization.[31] One point of agreement among all inter-

26. That is, no significant tomb offerings that could plausibly be connected with hero cults have been found from the time of the tombs' origins in the Bronze Age until the eighth century.

27. Snodgrass 1982, 107–08.

28. Whitley 1988; see also Alcock 1991, who likewise argues for the hero cults as tools of elite legitimation in the late classical period.

29. By later periods, at least, it seems clear that the maintenance and control of such cults was an elite phenomenon; see, e.g., Carstens 2002.

30. Hiller 1983, 10. Others see hero cult in terms of an unbroken lineage dating from the Mycenaean period, such as Andronikos (1968) and Nilsson (1967, 378–79; see discussion and references in Price 1973, 130). See also Coldstream 1976, 17, but cf. Antonaccio 1994, 402.

31. Hiller 1983, 14.

preters, however, is that the hero cults began as a highly politicized affair, which involved claims and rival claims to identity and power. As Antonaccio argues, a shift in authority structures from the end of the Bronze Age through the Iron Age—from "kings" to tyrants and aristocrats—necessitated shifting bases of power, and for the king (*basileus*) in particular, the inability of genealogy to secure a position of power may have increased the value of cults of ancestors generally (and heroes specifically) as a "legitimating device." "In the polis, hero cult creates a civic kinship that may serve individuals or the needs of the state to foster a new group identity."[32]

Glances at Hero Cult in the Iliad and Odyssey

Regarding the difficult question of the relationship of texts to the archaeological materials, we find no easy answers, but it is important for our purposes here to notice the variety of ways that concepts of the hero as a cult figure are embedded in early epic texts. In what follows I focus on only two examples, from the *Iliad* and *Odyssey*—though obviously other materials clearly belong to the extended discussion at hand[33]—to show how the dual identity of the hero as an actor in epic and in cult can be found in major, early, sustained literary productions. In particular, I follow the interpretive paradigm laid out by G. Nagy in *Best of the Achaeans, Greek Mythology and Poetics*, and elsewhere,[34] invoking his language of "hero of epic, hero of cult" and the primary examples used to posit the reality of this dichotomy in the texts.

First, in *Iliad* 23 (recording the lamentation and funeral games of Patroklos), we find several meaningfully loaded references to the *sēma* (σῆμα, "marker," "tomb") of the hero, where the *sēma* refers not only to the heroic burial mound in the story, but also to the point around which chariots turn in the ritual chariot race and, ultimately, to the mystical point of veneration and source of heroic blessing from the afterlife.[35] In *Il*. 23.45, Achilles repeats his vow not to wash until he has heaped up a *sēma* for the fallen Patroklos; this will be Patroklos' final resting place, but its presence also foreshadows Achilles' own fate—as Achilles' "ritual double" and substitute, Patroklos' demise and burial is the cue for understanding Achilles' actions and future. As

32. Antonaccio 1994, 409–10.

33. E.g., Hesiod; various tragedies, e.g., *Oedipus at Colonus*; Herodotus; Philostratus' *On Heroes* (Philostratus 2001), etc. See, e.g., Henrichs 1993; Vandiver 1991, passim (e.g., *Hist*. 1.167–68, 2.44, 5.47, 67, 104–14, 6.34–38, 7.117). For Hesiod, see Nagy 1999b, 151–73.

34. In Nagy 1999b, see part II, pp. 67–201, esp. 114–19 for some of the language and examples used here, as well as Nagy 1990a, 202–22; 2006; 2009b.

35. Nagy 1990a, 214–15; Sinos 1980; Nagy 2006, §100–103. See also *Od*. 11.126–137; Frame 1978.

Nagy states, "Achilles himself simply presides over these events [in *Iliad* 23] as if he were already dead, having already achieved the status of the cult hero who will be buried in the *sēma* to be shared with his other self, Patroklos."[36] The status of Achilles in this part of the narrative nicely illustrates Achilles astride two worlds: the living and dead. Moreover, subsequent references to the *sēma* in *Iliad* 23 give further nuance to the meaning of the term and to heroic fate. In 23.326–31, *sēma* refers to a turning post in a chariot race, which itself is then conflated with the possibility of a *sēma* as tomb marker for an anonymous hero of bygone days. Achilles' own "turning" signifies not only the completion of an athletic contest, but also a "mystical" turning, from epic to cult (and back again), when his continued existence in his own *sēma* will act as a source of power for future generations.[37]

The second example, from the *Odyssey* 11, involves a similar dichotomy of meanings for the *sēma* and invokes the same heroic duality, of the hero in epic and cult.[38] In 11.75, Odysseus' colleague Elpenor appears in the underworld to beg that a *sēma* be set up for him on the sea-shore (though the marker is not explicitly one of heroic blessing from the afterlife, but rather "in memory of an unlucky man"). Teiresias, however, rises out of Hades and alerts Odysseus to "a certain sign" (*sēma*, 11.126), which will prompt Odysseus to finally return home, only after which his people will be prosperous around him (11.136–37). This *sēma*, then, is a "signature," marking on the surface a blessed contact with the hero's family upon his return, but, on another level, marking the prosperity brought by the hero as a powerful cult figure.[39] Thus we have here an image of the "unlucky" hero and of the lucky one, the latter (Odysseus) bringing prosperity to the people after his return "home," that is, his death and reincorporation into the earth.[40]

Through these texts, we are given a tantalizing glimpse into the complex presentation of heroes inhabiting two worlds simultaneously. To be

36. Nagy 2005, 316 (cf. the updated version of this same article, Nagy 2009a). For another "heroic pair" in epic poetry, one may compare Gilgamesh and Enkidu in various incarnations of the third–first millennium Gilgamesh Epic.

37. Nagy 2005.

38. Even Farnell (1911, 11), who generally denied that Homer had meddled with notions of hero cult, admits that such themes are hard to ignore in the *Odyssey*. Admittedly, in *Odyssey* 11 we do find the heroes living after death, but they seem to be accorded no special place; rather, they come out of the horde with the rest of the deceased (see esp. 11.475–76, 489–91). But cf. West 1997a, 164, and the discussion of Ezekiel 32 infra.

39. Nagy 2006, §103.

40. Drawing on the work of Frame (1978), Nagy (1990a, 218–19) has shown how this journey home itself (*nóstos*) in the Odyssey is, in fact, representative of the dichotomy of epic and cult writ large across the tradition: Odysseus' *nóstos* is a journey to "light and life," to family, but also a return from death.

sure, the examples given here are multifaceted and nuanced, and we cannot expect to find such detail or precision in all contexts where hero cults were observed in antiquity. Nevertheless, from these Greek texts we learn to expect the dual appearance of heroic warriors in contexts of epic and cult, as figures who straddle the divide between action in life and action beyond.

II. Hero Cults in the Ancient Near East?

Having now reviewed some Greek materials, we are prepared to inquire whether such concepts functioned in the East, and if so, how and where they appear. Contact between these two realms that could have spread specific notions of heroic cult is indeed attested. As A. Yadin points out, the eighth-century rise of Homeric epic in the Aegean brought with it a heightened focus on the heroic world and an intensified exchange of ideas in this regard, and this influence was evidently present in heroic burial customs, as illustrated in the "Homeric"-style burials uncovered in Salamis, Cyprus.[41] Such burials, if they are genuinely "heroic" in style and purpose, suggest not only the raw physical exchange of funerary architecture but also the possibility that religious and cultural ideas that go along with such burials were exchanged as well. The Salamis burials may be indicative of the same search for identity and meaning that apparently consumed the eighth-century Greeks who adopted Mycenaean tombs as raw material in their own antiquarian quest.[42] This turn to antiquity in antiquity was not limited to Greek contexts. During this same time period (eighth–sixth century), Mesopotamian kings such as Sargon II, Assurbanipal, Nebuchadnezzar, and Nabonidus engaged in library collection, archaizing, and even archaeological excavation in an attempt to re-connect with a better past, and archaizing tendencies of a similar kind appear prominently in materials from twenty-fifth- and twenty-sixth-Dynasty Egypt.[43]

41. A. Yadin 2004, 383–85. See the first announcement of these finds in Karageorghis 1962, and later Karageorghis 1995, as well as Hughes (1991, 69), who is skeptical of Coldstream's interpretation of the Salamis burials (as expressed in Coldstream 2003, 349–50). Karageorghis (2006) has recently re-affirmed his views.

42. A. Yadin (2004, 384–85) argues that the "turn toward the heroic past" in Greece spread eastward, the evidence for which may even be found in certain Philistine inscriptions and ostraca (where a revival of Greek style personal names may indicate a reaching back toward a Greek past, as opposed to Semitic assimilation). Yadin cites the name 'kyš ("the Achaean"?) in the Ekron inscription, as well as ostraca and a seal from Tell Jemmeh allegedly demonstrating a shift from Semitic toward Greek names (ending in -s). It is not at all clear, however, that these linguistic features are straightforward evidence for an archaizing tendency.

43. See brief comments on this, e.g., in Albright 1957, 316–17, and also Beaulieu 1994; Der Manuelian 1994. I discuss these antiquarian interests in more detail, with additional bibliography, in Chapter 5.

The Gilgamesh Traditions

Bearing these possibilities in mind, we may look in several directions for "bridges" of contact between the Aegean and Israel regarding hero cults. One starting point is the figure of the quintessential Mesopotamian "hero,"[44] Gilgamesh, whose presence as both an actor in epic and a recipient of cult is well attested.[45] In the third millennium Gilgamesh plays some role in funerary rituals, and we find reference to a du_6 ^{d}bil.ga.mes^{ki} ("mound" or "cult-platform, shrine" [?] of Bilgamesh) in central Sumer—which, as a geographical reference, could be a certain ancient tell or even some kind of hero shrine.[46]

Within the Gilgamesh epic itself, the offerings for the dead prescribed in tablet XII (as well as in "Bilgames and the Netherworld") could be actual reflections of, or instructions for, ritual use of some kind.[47] Moreover, parts of the Gilgamesh epic tradition point beyond the "historical" life of the hero and forward to the ongoing significance of the characters and events in the tradition. As P. Michalowski has argued, the reference to the lapis lazuli tablet box in *Gilg*. I.24–29, situated at the foundation of the city walls of Uruk, is a token simultaneously of epic self-referentiality (i.e., the story is about the story) and also a reminder to behold the very walls that Gilgamesh himself was said to have built.[48] The story itself has thus become, at least in its first millennium forms, a type of *sēma*, indicating the hero's deeds in epic and also pointing "forward" to his death beyond the epic proper and toward his ongoing life in the present of the audience.

Anatolia

Another point of contact in the East reflecting something that can be compared, even if tangentially, to Greek hero cult is the traditions involving

44. Gilgamesh's partially divine lineage and superhuman size/ability, combined with his great exploits, journey to far away places, and royal status all place him squarely within the heroic conversation from a typological standpoint. See, e.g., Wolff 1969, with explicit correlations to scenes in Homer, and Kramer 1946; Westenholz 1983; West 2000, I/II: 40–41; Evans 1901, 55.

45. On Gilgamesh as a cult figure who is particularly associated with the dead and invoked in ancestor rituals, see *Gilg*. 1, 123–35, as well as M. Cohen 1993, 53–54. On ritual involving the dead generally, see the review in Hallo 1992.

46. *Gilg*. 1, 123–24. The meaning of this reference is disputed and not at all certain.

47. *Gilg*. 1, 52–54. Parpola 1993 also speculated on the mystical significance of the Gilgamesh traditions as a source of esoteric knowledge regarding eternal life; see also Parpola 1998 and Cavigneaux 2000 (to which I have not had access, but cited in *Gilg*. 1, 53).

48. Michalowski 1999, 80. This dynamic may be compared with Achilles' status in the *Iliad*, where the hero's cultic meaning is inscribed throughout the text itself (as discussed supra).

stelae and ancestor cults in ancient Anatolia.[49] In the various Hittite texts, we are hard pressed to find clearly "heroic" figures along Greek lines, though of course the Gilgamesh epic was translated and preserved in Hittite. In a very recent review of the possibilities for Hittite heroes and epic, A. Gilan casts grave doubt on the possibility of native, Hittite heroic poetry, though he is able to locate a potential native Hittite term for "hero" (*haštali*) and cites the adoption of Sargon legends in Hittite and some aspects of Hattušili I's "manly deeds" (*pešnatar*) as variations on heroic motifs.[50] The recently discovered eighth-century "KTMW stele" from Sam'al with an Aramaic inscription gestures toward a type of ancestor cult with features in common with heroic cult, such as the notion that the dead live on in specific locales (i.e., at the monument),[51] periodic feasting at the tomb, and the designation of monuments only for certain, important individuals.[52]

However, other, earlier Hittite funerary ritual bears resemblance to the ritual scene involving Patroklos' death and funeral in *Iliad* 23. M. Kitts argues for at least three correspondences:[53] the use of a ritual substitute (Hit. *tarpanalli*; cf. Gk. *therápōn*), killed in place of a king, which involves the victim dressing in the other's clothes and becoming a type of "alter ego"; the mourning ritual after Patroklos' death, which closely mirrors attested thirteenth-century Hittite mourning rites; and the treatment of the bones of the dead (collected, treated with oil, wrapped in cloth, etc.). In the Greek epic context, these features creatively developed into religious symmetry with the ideology of hero cult, while in the Hittite context the tradition apparently did not undergo this development.

Ugarit

Before moving on to the biblical materials, we have one more conduit to

49. On Hittite ancestor cult, see, conveniently, Haas 2000, III/IV: 2027–29; Hallo 1992, 383. Hallo (1992, 384) also mentions second-millennium material from Ebla, where Matthiae (1979) has claimed to find a set of cultic sites and graves dedicated to ancestor worship in parallel with the way the Ugaritic *rp'um* and even the biblical רפאים were venerated. See the updated archaeological analysis of Pinnock (2001), with discussion of the royal ancestor worship locations.

50. Gilan 2010, 52–55.

51. See the KTMW stele, line 5, where the speaker requests offerings "for my 'soul' that (will be) in this stele" (*lnbšy zy bnṣb zn*) and also line 11, where the sacrifice will be conducted "in (proximity to) my 'soul'" (*bnbšy*). See Pardee 2009, 62–63.

52. On the KTMW stele and other similar funerary expressions, see Struble and Herrmann 2009. In this stele and other, similar Syrian-Anatolian monuments, we lack the dimension of epic—there was clearly no "Epic of KTMW"—and even of heroic action attributed to the deceased, as the funerary monument was likely erected as part of a broader pattern of ancestor cult.

53. Kitts 2008, 222–24 (following Van Brock 1959). See Vermeule 1981, 224–25 n. 27 for further suggestions on similarities between Hittite and Mycenaean funerary custom.

explore at some length, through which notions of heroic cults of the dead may have passed in the Late Bronze Age Mediterranean world: Ugarit, specifically in the form of various texts invoking beings called, in the plural, *rp'um* (in the nominative, *rāpi'ūma*; sg. *rp'*, *rapi'u*[54]).[55] Due to the ambiguity of the texts in which these figures appear, no clear consensus has been reached regarding the status and meaning of the *rp'um*. What I suggest here, however, is that the *rp'um* are best read as deceased and quasi-deified ancestors who have acquired some military connotations (allowing that some expressions may diverge from this concept), and I will contend that what seems to be confusion or multivalence in the Ugaritic sources regarding the living or dead status of the *rp'um* is in fact significant and meaningful along the lines of interpretation of the hero in epic/cult continuity I have been so far developing in this chapter.[56]

A brief history of scholarship. Though I cannot review all of the Northwest Semitic references to the *rp'um* in detail here,[57] we may begin by noting the ambiguous nature of many of our textual examples.[58] Many view the *rp'um* as deceased ancestors of the Ugaritic monarchy (or as ancestors of other notables), though many other issues are highly contested, such as the etymology of the term, the exact status of the *rp'um* as divine or quasi-divine, and the possibility that *rp'u* could also be a designation of a living individual. We know, at least, that *rp'u* was a deity (mentioned in *KTU* 1.108.1,19,22),

54. I am following the vocalization here of Huehnergard 2008, 2.

55. Though the exact channels through which Ugaritic literary motifs made their way into Canaanite culture generally and into the Hebrew Bible (even sometimes in relatively late texts) are not fully clear, it has been sufficiently shown that many such motifs have indeed been transmitted; see, e.g., the clear summary of some parallels in P. Day 2002, 234–36.

56. In reading the Ugaritic *rp'um* in the context of military expressions, I explicitly follow the views of Horwitz (1979) and M. Smith (2001, 233 n. 10), who endorses Horwitz's formulation. The conception of the *rp'um* as reflecting a broader Mediterranean pattern of hero cult has been suggested by several commentators—e.g., Spronk 1986, 227–31; de Moor 1976, 336 and n. 82; Schmidt 1996, 90–93, 267–73; Lewis 1989, 14.

57. *Rp'um* appear in Ug. materials in the following forms (references here taken from *UDB*, which corresponds with *KTU* and corrects many errant readings in *KTU*): *rp'um*: RS 2.[019] = *CTA* 21 = *KTU* 1.21 = *UDB* 1.21 (21:II:2,3,11); RS 2.[024] = *CTA* 22 = *KTU* 1.22 = *UDB* 1.22 (21:I:8,21,23; 21:II:10,20,21,25); RS 34.126 = *KTU* 1.161 = *UDB* 1.161 (1.161.8,24); RS 3.348 = *CTA* 20 = *KTU* 1.20 = *UDB* 1.20 (20:II:1,6); *rp'im*: RS 5.155 = *CTA* 6 = *KTU* 1.6 = *UDB* 1.6 (6:VI:46); RS 2.[019] = *CTA* 21 = *KTU* 1.21 = *UDB* 1.21 (21:II:9,11); RS 2.[024] = *CTA* 22 = *KTU* 1.22 = *UDB* 1.22 (22:II:8 [3x],19[2x]); *rp'u*: RS 2.[024] = *CTA* 22 = *KTU* 1.22 = *UDB* 1.22 (22:I:8); RS 24.252 = *KTU* 1.108 = *UDB* 1.108 (1.108:1,19); *rp'i*: RS 34.126 = *KTU* 1.161 = *UDB* 1.161 (1.161.9); RS 3.345 = *CTA* 15 = *KTU* 1.15 = *UDB* 1.15 (15:II:3,14); RS 2.[004] = *CTA* 17 = *KTU* 1.17 = *UDB* 1.17 (17:I:17,35; 17:II:28; 17:V:5,14,34,52); RS 24.252 = *KTU* 1.108 = *UDB* 1.108 (1.108:21,22); RS 3.366 = *CTA* 19 = *KTU* 1.19 = *UDB* 1.19 (19:I:20,37,39; 19:IV:13); *KTU* 1.166 = *UDB* 1.166 (1.166:14).

58. For summaries and bibliography, see esp. Shipp 2002, 114–27; Lewis 1989, 217–19; Spronk 1986, 161–96; Wyatt 2010, 75–78; Schmidt 1996, 71–92; Caquot 1985; Healey 1986.

and it seems fairly clear that a series of parallel terms in *KTU* 1.6:VI:46–49 (*rp'im*/*'ilnym*/*'ilm*/*mtm*) connect the *rp'um* with the dead and with divine figures.[59] M. Smith has elaborated a promising view of the *rp'um*, suggesting they are ancient tribal ancestors and markers of "cultural identification" for Ugaritic kings. Moreover, he proposes that the royal invocation of these figures in a text like *KTU* 1.161 (see below) demonstrates the need for a continuity of political identification and power felt by the Ugaritic dynasty.[60] In this line of interpretation, the *rp'um* would have functioned somewhat as the heroic generation did for Greek elites, i.e., as a basis for cultural and political authority, as well as personal legitimacy.[61] In some Ugaritic texts, the *rp'um* seem to be "tribal predecessors," to use M. Smith's terminology, of the deceased kings of Ugarit. Regarding a derivation for the name, many endorse the "healer" etymology, which seems to be the most straightforward reading, though other options are possible.[62] The relationship between the *rp'um* as a group or retinue of some sort and the singular *rp'u* is unclear, but the two seem to be related in *KTU* 1.22:I:8 and 1.108:1,19. *KTU* 1.161 (discussed below), however, seems to distinguish between an older group of "tribal ancestral heroes" (again, in Smith's words) and the recently dead kings.[63]

The dead Rapiuma. In order to argue that the Ugaritic *rp'um* reflect something of the range of meanings later invoked in Mediterranean hero cults, we must demonstrate the simultaneous role these figures could play as agents of blessing, prosperity, and legitimation from their position after death and as "heroic" military agents in life. The role of *rp'um* as ancestors who have achieved a preternatural status after death—a status that may not have been strictly limited to kings or other special persons—is easier to demonstrate.[64]

59. Cf. Ps 88:11; Isa 26:14,19 for a similar parallel between רפאים and מתים (as pointed out by Healey 1989, 37).

60. M. Smith 2001, 69.

61. Words such as "authority" and "legitimacy" often seem to suggest that those seeking authority and legitimacy do not really believe in the truth of their claims. Very often, the opposite is the case. See Schloen 2001, 88–89.

62. Cf. Spronk (1986, 195), who sees the *rp'um* as deified royal ancestors, and specifically "as *rp'um* the deified dead appear as warriors (cf. *KTU* 1.20:II.2–3; 1.22:I.8–9; II.6–8), but more important seems to be their help as healers (cf. *KTU* 1.124) and in securing the welfare of the city (cf. *KTU* 1.161:31–34)." Note also Ginsberg 1946, 41, and J. Day 2002, 217–19. But as Healey (1989, 39) points out, there is no clear contextual reason to endorse the etymology; one must look to analogous healer-savior figures to flesh out the argument. Lewis 1989, 14 and L'Heureux 1979, 216–17; 1974, 269–70 follow F. M. Cross 1973, 20–21 in reading *rapi'u* statively, with the meaning "one who is hale, hearty, robust, vigorous." At Cross' suggestion, Lewis (1989, 14) even ventures to state that Ug. *rp'u* may have the same semantic range as the Gk. *hērōs*. Note also Schmidt 1996, 92, who suggests a parallel with Akk. *rabā'um*, "to be large, great," and the derivative *rabium*, "leader, chief."

63. M. Smith 2001, 68. Cf. L'Heureux 1974, 270–71.

64. I borrow the idea of the "preternatural" status of the dead from Lewis (1989, 47–52). By

The most famous and revealing of the Ugaritic texts mentioning the *rp'um* in this regard is *KTU* 1.161, the so-called "Royal Funerary Text."[65] The first ten lines of this ritual text invoking the *rp'um* are worth translating here:[66]

1) *spr.dbḥ.ẓlm*	Book of the sacrifices of the night[67]
2) *qritm.rpi.a[rṣ]*	You are summoned,[68] O Rapiu of the "earth"[69]
3) *qbitm.qbṣ.d[dn]*	You are invoked, O Gathered Ones of Didanu
4) *qra.ulkn.r[pu]*	Ulknu the Rapiu[70] is summoned
5) *qra.trmn.rp[u]*	Trmn the Rapiu is summoned
6) *qra.sdn.w.rd[n]*	Sidanu-wa-Radanu is summoned
7) *qra.ṯr.'llmn*	Bull-'llmn is summoned
8) *qru.rpim.qdmym*	The Rapiuma of old are summoned
9) *qritm.rpi.arṣ*	You are summoned, Rapiu of the earth
10) *qbatm.qbṣ.ddn*	You are invoked, Gathered Ones of Didanu...

Several features of interest here may be highlighted. Pending the translation of *ẓlm* in line 1, the ritual seems to occur at night, a seemingly appropriate

"preternatural," I mean beyond the "normal," mundane, continued afterlife existence of non-royal or non-heroic individuals.

65. The editio princeps is Caquot 1975–1976, 427–29, and the first photograph of the tablet appeared in Schaeffer-Forrer (1978), 399–405 (pl. VII–IX), but see the newer edition of Bordreuil and Pardee 1982. The most involved study is that of Lewis 1989, 5–46, but other analyses include: del Olmo Lete 1999a, 192–98; Good 1980; Healey 1978; Levine and de Tarragon 1984; Pitard 1978; 1987; Pope 1994.

66. The readings and translation here are my own, but often follow Lewis 1989, 7–28.

67. *ẓlm* is a difficult word. Pitard (1987, 78) and Levine and de Tarragon (1984, 651–52) connect *ẓlm*, "shadow, shade," with shadows, and suggest the connotation of "protection," translating the term as "the Protectors" (cf. Gen. 19:8). However, to have a plural here, we would expect the (transitive) participle *ẓālilīma*. Others have suggested *ẓlm* means "statue." I follow Lewis (1989), who reads "nocturnal sacrifices," with *ẓlm* meaning "darkness," along the lines of Heb. *ṣēlmāwet*, "shadow of death." The root *ẓlm* ("darkness") is well attested in Akk., Arab., and Eth. See Tropper 2008, 145.

68. I analyze the verb here and in line 10 as a 2mpl Gᴾ, *qura'tumū*; see also Tropper 2008, 98. Many translated *qritm* and *qbitm* (see also lines 9–10) as a 2mpl SC, "you have invoked...you have summoned," or even a "prescriptive perfect," "you all will have invoked/summoned..." Pitard (1978, 68) reads these verbs as 1cs SC with enclitic -*mi*, "I have called/summoned," and Levine and Terragon (1984, 652) thought the passive was less dramatic—the narrator should be exhorting the *rp'um* to come to the sacrifice. Yet Lewis (1989, 13) effectively argues for a speech act, analogous to the Akkadian *Koinzidenzfall* (performative), "epistolary perfect."

69. In this context, especially, "earth" must indicate the underworld. See also lines 21–22:

b'lk.arṣ.rd.arṣ	your lord, descend into the earth, into the earth
rd.w.špl.'pr.tḥt	descend, and down to the dust, down under

Cf. also Akk. *erṣetu* (*CAD* 4, 310–11, with examples), and Heb. אֶרֶץ (e.g., Exod 15:10,12; Num 16:32–34; Isa 26:19; Jon 2:7; Pss 88:13, 139:15, 143:3; Job 10:21–22, etc.).

70. Given that the end of the line is broken here and in line 5, one could reconstruct the pl. *rp'im*. Moreover, the *rp'u* element in these names could be part of the proper name itself, as lines 6–7 have compound names.

time to invoke the dead.[71] The *rp'um* are the first group summoned to the gathering, and in lines 2–3 the *rpi arṣ* stand in parallel to the *qbṣ ddn*. The exact meaning of *ddn* here is unclear; an Akkadian lexical text has *da-at-nu* = *qar-ra-[du]*,[72] but more scholars now view *dtn/ddn* as an old Amorite tribe, Ditanu, or its eponymous ancestor.[73] These views are not mutually exclusive, however, as the Amorite tribe could have been designated as a warrior clan of some kind.[74] In lines 4–7 a series of names appears, none of which can be identified with any known figure from Ugaritic history; these may be anonymous tribal heroes, later ancestors of the *rp'im qdmym* mentioned in line 8. Indeed, these "Rapiuma of Old" would seem to include the totality of such heroic figures from the distant past, who are called to assemble with the current company of the ritual in question.[75] If, as I assume here, the actions in *KTU* 1.161 were conducted under the auspices of Ammurapi (III) (c. 1195–1175 BCE), Ugarit's last king, on behalf of his predecessor Niqmaddu III (c. 1210–1195),[76] then there is a special pathos attached to this particular text, as the king invokes a heroic past—even possibly in desperation—on the eve of the destruction of the once powerful city and the end of its dynasty of kings.

The living Rapiuma? KTU 1.161 clearly reveals the status of the *rp'um* as figures from the Underworld. What is more difficult to discern, however, is the possibility that the *rp'um* in other texts were living humans of some kind, and perhaps even members of some aristocratic or military guild.[77] Straightforward evidence for living *rp'um* at Ugarit is scant, as some have noted,[78] though two enigmatic references may be considered. An administrative text (*KTU*

71. For night rituals in the Bible, see, e.g., 1 Sam 28:8; Isa 45:19, 65:4.

72. Cited in Lewis 1989, 16.

73. דדן is an individual, tribe, or geographic locale in the Hebrew Bible in Gen 10:7, 25:3; Jer 25:23, 49:8; Ezek 25:13, 27:15,20; 1 Chr 1:9,32. See D. Graf 1992. In a study that has only recently come to my attention, Annus 1999 argues for an equivalence between the Ug. terms *dtn* and the Greek *Titanes*. Annus participates very deeply in the "etymological" stream of Greek-Semitic comparison I described in Chapter 1, though some of the correspondences he describes are compelling (or at least provocative).

74. Lewis 1989, 16 n. 51. In the Bible, קבץ can mean "muster for war" (Josh 10:6; Judg 12:4).

75. Levine and de Tarragon (1984, 655–56) argue that the kings here are not necessarily to be identified as the *rp'um*, especially in lines 10 and 24. The *rp'um* could include royal figures, but the two are not automatically identified with one another.

76. On the attribution to Ammurapi III, see, e.g., Healey 1978, 86 n. 18; Lewis 1989, 32. Note the references to Niqmaddu in *KTU* 1.161:12–13, and to Ammurapi in line 31.

77. This issue is aptly summarized in Shipp 2002, 114–23 and Ford 1992, passim. L'Heureux (1974, 271–72; 1979, 219–21) and Margalit (1989, 252, 300) both see the *rp'um* as members of a "warrior guild."

78. Ford (1992) has been most strident in this position, though actually he only attempts to make a specific argument that the full expression *rp'um arṣ* refers exclusively to the dead.

4.232:8) mentions *bn.rp'iyn*, where *rp'iyn* may be a variant of *rp'um* (or at least derived from *rp'u*); these figures are part of a group that receives a stipend from the king.[79] Another economic text (*KTU* 4.69:I:1, II:9), listing groups of warriors under the heading *mrynm* (I:1), includes the *b[n.]dtn* (II:9), and still another text refers to the *bn.rpiyn* (4.232:8) in the same list as the *mrynm* (possibly "charioteers," 4:232:33).[80] Schmidt proposes that both the *bn rp'iyn* and the *bn dtn* were "contingents of living warriors in the service of the royal court at Ugarit," and posits a specific historical development, viz. Ugarit's need to strengthen its defenses upon the loss of regional Hittite hegemony just before the Sea Peoples' invasion, as the impetus for establishing such forces.[81] This is plausible, but Schmidt's further conclusion that these political developments led to many such troops dying and thus the *rp'um* at that time took on a "specifically postmortem dimension as expressed exclusively in the epithet *rp'im qdmym*" is misguided.[82] The *rp'im qdmym* are certainly not recently deceased figures in the ritual of *KTU* 1.61, though it is certainly possible that the *rp'im qdmym* are ancient military heroes who achieved a special status upon death.[83]

The Rapiuma as warriors. Other references do make clear, however, the connection between the *rp'um* and military imagery on a broader scale.[84] W. Horwitz went so far as to declare that all the *rp'um* functioned as soldiers, leaning heavily on the imagery in the "Rephaim Texts" (*KTU* 1.20–22).[85] For example, KTU 1.22.B/I:8–10 reads, in part:

79. See discussion in Schmidt 1996, 89.

80. Schmidt 1996, 90 is slightly misleading here when he says the *bn rp'in* are listed "alongside the *mrynm*"—many lines separate the two references. One might be able to say, at most, along with L'Heureux (1979, 220), that the *rp'um* as a warrior class may have partly overlapped in function with the *maryannu*. Cf. Healey 1989, 37–38. *Maryannu*, incidentally, is derived from a widely-accepted Indo-European root (cf. Sanskrit *marya*, "young warrior"); see Drews 1988, 59.

81. Schmidt 1996, 90–91.

82. Schmidt 1996, 91.

83. Cf. Spronk 1986, 174: "It is possible to think here of the soldiers who died as heroes on the battlefield. In ancient Greek religion all soldiers who died in battle were venerated as heroes and in the Akkadian 'Genealogy of the Hammurapi Dynasty', which mentions the dead persons who receive funerary offerings, 'the soldiers who fell while on perilous campaigns' are listed among kings and princes."

84. See Miller 2006, 43–44 and Spronk 1986, 171–74. Military imagery is also deeply embedded into Ugaritic myth; according to M. Smith (2009), the Aqhat epic is "suffused with warrior concerns," e.g., Aqhat's death as a "heroic" figure mirrors Ba'al's death in the Ba'al epic (*KTU* 1.18:IV:40–42; 1.5:VI:8–10) in the use of the word *ḥlq* ("perish") and in Anat's subsequent lament for the fallen hero.

85. Horwitz 1979, 39–40. The readings I adopt for these texts are taken from the superior edition of Pitard (1992). See also Spronk 1986, 161–77; L'Heureux 1979, 129–59; and Lewis 1997.

ṯm.ṯmq.rpu.bʿl.mhrbʿl	There Rapiʾu Baal rose up, the warrior(s) of Baal
wmhr.ʿnt.ṯm.yḥpn.ḥyl	and the warrior(s) of ʿAnat. There the army encircles
y.zbl.mlk.ʿllmy...	the eternal royal princes.

The phrase *rpu bʿl* may here indicate that *rpu* is an epithet of Baal (similar to *ʾalʾiyn*), and Baal is being described here in his role as the preeminent *rpʾu*.[86] One may then assume, along with Horwitz and others, that the *rpʾum* here are warriors. These lines make it sound as if the *rpʾum* are a divine warrior retinue charged with guarding the "eternal royal princes," a role earned by their mighty deeds as military heroes before death.

The overall image of the *rpʾum* in KTU 1.20–22 is one of action and military procession, as these figures are associated with horses and banquets. The opening line (KTU 1.20:I:1–3) presents a relatively clear mise-en-scène:

[rp]um.tdbḥn	The Rapiuma will feast
[š]bʿd.ilnym	Sevenfold, the spirits,
[ ] *kmtmtm*	[ ] like the ancient dead[87]

In this funerary ritual context, further clarified in 1.20:I:6–7 ("the spirits will eat...will drink"), the *rpʾum* appear at a shrine (*aṯr*[88]) in 1.20:II:1–2 and 1.22:II:5–6, to which they have ridden on horses and/or horse-drawn chariots (here quoting 1.20:II:1–4):

...r[pum.aṯrh.]	The Rapiuma, to his shrine
tdd.aṯrh.tdd.ilm[.mrkbt.]	they hastened, to his shrine hastened the spirits; chariots
asr.sswn.tṣmd.dg[lm.tšu.]	they hitched, they yoked the horses, they raised the standards.
tʿln.lmrkbthm.ti[tyn.ʿrhm]	They mount their chariots, they come on their stallions

The *rpʾum* then proceed to a threshing floor (*grnt*) and field (*mṯʿt*) in 1.20:II:6–7, where they are apparently fed and are later invited by El into his palace for a feast.

Though it cannot be proven that the *rpʾum* were an active, living warrior class in the Late Bronze context, it does seem clear that the *rpʾum* were

---

86. Following Spronk 1986, 173. Lewis 1997, 203 has "the shades of Baal..." This issue is a difficult one and any solution must remain tentative. M. Smith (2009) suggests that the title "warriors of Baal, warriors of Anat" might indicate that Baal and Anat were "patrons" of human *rpʾum*.

87. Again, following Lewis (1997, 197), here and in subsequent citations of KTU 1.20–22.

88. Cognate with Akk. *ašru*; see Tropper 2008, 8.

associated with military imagery, and we can only assume this is intention-al and draws on some real aspect of how these figures were understood.[89] The variation in *rp'um* imagery I have suggested here is consistent with the premise advanced by previous interpreters that the *rp'um* were a class of leg-endary warrior figures who were venerated at special moments after death, but the available evidence cannot definitively prove such a view.

My working hypothesis, then, is that the *rp'um* were indeed once thought to be heroic warriors of old, and that these figures played an important role in funerary ritual as markers of monarchic legitimation and heroic identifi-cation. I am further inclined to agree with Spronk, who draws the Ugaritic *rp'um* phenomena into the orbit of Greek hero cult,[90] and I would emphasize the pattern of religious similarity between the two expressions: dead mili-tary heroes of a period thought to be in the distant past are invoked at local cult shrines, food and drink are offered, and the hero acts in some way—perhaps by guaranteeing fertility of land or empire,[91] or some other status of legitimation—to benefit the supplicant. But this type of cult is to be dissoci-ated in the Ugaritic context (as it is for the Greek context) from veneration of, or care for, the dead generally. We possess no "epic" of the *rp'um* from Ugarit to confirm their role in great battles of bygone eras, but what mate-rial we do have points toward their legendary status in martial contexts.

III. The Biblical Giants and the Narrative Sublimation of a Heroic Pattern

I now return to the meaning and fate of the giants in the biblical narra-tive. Specifically, I argue that the continuity between the hero in epic and cult traced above in a variety of materials can effectively serve as an inter-pretive paradigm to understand a problem in the Hebrew Bible involving giants, viz. why the word Rephaim (רפאים) appears to describe both a liv-ing, "historical" ethnic group in the land and a variety of inhabitants in the underworld.[92] Moreover, echoes of this dual presentation of giants appear

89. I.e., as opposed to the view that the horse/chariot and military references are simply stock imagery applied to any lower divinity.

90. Spronk (1986, 167; citing Herrmann 1959, 60) notes that Greek heroes could also be depicted with horses at the moment of heroic sacrifice.

91. E.g., Horwitz (1979, 42–43) emphasizes the connection between the *rp'um* and fertility in particular. Cf. the potential for invoking the dead as a blessing in the Hammurapi Genealogy, published by J. Finkelstein (1966).

92. To review: in the Hebrew Bible, Rephaim as a people group appear in Gen 14:5, 15:20; Deut 2:11,20[2x], 3:11,13; Josh 12:4, 13:12, 17:15; 1 Chr 20:4; cf. Raphah in 2 Sam 21:16,18,20,22 (רפה) and 1 Chr 20:6,8 (רפא); cf. רפא in 1 Chr 8:2 and רפה in 1 Chr 8:37, and the Valley of Rephaim in Josh 15:8, 18:16; 2 Sam 5:18,22, 23:13; 1 Chr 11:15, 14:9,13; Isa 17:5. Rephaim in the underworld appear in: Isa 14:9, 26:14,19; Ps 88:11; Job 26:5; Prov 2:18, 9:18, 21:16; possibly 2 Chr 16:12.

outside the Rephaim texts, for example, in specific references to Gibborim (גברים) as majestic—and perhaps giant—warriors in a primeval age (Gen 6:4) as well as gloomy, impotent residents in Sheol (Ezekiel 32), and also through the connection between the Nephilim (נפלים; Gen 6:4) of the ancient past and the giant Anaqim (ענקים) who oppose Israel's entry into the land.[93] Even though this latter connection is arguably the work of a late glossator in Num 13:33, it nonetheless demonstrates that at least some biblical author was thinking in terms of linking groups of living giants with those who had been long dead, and some modern commentators have speculated that the origins of the Nephilim lie in some notion of an ancient warrior class or cult of dead, "fallen" heroes.[94]

Death Cults and Hero Cults in Ancient Israel

We should begin here by noting the pervasive nature of cults of the dead in ancient Israelite society. I am inclined to agree with R. Hallote, who has recently declared that the Israelite "cult of the dead" was "one of the most active domestic cults in the biblical period."[95] Likewise, E. Bloch-Smith summarizes the results of her synthesis of archaeological and textual data regarding ancient Israelite views of death and afterlife as follows: "A picture emerges of a widespread, flourishing cult of the dead, practiced in Jerusalem as in the rest of the country, which persisted throughout the Iron Age."[96] These views represent the dominant, current approach to the question, though there have been notable dissenters from this position.[97] The biblical evidence itself suggests that the status of the dead was a live question, and prohibitions against certain forms of death cult indicate the fear of widespread participation in just such rituals.[98] Let us look, even if briefly, at some examples.

93. Num 13:28; Deut 1:28, 2:10,11,21, 9:2; Josh 11:21,22, 14:12,15, 15:13,14, 21:11; Judg 1:20.

94. E.g., Hendel 1987b, 21–23.

95. Hallote 2001, 54.

96. Bloch-Smith 1992, 23. Reviews of of this topic can be found in many studies already cited: Schmidt 1996, 132–73; Lewis 1989, 99–170; 1992, II: 101–05; Spronk 1986, 3–12, 25–53, 65–81, 237–43; Smith and Bloch-Smith 1988; van der Toorn 1996. Cf. J. Levenson (2006, esp. 60–63), who argues for a deeply rooted ancient Israelite belief in life after death but does not think death cults were as prevalent or influential as many other recent interpreters.

97. E.g., Johnston 2002, 70 and Schmidt 1996, 274, 282, etc. The reluctance of each of these authors to take the archaeological and comparative data seriously, however, represents a critical flaw in both of their studies, though each raises appropriate cautionary notes regarding methodological issues.

98. The mere number or fury of pronouncements does not, in and of itself, indicate widespread practice. An analogous caution is raised by Tigay (1986, 39–40) regarding Israelite injunctions against polytheism. Tigay argues that even a very small percentage of Israelites practicing polytheism would have been enough to cause the problem "to loom large in the minds of those who were sensitive to the issue." However, in the case of Israelite death cults,

Legal materials abound with various prohibitions, including Deut 18:10–11, which represents a characteristic injunction:[99]

> (v. 10) Let there not be found among you anyone who makes his son or his daughter pass through the fire, or who practices divinations, witchcraft (מעונן),[100] auguries, or sorceries, (11) one who practices spells, consults a ghost or spirits (ידעני),[101] or who seeks information from the dead. (12) For anyone who does these things is an abomination to YHWH, since it is for these abominations that YHWH your God drove them out before you.

Death cults are styled as acceptable only to the pre-Israelite, Canaanite inhabitants of the land, along with so many other things. Various prophetic texts, as well as references elsewhere, confirm this general picture;[102] Isaiah of Jerusalem seems to harbor a particular hatred of illicit death cult rituals, and rails in Isa 8:19 against those who advocate that a people "consult their gods, (viz.) the dead on behalf of the living, for teaching and testimony."[103]

One must take into account, however, what is *not* prohibited in such texts. Feeding the dead is nowhere proscribed (Deut 26:14 only prohibits offering tithed first-fruits to the dead), and it is not clear that consulting the dead directly (as opposed to using a professional intermediary) was prohibited, either.[104] This ambivalence, or ambiguity, regarding what is allowed and not allowed concerning the role of the dead is perhaps most strikingly highlighted in 1 Samuel 28:8–19: after banning all of the ידענים and אבות (apparently two technical terms for those who can contact the dead) from

---

it is the combination of textual witnesses in the Bible, archaeological remains, and both text and artifact from surrounding regions (especially Ugarit, as Lewis [1989] has shown, but also Anatolia, Syria, and elsewhere) that serves to solidify the case.

99. See also Lev 19:26–32, 20:6,27; Deut 14:1, 18:9–14, 26:14.

100. Lit. "one who raises up / makes a cloud" (?), perhaps some reference to a type of magical conjuring.

101. The root ידע here obviously implies "knowing" of some kind; 1 Samuel 28, at least, seems to operate on the basis of this term (along with אבות) signifying one those who consult the dead.

102. Isa 8:19–20, 19:3, 28:15,18, 29:4, 45:18–19 (where the phrase ארץ חשך may refer to the "land" of the dead, so Lewis 1989, 142–43), possibly 57:1–10, 65:4; Ezek 43:7–9 (if the פגרי מלכיהם במותם in 43:7 refer to a mortuary stele of some kind, as Lewis [1989, 139–42] suggests); 1 Sam 28:3–25; 2 Kgs 21:16, 23:24; Psalm 106:28, etc.

103. These verses phrase the statement as a rhetorical question (הלוא עם...), not in the form of the statement I have here. The effect is the same. I am assuming that the author is here equating אלהיו with המתים; see 1 Sam 28:13 for a similar use of אלהים to describe the dead.

104. See Bloch-Smith 1992, 126–27. Brichto (1973, 28–29) even suggested that Deut 26:14 "attests that normative biblical religion accorded [such rites]...the sanction of toleration, and that the command to honor the father and mother in Exod 20:12 was primarily an order for respect 'after their death'" (Brichto 1973, 30–31; italics are Brichto's). But cf. Levenson 2006, 62.

the land, and after YHWH refused to answer Saul through sanctioned channels (dreams, Urim and Thummim, or prophets), Saul turns to a female medium at Endor. The form of Samuel appears—the woman identifies him as an אלהים—and an accurate message is delivered.[105] Thus, this particular narrative simultaneously demonstrates two different (though by no means incompatible) aspects of communicating with the dead or seeking their power: it is forbidden, but it works.

Bloch-Smith has sufficiently demonstrated the archaeological reality of ancient Israelite beliefs about the dead that receive only passing allusions in the text of the Hebrew Bible. She points to the rise in popularity of a certain kind of burial practice, viz. "bench tombs," which became the "overwhelming southern highland preference."[106] These bench tombs "were designed to resemble residences" (i.e. with skeumorph wooden beam "ceilings") and seem to have been a prerogative of the relatively wealthy—especially in the eighth–sixth centuries BCE.[107] Bloch-Smith claims the design of the tombs (i.e., to resemble the residences of the living) vividly demonstrates a belief in afterlife concepts, and can be positively correlated with Judahite religion. The archaeological record also shows that the cult of the dead at Ugarit was alive and well in actual practice; intramural funerary installations were common in Late Bronze domestic settings, and pipes or other shafts leading down to the places of burial were almost certainly used for libations.[108]

The correlation of these lines of evidence strongly suggests that cults of the dead were a reality; but where does this leave us on the question of hero cults, specifically, in Iron Age Israel? In a much discussed 1956 essay, "The High Place in Ancient Palestine," W. F. Albright offered a bold hypothesis that would bring the world of hero cult and local heroic veneration directly into the discussion of ancient Israelite religious expression.[109] Earlier in his career, Albright maintained that the cult of the ancestors was a minor phenomenon in Israel, but he later asserted that "there was a flourishing cult of

105. See the extended analysis in Lewis 1989, 104–17, with sources cited there. For a newer review, see Arnold 2004, 200–207.

106. Bloch-Smith 1992, 51.

107. Bloch-Smith 1992, 43, 51. See also Ussishkin 1993, and some comments in J. Osborne 2011, 50. The specific time frame in which these types of burials seemingly became popular among Judean elites corresponds with the rise of Deuteronomic death cult rhetoric, Homeric epic, and Greek hero cult during these same centuries. These concomitant phenomena are likely related, though more needs to be said on this front (see Chapter 5).

108. Lewis 1989, 97–98; see 97 n. 2 for primary sources on the Ras Shamra excavation reports. This interpretation of the Ugaritic burials is not uncontested, though; cf. Pitard 1994.

109. Albright 1957b. Albright's views on this topic were repeated in varying forms in later publications, including Albright 1968, 204–06, and he acknowledges that he was preceded in his interpretation of the מצבה as funerary stelae by Meyer (1913, 423–24); Albright 1957b, 243 n. 2.

'heroes' in second-millennium Palestine, which perpetuated both ancestral Hebrew and Canaanite practices."[110] Albright's review of the archaeological evidence as he saw it, combined with certain crucial texts from the Hebrew Bible (particularly Isa 53:9), emended to read:

וַיִּתֵּן אֶת רְשָׁעִים קִבְרוֹ וְאֶת עָשִׁיר בֹּומָתוֹ

His grave was put with the wicked, and his funerary installation[111] with the demons

led him to associate the במה, "high place,"[112] i.e., an open air cult site of some sort, with מצבות, "cairns," as a place of heroic burial and veneration along Greek models.[113]

Reactions to this proposal were largely negative,[114] and the archaeological excavations of the supposed locations of "high places" have not yielded conclusive evidence to confirm their function as the site of a hero cult.[115] It appears, then, that Albright's line of inquiry has hit an impasse, though we are still left with other tantalizing clues regarding the possibility that the ideology of hero cult made its way far and wide across the Mediterranean world. As I have mentioned, we do have some historical avenues by which such ideas could have been exchanged among Mesopotamia, Greece, and the Levant, and Schmidt has even briefly traced some parallel transformations that occurred between the evolution of Greek afterlife beliefs leading to hero cults and the development of Israelite "spirit worlds" in the seventh–sixth centuries and on into post-exilic Judaism. On the one hand, the rise and evolution of the Greek polis and a Pan-Hellenic identity required the veneration of heroes as both a link to the past and a religio-political answer to the question of elite legitimation, while in Israel the Assyrian and Babylonian crises

110. Albright 1968, 204.

111. Albright (1957b, 245) claims that this very form (בֹּומָתוֹ), with the ô, is found six times in the Qumran materials; since the original vowel was long in proto-Hebrew (*bahmatu > bâmatu), the spelling here in the emended reading and at Qumran is correct, according to Albright. See also 2 Sam 18:17–18.

112. The most clearly identified במות in the Hebrew Bible are those of Jeroboam at Bethel (2 Kgs 23:15, torn down by Josiah), and the one associated with Solomon at Gibeon (1 Kgs 3:4; 1 Chr 16:39, 21:29; 2 Chr 1:3); other במות are mentioned (derisively) in 1 Kgs 11:7; Jer 7:31, 48:35; Ezek 20:29.

113. Albright 1957b, 253, 257.

114. E.g., Fowler 1982. Lewis (1989, 140–41) supports the connection of Israelite death cult with Greek heroic ideas, even though he rejects Albright's interpretation of the במות.

115. Lewis 1989, 141. The lack of "conclusive evidence" to confirm such cults, however, raises the difficult question of what, exactly, one would expect to find at these sites in order to confirm the hero cult intepretation. Presumably, one would look for inscriptional evidence and certain burial styles at the site—but regarding the issue of physical burial, recall that in the Greek examples reviewed supra, there is never (?) a literal heroic body at the veneration site.

inevitably led to a reinvention of social and political structures that included the rise of the spirit world as a new site of meaning-making.[116] Such things suggest it is appropriate to investigate aspects of these two religio-cultural worlds in light of one another when it comes to issues of the dead.

The Biblical Giants of Epic and of Cult

Another avenue remains to be explored, one that takes us back to the hero of epic/cult model and the texts we reviewed at length in Chapter Three involving various groups of living giants.[117] Simply put, I suggest that Israelite authors drew upon a storehouse of epic and mythic tropes that were popular and current in the eighth–sixth centuries BCE and, in a twist of motifs that is unique to the biblical corpus, fused together the meaningfully loaded figure of the giant with some aspects of Mediterranean heroic ideology. The question of why, exactly, ancient Israelite authors would have conflated Palestine's aboriginal giants with these heroic tropes might be addressed in several ways. The status of Israel's giant enemies could have functioned on two interrelated fronts: on the one hand, the giants' size emphasizes their formidability, and thus the formidability of those who defeat them. But it also lends a sense of awe and "otherness" to the time period in which the giants appear, as if they were fearsome and even popularly recounted relics of an ancient, bygone era. Taking up the idea that the Canaanites could have fostered some notion of a hero cult, de Moor suggests the Israelites would have come into contact with stories of primeval giants, and, in particular, "one aspect of that cult kept occupying their minds: the presumed supernatural tallness of the heroic rulers."[118] As I demonstrated in Chapter One, there is a native and broadly shared Near Eastern tradition of imagining both deities and prominent warriors in battle as literally huge, and monumental artistic depictions of various kinds, which would have been visible to travelers and traders across the Near East and Egypt, portray images of giant beings who loom at sometimes double or triple the height of their conquered foes.[119]

If the image of the giant became bound up with the image of the heroic warrior, then we should not be surprised to find some echoes of the epic and

---

116. Schmidt 1996, 283–84. See also Niehr 2002.

117. I will not repeat the basic text-critical assessments, translation, and commentary to be found in Chapter 2 in my treatment below, but rather my earlier work will serve as the basis for my comments here.

118. de Moor 1976, 337.

119. Recall the huge size of Gilgamesh (*Gilg.* I.53–61), Eannatum, Naram-Sin, and Ramses II, as well as the textual and iconographic images of giant deities (e.g., the Hittite relief from Yazilikaya, the 'Ain Dara temple, and Isa 6:5; see images in Chapter 1).

cult symbiosis inscribed into the Bible's story of giants—even if what we do find are indeed only echoes, glimpses, or hints of the epic/cult correlation. In what follows, my evidence for hero cult ideas in the Hebrew Bible takes a two-pronged approach, illustrated by two primary examples (along with several other related texts). First, we must analyze the dichotomy between the living and dead Rephaim in the Hebrew Bible. Second, by revisiting the meaning of the Nephilim of Gen 6:4, we are led to a fascinating description of the "fallen" warriors, both contemporary and in the archaic past, in Ezekiel 32, which bears directly on the characters that stand at the center of my investigation and reveals something of the way these heroic tropes were viewed by at least the sixth century BCE.

Og of Bashan and the living Rephaim. The most conspicuous group of giant, "heroic" figures in the Hebrew Bible who straddle the divide between living, military action and a prominent place in the world of the dead are, as I have proposed, the Rephaim, embodied as living beings by name in the person of their purportedly final living representative, Og of Bashan. The repeated references to the victory over Og in the Hebrew Bible, along with Og's giant subjects, the Rephaim, suggests that the living Rephaim played a prominent and fearsome role in the Israelite imagination.[120]

Even outside of the Bible, we have (at least) two texts that have been thought to refer to Og in some way, which would imply that Og was a known figure in the pre-Israelite Transjordan. One of these texts, a fifth-century funerary inscription from Byblos, almost certainly does not refer to Og,[121] but

120. Num 21:26–35, 32:33; Deut 1:4, 3:1–3, 4:47; Deut 29:7, 31:4; Josh 2:10, 9:10, 12:2–5, 13:10–12,27–31; 1 Kgs 4:19; Pss 135:11, 136:19–20; Neh 9:22. Og is associated specifically with the Rephaim in Deut 3:11; Josh 12:4, 13:12.

121. The Byblos inscription has been read in such a way as to involve a figure named Og (or "The Og"). The editio princeps is Starcky 1969. Starcky read the portion of the fragmentary text (line 2) in question as follows: [lpth ']lt 'rn zn wlrgz 'ṣmy h'g ytbqšn h'dr wbkl d[ ] ([...to open] this sarcophagus and to disturb my bones, the Og will seek/avenge me, the Mighty, and in all...). Og would thus appear as a vengeful, mighty spirit, ready to protect the coffin. If h'g is a personal or divine name, then it should not have the definite article. However, a solution here may be found in the etymology of the name. Del Olmo Lete (1999b, 638–39) suggests the Hatraean 'g', "Man," which would have some correspondence to the "Northwest Semitic tradition ('īš, amēlu, mt) in relation mostly to military activity, the most striking case being mt rpi, applied to king Aqhat...The title would have finally turned into an eponymic divine name." Del Olmo Lete (1999b, 638–39) also points to an argument by van der Toorn (1991, 93) that the Anammelek (עֲנַמֶּלֶךְ) in 2 Kgs 17:31 is actually 'gmlk, "Og-Melek," a chthonic deity to whom children were sacrificed (and thus endorsing h'g's chthonic role in the Phoenician inscription).
Alternatively, Cross (2003) analyzes the most difficult part of the line quite differently. Noting that there is no space after the g, and reading z for y where Starcky read ytbqšn, he renders the line this way: [w'm kl 'dm ybqš lpth ']lt 'rn zn wlrgz 'ṣmy h'gzt bqšn h'dr wbkl dr [bn 'lm...] ("...and if anyone seeks to open this sarcophagus or to disturb my mouldering bones, seek him

the other, a fragmentary Ugaritic reference in *KTU* 1.108.1–3, does offer a likely parallel to the biblical description of Og's territory in Josh 12:4 and 13:12. In the *KTU* 1.108.1–3, it is the god Rapiu, patron of the Rapiuma, who rules at Ashtaroth and Edrei:

> [...]*n.yšt.rpu.mlk.ʻlm.w yšt*
> [*il*]*g̱tr.w yqr.il.ytb.b'ttrt*
> *il tpt. b hdr'y.d yšr.w ydmr*
> *b knr...*

> May Rapiu, king of eternity, drink wine, may he drink,
> the powerful and noble god, the one who rules in Athtarat,
> the god who reigns in Edrei (?), who sings and plays
> on the lyre...

This interpretation of the phrase *il ytb b'ttrt il tpt b hdr'y* has come under some criticism. In biblical Hebrew, at least, Edrei is spelled with an *aleph* (אדרעי), not *h*, and the description of Rapiu singing and playing the lyre seems odd. J. Day, for example, proposes that the *il* in 108.2–3 may be El, and that he is sitting at a banquet scene along with *hd r'y* ("Hadad the shepherd"?).[122] Day does admit, however, the fact that *ytb* in Ugaritic never means "sit alongside with," and the spelling *hdr'y* may simply be a mistake or an otherwise unattested Ugaritic term.[123] Though the Heb. שפט (= Ug. *tpt*, "judge") is not used of Og in the Bible,[124] ישב (= *ytb* in *KTU* 1.108.2, "sit, dwell")

---

out, O [Baʻl] Addīr and with all the assembly of the gods..."). "The expression *h'g* is bizarre and cannot be correct," Cross charges; moreover, "*ytbqš* does not exist in Phoenician, and if it did would be reflexive and intransitive, making the suffix *-n* a further anomaly, and the meaning unthinkable" (Cross 2003, 282–83). In addition to these problems, it is not clear why the epithet "the Mighty" would be separated from the subject by this anomalous verb. Despite these decisive problems, there remain others who endorse Starcky's reading, e.g., Weinfeld 1991, 184; del Olmo Lete 1999b, 639; and Spronk 1986, 210–11.

Finally, relating to Og outside of the Bible, see also Noegel (1998), who suggests a connection between Og of Bashan and the Greek flood hero Ogygos of Boeotia. On the most general levels, both Og and Ogygos are pejoratively styled as enemies of the divine and engage in military pursuits, and in both characters we find links to the underworld (e.g., Og's people are conspicuously called the same name as residents of Sheol in the Bible, and Ogygos is associated with Gaia and Tartaros). Noegel offers other, more obscure connections, many of which appear tantalizing, but are often strained and even wildly implausible. E.g., the "necklace" connection, linking Og to the Anaqim (ענקים) as "necklace people" (Noegel 1998, 420) and then the Anaqim to the Greeks, is particularly unhelpful—and nowhere is Ogygos associated with any of this except that he is a Greek (?). See also Brichto 1998, 136 and Wyatt (2005, 207–09), who endorses Noegel's hypothesis.

122. J. Day 2002, 50. See Wyatt 2010, 88 n. 16, for further bibliography on this debate.

123. J. Day 2002, 50. Pope (1994, 198) succinctly dispenses with the argument that *ytb* can mean "sit beside."

124. There is arguably far less a distinction between שפט and מלך (used of Og in Josh

appears in Josh 12:4 and Deut 1:4, deepening the connection between the image of Rapiu in *KTU* 1.108.1–3 and the biblical Og. If this reading of Athtarat and Edrei is correct, however—and it is the most straightforward and reasonable reading—then we have here a stunning correlation between the geography of Og's and Rapiu's kingdom in the Transjordan.[125]

Wyatt has gone so far as to completely equate Rapiu with Og, a move that is unnecessary.[126] What *KTU* 1.108 vis-à-vis Josh 12:4, 13:12 does tell us, however, is that some biblical authors imagined Og living at the gateway to the land, as a final, giant obstacle to overcome before crossing the Jordan. Og dwells in a mythic geography; if he is a true figure of history, the memory is faint and now inextricable from the biblical picture of a giant. In the mindset of the ancient Israelite authors, a native Israelite concept of an aboriginal human enemy, Og, was bound up with local myth in the Transjordan wherein this particular region as a site of various underworld kings, such as Rapiu and perhaps also *Mlk*.[127] As a powerful, giant king of this region, Og becomes a sort of King of the Dead, ruling from a Canaanite Hell; he is last of the living Rephaim, while simultaneously imbued with the mythological resonances associated with the notable dead (not least of which include the deceased Rephaim, as they are conceived in some texts; see below).[128] As a powerful enemy within the Israelite epic of conquest, he could well be called an epic hero—or perhaps better, in the biblical conception, a reverse image of YHWH's chosen people, a degraded counter-hero.

The dead Rephaim. Though Og and his generation passed away as a human

13:12) than might be supposed. See, e.g., Judg 8:18 and 9:6, where the noun מלך is used of a שפט before the institution of kingship has "officially" come to fruition.

125. See also Rainey (1974, 187), who finds *KTU* 1.108.3 to be "certainly reminiscent" of Gen 14:5, Josh 12:4, and 13:12. Stavrakopoulou (2010, 68) sees an equivalency between Og's cities and *KTU* 1.108.3. Wyatt (2010) affirms the Athtaroth/Edrei reading, as does del Olmo Lete (1999b) and Pope (1994, 198). De Moor (1976, 338) makes the odd but original suggestion that the Israelites actually read a real inscription on Og's bed (in Deut 3:11), which described Og as *hyšb b'štrt wb'd r'y*, "who thrones with Astarte and with Adda (Adad), his Shepherd." According to de Moor, however, the Israelites *misread* the (hypothetical!) inscription and interpreted it as" the one who dwelt in Ashtaroth and Edrei." Though de Moor's suggestion is quite adventurous, it is certainly within the realm of possibility.

126. Wyatt 2010, 76: "Og = Rapiu: from a biblical perspective they are one and the same character."

127. See discussion in del Olmo Lete 1999b, 638–39, which notes that Ashtarot is the dwelling of *mlk* in *KTU* 1.100:41, 1.107:17, and RS 86.2235:17. See also J. Day 2002, 46–47.

128. I borrow the phrase "Canaanite Hell" from del Olmo Lete 1999b, 639. Obviously, the Christian concept of "hell" is foreign to the authors of the Hebrew Bible. And yet the territory East of the Jordan does represent the death and aridity associated with the Wilderness wanderings before entry into "paradise," the Promised Land. On this, see Stavrakopoulou 2010, 65–66, 68–69, and other sources cited there.

population of giants, we find what might be a continuation of the lives of these figures in the shadowy post-mortem image of the Rephaim (Isa 14:9, 26:14,19; Ps 88:11; Job 26:5; Prov 2:18, 9:18, 21:16; 2 Chr 16:12). Aside from the cognate *rp'um* from Ugarit, we also have other Northwest Semitic references to the Rephaim as residents in the underworld in Phoenician. Two fifth-century BCE royal Sidonian tomb inscriptions mention the Rephaim, on the sarcophagi of Tabnit (*KAI* 2:17–19) and Eshmunazor (*KAI* 2:19–23).[129] In both instances, Rephaim is a general designation for *all* of the dead, and is opposed to the totality of the offspring listed at the very end of the Tabnit inscription of all those who live "under the sun."[130] Indeed, about half of the biblical references to Rephaim as the dead operate under the assumption that Rephaim has become a term that refers to the common mass of departed spirits. For example, Ps 88:11:

הלמתים תעשה פלא אם רפאים יקומו יודוך סלה

Do you work wonders for the dead—do the Rephaim rise up to praise you? Selah.

Prov 2:18, 9:18, and 21:16 all seem to imply that going down to die among the Rephaim is a decidedly negative fate, a fate that will specifically befall the unwise:

כי שחה אל מות ביתה ואל רפאים מעגלתיה

(2:18) For her house [i.e., of the "Strange Woman"] bows down to Death, to the Rephaim her paths.

ולא ידע כי רפאים שם בעמקי שאול קראיה

(9:18) He [one who eats "stolen water" and "bread in secret"] does not know that the Rephaim are there, in the depths of Sheol are her guests [lit. "called ones"[131]].

אדם תועה מדרך השכל בקהל רפאים ינוח

(21:16) The man who wanders from the road of discernment will rest in the assembly of the Rephaim.

In these references, the point is not that the Rephaim are a special class of particularly dishonorable dead, but rather that action not in accordance with

---

129. See McCarter 2003a; 2003b for translation and notes.

130. See also Healey 1989, 39–40, 43.

131. Cf. *KTU* 1.161.2, etc., where the passive *qura'tumū* is used to invoke the assembly of the dead.

prudence and wisdom leads to moral (and perhaps even literal) death—a death that can be averted through right behavior.[132]

Two appearances of the Rephaim in Isaiah 24–27 may present this group as a specific class within the world of the dead. Consider, first, Isa 26:14:[133]

מתים בל יחיו רפאים בל יקמו
לכן פקדת ותשמידם
ותאבד כל זכר למו

The dead do not live, the Rephaim do not rise,
therefore you have punished and exterminated them,
and obliterated all memory of them.

The first part of the verse echoes sentiments found elsewhere regarding the finality of death,[134] while at the same time seeming to indicate that the מתים ("dead ones") and רפאים (Rephaim) have been punished, as if those who have died and become the מתים and רפאים have committed some infraction. In v. 15, the speaker turns back to Israel, to affirm YHWH's ability to "increase" (יסף) the nation, which may indicate that the Rephaim in v. 14 are the dead of *other* nations—it is they who will not be remembered. In Isa 26:19, the speaker mentions the מתים and רפאים again:

יחיו מתיך נבלתי יקומון
הקיצו ורננו שכני עפר
כי טל אורת טלך וארץ רפאים תפיל

Your dead will live, your corpses[135] will rise;
Wake up and shout for joy, dwellers in the dust!
For your dew is a dew of lights (?)[136] and you will make it
    fall upon
the Land of the Rephaim.

While the reference to a notional or literal resurrection here cannot be denied, the meaning of the "dew" imagery and the implication of dew falling upon the ארץ רפאים ("land of Rephaim") are unclear. Presumably, the "dew

132. Though M. Fox (2000, 122) does not make any comments on the implications of the רפאים here in this wisdom context, he does not attach any special meaning (beyond "ghosts") to the term.

133. For comments and bibliography, see, e.g., Childs 2001, 171–98; Wildberger 1997, 439–602; Millar 1976.

134. E.g., Isa 38:18; Job 14:12; Pss 6:6, 88:6,11–13, 115:17; Eccl 3:18–22, 9:4–6,10.

135. Emending נבלתי to נבלתיך. See Millar (1976, 53), who also also points to the connection between dew and life in Ps 137. Cf. Wildberger 1997, 556, 567–68; Childs 2001, 187–88.

136. See comments in Wildberger 1997, 556. נפל as a noun can refer to "miscarriage," in which case we would be dealing with an unsuccessful birth (see *BDB* 658, e.g., Job 3:16; Eccl 6:3; Ps 58:9)—but this seems not to fit the context here.

of lights" is a life-giving element,[137] and its power over the רפאים (if we are to imagine the dew in a resurrective capacity for the Rephaim) could suggest the רפאים here are the dead generally, i.e., the totality of those who will rise again.

Two references to the Rephaim imply something of the physical location of the dead beneath (or in) a watery setting. The extended context of Ps 88:11 makes this clear, specifically in v. 7:

שתני בבור תחתיות במחשכים במצלות

> You have placed me in the Pit below, in the darkness of the watery deep.

Job 26:5 draws upon this same imagery, as mentioned above: "The Rephaim writhe below the waters and their inhabitants" (הרפאים יחוללו מתחת מים ושכניהם).[138] The overarching theo-cosmological picture in Job 26:1–14 sets in opposition water and void (תהו) over and against Zaphon, i.e., the notion of an organized, cosmic mountain of God (esp. in vv. 6–7, 10–13). In this sense, the land of the Rephaim is clearly linked with the forces of chaos that must be conquered for "Zaphon" and the earth to exist (v. 7). One could also appeal to the general symbolic import of being buried beneath the sea, i.e., removed at the farthest length possible from YHWH and the land of the living,[139] or one could forge a connection between the symbolism here and a Tartaros-like setting for awful offenders, sunk deep beneath sea and land.[140]

In other passages, however, we find references to the Rephaim that more clearly draw on the term's special significance to designate specific types of dead, such as kings or healing spirits of some kind. Isa 14:9 contains the clearest reference to the Rephaim that seems to follow along the Ugaritic model:

שאול מתחת רגזה לך לקראת בואך
עורר לך רפאים כל עתודי ארץ
הקים מכסאותם כל מלכי גוים

---

137. Millar (1976) also points to the connection between dew and life in Psalm 137. Cf. Wildberger 1997, 556, 567–68, and Childs 2001, 187–88.

138. Alternatively, we could read these words as a pair of synonymous phrases: "The Rephaim writhe below, (so too) the waters and their inhabitants." Either way, the Rephaim are associated with the watery depths.

139. As in Amos 9:3, where the קרקע הים ("floor of the sea") marks a cosmological boundary to which fleers might flee.

140. E.g., as in the Greek myth of the Titans, Giants, and others being banned to the lowest place. On the geography of Tartaros in this respect, see Fontenrose 1980, 224–25. The Greek translation of רפאים in Job 26:5 as γίγαντες would have clearly resounded with this meaning. See Annus 1999, 22–24.

> Sheol beneath trembles excitedly to greet you when you
>   come;
> it arouses the Rephaim for you, all the leaders of the earth,
> it raises up from their thrones all the kings of the nations.

Many studies attempt to sort out just which Near Eastern or Greek mytho-logical tropes best serve as the background for the fallen king in Isaiah 14. Inspiration ranging from the Gilgamesh Epic to the Greek Phaeton myth has been cited, and many promising resonances in the Ugaritic corpus have been discovered.[141] It is clear that the mocking dirge for the fallen, anonymous king of Babylon in this chapter bears similarities with many literatures and is not to be identified in a strict sense with any of them.

The Rephaim of Isa 14:9 are clearly immersed in a context of dead roy-alty. Three descriptions of the dead that rise up to greet the humiliated king appear: עתודי ארץ, "leaders of the earth" (with ארץ signifying a double en-tendre, i.e. of the physical "earth" and the ארץ as "underworld"[142]), מלכי גוים, "kings of the nations," and רפאים (Rephaim). One can only assume here, then, that the Rephaim in this passage maintain an older, more specific mean-ing: the deceased notables, comprised here of various leaders and probably thought to encompass a broader range of kings, heroes, and other outstand-ing figures. The notion that the deceased royalty have their thrones in the underworld (הקים מכסאותם) is expressed also in *KTU* 1.161, where in line 13 the throne of Niqmaddu is commanded to weep (*ksi.nqmd.tbky*, "throne of Niqmaddu, may you weep"), and in lines 20–21 there is a descent from the throne (or possibly *by* the throne itself?) into the Underworld.[143] The author of Isa 14:9 thus seems to understand the Rephaim along the lines of *KTU* 1.161, as distinguished leaders of the past among whom a dead king would like to keep company. The summary statement in v. 20, however, provides a twist on the Babylonian king's categorization within these ranks of the significant dead:

> לא תחד אתם בקבורה
> כי ארצך שחת עמך הרגת
> לא יקרא לעולם זרע מרעים

---

141. The most recent, major study is that of Shipp (2002), who makes broad and repeated appeal to the Ugaritic materials. See also Heiser 2001; Craigie 1975; Poirier 1999; O'Connell 1988.

142. A feature also noticed by Talmon 1983, 247.

143. *KTU* 1.161.20: *aṯr.[b]'lk.l.ksi.aṯr b'lk.arṣ.rd.arṣ* ("After your lord, from the throne [?], after your lord, descend into the earth, into the earth"). The tablet is partly damaged in line 20, so that what I have transcribed here as *ksi* (*kissi'i*) could be read as *ksh* (*kāsihu*, "his cup").

> You will not be joined with them in burial,
> for you ruined your land, you killed your people;
> may he never again be invoked—a seed of evildoers![144]

Thus he will not join the Rephaim, or be included among their ranks—a denial that alerts us to the specific status the Rephaim were thought to have in this text, written before the concept of the Rephaim had become generalized to all the dead.[145]

A final reference to the special status of the Rephaim appears in 2 Chr 16:12, the second half of which has no parallel in Samuel-Kings:

ויחלא אסא בשנת שלולים ותשע למלכותו ברגליו עד למעלה חליו וגם בחליו לא דרש
את יהוה כי ברפאים

Asa became diseased in his feet in the thirty-ninth year of his reign, and his condition worsened—but even in his pain he did not seek YHWH, but rather[146] (he sought help) through the רפאים.

The Masoretic Text vocalizes the agents of healing as בְּרֹפְאִים, i.e., as a participle from רפא, "heal" (LXX ἰατρούς), a form found elsewhere (but not particularly common) in the Hebrew Bible.[147] רֹפְאִים only appears two other times in the Bible (both in the same verse, Gen 50:2) and describes "embalmers," while רֹפֵא, "the one who heals," is relatively common, and thus רֹפְאִים in the plural as "embalmers" is an otherwise unattested term. A better solution here is to read רְפָאִים, drawing on what I have already discussed as the most likely (though by no means certain) etymology of the word, i.e., as those who heal.[148]

---

144. Though it is not clear that this last line goes with the preceding material, I have chosen to read it as a denial that the shamed king will ever be invoked (קרא) in his ritual capacity as a dead king—i.e., as other רפאים would presumably be invoked.

145. Cf. Wildberger 1997, 60–61, and de Moor 1976, 341.

146. Clearly the כי here is adversative; see *GKC* 163a–b.

147. Gen 50:2 (2x), הָרֹפְאִים; for רפא as a verb ("heal"), see, e.g., Gen 20:17; Exod 21:19; Lev 13:18; Num 21:13; Deut 32:39; 1 Sam 6:3; 2 Kgs 8:29; Isa 6:10, 57:19; Jer 30:17; Hos 5:13; Ps 30:3. The preposition ב here in ברפאים is difficult to understand; it may signal the agency of the רפאים, i.e., "(he sought help) *through* the Rephaim" (compare the phrase ביהוה in, e.g., Isa 26:13; Hos 1:7; Pss 18:30, 44:6, etc.) or "*among* the Rephaim." See Waltke and O'Conner 1990, 198, 200 and *BDB* 88–89.

148. Among those who endorse this reading are Rouillard (1999, 700) and Wyatt (2010, 87 n. 7). An equally acceptable solution, proposed by de Moor (1976, 340–41), is to read רֹפְאִים here, which attests to the earlier vocalization and understanding of the רֹפְאִים as "healers"; the effect is the same, viz. that the רפאים in this passage are not human doctors. It is possible that the Chronicler has offered a midrashic expansion on his source (which was identical with Kings at this point) by way of explaining Asa's illness: the reference could be a pun on Aram. אסי ("doctor") and the name of Asa. See Cogan 2001, 402; Japhet 1993, 737–38; J. Gray 1976, 355–56.

The Rephaim as beneficial spirits of healing and fertility in ancient Israelite society could be inferred from three directions. (1) The Ugaritic texts (*KTU* 1.124:1–15) refer to a healing enacted by *Dtn*, an eponymous ancestor connected to the *rp'um* in *KTU* 1.161 and elsewhere.[149] (2) As noted above, Greek hero cult carried with it a well attested set of beliefs regarding fertility, growth, and healing, and these aspects may well have been shared with (or borrowed from) other, Eastern Mediterranean cultures where similar ideas were present. (3) The repeated reference to YHWH as healer (using the root רפא, in particular), as in Deut 32:39, Jer 33:6, 51:9, Hos 5:13, 61, etc., can be read as *counter claims* against other sources of רפא (healing), against *all* human and rival divine attempts to heal sickness. Though, oddly enough, prayers and incantations for healing the sick play a relatively minor role in the Hebrew Bible in comparison to what we know of other contemporary cultures, and ancient Israelites could apparently be forbidden from seeking any source of healing other than following YHWH completely (Exod 23:25–27!).[150] One can only guess as to which practices and cults supplemented Yahwism in widespread practice, but it is quite possible that the Rephaim from beyond death could be consulted, as could their counterparts in Ugarit and Greece, to provide relief from pain and illness.

Thus far, our review of the evidence from the Hebrew Bible and elsewhere has clearly demonstrated the dual existence of the Rephaim as both a living, aboriginal population in the Transjordan and a designation for the dead of various kinds—a dual existence that has raised an intractable problem for biblical scholarship. Typical solutions—in fact, nearly all solutions offered to this point—posit a *transference of meaning*: either the Rephaim were first a living group, whose title was later bestowed upon the dead, or the dead Rephaim receive priority, from which the term was extended as an ethnic description for a perceived or real people group.[151] For example, before the discovery of the Ugaritic materials, F. Schwally (in 1892) argued that the Rephaim first applied to the dead, and only afterward did the frightening legend of the Transjordanian giants receive the title.[152] Later work essen-

---

149. See Spronk 1986, 193–95, and also Liwak 2004, 607.

150. In no other statement of covenant benefits (e.g., Lev 26:3–10, Deut 11:13–15, 28:1–13) do we find such a sweeping or surprising statement (to which, e.g., Propp 2006, 289, in a recent two-volume, 1500 page commentary on Exodus, devotes not a single word). Many commentators are quick to assert that the Hebrew Bible nowhere condemns the physician's trade (e.g., Myers 1965b, 95, citing Exod 21:19; Jer 8:22; and Isa 38:21. None of these citations, however, clearly endorses a professional class of healers).

151. Schmidt (1996, 267–73) summarizes some attempts to connect the living and dead Rephaim.

152. Schwally 1892, 64–65 n. 1. See Rouillard (1999, 699), who notes that Schwally connected the רפאים to תרפים (Judges 17–18; 2 Kgs 23:24; Ezek 21:26; Hos 3:4; Zech 10:2), for which

tially took up this same line of thought. Caquot suggests that the Rephaim began as powerful afterlife spirits whose reputed danger haunted Israel's historiography in the form of the living ethnic group,[153] though S. Talmon, while finding correspondences between the Rephaim as the dead and the Ugaritic texts but *not* between the ethnic-geographical Rephaim, prefers to explain the latter with no connection whatsoever to the former.[154]

What I am suggesting here, however, is that these solutions are arbitrary and thus unsatisfying. The two sides of the Rephaim equation are, in fact, linked, as others rightly saw, but they are linked on another level—not of subsequent transportation of one group's existence to the other, but rather as an *interpenetration of religious meaning*. In parallel to the individual existence of the Greek hero, whose life is filled with valorous battle and so on, we have the living Rephaim, represented by Og; and, in parallel to their continued existence as the powerful dead, we have the dead Rephaim (as in Isa 14:9). The Rephaim who live in the Transjordan are, in a sense, the same Rephaim who appear as the dead in Isa 14:9—a heroic tribe or group of kings whose notables rank among the powerful and active dead in Palestine. Og's own life appears in the Bible as a relatively sorry affair, as he exists only to be killed by the Israelites and memorialized by his giant bed.[155] But I suspect he was a well-known figure in the Iron Age Levant; it is fully possible that tales of Og's deeds and a protracted account of the Israelite engagement with the Rephaim could be found in the ספר מלחמת יהוה ("Book of the Wars of YHWH," Num 21:14) or the ספר הישר ("Book of the Upright," Josh 10:13),[156] and thus Og would belong to a constellation of Transjordanian heroes, kings, and cultic functionaries who, like Balaam, appear in the Hebrew Bible in prominent roles, but also in native, detailed, independent Canaanite traditions.[157] Even though the Bible never explicitly links the living Rephaim with the Rephaim as the dead, Og's prominent place in the conquest narratives and the hints that Og was known as part of a larger, non-Israelite tradition

---

an implausible linguistic argument must be made (i.e., the loss of the א and the additional of a prefixed -מ). See also Karge 1917, 620.

153. Caquot 1985, 350.

154. Talmon 1983, 236–41, 247. If these two groups had *no connection* to each other, except by *coincidence* in the final form of the biblical text, then this would be an amazing coincidence indeed, which defies the effort of any scholarly investigation.

155. As Nagy (2006, §67) and Hendel (1987b, 21) put it, the Rephaim "exist in order to be wiped out."

156. Recall that Mowinckel (1935), at least, thought these references point to detailed, ancient Israelite epic sources.

157. And we know for certain that such traditions existed for Balaam; see, e.g., Hackett 1980.

in the region give us the necessary clues to surmise a link between the two Rephaim.

Like the Greek heroes, then, Og and the once living Rephaim live on in the dead Rephaim, whose own exact status is repeatedly muted or suppressed by omission. We have witnessed something of this same dichotomy in the Ugaritic texts, a dichotomy not between a living, human group of *rp'um* and the long dead *rp'um*, but rather, between the *rp'um* as notable heroic ancestral figures from the distant past and the ongoing role of these figures in present cultic settings. The biblical dichotomy operates in a similar fashion, yet with crucial differences: the Rephaim as an aboriginal group of giants, with one primary figure as representative (Og of Bashan), are given a narrative explanation, succinct and enigmatic though it may be,[158] while the Ugaritic figures mentioned in *KTU* 1.161 are given only a name here or there with no narrative,[159] and the biblical Rephaim as figures in cult are only revealed as such through polemic and hints.

The biblical presentation may thus shed light on the Ugaritic situation, and suggests that non-extant Ugaritic texts did record epic-like materials describing the battles and exploits of past *rp'um*. Presumably such records would have presented the *rp'um* in a positive light, unlike the doomed biblical Rephaim. In the biblical record, we find a tendency to bring the giants, their origins, and their demise into the stream of Israelite "history"—Og's mythological existence in the Transjordan as a deceased, deified king or hero was picked up and transformed into a fact of Israel's story in the Deuteronomistic narrative. In this way, through the figures of Og and the Rephaim, we have a continuity of living and dead heroes that mirrors the situation in Greek hero cult.

The Nephilim—fallen warriors? Another avenue for positing this continuity between the status of the giants as living "heroes" and their status as actors in the world of the dead comes through an even more oblique channel: the Nephilim and the Anaqim. Num 13:33, which succinctly forges a genealogical connection between these two groups, might seem to provide just the clue one would desire, though obviously this reference cannot bear much

---

158. M. Smith (1992, V: 675) puts the issue slightly differently, but, I think, with the same point: "The Rephaim as a line or group of heroes and monarchs at Ugarit corresponds to the biblical view of them as people or nation. As heroes and monarchs, the Rephaim survived in the Bible as giants or warriors."

159. Of course, there is Danel, who is called *mt rp'i*, "Man of Rapiu" (*KTU* 1.20) and Aqhat, who is called *'aqht ǵzr*, "Hero Aqhat" (e.g., *KTU* 1.17:VI:25–38, etc.; as many suspect, Aqhat's epic is connected to the *rp'um* texts). See Spronk 1986, 151–60.

interpretive weight.[160] There are, however, some lines of interpretation that could take us back to the significance of the Nephilim as actors in a hero cult. In a relatively obscure Festschrift article in 1973, H. Gese made a stunning, even if mostly conjectural, argument regarding the place of Gen 6:1–4 and specifically the Nephilim as giant heroes.[161] Beginning with the Rephaim tradition centered around Bashan, Gese argues for a flourishing Canaanite cult of heroes, in whose presence the biblical authors felt compelled to respond. Gese claims that some concept of heroic cult is the religious background behind Gen 6:1–4, and, specifically, the etiological thrust of this fragment of myth comprised an attempt to sanitize and circumscribe the ideological power of hero cults: semi-divine heroes are indeed begotten by divine-human miscegenation, but their lifetimes are limited, their power cut off by YHWH.[162] The mythological possibility of an active, legitimate hero cult, Gese contends, brought the Yahwist face to face with a dire threat of disorder ("einer drohenden Unordnung"), just as in Gen 3:22, and the divine response was to cut off the source of chaos from unrestrained life.[163] In this reading, then, the biblical author is openly acknowledging the power the Nephilim, Gibborim, and others were thought to possess in their ongoing existence in either popular belief or even organized cult, but, in his countermeasure, the biblical author risks partly endorsing the very religious ideas he criticizes by bringing the problem out into the light of the counter-myth.

All of this takes us back to the problem of the identity of the Nephilim, and to the etymology of the word itself (נפלים), which is unlikely to receive a unanimous solution.[164] One productive suggestion was offered by Albright in a discussion of Balaam's vision in Num 24:4, where the word נפל may be translated (according to Albright) as "unconscious."[165] Albright suggested an underlying form, *napîl "dead hero or shade," comparing Akkadian *nabultu* ("corpse").[166] Apparently unaware of Albright's hypothesis, Hendel

---

160. Num 13:33 reads: "We also saw the Nephilim there—the sons of Anaq are from the Nephilim—and we seemed like grasshoppers in our eyes and likewise we were in their eyes!" See the discussion in Chapter 2. Talmon (1983, 238) calls this reference a "historization of myth," which, if true, would call for an explanation of *why* this myth was historicized in exactly this way (which Talmon does not give).

161. Gese 1973, 83–85.

162. Gese 1973, 84.

163. Gese 1973, 85.

164. For possible etymologies, see Hendel 2004, 21–22; Hess 1992, IV: 1072; Coxon 1999b.

165. Num 24:4: "An oracle of the one who hears the utterances of El, one who sees the vision of Shaddai, who 'falls down'(נֹפֵל), but with uncovered eyes."

166. Albright 1944, 217 n. 61. But cf. *CAD* XI: 296, 328, for uncertainty regarding the meaning of *nabultu/napultu*; the term may be a variant of *napištu* ("life, throat," etc.) or could also mean "crushed" (and perhaps, by extension, a crushed one, i.e. a corpse).

proposed a very similar solution to the term in his discussion of the meaning of the נפלים in Gen 6:1–4: the "fallen" sense of נפל refers to "ones fallen in death," a meaning found in several other significant passages.[167] Hendel cites, for example, what may be rightly considered a heroic-style lament by David in 2 Sam 1:19,25,27: איך נפלו גברים/גבורים, "How the Gibborim have fallen!", meaningfully linking the words נפל and גבור (note also Jer 6:15, 8:12, 46:12, etc.).[168] These examples begin to indicate that the Nephilim of Gen 6:4 may have originally referred to the fallen, powerful, heroic dead, whatever else the term came to mean to later interpreters. Though not conclusive, Gese's and Albright's (separate, yet compatible) hypotheses begin to suggest a plausible interpretation of fallen warriors and hero cults that can be brought to bear on the meaning and origins of the Nephilim traditions.

The fallen, (un-)heroic dead of Ezekiel 32. This discussion of the Nephilim as the "fallen" dead leads us directly to Ezekiel 32:17–32, which is perhaps the most significant, extended context in which the verb נפל (*nāpal*, "fall") is meaningfully linked to the Gibborim (with the hint of a heroic context in the afterlife).[169] Little scholarly attention has been paid to Ezekiel 32, which is surprising since the text provides the most explicit tour through the land of the dead available in the Hebrew Bible, and is rich with imagery describing the fate of fallen enemy hordes. The context of the lament in Ezek 32:17–32 within the book of Ezekiel and within the broader corpus of prophetic books is notable. Many have noticed the form of (parody) lament for a foreign ruler present here, combined with the descent-to-the-underworld motif, which can be compared with other such forms in Ezekiel (e.g., Tyre in 26:1–21) and elsewhere (Isa 14:4–21, discussed above).[170]

167. Hendel 1987b, 22. See also Spronk (1986, 227), who endorses the fallen warrior interpretation. Other passages not noted above where the participle נפלים denotes warriors fallen in battle are: Josh 8:25; Judg 8:10, 20:46; 1 Sam 20:46, 31:8; 1 Chr 10:8; 2 Chr 20:24, as well as three other times in Ezek 32 (vv. 22, 23, 24). The verb נפל is used elsewhere to refer to the fallen dead in a significantly plentiful number of contexts, e.g., Exod 19:21; Isa 3:25; Ezek 5:12; Amos 7:17; Job 1:15; 2 Chr 29:9.

168. Hendel 1987b, 22.

169. See the brief dicussion in Chapter 2, and my more extended, forthcoming analysis in the *Journal of Biblical Literature*, "Ezekiel's Topography of the (Un-)Heroic Dead in Ezek 32:17–32." For other treatments, note Cassuto 1961, 298; Kraeling 1947b, 196, 202–03; Hendel 1987b, 22; Coxon 1999a, 619; V. Hamilton 1990, 270; Hanson 1977, 209–10; Westermann 1984, 378.

170. E.g., Jahnow 1923, 231–39; Shipp 2002, 46. Ezek 31:15–18 also resounds with the imagery of the underworld and makes reference to Pharaoh. For general commentary on the Ezek 32 passage, see Zimmerli 1983, 163–78; Greenberg 1997, 659–70; Eichrodt 1970, 435–41; Joyce 2007, 187–89; Block 1998, 2: 215–34; Cooke 1936, 350–59, and the more specific studies of Launderville (2007, 309–12) and Boadt (1980, 154–61). The comparative analysis of

In summary, the passage describes Pharaoh's descent to the nether-world, where he will be ignominiously greeted by the hordes of fallen (נפל) dead. Vv. 21, 26–27, and 32 represent particularly relevant scenes:

(v. 21) The rulers of the Gibborim (אלי גבורים)[171] will speak to him from the midst of Sheol, along with his helpers: "They have come down, they lie down, the uncircumcised, slain by the sword!"

(v. 26) Meshek and Tubal are there, and all her horde, her graves all around, all of them uncircumcised, those slain by the sword, for they spread their terror (חתיתם) in the land of the living (בארץ חיים).

(v. 27) But they do not lie down with the fallen Gibborim of ancient times (גבורים נפלים מעולם),[172] who went down to Sheol, with their weapons of war, their swords placed under their heads, and their iniquities upon their bones (עונתם על עצמותם), for the terror of the Gibborim (חתית גבורים) was in the land of the living (בארץ חיים).

(v. 32) But I [YHWH] will spread my terror (חתיתי)[173] in the land of the living (בארץ חיים), and he will be laid down in the midst of the uncircumcised, with those slain by the sword, Pharaoh and all his horde, declares the lord YHWH.

Several features in Ezek 32 reveal affinities—and intentional disjunctions—with Aegean concepts of the heroic dead. Specifically, I would suggest several areas in which themes of heroic power and afterlife appear in our text at hand, and I will briefly discuss how the author of Ezek 32:17–32 (whom I

Launderville (2007) in particular is closest to the spirit of my own views here in several important respects.

171. Gk. γιγάντες, also in vv. 12 and 27. By the time of the Greek translation, v. 27 was understood in the context of a gigantomachy:

> καὶ ἐκοιμήθησαν μετὰ τῶν γιγάντων τῶν πεπτωκότων ἀπὸ αἰῶνος οἳ καὶ κατέβησαν εἰς ᾅδου ἐν ὅπλοις πολεμικοῖς καὶ ἔθηκαν τὰς μαχαίρας αὐτῶν ὑπὸ τὰς κεφαλὰς αὐτῶν καὶ ἐγενήθησαν αἱ ἀνομίαι αὐτῶν ἐπὶ τῶν ὀστῶν αὐτῶν ὅτι ἐξεφόβησαν γίγαντας ἐν γῇ ζωῆς

> ...and they lay down with the giants, fallen long ago, the ones who went down to Hades by weapons of war, and they placed swords under their heads and the lawless acts that they created were upon their bones, since they terrified giants in the land of the living.

The meaning of the last clause here is unclear; see Doak ("Ezekiel's Topography...", forthcoming); Kraeling 1947b, 204–05.

172. Following the Gk. here, τῶν γιγάντων τῶν πεπτωκότων ἀπὸ αἰῶνος. Though the characterization of the גבורים as ערלים, "uncircumcised," would fit with imagery throughout the passage, the original reading here is very likely מעולם, "from ancient times," and in fact it is the repeated appearance of ערלים in these verses that prompted the error in the first place.

173. Reading the *qere* (MT חתיתו).

presume to be the prophet Ezekiel himself in the sixth century BCE) adopts, reconfigures, and adapts these themes for his own purposes.[174] First, the fact that we have here military figures who are very clearly presented as actively inhabiting or straddling the dichotomy between the worlds of the living and the dead in Ezekiel 32 is, on the most basic level, an important similarity between the basic religious ideology of this text, the Ugaritic *rp'um* texts, and the evidence for Greek hero cult.[175] One gets the distinct impression, however, that, unlike the *rp'um* or the Greek *hērōs*, these "heroes" are stuck in the underworld—the most they can do is glibly rise up to meet the next of their comrades, Pharaoh (v. 21). The imperative used in v. 18 to induce the lament, נהה, suggests a formal lament category, and indeed the act of heroic lament is well attested throughout the Mediterranean world, encountered in the Aegean most prominently and earliest in the Homeric corpus) e.g., *Iliad* 24), and belongs to a "heroic code" linking death, glory, and immortality in epic.[176] Given the degraded status of the dead in Ezek 32, however, Ezekiel's "lament" can only be a parody. The inversion of the reverence and awe inherent in heroic lament nevertheless reveals the prophet's familiarity with this mode of discourse as specifically applied to the heroic context.

The term חתית ("terror") appears six times in Ezek 32 (vv. 24, 25, 26, 27, 30, 32) as well as in another lament in Ezek 26:17 to describe the city of Tyre. We could justifiably translate חתית in Ezek 32:17–32 as "terror," as I have above, and we often find just such a use of this root attached to military contexts. Soldiers may become "terrified" or be "thrown into a panic," and the Israelites are warned against falling into just such a state as they approach the land (e.g., Deut 1:21). In other places (e.g., Jer 51:56), חתת refers to warriors thrown into a frenzy, as if by divine force, and Gen 35:5 describes a חתת אלהים ("terror of God") that falls upon the cities through which Jacob travels. This notion of חתה as a "divine panic" from God is intriguing, and displays overlap with the Akkadian cognate *ḫātu, ḫattu, ḫa'attu*, "terror, panic."[177] Specifically, these Akkadian terms describe panic as a type of induced, supernatural terror, i.e., the panic that comes from a divine authority

---

174. Cf. Zimmerli 1983, 170–74.

175. The notion that those killed in heroic battle have a special place in the afterlife is a shared feature of Ezekiel 32 and Greek heroic literature, even as Ezekiel 32 may be the only text in the Hebrew Bible to give such a detailed description of this geography. There is a hint of a similar conception in Isa 14:4–21. See Eissfeldt 1950. Note the gloomy underworld scene in *Odyssey* 11, which is seemingly not the standard ancient Greek view of heroic fate—but West 1997a, 164–66 nevertheless productively compares the state of monarchs in the underworld in Ezekiel 32 with Achilles' status as ruler in the underworld in *Odyssey* 11.

176. See Nagy 1999b, 94–117; Perkell 2008; Burke 2008. I borrow the phrase "heroic code" here from Perkell 2008, 94.

177. See *CAD* 6, 150–51.

(or even a king), as well as "panic" as a mental illness or a symptom of sickness. The word ḫa'attu, particularly, is almost exclusively connected to a panic or terror caused by ghosts or witchcraft, e.g.:

šumma amēlu eṭimmu iṣbatsu [...] u ḫa-a-a-at-ti eṭimmi irtanašši

If a ghost takes possession of a man...if he has repeated attacks of panic (caused by) a ghost...[178]

I would suggest the possibility that the use of חתית in Ezekiel 32 reflects something of this supernatural, ghost-induced panic, in that our author is specifically *denying* the fallen dead any power of חתית over the living. In our passage, the "terror" was always *in the land of the living*, which is to say that the "fallen" (נפלים) were only able to spread their panic while they were alive, as emphasized repeatedly in vv. 23, 24, 25, 27, 29, and 32.

In v. 27 particularly, we learn that even the Gibborim of the ancient world, who may have held some powerful status in Israelite religious thought (Gen 6:4), are only effective in their historical epoch and not beyond. The insistence that the only "terror" these figures have left is in powerless human memory comes in vv. 28–29, where the author drives home with repeated and clear imagery the nature of the warriors as broken (שבר), lying down (שכב), and in the Pit (בור). The atmosphere is one of total impotence, suggested even if obliquely by the notion of un-circumcision throughout the passage. The specific power of this image must, I contend, lie in a *counterimage*, viz. a concept of the fallen dead who are thought to have the power of spreading חתית as a divine or semi-divine panic from the grave into the land of the living. Verse 27 is most notable here, with its explicit connection among the ancient Gibborim (גבורים נפלים מעולם) and their "terror" (חתית). YHWH's commanding position over and against his terror-spreading rivals is made clear at the end of the oracle in v. 32: "But *I* will spread *my* חתית (terror) in the land of the living..."

The idea that the dead hero has the power to cause terror and to harm in the "land of the living" is clearly exemplified in the Greek epic tradition. Two examples from the world of tragedy must suffice. In Aeschylus' *Orestia* trilogy, the figures of both Agamemnon and Klytemnestra prove potent from beyond death, as a visit to Agamemnon's grave in the *Libation Bearers* (554ff.) begins a cycle of violence leading to the murder of Klytemnestra and her lover, while the murder of Klytemnestra brings about (in the form of the Erinyes) an attempt at vengeance. A more direct illustration of the hero's fury (as opposed to blessing) after death comes in Sophocles' *Oedipus*

178. *KAR* 267:2, as cited in *CAD* 6. Cf. Job 7:14.

at Colonus: Oedipus promises that his vengeful spirit will brood against Creon and his land forever (784ff.), while, alternatively, his heroic body will serve as a blessing for the location of its rightful burial (552, etc.), and Oedipus promises Athens blessing in return for defending him as opposed to disaster for their enemies, Thebes (450–60).[179] Samuel's appearance to Saul in 1 Sam 28:15–19 may also be considered as an instance of the power of the dead to haunt the living, though in Samuel's case the prophet only recounts the decision of YHWH that seemed obvious throughout the preceding narrative.

Finally, we may note the special attention Ezekiel pays to the bones of dead in v. 27.[180] As Spronk points out, the bone (עצם) is an important image in the Ezekielian world, and the burying or revivification of bones plays a critical function in what can be read as a two-part drama in Ezek 37:1–14 and 39:11–20. In the first instance, in the midst of a valley of dry bones (37:1), the breath of YHWH sweeps in and brings the dead, Israel, up out of their graves. In 39:11–20, we find the only other reference in Ezekiel to the Gibborim (39:18,20), and it comes in a context where the term may best be read in the sense of the departed, heroic dead (vv. 11, 14).[181] The location of the "Oberim" (עברים), east of the Jordan (v. 11), coincides with the homeland of the Rephaim in Numbers – Deuteronomy, and the Ugaritic *'brm* is a parallel term to describe the *rp'um* who "cross over" from the underworld (*KTU* 1.22:1:15).[182] The scene in Ezekiel 32 may have provided inspiration for, or been conceived as a thematic counterpart to, the presentation in Ezek 37:1–14/39:11–20, as these scenes are connected together not only via references to bones and the place of the dead, but also by other specific vocabulary.[183]

The author of Ezek 32:17–32 clearly seems to be exploiting an established correlation between Nephilim (here in the verb נפל) and ancient Gibborim (vv. 20, 22, 24, and especially v. 27). These concepts, then, could be

179. See also lines 1380–85, where Oedipus speaks of the κράτος ("power") of his curse after death against those who mistreat him.

180. There is a text-critical problem here, as many want to emend עונתם to "their shield" (presumably either מגניהם or צגנתם/צנותם?), which would make sense on two levels, viz. the parallel with swords under heads in the preceding line, and the possibility of graphic confusion between עונתם and צנותם. The practice of burying warriors with their weaponry is apparently a very ancient custom in the Levant; see, e.g., Garfinkel 2001, 143–61. See discussion in Zimmerli 1983, 168, and Pohlmann 2001, 435, but cf. Greenberg 1997, 666. Other factors militate against this emendation. The notion of "iniquity" bound up in the bones of the dead heroes may preserve a polemic against a widespread notion that the powers of blessing and fertility were bound up with heroic bones. On such objects of power, see Pfister 1909–1912; Nagy 1990b, 177; McCauley 1999, 94.

181. See Spronk 1999, 876–77.

182. Spronk 1986, 229.

183. As pointed out by Spronk 1986, 229–30.

conceived of in terms of one another at least by the early sixth century BCE, if not far earlier. The passage in Ezekiel 32 thus bears an important witness to the conflation of these significant traditions, as the author seems to be intentionally moving *beyond* simply using a common word, נפל (*nāpal*), to describe the dead in battle, but rather is alluding either to a broader tradition of "fallen" Gibborim in a manner reminiscent of the fragmentary reference in Gen 6:1–4 or to the very text of Gen 6:1–4 itself.184 The Nephilim and Gibborim are thus presented with an aura of reverence and the significance that was attached to the distant past.185

The haunting power of the Gibborim of Old, set alongside the less mythically fearsome and impotent hordes of Israel's current enemies, presents a paradox of heroic ideologies, and it seems that something of this religious conflict is built into the fabric of Ezekiel's symbolic world. On the one hand, the prophet recognizes and even endorses the trope of heroic power from the grave, and on the other he seeks to extinguish it for specific populations. Even as the author of Ezek 32:17-32 *divests* the fallen heroes of their power to act, and thus *denies* his audience any notion of an active, real hero cult with its terror, it is important to notice the ways in which he still *invests* these figures with some resonance of traditional power at the critical turning point of v. 27.

The unity and nature of this heroic portrayal in the chapter as I have described it lends credence to those who have argued for a distinct theology of history and the heroic dead in Ezek 32:17–32,[186] and a more robust recognition of the features pertaining to heroic dualities of living action and, in this case, *inaction*, in the world of the dead further helps to identify some aspects of the shared heroic ideology circulated in the eighth–sixth centuries in the Mediterranean. Though Ezekiel speaks the language of this Mediterranean *koine*, he participates in an exilic and post-exilic trend in the Hebrew Bible toward the *denigration* of heroic concepts and ideals.[187] Indeed, in these later periods, the only "hero" one will be able to speak of is God alone, while the valor of humans recedes, like the fallen Gibborim of old, into the shadowy past. God becomes Israel's only meaningful actor, separating Israel from every other nation. This distinction determines how later interpreters would come to read a passage like Ezekiel 32; as stated in *Sifre Deut.*, commenting on Deut 32:8 (Pisqa 311, "When the Most High gave to the nations their inheritance..."):

184. See Block 1998, 2: 228, who finds this connection "shocking."
185. Eichrodt 1970, 438; Spronk 1986, 280.
186. E.g., Zimmerli, 176; Eichrodt, 441.
187. See, e.g., Jer 9:22; Zech 6:4; Pss 33:16, 52:3; Prov 16:32, 21:22; Ecc 9:11, and the discussion of these texts and others in Chapter 5.

When the Holy One, blessed be He, gave the peoples their inheritance,
He made Gehenna their portion, as it is said, *Asshur is there and
all her company* (Ezek. 23:33), *There are the princes of the north,
all of them, and all the Zidonians* (Ezek. 32:30), *There is Edom, her kings*
(Ezek. 32:29). Should you ask, who will possess their wealth and
honor? the answer is, Israel...[188]

Other glimpses of hero cult ideology in the Hebrew Bible? If the preceding arguments
have any validity, then it stands to reason that we might catch other glimpses of the ideology of hero cult in the Hebrew Bible. Two possibilities may be
mentioned. As I have already discussed in Chapter Two, some have speculated that the figure of Goliath played some role in Israel's cult, as a giant
Chaosmacht in ritual opposition to YHWH.[189] The position of Goliath's sword
at the Nob sanctuary in 1 Sam 21:10 reveals something of the importance
attached to Goliath's relics—indeed, in a Homeric-type scene, David returns
to the site of their single combat to strip his enemy of his gear (1 Sam 17:54).
Another possibility comes through the drama surrounding the burial, transfer, and reburial of Saul's bones in 1 Sam 31:1–13 and 2 Sam 21:1–14, which
could be fruitfully compared with what is known about the importance of
heroic relics—specifically the bones of the hero—and the politics of hero
cults in the Iron Age Aegean.[190] The attention given to the power of the bones
and the dead body in this biblical account is analogous to certain Greek stories drawing on the power and imagery of hero cult, as both contexts reveal
situations in which the location of a hero's body has significant implications
for either blessing or disaster for the possessors of that body.[191]

IV. Conclusion

In this chapter I have argued that some very striking dualities present in
the biblical picture of giants, viz. their presence as both living groups (perhaps embodied most clearly in the Rephaim, but also others, such as the
Nephilim, and Gibborim) and as shades of the dead, have their origin in a

188. Hammer 1986, 317.

189. This idea was proposed by Grønbaek (1957; 1971, 94–95), and endorsed by Hertzberg
(1964, 152).

190. Cf. Weinfeld 1993, 14–15, and my own extended, forthcoming treatment of this issue in *Harvard Theological Review*, "The Fate and Power of Heroic Bones and the Politics of Bone
Transfer in Ancient Israel and Greece." The movement of Jacob's and Joseph's bones in Gen
50:4–14, 50:25; Exod 13:19; Josh 24:32 may also resonate with notions of heroic identity.

191. See McCauley 1999. In addition to these possibilities regarding Goliath and Saul,
note also the בית הגברים in Neh 3:16, which may be a simple meeting house for soldiers, but
could also refer to heroic or royal graves (see also the קברי דוד in the same verse); see Wifall
1975, 298.

pan-Mediterranean style of religious thought regarding heroic warriors and their fate and meaning after death. In this ideology, the death of the hero is only a pretext for his true birth: to paraphrase Rilke, a birth into an existence of blessing and activity as the object of heroic cult.[192] The biblical reflex of this thinking, however, as opposed to the Greek model, takes a very different turn. Though the giants could have a prominent place in the epic of conquest, their status is severely downgraded (and often eliminated entirely) in their subsequent appearance on the other side of death. Even so, we are still left with several tantalizing passages—Gen 6:1–4, Deut 3:11, and Ezek 32:27 most primary among them—wherein echoes of ancient wonder are still attached to the austere, giant, heroes of old. At this point, then, the specific term "hero" applies to the biblical groups of giants in significant and productive ways, insofar as these figures fulfill the pattern of conquest/cataclysm in parallel with the Greek heroes in the *Iliad* and related heroic/epic traditions, and also insofar as the appearance of these groups in the dual context of "epic" and "afterlife" (cult) can be shown to be relevant both to the Greek materials and, in narrative sublimations writ large, across various elements of the biblical corpus.

We have now observed two strategies used by the biblical authors to deal with the presence of these figures: (1) to cut them down in battle during their lives, or, (2) in a sense, to drive them *underground*, where the tactic is humiliation, impotence, and utter powerlessness. A striking turn of approach is present in all of this, since in the Pentateuch and Deuteronomistic History it was very important to make these giants look as powerful and fearsome as possible, whereas, in the second strategy, their role is reversed—the Rephaim can raise their mocking, ghost-like voices to welcome useless foreign kings into Sheol (Isaiah 14), but that is all; the chiefs of the Gibborim and Nephilim can rule over the dead (Ezekiel 32), but their time in the land of the living is over. We also have had occasion yet again, as in the previous chapter, to notice the "slippage" between the biblical giants as giants and their affinities with aspects of the heroic traditions shared by cultures in the historical and geographical stream of the Mediterranean *koine*. This interplay between "giant" and "hero" seems to be a natural part of the biblical text, which demonstrates fluidity between the two concepts.

This merger between giant and hero has not reached the point of complete or easy identity, and no one should expect that it would. Rather, I have argued that the Bible's fusion of giant and hero belongs to a religious conversation shared with ancient Aegean cultures. The Bible's reverse image of the hero in cult relies on a counter image, the "Canaanite" hero cult ideology

---

192. Rilke 1989, 153; quoted as the epigraph for this chapter.

that was shared throughout the Mediterranean beginning at least in the eighth century (as endorsed by A. Yadin, Albright, and others discussed above) but very possibly sooner—certainly earlier at Ugarit, if my analysis is correct. The very fact that such ideas (including those regarding death cults generally) receive polemical treatment by biblical authors demonstrates their powerful status in the minds of the biblical audiences stretched across time. The biblical presentation is defined and circumscribed by its broader religious context, its images formed in relation to counter-images. This broader cultural process finds a parallel in the very dynamics of epic itself, which relies upon tension, perpetual enemies, and counter-images for its own survival.

Consider, for example, the meditation on this point by Hendel by way of Alain (Émile-Auguste Chartier):[193]

> The object that belongs to the hero and shapes the hero is the enemy; that is to say, the equal, the much-praised equal, the rival, a rival whom he judges worthy of himself. Therefore there can be no complete hero without a solemn war, without some provocation, without the long anticipation of another hero, subject of fame and legend.

Hendel elaborates: the "self is defined by the other; the other, in religious terms, is God; therefore mythological encounters are inevitable...The hero and the other are also opposites; from their encounter comes the harmony we call epic."[194] When the biblical authors wrote of our giants as epic (enemy) heroes on the battlefield, the heroic counter-image of the powerful hero in cult was dragged along, a kind of reptilian tale, an inevitable shadow image. With each renewed effort to describe the hero and the heroic age, the counter-image follows, implicitly reminding the audience of the "other" side, the myth, the cult they were to avoid. In such a presentation, we find something deformed and something whole, something hidden, and something blindingly open.

Although I have suggested the distinct possibility that notions of hero cult were actively present in Israel as part of their inherited Canaanite religious milieu, I have not forcefully claimed that heroes were actively worshipped as local divinities. Rather, I have suggested that the signals of hero cult are woven into biblical texts dealing with giants, and that there must have therefore been religious space for such a presentation to exist. J. Assmann has recently argued that heroic myth and the accompanying ideologies of hero cult could not develop in either the Mesopotamian or the

---

193. Alain 1974, 113, quoted in Hendel 1987a, 101.
194. Hendel 1987a, 102.

Egyptian contexts, since the figure of the king in these societies (at least in some periods) left no room in the religious economy, so to speak, for humans to achieve divine or semi-divine status except for the king/Pharaoh.[195] If his line of reasoning is accurate, then we may surmise that the residuum of hero cult that found expression in the Hebrew Bible was allowed to operate precisely because of the position of Israel's kings, i.e., as distinctly non-divine extensions of existing tribal arrangements.[196] In this sense, the structures of political leadership in Israel allowed religious space for humans to achieve an extraordinary status, just as in a different, yet parallel manner the structure of the Greek polis held market opportunities for cults of heroes. Of course, in normative Israelite religious expression YHWH was to crowd out *all* other competitors, be they human, semi-human, or divine, and the biblical bans on all mediums, diviners, and the like all bear witness to YHWH's monopoly over the system.[197] There would seem to be no real possibility, then, for chthonic deities to exist in a monotheistic system; ancient Israelite religion, insofar as it is a true monotheism, cannot have a Nergal running around.[198] And yet we come back to our point above: epic relies upon tension, so the presence of the giants cannot be eradicated entirely; epic cannot tolerate

---

195. Assmann 2009. Or, perhaps more accurately: the king in these contexts *becomes* the hero. See, e.g., the Qadesh battle accounts and reliefs of Ramses II, or the Epic of Tukulti-Ninurta I (for the latter, see Machinist 2006).

196. I do not mean to suggest here that kingship in Israel was entirely un-Mesopotamian or un-Egyptian, as the pan-Near-Eastern symbolism of kingship found its way very deeply into the heart of Israelite expressions (e.g., in the Temple–Palace complex, and in some of the language of monarchic identity vis-à-vis the deity, e.g., 2 Sam 7:14; Ps 2:7, 45:6). Nor would I endorse the viewpoint of Mendenhall (1962, and several later works) and others who see biblical faith as opposed de jure to any "Canaanite" model of kingship. Nevertheless, these motifs elevating the king to divine status are more restrained in Israel than one finds elsewhere in the historical region, or more restrained, at least, than one might have expected them to become, to the point where the Israelite ideal of kingship is a novum for its time and place.

197. Prophets and priests are obviously the only exception to this rule, though their tactics supposedly did not include the mechanistic derivation of YHWH's will or the operation of the cultus.

198. Epic conflict relies upon the tension between more or less equally matched powers—i.e., a polytheistic milieu. On this point, consider Louden (2007, 90–95), who defines an "epic triangle" of divine actors in relation to the hero, i.e., a sky god who presides over the divine council to decide the hero's fate; a mentor deity for the hero; and a third, antagonistic deity who opposes the hero. This triangle is apparently not only in Greek epic, but also in the canonical Gilgamesh tradition, where we find Anu, Shamash, and Ishtar, respectively, in the three stereotyped roles. If this inherently polytheistic triangle (or something like it) is endemic to epic qua epic—which is to say, if this conflict of divine interests and axes of power is necessary for epic to function—then the genre of epic can only stand in continual tension with the ideals of monotheistic power. Note also Lamberton 2010, 36, 38–39 on Hellenistic and Christian efforts to deal with polytheism and monotheism vis-à-vis epic.

the centralization of power that the Bible claims YHWH should have, and thus strong opponents must remain on call. The giants have therefore led us into a trap. We must have them, yet we cannot have them. They are left in an ambivalent position, the chaos they represent managed by way of doubleness. They are alive and dead, powerful and powerless.

In their distinct presentation of these characters, the biblical authors acted as true innovators, and we have already begun to see a certain kind historiography developing, which is a meditation on the fate of the Late Bronze Age societies: the victors become the victims, the victorious, heroic Rapiuma become the biblical Rephaim, and the heroic age both recedes far into the past even while certain elements of it are continually kept alive in the present. It is to this final chapter in the story of our heroic giants and their role in demarcating Israel's "heroic ages" in the historiography of the Hebrew Bible that we now turn.

Chapter Five

The Historiography of Biblical Giants: Emergence, Submergence, and Resurrection

I. Introduction

I N THIS CHAPTER, I retrospectively explore the giants' place in the historiography of the biblical stories in which they are embedded. In existing scholarship, giants are neither a question nor a problem to be dealt with on a historiographic level; at most, giants have been styled as merely the oversized enemy, an "other" against which Israelite heroes can fight in single combat (thus evoking the giants in association with a "heroic age" concept).[1] There was, of course, a traceable history of Israelite emergence and action in the land, beginning probably in the mid-thirteenth century BCE, but the giants we have been discussing throughout this study played no role as human actors in this history. *Pace* Herodotus, Augustine, and others, there are no Brobdingnagian bones to be dug up, and the origins of Israel's giant traditions do not lie in exaggerated memories of physical conditions of freak gigantism and so on. Rather, the giant takes his place in the historiography of cultural memory, as a symbol in the narrative of a people in the act of rendering account of its past to itself.[2]

In what follows, I argue that giants serve as historiographic punctuation marking a series of heroic ages—or perhaps better, heroic *moments*—in ancient Israel. This task has already been initiated, in different ways, in Chapters Two and Three, where I explored the place of giants at three different, critical junctures in the biblical storyline (Flood, conquest, and monarchy), and where I compared the end of the giants' era to the demise of the mythological Giants and Titans and the heroic generation in ancient Greek literature. There is no single "heroic age" in the Hebrew Bible; rather,

---

1. As recently by Mobley (2005, 50).

2. Here I am obviously paraphrasing part of Huizinga's famous definition of history as "the intellectual form in which a civilization renders account to itself of its past" (Huizinga 1963, 9). Huizinga's concept has also been effectively used to explore the biblical materials by Van Seters (1997, 1–7). By invoking the concept of "memory," I allude to recent studies dedicated to the concept of biblical historiography as cultural memory; see, e.g., Leveen 2008; P. Davies 2008; Hendel 2005; M. Smith 2004.

there are several, and the giants are a part of each one, where they create both specific moments of historical crisis and eternal "moments" in the historiographic maintenance of the ordered cosmos of God's deliverance and justice. This technique of periodizing is not exactly "cyclical,"[3] nor is it strictly linear, if by "linear" one means a unidirectional, salvation history culminating in a decisive eschaton.[4] Rather, we find the historiography of *periodic irruption*, a "rattling of the chains at intervals,"[5] a breaking in of threat followed by responses to the threat through events of divine ordering.

As we have already observed, the Bible presents us with potentially conflicting notions of the heroic and the gigantic—as both historical and mythic phenomena.[6] For example, before Joshua or Kaleb or anyone else crosses the Jordan, the promised land is a real geographical place, but it is also symbolically fearsome (Num 13:32) and wildly fertile (Num 13:23), and the giants who live there are represented simultaneously as ethnic groups (Anaqim) and as descendents of a mythic, antediluvian race (Nephilim). So too, in Deuteronomy 2–3, the existence of giant Rephaim and their congeners is rolled out as a mundane ethnographic fact, with the author of Deut 2:10–11 taking particular pride in relaying comparative data about the names and categorization of these groups. The giants are thus presented in terms of a feasible "historical" narrative by ancient standards, bound up in a recognizable conquest trope of the new-good vs. the bad-old, and yet other dynamics are at play. The giants signify much beyond their brute physical existence; they embody a spirit of anti-divine chaos, opposed to God's boundaries in the heavens and on earth. Their potential for continued existence, in the form of the dead Rephaim (as discussed in Chapter Four), sets up the underworld as a cosmic, opposing counterpart to the heavens. There is a human conflict, between giants and their Israelite slayers, which, ultimately, points both forward (within the biblical narrative) and backward (from beyond it) toward the power of kingship at a real moment in Israel's history, but this

3. See Albrektson 1967, 93–97.

4. On the problems associated with linear or cyclical historiographic schemes, see Tucker 2001, 47.

5. I steal this phrase from Wellhausen (1878, 114), who uses it to describe part of what he considers a pessimistic "antique philosophy of history" pursued by the Yahwist in his use of myth at intervals in Genesis 1–11.

6. By invoking these often opposed categories of "history" and "myth" I am not, at this point, making any assumptions regarding the suitability of either category as a ruling concept in the biblical presentation of any particular topic. Nor is it suitable, as demonstrated by Albrektson (1967) and Roberts (2002), to conveniently credit Israel with an historical outlook vis-à-vis the rest of the ancient Near East. Rather, it is the Bible's mélange of these categories of history and myth (each of which is problematic in and of itself) that is notable, especially, in terms of my project, in the figures of the giants-as-heroes.

same conflict is something supra-human and omnitemporal. It is a struggle between divine limit, on the one hand, and human-daemonic transgression, on the other, acted out on earth through God's human agents and also in the primeval age where only God was king and where the wayward acts of giants were dealt with by God alone (Gen 6:1–4). Insofar as the giants come packaged as identifiable human societies, such as the Anaqim, Rephaim, Emim, and so on, they pass away, but as a mythic possibility, they do not—indeed, they *cannot*.

This interplay between ethnography and myth signals a moment, I contend, to which we should pay attention in terms of historiographic strategy. Indeed, the periodization of the existence of giants into the antediluvian world, pre-Israelite Canaan, and pre-monarchic Philistia suggests yet another important heroic concept, viz. the notion of a "heroic age." By way of addressing the role of the giants in the conception of a heroic age, I briefly discuss the concepts of historiographic periodization, heroic ages in a variety of cultures, and the question of a heroic age as an "axial" category. Having established this base, I proceed to examine specifically the concept of a heroic age in both ancient Greece and Israel. In the Aegean formulation, the heroic age terminates with the Trojan War, and, while the identity and terminus of a heroic age in the Hebrew Bible are not as easy to identify, we still find several promising avenues of exploration. Moreover, the biblical conception of the role of giants in the organization of historical epochs finds dual expression in the exilic and post-exilic period, where we find sources that participate in the denigration of heroic concepts and also later sources that revive the purely mythic dimensions of giants and their attendant heroic tropes, thus resurrecting the giant into continuing service in opposition to Israel's God.

II. Periodization and the Heroic Age

Sophisticated attempts at historical periodization are an old phenomenon in the ancient Near East, and periodization seems endemic to any human conception of the past as such.[7] Indeed, some of the very first written royal propaganda, under Naram-Sin (c. 2254–2218 BCE), uses a very simple periodization technique to speak of the god-king's rise to prominence. I refer here to the reference to "nine battles in one year" (10.LÁ.1 KAŠ.ŠUDUN [*tāḥāzī*] in MU 1) recorded in the famous Basetki inscription and elsewhere, which is very likely a utilization of the schematized number nine as a symbol of totality.[8] In this reference we already see awareness, however scant, of

7. See Green 1992; 1995.
8. See example in Frayne 1993, 2: 111–12, E2.1.4.9. Cf. the Egyptian motif of the Pharaoh

abstract, symbolic values, as the ruler conceives of, and attempts to justify, his achievements in terms of a known trope. A more intricate, early periodization can be found in the so-called Sumerian King List, editions of which circulated as early as c. 2300 BCE and were composed as late as 1900–1850 BCE.[9] Here, eras of kingship begin after the institution descended from the heavens. In the earliest, antediluvian era, kings rule for tens of thousands of years each, but a decisive break occurs "after the flood had swept over," at which time more modest reigns occur.[10]

In the first millennium BCE, increasingly, we find further, and often more sophisticated, attempts at periodization, the most notable of which in the Greek world is Hesiod's progression of metallic ages in the eighth century.[11] A second-century portion of the biblical book of Daniel (2:31–45) also famously takes up a succession of metallic ages, and this was apparently a popular way to view the progression of human history in ancient Iranian lore and later Jewish writings (e.g., the six metal mountains of 1 Enoch 52).[12] Other methods could be used, such as genealogies: the so-called "Uruk Apkallu List" is a sort of scholarly genealogy, dating to the Seleucid period (c. 165 BCE) but with precedents throughout the late second and first millennia BCE, and provides what A. Lenzi calls a "mythology of scribal succession."[13] This text lists seven antediluvian kings with their counterpart *apkallu* ("sage, wise man"), and eight further postdiluvian kings with counterpart *ummânu* ("scholar, specialist"). Clearly, these scribes sought to associate the profession of the contemporary *ummânu* with that of the ancient *apkallu*, forming a succession of scholarly ages from the pre-flood world through their present time.[14]

The flourishing of these and other complex manners of historical pe-

---

enthroned atop the nine enemies or nine bows in Egyptian art, as well as the listing of nine conquered nations in Ps 83:5–7; see images, discussion, and references in Hossfeld and Zenger 2005 (342–44, plates 1–2). For further analysis of the developing historiography of early Akkad, see, e.g., Tinney 1995 and Michalowski 1993.

9. Glassner 2004.

10. To be sure, the Epic of Gilgamesh also nods toward the pre-flood/post-flood periodization, where Gilgamesh acts as a mediating figure (i.e., in bringing back information from the lone survivors of the antediluvian world). It may further be argued that in the figures of Gilgamesh and Enkidu, as well as in the early monarchs in the Sumerian king list, we have a conception of a "heroic age" in which extraordinary individuals lived and acted in a way that later audiences no longer thought possible in the present. Such a concept is explicitly marked in the Sumerian King List by the extraordinary age of the antediluvian kings, and also in the Gilgamesh epic by Gilgamesh's own extraordinary status (i.e., his size, ability, and exploits).

11. This text, in *Works and Days* 106–201, was discussed in Chapter 3, and will be taken up again below.

12. See, e.g., Black 1985, 215.

13. Lenzi 2008, 143.

14. Lenzi 2008, 164–65. For the possible influence of the *apkallu* tradition on Enoch and Genesis, see Gmirkin 2006, 109–110.

riodization in the first millennium could be considered in terms of Karl Jasper's famous concept of the *Achsenzeit*, or "Axial Age," a time period ranging from c. 800–200 BCE—but culminating around the year 500 BCE—in which all current "fundamental categories" of history and religion were supposedly born.[15] In the West, Homer and the Greek philosophical tradition flourished; India witnessed the era of the Buddha and the Upanishads; Iranian Manichaeism was born under Zarathustra; and in Israel, the prophetic voices of the ninth–sixth centuries emerged. For Jaspers, in all these traditions a series of fundamental changes took place:[16]

> man becomes conscious of Being as a whole...He experiences the terror
> of the world and his own powerlessness. He asks radical questions.
> Face to face with the void he strives for liberation and redemption. By
> consciously recognising his limits he sets himself the highest goals. He
> experiences absoluteness in the depths of selfhood and in the lucidity
> of transcendence...spiritual conflicts arose, accompanied by attempts
> to convince others through the communication of thoughts, reasons
> and experiences. The most contradictory possibilities were essayed.
> Discussion, the formation of parties and the division of the spiritual realm
> into opposites which nonetheless remained related to one another created
> unrest and movement to the very brink of spiritual chaos.

The opposition between a "transcendental" and "mundane" order is at the heart of such of a conception, though it is not immediately clear what these terms mean. For Benjamin Schwartz, all axial movements participate in a "strain towards transcendence," where transcendence is defined as "a kind of standing back and looking beyond—a kind of critical, reflective questioning of the actual and a new vision of what lies beyond."[17]

Another explicator of the axial phenomena, S. Eisenstadt, argued that during the Axial Age,

> a new type of intellectual elite became aware of the necessity to actively
> construct the world according to some transcendental vision. The
> successful reinstitutionalization of such conceptions and visions gave rise
> to extensive re-ordering of the internal contours of societies as well as
> their internal relations.[18]

Eisenstadt cites several factors within the rise of clerical and intellectual

---

15. Jaspers 1953. The secondary literature on this topic is immense; e.g., Eistenstadt 1986a; Arnason, Eisenstadt, and Wittrock 2005; and the recent summary in S. Smith 2011b. Note also the semi-popular book by Armstrong 2006.

16. Jaspers 1953, 2.

17. Schwartz 1975, 3.

18. Eisenstadt 1982, 294; 1981; 1986a.

groups that gave rise to the axial re-ordering. Tension developed between "'traditional' modes of legitimation and more 'open' (rational, legal or charismatic) ones";[19] the concept of the god-king gave way to the "secular ruler," who was accountable to the divine;[20] new levels of social conflict emerged, with "highly ideologized, generalized and sometimes even universalized" struggles.[21] Drawing explicitly on Eisenstadt's concept of these new elite actors, A. Joffe has analyzed the rise of "secondary states" (e.g., Phoenicia, Israel, Edom, Moab, Judah, etc.) in the first millennium as the result of ethnic identities assuming a political role after the breakdown of the Late Bronze empires. In these secondary states, Joffe argues, independent "axial elites" for the first time play a pivotal role in transmitting historical memory, revising laws, and influencing religion.[22]

The question of whether we can speak of axial phenomena in Israel or in the Near East more broadly would seem to have been decided, in the first instance, by Jaspers himself, who made the Israelite prophetic movement as embodied in Jeremiah and Isaiah one of the cornerstone examples of axial transformation.[23] On the Mesopotamian front, there have been few but notable studies. Voegelin's *Order and History* dealt with such concepts as "leaps of being," self-consciousness, and abstract thought in Mesopotamia,[24] and L. Oppenheim spoke of a Mesopotamian stretch into abstraction but found no existence of Mesopotamian polemic against intellectual enemies or expressions of uniqueness.[25] H. Tadmor saw a limited connection between emerging "elite groups" in Assyria and Babylon who could act as purveyors of royal accountability, though these figures did not approach the level of biblical prophecy.[26] Addressing the question from a different angle, P. Machinist concludes that in Mesopotamia we do find abstract stereotyping, through the bifurcation of city versus the savage, and certain categories such as "nomad," "mountaineer," "foreigner," and so on.[27] Moreover, there may be found "hints of self-consciousness" in various literary sources, and

19. Eisenstadt 1982, 300.

20. Eisenstadt 1982, 303.

21. Eisenstadt 1982, 304.

22. Joffe 2002, 455–56. See also Knohl (2005), who speaks of specific priestly schools enacting Axial Age transformations in the eighth century BCE.

23. Jaspers 1953, 2. See also Eisenstadt 1986a; Uffenheimer 1986; Weinfeld 1986.

24. Though he does not refer to Jaspers or axiality specifically, Voegelin uses axial-sounding phrases such as "Mosaic leap in being" when discussing Israelite religion and "the aptitude of various civilizations for development in the direction of the 'leap in being'" with reference to Mesopotamia. See Voegelin 1969, 501 and 38, respectively, and discussion in Machinist 2001, 26–32.

25. Oppenheim 1975, 38, 42; cf. Garelli 1974.

26. Tadmor 1986.

27. Machinist 1986.

Mesopotamian mathematical thinking and scribal lists clearly evince analytical, abstract formulae.[28] Machinist concludes that the cuneiform record does conform somewhat to the axial categories of self-criticism and self-consciousness, but not as fully as the classical examples of axiality. In the end, he categorizes Mesopotamian cultures as "traditional," an ideal-type classification opposed to innovative, "rational" societies.[29] In other words, traditional societies by nature typically do not allow the type of heterodoxy axiality would seem to require for the operation of its breakthroughs of rigorous prophetic or philosophical critique.

More recently, P. Michalowski has built on certain aspects of the dichotomy between traditional and axial societies described by Machinist and taken the argument further, making the provocative suggestion that Babylonian intellectuals created a "counter-axiality" as a way of resisting "the axial institutionalizations that were taking shape all around them" in the Persian and Seleucid periods. This counter-axiality was, according to Michalowski, "ironically, both sociologically and structurally, homologous to the nascent axial movements in other societies."[30] To illustrate one possible counter-axial/axial movement in Mesopotamia, Michalowski offers the example of Nabonidus' reworking of the cult of the moon-god at Harran. Nabonidus apparently sought to use his own scribal training and religious knowledge to promote novel readings of astronomical texts and radically alter Babylonian religious tradition, actions that resemble the heterodox, autonomous elite of axial innovation.[31]

Rather than pursuing the reductionist interpretation of cuneiform literature in the sixth century and onward solely as a culturally regressive shield put up toward the onslaught of religious and political upheavals, Michalowski argues that the peripheral location of scribal culture in this socio-political context—situated as it was on at least the cultural, if not geographic, periphery—comports well with the observations of those who have located the rise of axial responses on the "outskirts" of a given civilization (as opposed to its cultural center).[32] It is important for our purposes here to note that this same sixth-century context also saw the flourishing of what might be called

28. Machinist 1986, 196–98.
29. Machinist 1986, 201–02.
30. Michalowski 2005, 177.
31. Michalowski 2005, 177–79.
32. Michalowski 2005, 177, drawing on the work of Wolf (1967, 462). Moreover, along with Michalowski, I have preferred to use the phrase "axial phenomena" rather than "Axial Age," so as not to omit smaller-scale or subtler axial-like movements or innovations, and also as a way to partly avoid the sometimes domineering homogeneity with which Jaspers could speak of the *Achsenzeit* topic.

a certain kind of "antiquarianism," marked by the collation of artifacts from the past (such as inscriptions, artistic monuments), archaeological excavations, and possibly even an organized forum—a type of "museum"—where such artifacts were displayed.[33] This phenomenon, too, had taken on a distinct character, as critical, heterodox expression, placing it squarely within the conversation of axial consciousness.[34]

I have thus far attempted to show some possibilities regarding the interface between axial breakthrough phenomena and the manner in which the past was imagined, in terms both of periodization and of the implications of antiquarian interest. These topics of periodization and antiquarianism may now be brought to bear on the notion of periodization via a "heroic age," a common structuring technique recognized in many geographic regions and historical traditions.[35] Indeed, much has been written on the topic of a heroic age, and elaborate concepts of the hero and epic literature are adduced for an increasing number of languages and literatures throughout the world, both ancient and modern.[36] For example, even though some of the standard Ugaritic texts had received the "epic" label for some time (e.g., the "Baal Epic," Kirta, Aqhat, etc.),[37] there is a renewed interest in viewing various ancient Mesopotamian literatures through an "epic" lens, as well as some Egyptian texts.[38] Roman epic re-created its own version of the Greek heroic age (e.g., Ovid's *Metamorphosis* and Virgil's *Aeneid*),[39] and the Indo-European stream, including the Sanskrit *Mahābhārata*, some Hittite texts, and the Persian *Shāhnāma* ("Book of Kings"), have all been studied in terms of their conception of heroes and a heroic age.[40] Old European texts of the Common

33. See Beaulieu 1994; Winter 2010; Michalowski 2003; 2005, 175, who also cites Bernbeck 1996 and Klengel-Brandt 1990. A parallel development also occurred in the twenty-fifth and twenty-sixth Dynasties of Egypt (mid-eighth–late sixth centuries BCE); see Der Manuelian 1994.

34. Michalowski 2005, 176.

35. The two major studies of the heroic age phenomenon in the twentieth century are Chadwick 1912 and Bowra 1957. Note also Bowra 1952, 1–47; Gladstone 1869; Huxley 1976; Hatto 1980–1989. For Hebrew Bible studies, see now Echols 2008, esp. 135–56 and 157–202, as a reminder that the biblical text did indeed engage in ruminations on actors in a heroic age, and that the study of heroic themes in the Hebrew Bible can open up productive comparative vistas with other literature.

36. Outside of the examples from the Mediterranean, Mesopotamia, and Old Europe cited below, see, e.g., Araki 1962; Chan 1974; Biebuyck 1976; Ingham 1993; Spaulding 2007.

37. See the collection of primary texts in Parker 1997; 1989.

38. For recent updates on Mesopotamian epic, see, e.g., Sasson 2007; Noegel 2007; Alster 2007; J. Klein 2007; and several new essays in Konstan and Raaflaub 2010, 7–85. But note already Kramer 1946. On ancient Egypt, see Loprieno 1996; Spalinger 2002.

39. See, e.g., Farrell 2007; Momigliano 1957; Horsfall 1994; Suerbaum 1999.

40. Generally, see Katz 2007; on the Indic epic, see Fitzgerald 2004; Brockington 1998;

Era—most famously the *Nibelungenlied* and *Beowulf*—enter the tradition of heroic literatures inspired by earlier Mediterranean epic, representing the apex of heroic age reminiscence in pre-modern Europe.[41]

Previous references to heroic ages vis-à-vis axial phenomena have been conceived in terms of radical *difference*, pushing the heroic age and the axial age toward two opposite ends of a pole.[42] Such a polarization can be heuristically useful or misguided, depending on how it is configured. On the one hand, one must recognize that the historical era in which the recollection of a heroic age is *composed* is never coterminous with the historical epoch in which the heroes putatively *lived*—rather, the conception comes later, in retrospect, and thus could be read either as an endorsement of heroic values only insofar as they are relevant in the present age of the authors or as a condemnation, even if oblique, of the heroic age. If the latter is the case, then the formulation (as denigration) of a certain kind of heroic age could very much fit the standard concepts of axiality. If the heroic age is viewed positively, and therefore allegedly in opposition to the axial age, the very "past-ness" of the heroic age could still be interpreted as a signal that this age is confined to the museum of past eras, and cannot break out upon the world again. On the other hand, the intellectual environment of axial elites might demand a direct and unmitigated criticism of *any* past represented by traditional heroes in a heroic age. If the condemnation of the past is necessary for the heterodox, self-conscious criticism of the present, then, to borrow a quip from Nietzsche, every past is worth condemning.[43]

III. The Heroic Age of Ancient Greece and the Giants of the Hebrew Bible

As is well known, in Greek epic thought the Trojan and Theban wars marked the end of the Greek heroic age.[44] This meditation on the end of the age of heroes in diverse texts that may not have directly influenced one another at

McGrath 2004. Specifically, for heroic age themes in contact with ancient Greece, see the analysis of *Mah.* 11.8.26 in Dumézil 1986, 195–96 and de Jong 1985, 397–400. For the Hittites, see Beckman 2007 with sources cited there, and Gilan 2010. For Persian epic, see Davidson 2007; 1994; Skjærvø 1998.

41. Se the new edition of the *Nibelungenlied* with interpretation and bibliography by Reichert 2005; on Beowulf, see F. Robinson 1991; for Old French, Germanic, Irish, Icelandic, Indian, Persian, Slavonic, and some non-Indo-European materials, see de Vries 1978, 22–163; Glosecki 2007; Brault 1978.

42. E.g., Ferwerda 1986, 112. Strathern (2009) characterizes the heroic age insofar as it appears in Armstrong's popular work on the topic as "transcendentalism's shadow," an "unsustainable, unbearable" age that could only be remedied by a peaceful, ethically renewed Axial Age.

43. Nietzsche 2005, 21.

44. For comments similar to some of what follows, see Finkelberg 2004; 2005, 161–69.

the earliest level of their production indicates, as M. Finkelberg puts it, "the destruction of the Race of Heroes was an all-pervasive theme which crossed the boundaries between epic traditions."[45] The *Cypria* (1-2; Schol. [D] *Il*.1.5) for example, explicitly places Zeus at the center of instigating the Trojan War—his destructive plan (the βουλή of *Il*. 1.5) is a quest to wipe the heroic generation from the face of the earth.[46] At the end of Hesiod's *Catalogue*, we again find the theme of the sharp break between the heroic age and later history, and indeed, in classical Greek thought, the recognizable "modern history" of the sixth-century polis and onward begins with end of the heroic age. Hesiod's formulation in *Works and Days* (106-201) is most explicit here. The periodization of the past in terms of metallic ages is interrupted (artificially, as many have argued[47]) by the fourth generation of "of men heroes" (ἀνδρῶν ἡρώων), characterized as "demigods" (ἡμίθεοι; lines 156-73), and it is these figures who are identified with the Trojan and Theban heroes—over and against the ignominious "Bronze Age" brutes.[48] Homer, too, participates in this stream of recognizing the terminus of heroic activity, even if his ultimate presentation of the heroic age seeks to forge continuity between this age and the living generations of the classical period.[49] The reference in *Il*. 12.23 to the "demigods" (ἡμιθέων γένος ἀνδρῶν), linked as it is with the imagery of flood and the retrospective view of the end of the Trojan War, suggests Homer was in fact aware that the heroic age was comprised of individuals of a different quality from contemporary humans, and that the end of this age marked a periodizing break in the history of the region.[50]

45. Finkelberg 2004, 13.

46. I discussed these references, as well as the following texts in Hesiod and Homer, at some length in Chapter 3.

47. See Walcott 1966, 81-86 and Querbach 1985, 1-2, to cite but two examples.

48. Recall that in Hesiod's Bronze Age (*Works and Days*, 143-55), the warriors are nameless warmongers, doomed to the "dank house of chilly Hades," whereas the "race of men-heroes" in the next generation (156-73) is "more just and superior." Selected elements of this latter race dwell on the Islands of the Blessed as "happy heroes" (ὄλβιοι ἥρωες).

49. We do not know, of course, what role such continuity played in any putatively "original" *Iliad*, but we do know that by the sixth century the important Panathenaic performance of the *Iliad* and *Odyssey* made the link between the heroic past and the political present a permanent, constitutive feature of the Homeric corpus. Finkelberg (2004, 19-24) has argued that Homer intentionally suppressed the theme of the end of the heroic age by way of making just such links with contemporary audiences. Cf. Nagy 1999b, 7-9, 115-21, 139-42 on the role of the *Iliad* and *Odyssey* vis-à-vis Panhellenism.

50. One may also cite as evidence of this awareness the reference in *Il*. 5.302-04, where the narrator reveals his opinion that a great gulf of size and strength separates the heroes from those in the epic audience. So too, in 1.271-72, Nestor recounts a battle fought long ago in which he asserts "mortals now on the earth" (i.e., even in the time of the *Iliad*?) could not have contended, revealing further awareness of the qualitative distance between heroic individuals living in different eras.

The clear periodization into heroic and post-heroic ages in these accounts reflects a kind of antiquarianism, a concern with the way past epochs of humankind developed, acted, flourished, and died away. Hesiod's schema presciently recalls at least two of his historical ages, the Bronze and the Iron, in the very same terms that came to be adopted by archaeologists to describe those cultures living on either side of the period of historical chaos and change in the Mediterranean world from c. 1300–1200 BCE (though the use of these exact metals in the modern, archaeological categorization was never particularly exacting, even if it is representative of the types of prestige weaponry metal in each era). Homer displays his own antiquarian flair generally by speaking of the end of this heroic age as well, and specifically by his penchant for mentioning a few details about weaponry styles, cultural values, and so on that could represent real historical memories of the "heroic" Mycenaean civilization.[51]

But the relatively sudden end of this heroic age in the triumphant battles of yore in epic serves as a mask, covering the face of a complicated, drawn-out historical process: the breakdown and eventual collapse of the Late Bronze civilizations across the Mediterranean world. It is at this obvious—yet often overlooked—point that what little we do know of the historical record contradicts the notion of Trojan War as a comprehensive, totalizing event; the demographics of mainland Greece radically shifted by some still mysterious dynamic of population change, prompted perhaps by natural cataclysms, famines, or broader political unrest in the macro-region.[52] The heroic age accounts, composed only after a 400–500 year hiatus when certain regions had made a cultural recovery, are the media by which epic chose to look back at the end of the Bronze Age heroic cultures; and thus Homer, Hesiod, and others now stand as the voices who most poignantly captured the memories of this period (even if in distorted forms).[53] The stories of the heroic age became the central memory and the primary idiom for describing the break

51. E.g., Nestor's cup in *Iliad* 11 and the leather helmet with boar tusks in *Iliad* 10 have archaeological parallels dating specifically to the Bronze Age, etc.

52. See the overview in Morris 2006 and also Finkelberg 2005, 167–68, which discusses this very point in some detail. As Finkelberg 2005 also points out, Greek tradition did attempt to account for issues of population change through other types of epic (e.g., the lost *Aigimios* and *Melampodia*) which did not achieve the status of Homer or Hesiod.

53. Morris 2006, 73. Finkelburg (2005, 169) puts the issue similarly: "The painful historical events that accompanied the end of Mycenaean Greece were replaced in this tradition by the story of a war specially designed by Zeus to put an end to the Race of Heroes. As a result, it was the Trojan War rather than the population movements that shook Greece at the end of the second millennium BC that became universally envisaged as the main if not the only factor responsible for the catastrophe that brought about the end of the Heroic Age."

between eras; in biblical terms, the fall of Troy and the eradication of the semi-divine heroes are at once the Greek "flood" and the Greek "conquest."

Turning to the Hebrew Bible, we are now in a position to observe the way various biblical authors participate in a striking re-imagination of the collapse and regeneration surrounding the crucial breaking point c. 1200 BCE via the periodizing device of a heroic age. This re-imagination involves a heroic crusade against indigenous giants, among other groups, even as it is not only in the conquest narratives that giants are to be found. The biblical account of this collapse, just as in the Greek tradition, represents a charged heroic moment; a certain kind of existence, represented by a native population (cf. the Trojans in Homer), has come to an end. In Homer and Hesiod, this heroic age is valorized, but there were other contemporary traditions that charged the heroes with impiety, or at least of having incurred divine wrath, thus leading to their demise. In the Hebrew Bible, we find the valorization and the denigration woven into a single narrative, represented by two groups with clearly delineated moral values. Israel's rejection of the power of the aboriginal inhabitants, including the giants, and the suppression of their world instead of adopting it as legitimation, marks a sharp break with a heroic past, even as it seeks to use heroic categories (embodied, for example, in figures such as Moses, Joshua, and Kaleb). So too does the emergence of the monarchy in Israel fall into the idealized pattern of a heroic age, with David the ruddy chosen young man rising romantically through victory after victory, the swoons of young women (1 Sam 18:7), and his status as the chosen messiah after God's own heart. This process may in fact bear quite a bit more historical truth than has sometimes been assumed, though it cannot possibly bear the weight of being considered "history" in any modern sense.[54]

At any rate, interpreters have not sufficiently recognized the important role giants play at important periodizing moments in the heroic ages forged by the biblical narrative—moments that cut across the formal division of the Pentateuch and the Deuteronomistic History. The conquest and the Davidic monarchy are two options scholars have pursued in the past in discussing a heroic age in the Bible, though the Patriarchal narrative of Genesis 12–50 has been considered for inclusion among the broader corpus of heroic narrative,[55] and other moments in Genesis 1–11 and the book of Judges could

---

54. The debate over the historicity of David as a king and the extent of the United Monarchy has served as the flashpoint for many a debate between so-called "minimalist" and "maximalist" scholars of the Hebrew Bible. See, e.g., the denial of David's status as a historical character in P. Davies 1992, 12, and the more conservative treatment in Provan, Long, and Longman 2003, 215–38.

55. E.g., Hendel 1987; Gordon 1955; 1962, 26, 284.

qualify as well.[56] In several of these key heroic moments, giants take center stage opposite the Israelite hero, as representatives of native (anti-)heroic opponents: at the end of the old world of superhuman action in Gen 6:1–4, as a barrier to the Israelites entering the land at the conquest (Num 13:22–33, 21:33–35; Josh 11:19–22, 12:1–6, 14:12–15, 15:12–14), and at the beginning and end of David's reign (1 Samuel 17; 2 Sam 21:15–22 // 1 Chr 20:4–8).[57] Ancient Israelite authors invented the giants, as a manageable, if not ferocious, symbol of the past. Even as something of the majesty and power of the non-Israelite heroes of Canaan were preserved in Israelite stories of giants, these figures were transfigured into monsters, with the concomitant moral ugliness and arrogance that adheres to giants in so much myth and legend.

The heroic past of Canaan was a potentially usable past, though—one through which Israel could feasibly have claimed lineage (as did Greek elites, mutatis mutandis, in the classical period). Clearly, the Canaanite heroic past could have been profitably co-opted, as in the Ugaritic tradition of the *rp'um*, who represented cultural identification and legitimization for the monarchy and probably other elites.[58] Israel's Rephaim, on the other hand, are distinctly fashioned in terms of "disidentification," and as such they are strong markers of identity nonetheless: they are a *counter-identity*, a signal of that which is rejected.[59] It is the Deuteronomist, in particular, who seems to be most obsessed with constructing this heroic identity/counter-identity. He engages in a certain kind of antiquarianism regarding the giants, and the Rephaim in particular; he notes the territories they inhabit and the history of their own cycles of land possession and conquest (which may even serve as models for Israel's own actions), he pauses to provide linguistic notes on the various titles under which "Rephaim" are subsumed (Emim for

56. See, e.g., Bartelmus (1979), who sees Gen 6:1–4 as the birth of a *Heroenkonzept* in ancient Israel, which blossoms out in into other texts such as the Samson cycle and early monarchic tales, as well as the discussion of the conquest era in comparative perspective by Weinfeld (1993) and the assortment of heroic characters addressed in Mobley 1997; 2005.

57. Note also the appearance of the Rephaim, Zuzim and Emim in Gen 14:5–7; if they were considered giants by whatever author inserted them in this strange narrative (see discussion in Chapter 2), then Abram would be pulled into the orbit of heroes who fight giants (even though Abram is not directly involved with the giants here). In the book of Judges, we may even find one character that we could loosely categorize as a "giant," viz. Samson in his superhuman power and toppling of the giant Philistine structure. Though Samson is nowhere identified in terms of his height in the book of Judges, some later traditions would impute gigantism to him; see Mobley 1997, 229–30, nn. 55–56.

58. Here I refer back to my discussion of this topic in the previous chapter, and I borrow the language of "cultural identification" and "disidentification" from M. Smith 2001, 69, who phrases the basic issue here in much the same way.

59. This focus on disjunction with the past may be a natural result of Israel's often repeated and radical conception of "uniqueness"; see Machinist 1991, 420–42.

the Moabites, Zamzummim for the Ammonites; Deut 2:10,20), and he claims knowledge regarding the existence and possession of important artifacts (Deut 3:11). The significance of these musings, for the Deuteronomist, lies not only in the era of conquest, of course, but also in the battles of David and his men, where the giants are considered in terms of sheer arrogance (Goliath) but also physical freakdom (e.g., too many fingers, etc.).

The antiquarianism here must, in one sense, be the opposite of the kind we noted above for sixth-century Babylonian elites in their heterodox turn toward antiquity. For the link to the past, for Israel, is an anti-link. Israel represents a break from all previous humanity, and a triumph over its illegitimacy.[60] In both situations, however, images of the past are invoked as a reaction to the loss of empire; and if the Deuteronomist has toyed with the notion of a heroic age in his construction of both the conquest and the early monarchic eras, it is a manifestation of loss in response to Israel's new political situation in the sixth century, or even in the eighth century during the era of Assyrian domination.[61] As Israel gets smaller, its God gets bigger,[62] as do its heroes—as do its enemies. The utilization of a heroic age concept involving the eras of conquest and early monarchy and the antiquarian interest in giants may in fact be a part of the Axial Age phenomenon discussed above. The periodization into heroic ages shows a heightened degree of self-awareness regarding distinctive modes of human activity in the past as opposed, presumably, to the present. We might also consider the very existence of the Deuteronomist(s) as evidence of the rise of elite, partly heterodox, and relatively autonomous intellectuals and cultural interpreters in axial civilizations as discussed by Eisenstadt; these figures would have been responsible for drawing on cognate traditions regarding heroes and giants, characterizing certain past eras in the stylized, periodized idiom of the heroic age.[63]

60. This statement specifically pertains to the idea of the pre-Israelite (Canaanite) heroic past. Of course, the patriarchs represent a "legitimate," usable past in the Bible—but the selection of these figures, as opposed to others, represents a historiographic and theological *choice* for the biblical authors. Certain pasts are rejected, and others are embraced.

61. I assume here, as nearly all others do, that the "Deuteronomist" is not a single individual who penned all of Deuteronomy through Kings at one fell swoop. Several layers must be present in the current block of materials we now have, focusing on crucial moments over a long period of time from the twelfth–sixth centuries, with the late eighth-century Assyrian crisis representing one pivotal moment of reflection. See Cross (1973, 274–89) and Weinfeld (1972, 25), who saw Deuteronomic activity occurring from the time of Hezekiah through the exile.

62. Again borrowing a concept from M. Smith 2001, 165, where Smith speaks of the rise of monotheism in these same terms.

63. Weinfeld 1972 prominently attempted to interpret at least the book of Deuteronomy as the product of a "wisdom school" in ancient Israel, and such a group would fit the social

From the diachronic perspective of historical priority, the ruling image of the Israelite hero and the giant counter-hero for all of the biblical depictions of giants is that of David in his triumph—first over Goliath, in the act that initially propels him to prominence in Saul's court, and finally over the Philistine giants in 2 Sam 21:15–22 // 1 Chr 20:4–8, where the legendary status of David's mighty men in their role as giant-slayers appears in retrospect to confirm the greatness of David, his compatriots, and his era. As we have noticed earlier in this study, giants served as an important "book-ending" device in the conquest narrative as well: fear of the giant beings prevented Israel from entering the land, thus dooming the group to wilderness wandering (Num 13; Deut 1:28, 1:46–2:1,14), but finally resulting in a great victory under Joshua and Kaleb (Josh 11–15). One is tempted here to posit one of these two accounts as the model for the other, i.e., either the symbol of giants standing in the way of the conquest was imputed to David as a way of describing his "second conquest" of the Anaqim and Philistines to secure the unified nation, or as a symbolic trope that originated with the tales of David's glorious era read back into the conquest. Though it is impossible to prove with finality, I am inclined to favor the latter interpretation, which comports with an argument made throughout this study: the leveling of giants at the hands of David is a political symbol of law and of justice, and belongs most naturally to the symbolic world of chaos maintenance embodied in the monarchic complex—David's heroism would be the model for all Israelite heroes, his giant enemies the model for all enemy heroes.[64]

Even though we have observed several important moments wherein the heroic tropes of might and power are valorized in the biblical texts, beginning with the destruction of Jerusalem in 587 BCE, we understandably find a very prominent rise in a sub-genre of warnings *against* trusting in the power of the Gibbor and military heroism.[65] This is not to say that themes

---

profile of axial elites. There are other indicators of the Deuteronomist's axiality: he criticizes the power of the king (e.g., Deut 17:14–20; 1 Sam 8:7) in a matter than suggests his autonomous place in society (see the discussion here of Levinson 2001), and he displays what we could rightly call heterodox tendencies in his willingness to reject and improve upon earlier legal codes (e.g., the re-imagining of the Sinai encounter and the "ten commandments" in Deut 4:12–19, 5:6–18; innovations regarding the place of worship and the nature of altars in Deut 12:5 [cf. Exod 20–21]; the transformation of trials into purely secular events in Deut 12:15–25, 17:2–7 [cf. Exod 21:6, 22:8], and many other examples. On this, see Levinson 1997). Admittedly, the Deuteronomist makes these innovations *within the framework of past tradition*, seeming at times to roll out changes as though nothing has been altered—here we encounter the effects of the agglutinative nature of Israel's traditional society, as noted by Machinist (1986, 201) for Mesopotamia.

64. Noteworthy here is the fact that even Saul, as David's enemy, receives a rare and distinctive physical description: he is extraordinarily tall (1 Sam 9:2).

65. See Smith-Christopher 2002, 178–82.

of heroic power were always promoted *tout court* in all pre-exilic texts; reliance on the might of warriors above YHWH's own strength was never valued (see, e.g., Exodus 15, or the putatively eighth-century reference in Hos 10:13, which castigates its audience for trusting "in the abundance of your strength" [ברב גבוריך]; cf. Jer 9:22). But the multiplication of such sentiments in exilic and post-exilic texts is striking. We have already discussed the prophetic witness of Ezekiel 32, who relies on the mythological echoes of past heroic culture to affirm the impotence and permanent death of Israel's enemies. But their defeat is styled as a direct act of God, and the ultimate failure of the monarchy apparently curtailed faith in the notion that might and power is enough to defeat the monstrous. This feeling is captured succinctly and memorably in an oracle to the would be king Zerubbabel in Zech 4:6:

> He answered and spoke to me, saying, "This is the word of YHWH to Zerubbabel: 'Not by strength (חיל) and not by power (כח), but by my Spirit (רוחי), says YHWH of Hosts.'"

Such themes reverberate through the Psalms and wisdom literature (Pss 33:16, 52:3; Prov 21:22; Ecc 9:11), and Prov 16:32 is an excellent example of the way the moral virtues of patience and self-control could be extolled above any brave act of the Gibbor:

> Better is one who is slow to anger than a Gibbor, and one who has control of his temper than one who captures a city.

The changed political context between David's or Joshua's day and the post-exilic period is clearly the dominant cause of this switch to the rhetoric of self-mastery, and at the very least, the Proverbialist recognizes that one might look to more than swords to cut down the threat of hubris and chaos represented by a giant or any other imposing enemy.[66] At most, however, the voice of wisdom here explicitly criticizes any notion of heroic valor; one might even imagine the speaker here reading the books of 1–2 Samuel with pronounced antipathy.[67] In a study of the treatment of themes of heroism

66. Indeed, the Proverbialist's ideology in this respect represents a type of axiality, I would contend, parallel to (and compatible with) some of the categories I have outlined above: the hero has become a scholar, and the rise of clerical elites in the post-exilic period reflects an axial society's shift in emphasis toward the mediation of wisdom and transcendent categories. One might compare the presentation of Socrates' death in Plato's *Apology*, insofar as specific heroic categories and terminology are used to frame Socrates' philosophical life and martyrdom, and also in Plato's description of Socrates' death in the *Phaedo*. See, e.g., *Apol.* 17a–d, 28b–c, 36d, 38e–39b, 41b, 42a; *Phaed.* 60d–61b, 69c–d, 114c–115a, etc.

67. This critical reflection on the values of the heroic age suggests a type of axial phenomenon along the lines of our discussion above, as we have here a gesture toward critique of the past.

and the Gibbor in rabbinic interpretation, R. G. Marks notes an example of a move similar to that in Prov 16:32 in a midrash on Isa 3:1-7 (b. Ḥag. 14a), where R. Dimi comments on the meaning of the Gibbor and the "man of war" (איש מלחמה) as leading supporters or protectors of the community (Isa 3:2): R. Dimi sees the Gibborim here as "masters of tradition," and the man of war as "the scholar skilled in conducting himself 'in the war of Torah'" (במלחמתה של תורה).[68]

At the same time, however, as Marks notes, there is ambivalence about the role of the warrior in the later tradition—his great strength can still be cause for positive awe, even if the power he possesses is simultaneously a source of negative fear insofar is it is wrongly used or trusted. If the powerful excess represented by giants and of all heroic power would seem to have died forever at the fall of Jerusalem in 586 BCE, later periods witnessed a resurrection of the role of the giants in post-biblical sources of the third-first centuries BCE. In these texts, however, the giant does not continue to act as an ethnic group or historical individual in the contemporary world of the authors; the giant now lives solely in the past, as myth, and has been transmuted into a wild monster whose sole enemy is God himself. The tension between the giant as history and as myth that we found in a character like Og of Bashan or Goliath of Gath is therefore lost. Even though, in one sense, these post-biblical materials join the biblical post-exilic chorus denigrating heroic themes and the power giants represent—the giants, as we shall presently see, in Enoch, at Qumran, and elsewhere are all presented as corrupt in every way—they nonetheless revert to the representation of giants in detail, and thus explicitly re-integrate these figures into the storyline of Israel's religion in a meaningful way.

In 1 Enoch chapters 6–11, particularly, we find an interpretive retelling of Gen 6:1-4.[69] In 1 Enoch 6:1-2, two hundred "Watchers" (Aram. עירין, angelic heavenly beings) cohabit with mortal women, led by Shemihazah. These women bear giants (גבורים), who then bear the Nephilim and who in turn bear the Elioud (Enoch 7:1-2)[70]; these giant beings devour humans, and one

68. As cited in R. Marks 1983, 191.

69. Compare with Philo of Byblos (Attridge and Oden 1981, 42-43; see comments in Bartelmus 1979, 151-94): "He [Sanchuniathon] says, 'These discovered fire by rubbing sticks of wood together, and they taught its usefulness. They begot sons greater in size and stature, whose names were given to the mountains over which they ruled...From these,' he says, 'were born Samemroumos, who is also called Hypsouranios <and Ousōos>.' He says, 'They took their names from their mothers, since women at that time mated indiscriminately with whomever they chanced to meet.'"

70. This third generation, the Elioud (Ελιουδ), has proven quite elusive; Nickelsburg (2001, 185) speculates that term may have been על יהוה ("Anti-Gods") in Hebrew, or a corrupted word derived from עלי (denoting arrogance).

another (7:3–4), and teach all manner of astrology, sorcery, and cosmetics to the human race (8:1ff.). As a result of these transgressions, a series of angelic figures are assigned the task of destroying Shemihazah and his cohort. Though the Noahide flood is part of this destructive act (10:1–3), reference to the deluge plays only a small part in the Enochic tradition vis-à-vis the Watchers and Archangels in chapters 6–11.[71] In 1 Enoch 15, the giants appear again, this time in a direct address from the Lord to Enoch. It seems that the giants are condemned to live as evil spirits (15:6), since their origin in the congress of spirits and human women (15:4) created them, and yet they will continue to haunt the lives of mortals (15:11–12: "These spirits [will] rise up against the sons of men and against the women, for they have come forth from them.").[72]

The very popular postbiblical book of Jubilees assumes Enoch as a textual authority on the issue of the giants, to the point of simply quoting large tracts of material from it. However, where in Enoch the giants sin by coming down to earth to instruct humans in various technologies, in Jub 5:6 the Watchers are sent by God and their actions are viewed as a remedy for humanity's sinful post-fall state.[73] Other references to the events of Gen 6:1–4 in terms of giants reverberate throughout Second Temple texts. In 3 Macc 2:4, the giants "trusted in their strength and boldness" (ῥώμῃ καὶ θράσει πεποιθότες), and in Bar 3:26–28 the giants died by their "foolishness" (ἀβουλίαν), though they were "experts in war" (ἐπιστάμενοι πόλεμον).[74] The motif of the giants via Qumran and elsewhere made its way obliquely into the New Testament in 2 Pet 2:4 and Jude 6, where allusions to angelic figures (= the giants?) bound, imprisoned, and awaiting judgment appear,[75] and the Enochic giant motif even found a home in the Manichaean tradition.[76]

71. As Nickelsburg (2001, 183) aptly points out, the austere (or even admiring?) tone of Gen 6:1–4 gives way to an obsessive focus on the giants themselves as the locus of sin in 1 Enoch (as opposed to all humanity in Gen 6:5).

72. Translation from Nickelsburg and VanderKam 2004, 37. See comments on this in Stuckenbruck 1997, 38. Nickelsburg 2001, 269–80 reads the action here in Enoch 15 as representing a counter-theme to chs. 6–11. Whereas in the Book of the Watchers the giants are destroyed (via warfare), here "the giants' death is the prelude and presupposition for the *continued violent and disastrous activity of their spirits*, which goes on unpunished until the final judgment" (italics mine).

73. See the detailed discussion in Nickelsburg 2001, 71–73.

74. See also Wis 14:5; 3 Macc 2:4; Sir 16:7.

75. Note also Rev ch. 12, discussed in detail by Lichtenberger (2004). Indeed, speculation on the "fallen angels" trope in the NT and other literature found other sources in the Hebrew Bible, including Isa 14:12–13 and Ezek 28:11–19; on the former, see, e.g., Albani 2004.

76. Mani apparently utilized the Aramaic "Book of Giants" as the basis for the Manichaean Book of Giants; see Skjærvø 1995 and Reeves 1991.

Even though the giants do not act any longer as contemporary anti-heroes in these texts, their resurrection as widely used examples of impiety gives them a sort of second life, one bordering on the possibility that the giant could burst out into the contemporary world. At Qumran, for example, we find in addition to many Aramaic portions of Enoch a blossoming literature in an Enochic style devoted to giants (c. 150–115 BCE).[77] In *4QBook of Giants* (= BG)[a–b],[78] explicit references to the giants are plentiful, but the context is unfortunately broken and only tentative reconstructions are possible. What can be discerned of the narrative flow in BG[b] involves a dream had by the Giants (גבריא) and Nephilim (Nephilin), in which their destruction is decreed. Enoch appears as an interpreter (col. II.13–14), and hears the description of a certain 'Ohyah, who recounts a Danielic "judgment in heaven scene": the Lord is enthroned amongst a myriad of divine beings, books are opened, and a sentence proclaimed (col. II.16–19). The result for the Giants is utter fear. BG[c] seems to record some action prior to 'Ohyah's speech recounting the dream: in Frag. 5, we find the giants in what looks like an orgy of violence and wild eating (frag. 5.1–8):

...they defiled themselves... ...the Giants (גברים) and the Nephilin (נפיליא) and... ...they sired. And if all... ...in his blood. And according to the power... ... ...Giants (גברין), as was not enough for them and for their sons... ...and they wanted to eat much (ובעין למאכל שגיא)... ...the Nephilin (נפילין) destroyed it...

Here we see what could be an explicit—even if fragmentary—depiction of the giant in his traditional role as a defiling, over-eating monster, and these aspects of the giant in later literature are far more detailed than in the biblical images, where such notions are only symbolically implied.[79]

The historical-cultural matrix of *4QBook of Giants* fragments is partly revealed by the prominent place of Gilgamesh as a member of the giants in at least two fragments (Babylonia),[80] the participation of Enoch and his association with astrology (Hellenistic lore), and the biblical narrative (Gen

---

77. See García Martínez 1992; Stuckenbruck 1997, 1–40; VanderKam 1994, 37–39; Milik 1976. Quotations from the Qumran materials here taken from García Martínez and Tigchelaar 1997–1998. Note also *4QHistorical Work* (4Q183), "...[the daughters of] man and sired giant[s] for themselves [...], Frag. 2 (Martínez and Tigchelaar, 1997, 1: 374–75), which takes up the theme of giants in terms of Gen 6:1–4. On angels and demonology at Qumran generally, see Reimer 2000.

78. Abbreviated below as BGb/BGa, with column and line numbers following Martínez and Tigchelaar 1998, 2: 1063–69.

79. See now Goff 2010.

80. See Jackson 2007. One of Gilgamesh's monstrous enemies, Humbaba, also makes a cameo in the *Book of Giants* under the Hebrew name חובבש/הובבס. See *Gilg.* 1, 147.

6:1–4).[81] The question of why, exactly, these authors used the tradition of the giants so specifically is a difficult one; clearly, the Enochic literature and *4QBook of Giants* sought to affirm the guilt and punishment of the giants, but this tactic had already been achieved in Genesis, if not in other biblical narratives. The musing on the existence of the giants as spirits in Enoch (with some echoes in BG[b 82]) could reflect the growing importance of angelology and the arcane spirit world in the third–second-century context, and the insistence that the giants are powerless and defeated since primordial days is a kind of second-century update of ideas expressed in a text like Ezekiel 32 or in the references to the forlorn Rephaim and Nephilim as powerless denizens of Sheol.[83] Conversely, or additionally, the presumption of some power for the demonic spirits that pervades Enoch 15–16:4 (as opposed to chapters 6–11) assumes an *ongoing role* for the disembodied giants in the present age of the author—which is conceived as a wicked epoch with a fixed limit (along the lines of other apocalyptic works).[84]

The emergence of these materials in the third century BCE and onward in Jewish tradition could be interpreted, then, as a *novum*, i.e., authors in the Hellenistic period invented hitherto non-existent traditions of the giant and spirits of giants in accordance with broader religious trends of the day that tended toward this kind of esotericism and angelology/demonology. This simple explanation, though, ignores the strength of the biblical tradition regarding giants and the hints it contains that the lore surrounding these figures was far richer and older than the material we see in the Hebrew Bible. In short, detailed traditions regarding the giants were there all along, and resurfaced as part of the broader phenomenon of the re-emergence of myth in apocalyptic literature.[85]

81. Stuckenbruck 1997, 35, with reference to other studies in n. 134.
82. See references in Stuckenbruck 1997, 38; admittedly, however, this theme of giants as spirits is difficult to locate in BGb.
83. Here I echo some statements of Stuckenbruck (1997, 38–40).
84. See Nickelsburg 2001, 274 on this idea.
85. This is not an unusual phenomenon, and can be observed for a variety of other topics as well. Recall, for example, the discussion of Cross (1973, 135–36) on apocalyptic "recrudescence." For Gen 6:1–4, as I have already noted earlier in this study (Chapter 3), many commentators suspect that this "torso" of a story is only an edited down, "sanitized" excerpt from a much richer tale. E.g., Westermann (1984, 368) assumes that "there was once in place of v. 3 a direct intervention of God which punished the transgressors (on analogy with Gen 12:10–20 and 2 Sam 11). Childs' comments are particularly stark (Childs 1962, 57): "Even in the final state the mutilated and half-digested particle struggles with independent life against the role to which it has been assigned within the Hebrew tradition." Speaking of the giants more broadly, see Cassuto 1961, 300–01; 1973–1975, 81–82, 99–102. The submergence and re-emergence of the *Chaoskampf* provides an analogous situation; see the classic work of Gunkel (2006; 2009), and more recently J. Day 1985. A different kind of example that can illustrate the

IV. Conclusion

My approach to the problem of the heroic ages and the meaning of the giants has, through a comparative angle involving ancient Greek conceptions
and others, shown that it is not at all surprising to find ancient Israelite authors engaged in this project of the creation of a heroic age. The historical
diffusion of ideas in the eighth–sixth-century BCE Mediterranean context
involving heroic culture found a home in Israel as well as Greece, despite the
many differences that separate these literatures on this front, and the the
axial age concept may thus be a useful device for understanding the rise of
certain features inherent in these types of stories. It is this late eighth–early
sixth-century context that was the period of the literary development of
the Greek and biblical materials I have been describing here, and Israelite
intellectuals living in this period were responsible for the fusion of independent, native traditions about giants with broader Mediterranean patterns of
heroic ideology. Greece's heroic age lived on, in the form of hero cults and
the epic tradition itself, and Israel's giants lived on as well, though only in
the negative sense, as symbols of arrogance, pollution, and anxiety. The recrudescence of tales involving these figures in later Jewish traditions signals
that giants were looked on as never truly eradicated, and so as ever ready
to rise again.

As J. Cohen has asserted, "the giant appears at that moment when the
boundaries of the body are being culturally demarcated,"[86] and, as I have
been arguing throughout this study, the conflation of the biblical giant with
Mediterranean traditions of the hero stands meaningfully amidst situations
of narrative and historical change. The scholarly consensus that has developed on the meaning of heroic ages generally is that such ages are conceived
in times of social, religious, and political upheaval.[87] Insofar as the giants are
concerned in the Pentateuch and the Deuteronomistic History, Israel's story
of its past consisted of a succession of heroic moments, punctuated by the
threat and subsequent defeat of characters like the Nephilim and ancient
Gibborim, the Rephaim and Anaqim, Goliath and the Philistine giants.

Whether these "heroic moments" ever truly amount to something like
a full-blown "heroic age" is questionable. This is due, in part, to the fact that

---

same tendency for a symbol or group to regain momentum and significance in later periods
involves the "return" of the concept of "Samaritans" in exilic/post-exilic literature; the idea
here is that the Samaritan conflict was early, not begun for the first time in 1 Kings 17, and
represented a deep fracture not expressed in the Bible because of concern to present the nation as a unity until at least the end of Solomon's reign.

86. J. Cohen 1999, xiii.

87. See, e.g., Chadwick 1912, 359–60, 391, 414; Bowra 1957, 15, 21–22, etc. Cf. Ulf 2003, 262–
84.

both the giants and their human opponents play relatively limited roles, i.e., compared with what they could have become. Joshua is no Agamemnon, and Kaleb is no Achilles—Joshua and Kaleb possess nothing of the personality, the semi-divine lineage, or the dramatic glamor of any of the key players in the *Iliad*. This muted portrayal in the Bible is highly significant. David is another story, in some respects, and represents a different trajectory; he is ambiguously part of the divine family (Ps 2:7–9), and his name appears more than any other human name in the Hebrew Bible. Thus we see images of budding heroic ideals in a figure like David, even as other victors in Israel's ongoing gigantomachy are relatively anonymous players.

David is extraordinary, over against, say, Joshua and Kaleb, who are ordinary. David's role strains toward the universal, in that his messianic lineage extends to future kings and to a whole complex of monarchic promise (2 Sam 7:13). Kaleb, on the other hand, is local, or tribal, and his heroics recede into the past as one part of an ongoing divine plan. In Eisenstadt's conception of axiality, one sees the emergence of a "universal" deity, which is opposed, one must suspect, to the tribal hero or the local god in a polytheistic system.[88] The "Universal God" may not be as all-encompassing as "Transcendence," to be sure, and yet, in Israel, the universal deity also represents a move toward the centralization (or coalescence) of divine power in a single figure. This universalizing centralization comes in the form of monotheism and its attendant symbolism (e.g., one deity, one temple, one capital, one king), as opposed to epic categories of pluriformity, with multiple poles of divine and human power competing with one another with no end in sight. Such conflict is inherent in the genre of epic qua epic, and pluriformity of all kinds is a natural part of epic's political theology.[89] Emerging axial values of universality and monotheism in Israel were incompatible with (what was at least perceived as) the inherently polytheistic character of epic, and thus epic ultimately fell by the wayside[90]—but not without leaving its bright marks as an overwritten story in the layers of the palimpsest that became the Bible.

88. So also Eisenstadt 1986a, 128.
89. Here I follow the views of S. Smith (2011a); see also Lukács 1974, 88; Olender 1987.
90. See the comments on this in M. Smith 2001, 174; Talmon 1981, 50–53.

Conclusion

ONLY A FEW DECADES after the newly invented printing press revolutionized Renaissance Europe, a resurgence of popular, heroic poetry swept through late-fifteenth-century German literate circles.[1] Featured as the primary hero of this poetry was a certain Dietrich von Bern, and many Christian preachers of the era—from Martin Luther to many lesser known figures—seized upon the popular appeal of this literature and commented (usually in a negative fashion) on the spiritual worthiness of the materials contained therein. One of the criticisms leveled against the poetry was that the stories they contained were *untrue*, either historically or morally, though Luther, at least, clearly understood something of the historical heritage preserved in them.[2] Nevertheless, references to Dietrich and other heroes in the cycle appear frequently in sermons from the period, to appeal to audiences on the basis of their fashionable, even if degradedly pagan, interests. Luther, for example, referred to the pope as "ein mächtiger Reise, Roland und Kerl" ("a mighty giant, Roland, and lout"). It is important here to note that *Riese* in sixteenth-century German could mean both "hero" and "giant"[3]—the heroes (especially Dietrich and Hilderbrand) fought giants in some of the tales, and in the double meaning of *Riese* there always existed the possibility that one could simultaneously invoke both notions as a kind of wordplay: the hero and the giant, the epic victor and the epic enemy. The shrewd implication, for Luther's purposes, is that one perhaps cannot easily distinguish between them.

Likewise, in the Hebrew Bible, we have had occasion to observe some transpositions between the categories of "giant" and "hero," and we found the figure of the giant in a variety of situations, often pitted against the Israelite hero but sometimes identified as a legitimate, heroic participant in a shadowy, heroic past. In this study, I have attempted a thoroughgoing analysis of the meaning and function of these categories in the Hebrew Bible, which begins with the giant and moves into a comparative assessment of the

1. The information here is drawn from a short but fascinating article devoted to this very topic by Flood (1967); see also Wood 2008, 257.

2. Evidence for this can be found in Flood 1967, 654–55.

3. See also this excerpt from an Epiphany sermon by Luther, quoted in Flood 1967, 657 (see also n. 3 on the same page for other examples of the conflation in the fifteenth–sixteenth-century context).

biblical giant and the Greek hero. As there is no other comparable project (of which I am aware) that tackles the giants as a coherent literary, historical, cultural, or theological classification, I have found myself inventing some new categories of discourse and reappropriating many well-used ones along the way. In particular, I have highlighted the prominence of giants as they tower above the biblical landscape in a variety of settings, beginning in Genesis 6:1–4 with the mythical birth of the Nephilim and the Gibborim of the primeval period. If the fate of entire populations is bound up in their origins—a theological point that the anecdotes of Genesis 1–11 seem at pains to demonstrate[4]—then the role and destiny of the giants are made clear in the mythical scene of violence and sexual transgression against divine boundaries, followed by divine annihilation.

This oft-cited, and duly enigmatic passage in Genesis 6, however, is only the "beginning"—perhaps not historically, but at least in terms of the intra-biblical timeline—of the Bible's meditation on the figure of the giant. We found the giants residing iniquitously in Canaan, where the Anaqim and Rephaim had to be confronted and killed in order to rectify a generations-long problem of wrong land possession. These giants are characterized as both a vague, pervasive force throughout the entire hill country (Num 13:28; Josh 11:21, 14:12), as well as specifically residing in particular towns and regions (e.g., Deut 2:20–21, 3:13; Josh 14:15, 15:14). To be sure, biblical authors slide back and forth in their presentation of the giants in the era of conquest. The giants in the biblical depictions act, on the one hand, as oversized barbarians who austerely embody everything wrong that Israel will put to right when they occupy their promised home, and, on the other, enter the roll call of "real" ethnic groups (alongside other non-giants) that must be eliminated. Of special interest here is the work of the Deuteronomist in Deuteronomy 2–3, who embarked on a series of crude anthropological comments regarding the names of groups of giants in cross-linguistic perspective (Emim, Zamzummim, Rephaim), the history of their cycles of land possession and dispossession, and the museum artifacts proving their existence (Deut 3:11).

Though the Noahide Flood and the Conquest, in turn, should have eliminated these giants, they lived to fight another day (Num 13:33; Josh 11:22). David's encounter with Goliath at the very beginning of his military-political career (1 Samuel 17), and the brief but conspicuous notice of how his own trusted warriors defeated a series of giants and other excessive,

---

4. E.g., humankind in general in chs. 2–3, Ham's actions and Canaan's predicted fate in 9:22–27, the so called "Table of Nations" in ch. 10, and the position of Babel/Babylon in ch. 11.

physical mutants (2 Sam 21:15-22 // 1 Chr 20:4-8) serve as decisive moments in the history of the giants' existence. The finality of David's encounters, after which no giants appear in Israel's history, led us to argue that there is something special here, bound up with the nature of kingship, insofar as the establishment of the Davidic monarchy means the end of the threat of giants. The order, the *law* that kingship represents is the antidote to the anarchy giants embody. David's triumph thus marks a decisive moment in the historiography of Israel's struggle for national *eunomia*. His victory marks the end of one line of history and the beginning of another, i.e., the end of cycles of unjust, temporary reign and the beginning of a new period under the Davidic covenant.

Moreover, the biblical narratives cannot hide the fact that one must become a sort of giant in order to kill a giant. David is, I would contend, a giant gone good; the lawless chaos of his intermittent megalomania corresponds to the problem posed by giants.[5] But David is a reformed giant, or, perhaps more accurately, God's chosen giant. Other towering biblical leaders, such as Moses, fall into this same paradigm and contain the same narrative possibilities—their lawlessness, murders, and hubris have been transformed through a sometimes lengthy, agonizing, and ambiguous process, regulated within the framework of covenants and election.[6] In the dead body of each defeated giant, then, another countergiant lives on, just as the confrontation with the giant outside of the king is also an overcoming of the giant *inside* the king.

In tracing the contours of these progressive generations of giants, the specific contribution of this study has been to highlight the previously ignored currency of the giants in the religio-intellectual world of ancient Israel and its ancient heirs. Although the giants' resurgence in post-biblical materials (1 Enoch 6–11; *4QBook of Giants*, etc.) is in many cases a meditation on the past transgressions of the giants as an interpretative expansion of Gen 6:1-4, in other cases (specifically 1 Enoch 15) we find these figures caught up in esoteric speculations regarding the ongoing (even if not eternal) role in the evil spirit realm of the present age. The later developments in the Enochic and *4QGiants* corpora begin to make more explicit a development which we could already see developing in the earlier texts: the giant exists in "marvelous time," in a range of mythical and epic periods in the past, and in this modality of existence he can burst onto the scene again and again, in the now and forever more.[7]

5. See, e.g., 2 Samuel 11.
6. On Moses in this respect, see Machinist 2000b.
7. Here I draw on language and categories (*in illo tempore, illud tempus*) famously employed by Eliade 1996, 395.

As such, we have been justified in speaking about the giants in the terms of founding ritual, creation, and the ordered cosmos. The defeat of the giant in the past represents a creative period of ritual, a founding act, a meaningful storehouse of imagery that can be unleashed at any moment to re-enact the institution of primeval order upon which the divine society is built.[8] These patterns of recurrence, however, are in no way divorced from history as a mystical spiritual reality. Rather, as I have emphasized throughout this study, the appearance of the giant is intimately linked with two periods of decisive historical change during the biblical period, the Conquest and the establishment of the monarchy. In their reflection upon both periods, Israelite audiences were called upon to remember and re-imagine all of the menace of the threat and the triumphant defeat of that very threat by God and his chosen agents.

Having established these arguments and categories on the terms of the biblical texts themselves, I have attempted to interpret the giants within a specific comparative framework, vis-à-vis the presentation of heroes and a heroic age in the context of Greek epic. Though this comparison at first seems unnatural—perhaps because in the Bible, the giants are decidedly *anti*-heroes (insofar as "heroes" are imagined positively)—closer investigation reveals a series of deep connections between the presentation of these two categories in their respective literatures. Both were thought to represent a discrete "race" or *genos* of humans (or half-humans), both were thought to be larger and stronger than contemporary people, and both groups lived and flourished, in the historical imaginations of later authors, throughout the Bronze Age and ceased to exist at the end of this period (c. 1300–1100 BCE).[9] Beyond these categories, though, other patterns of meaning become apparent. The size, strength, and physical excess of the heroes and giants lead to hubris and subsequent judgment, symbolized through the "flattening" effects of warfare and flood. After their death, the heroes and giants retain possibilities for an ongoing life in cult (though this has become only a

8. Eliade 1996, 395–96.

9. The exception to this latter comparison in the biblical materials, of course, is the fact that giants live after the end of the Conquest period—but the Davidic giants are isolated figures, not members of communities of giants as in Numbers through Joshua. In Greek thought, some heroes lived after the decisive fall of Troy, but again, the primary heroic age ended with the collapse of that city (i.e., the epic representation of the end of what we now call the Late Bronze Age). As should be clear, I believe history and epic collide, however imperfectly, in the stories of the fall of Troy and the Israelite invasion of Canaan. Homer records echoes of a real event when he describes the destruction of some great Anatolian coastal city (see, e.g., Latacz 2004), and in the stories of conquest the authors of the Hebrew Bible attempted to describe what was obviously some real process by which Israel came to possess (at least some of) the land in the early Iron Age.

vestigial, sublimated reality in the Bible), and, in the retrospective creation of both Greek and Deuteronomistic literatures, the heroes and giants are positioned in a "heroic age."

The comparisons I have taken up in this study have, at times, partaken in a kind of "magic," harking back to the title of J. Z. Smith's essay, "In Comparison a Magic Dwells."[10] Our comparanda must be similar enough to compare—otherwise, why consider them in terms of one another at all?—and yet the value of the comparison must lie in difference. This recognition has led us, in every specific case, to make an attempt at establishing the historical and literary contexts of materials in their own right, while at the same time selecting details for the purpose of comparison that best exemplified the arguments at hand. The project of comparison is thus a type of loop, and ones hopes to re-emerge each time with a better understanding of all the details along the way. At any rate, I have argued that the similarities between our heroes and giants are not simply typological, but rather the result of the participation of both Greek and Israelite authors in a Mediterranean *koine*, a shared religious, historical, and cultural discourse in the macro region that began as early as the Late Bronze Age but which intensified particularly in the eighth–sixth centuries BCE. It is this creative period, I have argued, that led to the emergence of giants as a visible religious category in the Hebrew Bible, just as this same epoch witnessed the zenith of Greek epic in the West and an explosion of advanced symbolic expressions across the ancient world.[11]

Although there is no service rendered to the Bible in trying to shoehorn it into the mold of the Greek classics by affirming the existence of some ill-conceived "Hebrew *Iliad*," our project has shown the positive results that can come from looking westward to the interpretive categories of the Greek hero. In particular, the two-part destruction of the biblical giants via flood and totalizing warfare, along with the symbolic similarities between these two types of cataclysms, have taken on a more meaningful set of nuances in light of these same themes in the Greek texts (e.g., the flooding of the Achaean wall in *Iliad* 12), as we were able to interpret the Conquest of giants as a repetition of the cleansing power of the primeval Flood. Moreover, the existence of Greek hero cults and the ongoing lives of heroes after death prompted our investigation into the meaning of the Rephaim, Nephilim, and

10. J. Z. Smith 1982a.
11. I.e., as noted in Chapter 2, I would date the coalescence of the so-called "Deuteronomistic History" to the mid-sixth century, evan as earlier materials (from the mid- to late-eighth centuries BCE) are included.

Gibborim among the dead, and here also the Greek texts have helped us to reveal traces of a native Canaanite/Israelite heroic ideology in the Hebrew Bible that survived through groups classified as giants.

Initially, we defined the "giant" as a human being whose physical stature soared unnaturally above others of standard height. He may be the Brobdingnagian Goliath, the nine and a half-foot monster of the Septuagint and modern Bible translations, or even the subtler six and a half feet of the Goliath in the Masoretic Text. He may be like Og of Bashan, whose thirteen-foot bed offers a frightening indication of superhuman stature. He may be generically described as "great and tall" (גדול ורם) like the Anaqim and then drawn, through a series of seemingly ad hoc associations in Deuteronomy 2, Gen 6:1–4, and elsewhere into the murky interpretive history of the pre-Israelite giants. He may be a man of "notable measure" (1 Chr 20:6), or possess twelve fingers and twelve toes, or perhaps, like Saul, stand only a head taller than the rest.

Now, however, it appears we must expand our definitions marking the conceptual boundaries of the giant beyond mere physical height—his height is but one marker (and not always clearly indicated) signaling the horror of moral iniquity, of arrogance blossoming out beyond controllable limits, of the gargantuan desire to smother all living things beneath giant feet. The giant is that mythical spirit opposing the pristine order of creation and divine boundaries, the principal demon of disorder who reigns on the open battlefield of the Philistines, or the gargoyle standing watch at the gates of Canaan. In this expanded capacity, these giants represent inherent excess or surplus. They cannot help reappearing, transformed in name or other detail but constant in their function as *Chaosmächte*, opposing all human and divine order—they ensure the cosmos will always remain a *chaosmos*. The giants could be said to "represent" these qualities of opposition, but in fact they also *are* the opposition, even as their presence always seems to signal forces beyond the brute facts of their own personal size or actions. It is difficult to say whether such an effect is a carefully calculated move on the part of a series of innovative authors, all consciously attuned to the narrative value of giants, or whether the associations between the giants and sociohistorical chaos come as an almost involuntary, latent reaction.

Something of this ambiguity can be found in an odd digression in Augustine's *City of God* 15.23, where Augustine tries to persuade his audience to believe in the existence of giants not only in the past (i.e., such as those produced by the unholy union in Gen 6:1-4), but also in the present. Apparently there lived in Rome a particular woman in the years leading up to the sacking of the city in 410 CE, born of ordinary-sized parents, "who by her gigantic size overtopped all others."[12] According to Augustine, people flocked in droves to gawk at the giantess, even as the enemy hordes amassed at the gates—a grim commentary, it seems. This exact reference to the fall of Rome along with the woman in Augustine's account takes advantage of the power encapsulated in the figure of the giant, who acts as both a diversion and a focal point, a fraught avoidance of what lies just outside the city while acting simultaneously as a recognition of terror and the specter of the monstrous by a society obsessed with its own demise. In this latter sense, the woman *is* the barbarian horde. The Romans could not stop the invaders, just as they could not refrain from staring at the woman, who, in her celebrity, was a domesticated, manageable circus giant, a segue to real disorder and real death.

The eradication of an enemy horde in the real world is impossible, and no civilization can prevent the recurrence of such a threat. Indeed, the killing of giants in the biblical narrative is far from simple, even if floods or invading Israelites or Davids slinging stones seem to conduct their business with decisive swiftness. The complete nature of the eradication of giant races, whether stated directly or implied, is belied by the reappearance of these creatures beyond their putative extinctions. There is something quite telling in the progression of the destruction of giants as it appears in its three most critical moments in the biblical narrative: the first destruction, via flood, is enacted by YHWH alone; the second, at the conquest, is accomplished by humans (Kaleb, Joshua), accompanied by miracles, parting rivers, and angelic visitations; and the final annihilation through David is, by comparison, an astonishingly secular event, the product of monarchic triumph.

This is not to imply that David's era is not one in which YHWH is said to play some decisive role, or that ancient Israelites possessed anything like a modern notion of secularity. One must notice, however, the progression of divine power as it is invested in a single human being, as opposed to the community or the mythic world of the primeval history. Alternatively, we may speak of this progression as a move toward religious and political *centralization* in Jerusalem; again, the monarchic is a correction of the gigantic, and a concomitant rectification of epic, heroic categories of pluriformity. The multicentric epic narrative, as a historical reflection of the multicentric nation, is a fertile site of heroic conflict; this pluriformity is the tension upon which epic is built. The construction of the monarchy's political symbolism, combined with the gradual formation of a Yahwism shorn of powerful opposing deities, marks a narrative anxiety regarding multicentricity and

12. Augustine 2000, 512.

at the same time signals a profound conversion from aborted heroic, epic patterns to mono-monarchy and monotheism. Viewed in this light, giants are a narrative meditation on the problem of centralization of power, and their final demise amounts to the ultimate failure of epic as a dominating category of the biblical *Weltanschauung*. Epic conflict in the Bible receives a mortal blow in the body of Og, and finally breathes its last breath through Goliath and his Philistine comrades.[13]

At every stage in this journey of battles, the community stakes its claim to identity in the narrative. We are unique, the community affirms. We are God's people; we are not giants. Indeed, the giants lurk at the boundaries of some mystery of Israelite identity, constitutive of that identity itself and thus inseparable from it. They can be banished, by military campaign and by symbolic exorcism, as proof of their ultimate impotence as threats against God; in this way, they are like the plentiful existence of cruel, debased characters in the novels of Vladimir Nabokov, who himself defended their appearance as no more than "the mournful monsters of a cathedral façade—demons placed there merely to show that they have been booted out."[14] Should we believe Nabokov on this point? Should we believe the prophet Ezekiel in his own strong insistence (Ezekiel 32) that the heroic and gigantic dead have no power, that they have truly been booted out? As Timothy Beal has perceptively remarked:

> Whether demonized or deified or both, no matter how many times we kill our monsters they keep coming back for more. Not just Dracula but all monsters are undead. Maybe they keep coming back because they still have something to say or show us about our world and ourselves. Maybe that is the scariest part.[15]

In the Hebrew Bible, the giant is a potent signal of the anxiety inherent in situations of change and cultural liminality, and in this uneasy space both the threat of the monstrous and the power of faith reside; it is a fissure between madness and order, between the divine abode in the glorified landscape of Zion and the typological hell where dwell the vast hosts of the gigantic dead, Goliath and the Anaqim and Og, King of Bashan, the last of the Rephaim. Between these poles there is warfare. The Protestant and Catholic ministers in the sixteenth-century German context discussed above found their own sacred Scripture and the legacy of Christianity in *direct competition*

---

13. One can still find, however, clear traces of distinctly *mythic* conflict in the biblical materials after the "historical" conflicts of epic have passed. See, e.g., the role of the chaos monster in projected future engagements in Isa 27:1 or Dan 7.

14. Nabokov 1973.

15. Beal 2001, 10.

with the heroic legacy represented in the popular tales of Dietrich and others, and the sermonic appropriation of these stories sought, in one stroke, to use the heroic past to entertain and admonish while at the same time neutralizing its cultural power. One may well question whether both of these tasks can be effectively accomplished simultaneously—that is to say, once the giant and specter of the heroic past are introduced into the story, can they be controlled?

Bibliography

Abramson, Herbert (1979), "A Hero Shrine for Phrontis at Sounion?" *CSCA* 12: 1–19.

Aharoni, Yohanan (1979), *The Land of the Bible: A Historical Geography*, tr. A. F. Rainey, 2nd ed., Philadelphia.

Akurgal, Ekrem (1968), *The Birth of Greek Art. The Mediterranean and the Near East*, London.

Alain (Émile-Auguste Chartier) (1974), *The Gods*, tr. R. Pevear, New York.

Albani, Matthias (2004), "The Downfall of Helel, the Son of Dawn: Aspects of Royal Ideology in Isa 14:12–13," in: C. Auffarth and L. T. Stuckenbruck (eds.), *The Fall of the Angels*, Leiden, 62–86.

Albersmeier, Sabine (ed.) (2009), *Heroes: Mortals and Myths in Ancient Greece*, Baltimore.

Albertz, Rainer (1999), "Das Motiv für die Sintflut im Atramḫasīs-Epos," in: A. Lange, H. Lichtenberger, and D. Römheld (eds.), *Mythos im Alten Testament und seiner Umwelt. Festschrift für H.-P. Müller zum 65. Geburtstag*, Berlin, 3–16.

Albrektson, Bertil (1967), *History and the Gods: An Essay on the Idea of Historical Events as Divine Manifestations in the Ancient Near East and Israel*, Lund.

Albright, William F. (1926), "The Historical Background of Genesis XIV," *JSOR* 10.3/4: 231–69.

——(1928), "The Egyptian Empire in Asia in the Twenty-first Century B.C.," *JPOS* 8: 223–56.

——(1944), "The Oracles of Balaam," *JBL* 63.3: 207–33.

——(1950), "Some Oriental Glosses on the Homeric Problem," *AJA* 54.3: 162–76.

——(1957a), *From the Stone Age to Christianity: Monotheism and the Historical Process*, 2nd ed., Garden City, N.Y.

——(1957b), "The High Place in Ancient Palestine," in: *VTSupp* IV, Leiden, 242–58.

——(1963), "Jethro, Hobab, and Reuel in Early Hebrew Tradition, with Some Comments on the Origin of 'JE'," *CBQ* 25: 1–11.

——(1968), *Yahweh and the Gods of Canaan: A Historical Analysis of Two Contrasting Faiths*, Garden City, N.Y.

——(1972), "Neglected Factors in the Greek Intellectual Revolution," *PAPS* 116.3: 225–42.

Alcock, Susan E. (1991), "Tomb Cult and the Post-Classical Polis," *AJA* 95.3: 447–67.

Alighieri, Dante (1995), *The Divine Comedy*, tr. A. Mandelbaum, New York.

Alkier, Stefan, and Markus Witte (eds.) (2004), *Die Griechen und das antike Israel: Interdisziplinäre Studien zur Religions- und Kulturgeschichte des Heiligen Landes*, Göttingen.

Allen, Danielle S. (2003), "The Flux of Time in Ancient Greece," *Daedalus* 132.2: 62–73.

Allen, Nicholas J. (2004), "Bhīṣma and Hesiod's Succession Myth," *IJHS* 8.1/3: 57–79.

Al-Shorman, Abdulla (2010), "Testing the Function of Early Bronze Age I Dolmens," *NEA* 73.1: 46–49.

Alster, Brendt (2000), "Epic Tales from Ancient Sumer: Enmerkar, Lugalbanda, and Other Cunning Heroes," *CANE* III/IV: 2315–26.

Andersen, Francis I., and David N. Freedman (1989), *Amos*, New York.

Anderson, William P. (1990), "The Beginnings of Phoenician Pottery: Vessel Shape, Style, and Ceramic Technology in the Early Phases of the Phoenician Iron Age," *BASOR* 279: 35–54.

Andronikos, Manolēs (1968), *Totenkult*, Göttingen.

Annus, Amar (1999), "Are There Greek Rephaim? On the Etymology of Greek Titans," *UF* 31:13–30.

Annus, Amar, and Alan Lenzi (eds.) (2010), *Ludlul Bēl Nēmeqi: The Standard Babylonian Poem of the Righteous Sufferer*, Helsinki.

Anspaugh, Kelly (1995), "'Jean qui rit and Jean qui pleure': James Joyce, Wyndham Lewis and The High Modern Grotesque," in: M. J. Meyer (ed.), *Literature and the Grotesque*, Amsterdam, 129–52.

Antonaccio, Carla M. (1994), "Contesting the Past: Hero Cult, Tomb Cult, and Epic in Early Greece," *AJA* 98.3: 389–410.

——— (1995), *An Archaeology of Ancestors: Tomb Cult and Hero Cult in Early Greece*, Lanham, Md.

Apollodorus (1921), *The Library*, 2 vols., tr. J. G. Frazer, London.

Araki, James T. (1962), "Kôwaka: Ballad-Dramas of Japan's Heroic Age," *JAOS* 82.4: 545–52.

Armstrong, Karen (2006), *The Great Transformation: The Beginning of Our Religious Traditions*, New York.

Arnason, Johann P., Shmuel N. Eisenstadt, and Björn Wittrock (eds.) (2005), *Axial Civilizations and World History*, Leiden.

Arnold, Bill T. (2004), "Necromancy and Cleromancy in 1 and 2 Samuel," *CBQ* 66: 199–213.

Arnold, Bill T., and D.B. Weisberg (2002), "A Centennial Review of Friedrich Delitzsch's 'Babel und Bibel' Lectures," *JBL* 121.3: 441–57.

Ashley, Timothy R. (1993), *The Book of Numbers*, Grand Rapids, Mich.

Assmann, Jan (2009), "Der Mythos des Gottkönigs im Alten Ägypten," in: C. Schmitz and A. Bettenworth (eds.), *Menschen - Heros - Gott: Weltentwürfe und Lebensmodelle im Mythos der Vormoderne*, Stuttgart, 11–26.

Astour, Michael C. (1965), *Hellenosemitica: An Ethnic and Cultural Study in West Semitic Impact on Mycenaean Greece*, Leiden.

——(1966), "Political and Cosmic Symbolism in Genesis 14 and in Its Babylonian Sources," in: A. Altman (ed.), *Biblical Motifs: Origins and Transformations*, Cambridge, Mass., 65–112.

——(1992a), "Amraphel," *ABD* I: 217–18.

——(1992b), "Arioch," *ABD* I: 378–79.

——(1992c), "Chedorlaomer," *ABD* I: 893–95.

——(1992d), "Ellasar," *ABD* II: 476–77.

Aubet, Maria Eugenia (2001), *The Phoenicians and the West: Politics, Colonies, and Trade*, Cambridge.

Auffarth, Christoph (1991), *Der drohende Untergang: "Schöpfung" in Mythos und Ritual im alten Orient und in Griechenland am Beispiel der Odyssee und des Ezechielbuches*, Berlin.

Augusti, Johann Christian Wilhelm (1827), *Grundriss einer historisch-kritischen Einleitung in's Alte Testament / von Joh. Christ*, Leipzig.

Augustine (2000), *The City of God*, tr. M. Dods, New York.

Baikie, James (1914), *Lands and Peoples of the Bible*, London.

Bailkey, Nels M. (1950), "A Babylonian Philosopher of History," *Osiris* 9: 106–30.

Bakhtin, Mikhail (1968), *Rabelais and His World*, tr. H. Iswolsky, Cambridge, Mass.

Barker, Elton T. E. (2009), *Entering the Agon: Dissent and Authority in Homer, Historiography and Tragedy*, Oxford.

Barrois, G. A. (1974), "Rephaim, Valley Of," *IDB* IV: 35–36.

Bartelmus, Rüdiger (1979), *Heroentum in Israel und seiner Umwelt: eine traditionsgeschichtliche Untersuchung zu Gen. 6, 1-4 und verwandten Texten im Alten Testament und der altorientalischen Literatur*, Zürich.

Bartlett, J. R. (1970), "Sihon and Og, Kings of the Amorites," *VT* 20.3: 257–77.

Bažant, J. (1997), "TITANES," *LIMC* VIII.1: 31–32.

Beal, Timothy K. (2002), *Religion and Its Monsters*, New York.

Beaulieu, Paul-Alain (1994), "Antiquarianism and the Concern for the Past in the Neo-Babylonian Period," *BCSMS* 28: 37–42.

Becking, Bob (1999), "Rapha רפה," *DDD*, 687–88.

Beckman, Gary (2007), "Hittite and Hurrian Epic," *CAE*, 255–63.

Beekes, Robert, with Lucien van Beek (2010), *Etymological Dictionary of Greek*, 2 vols., Leiden.

Beloch, Julius (1894), "Die Phoeniker am aegaeischen Meer," *RMP* 49: 111–31.

Beltz, Walter (1974), *Die Kaleb-Traditionen im Alten Testament*, Stuttgart.

Bernabé, Albertus (ed.) (1987), *Poetarum epicorum Graecorum*, Testimonia et fragmenta, part 1, Leipzig.

Bernbeck, Reinhard (1996), "Ton, Steine, Permanenz. Erfahrungsraum und Erwartungshorizont in archäologischen Hinterlassenschaften des Alten Orients," in: H. -J. Gehrke and A. Möller (eds.), *Vergangenheit und Lebenswelt. Soziale Kommunikation, Traditionsbildung und historisches Bewußtsein*, Tübingen, 79–107.

Bernal, Martin (1987), "On the Transmission of the Alphabet to the Aegean before 1400 B. C.," *BASOR* 267: 1–19.

——(1987–2006), *Black Athena: The Afroasiatic Roots of Classical Civilization*, 3 vols., London.

Bernheimer, Richard (1952), *Wild Men in the Middle Ages: A Study in Art, Sentiment, and Demonology*, Cambridge, Mass.

Best, Jan (2000), "The First Inscription in Punic—Vowel Differences in Linear A and B," *UF* 32: 27–36.

Bethe, Erich (1966), *Der Troische Epenkreis*, Stuttgart.

Biebuyck, Daniel P. (1976), "The African Heroic Epic," *JFI* 13.1: 5–36.

Billington, Clyde E. (2007), "Goliath and the Exodus Giants: How Tall Were They?" *JETS* 50.3: 489–508.

Bittel, Kurt (*et al.*) (1975), *Das hethitische Felsheiligtum Yazilikaya*, Berlin.

Black, Matthew (1985), *The Book of Enoch or I Enoch, A New English Edition*, Leiden.

Blegen, Carl (1937), "Post-Mycenaean Deposits in Chamber-Tombs," *AE*: 377–90.

Blenkinsopp, Joseph (2011), *Creation, Un-Creation, Re-Creation: A Discursive Commentary on Genesis 1-11*, London.

Blickman, Daniel R. (1987), "Styx and the Justice of Zeus in Hesiod's 'Theogony'." *Phoenix* 41.4: 341–55.

Bloch-Smith, Elizabeth (1992), *Judahite Burial Practices and Beliefs about the Dead*, Sheffield.

Block, Daniel I. (1997–1998), *The Book of Ezekiel*, 2 vols., Grand Rapids, Mich.

Blümer, Wilhelm (2001), *Interpretation archaischer Dichtung: die mythologischen Partien der Erga Hesiods*, Münster.

Blusch, Jürgen (1970), *Formen und Inhalt von Hesiods Individuellem Denken*, Bonn.

Boadt, Lawrence (1980), *Ezekiel's Oracles Against Egypt: A Literary and Philological Study of Ezekiel 29-32*, Rome.

Boardman, John (1999), *The Greeks Overseas: Their Early Colonies and Trade*, London.

Bogan, Zachary (1658), *Homerus, 'Ebraizon sive comparatio Homeri cum scriptoribus sacris quoad normam loquendi*, Oxford.

Boling, Robert G. (1975), *Judges*, Garden City, N.Y.

—— (1982), *Joshua*, Garden City, N.Y.

Bordreuil, Pierre, and Dennis Pardee (1982), "Le rituel funéraire ougaritique RS. 34.126," *Syria* 59.1/2: 121–28.

Borell, Brigitte (1978), *Attisch geometrische Schlalen. Eine spätgeometrische Keramikgattung und ihre Beziehungen zum Orient*, Mainz.

Borger, Riekele (1956), *Die Inschriften Asarhaddons, Königs von Assyrien*, Graz.

Böttcher, Friedrich (1863), *Neu exegetisch-kritische Aehrenlese zum Alten Testamente*, Leipzig.

Bowra, Cecil M. (1952), *Heroic Poetry*, London.

—— (1957), *The Meaning of a Heroic Age*, London.

Boyd, Timothy W. (1995), "A Poet on the Achaean Wall," *OT* 10: 181–206.

Brault, Gerald J. (1978), *The Song of Roland. An Analytical Edition*, 2 vols., University Park, Penn.

Braun, T. F. R. G. (1982), "The Greeks in the Near East," in: J. Boardman and N. G. L. Hammond (eds.), *The Cambridge Ancient History*, 14 vols, Cambridge, 3.3: 1–31.

Brekelmans, Christianus (1959), *De herem in het Oude Testament*, Nijmegen.

Bremmer, Jan N. (1998), "Near Eastern and Native Traditions in Apollodorus' Account of the Flood," in: F. F. García Martínez and G. Luttikhuizen (eds.), *Interpretations of the Flood*, Leiden, 39–55.

—— (2004), "Remember the Titans!" in: C. Auffarth and L.T. Stuckenbruck (eds.), *The Fall of the Angels*, Leiden, 35–61.

Brettler, Marc Z. (2007), "Method in the Application of Biblical Source Material to Historical Writing (with Particular Reference to the Ninth Century BCE)," in: H. G. M. Williamson (ed.), *Understanding the History of Ancient Israel*, Oxford, 305–36.

Brichto, Herbert C. (1973), "Kin, Cult, Land and Afterlife—A Biblical Complex," *HUCA* 44: 1–54.

—— (1998), *The Names of God: Poetic Readings in Biblical Beginnings*, Oxford.

Broneer, Oscar (1942), "Hero Cults in the Corinthian Agora," *Hesperia* 11.2: 128–61.

Brønno, Einar (1943), *Studien über hebräische Morphologie und Vokalismus auf Grundlage der mercatischen Fragmente der zweiten Kolumne der Hexapla des Origenes*, Leipzig.

Brown, A.S. (1998), "From the Golden Age to the Isles of the Blest," *Mnemosyne* 51.4: 385–410.

Brown, John Pairman (1995–2001), *Israel and Hellas*, 3 vols., Berlin.

——(2003), *Ancient Israel and Ancient Greece: Religion, Politics, and Culture*, Minneapolis.

Brown, Robert (1898), *Semitic Influence in Hellenic Mythology*, London.

Brueggemann, Walter (1968), "David and His Theologian," *CBQ* 30: 156–81.

——(1972), "From Dust to Kingship," *ZAW* 84: 1–18.

Brunk, Samuel, and Ben Fallaw (eds.) (2006), *Heroes & Hero Cults in Latin America*, Austin.

Bryce, Trevor (2005), [Review: *Troy and Homer*, by J. Latacz], *NEA* 68.4: 195–96.

Budde, Karl (1883), *Die Biblische Urgeschichte (Gen. 1-12, 5)*, Giessen.

van Buitenen, J. A. B. (ed.) (1981), *The Bhagavadgītā in the Mahābhārata, A Bilingual Edition*, Chicago.

Burgess, Jonathan S. (1996), "The Non-Homeric Cypria," *TAPA* 126: 77–99.

——(2001), *The Tradition of the Trojan War in Homer and the Epic Cycle*, Baltimore.

——(2002), "Kyprias, the 'Kypria', and Multiformity," *Phoenix* 56.3/4: 234–45.

Burke, Aaron A. (2008), *"Walled Up To Heaven": The Evolution of Middle Bronze Age Fortification Strategies in the Levant*, Winona Lake, Ind.

Burke, Brendan (2008), "Mycenaean Memory and the Bronze Age Lament," in: A. Suter (ed.), *Lament: Studies in the Ancient Mediterranean and Beyond*, Oxford, 70-92.

Burkert, Walter (1992), *The Orientalizing Revolution: Near Eastern Influences on Greek Culture in the Early Archaic Age*, tr. M.E. Pinder and W. Burkert, Cambridge, Mass.

——(2004), *Babylon, Memphis, Persepolis: Eastern Contexts of Greek Culture*, Cambridge, Mass.

Butler, George F. (1998), "Giants and Fallen Angels in Dante and Milton: The 'Commedia' and the Gigantomachy in 'Paradise Lost,'" *MP* 95.3: 352-63.

Cairns, Douglas L. (1996), "Hybris, Dishonour, and Thinking Big," *JHSt* 116: 1–32.

Caldwell, Richard S. (1987), *Hesiod's Theogony*, Translated, with Introduction, Commentary, and Interpretive Essay, Cambridge, Mass.

Cambiano, Giuseppe (2002), "Catastrofi naturali e storia umana in Platone et Aristotele." *RSI* 114.3: 694–714.

Campbell, Joseph (1956), *The Hero With A Thousand Faces*. New York: Meridian, 1956; first published 1949.

Caquot, André (1975-1976), "Hébreu et Araméen," *ACF* 75: 427–29.

——(1985), "Rephaim," in: L. Pirot (ed.), *Dictionnaire de la Bible, Supplément*, Paris, X: 344-57.

Carey, John (1991), "A British Myth of Origins?" *HR* 31.1: 24–38.

Carlyle, Thomas (1902), *Les héros: le culte des héros et l'héroïque dans l'histoire*, 7th ed., Paris.

Carruthers, F. J. (1979), *People Called Cumbri: The Heroic Age of the Cumbrian Celts*, London.

Carstens, Anne Marie (2002), "Tomb Cult on the Halikarnassos Peninsula," *AJA* 106.3, 391–409.

Carter, Jane B. (1995), "Ancestor Cult and the Occasion of Homeric Performance," in: J. B. Carter and S. P. Morris (eds.), *The Ages of Homer: A Tribute to Emily Townsend Vermeule*, Austin, 285–314.

Cassuto, Umberto (1961), *A Commentary on the Book of Genesis. Part One: From Adam to Noah, Gen. I - VI 8*, tr. I. Abrahams, Jerusalem.

——(1971), *The Goddess Anath: Canaanite Epics of the Patriarchal Age*, tr. I. Abrahams, Jerusalem.

——(1973–1975a), "Biblical and Canaanite Literature," in: U. Cassuto, *Biblical and Oriental Studies*, 2 vols., tr. I. Abrahams, Jerusalem, 2:16–59.

——(1973–1975b), "The Israelite Epic," in: U. Cassuto, *Biblical and Oriental Studies*, 2 vols., tr. I. Abrahams, Jerusalem, 2:69–109.

Cavigneaux, Antoine (2000), "La fin de Gilgameš, Enkidu et les Enfers d'après les manuscrits d'Ur et de Meturan," *Iraq* 62: 1–19.

Cerutti, M. V. (1998), "Mito di distruzione, Mito di fundazione; Hes. Fr 204, 95–103 M.-W.," *AA* 11 (1998): 127–78.

Chandrasekhara Reddy, R. (1994), *Heros, Cults and Memorials: Andhra Pradesh, 300 A.D.-1600 A.D.*, Madras.

Chadwick, H. Munro (1912), *The Heroic Age*, Westport, Conn.

Chambert-Loir, Henri, and Anthony Reid (2002), *The Potent Dead: Ancestors, Saints and Heroes in Contemporary Indonesia*, Honolulu.

Chan, Marie (1974), "Chinese Heroic Poems and European Epic," *CL* 26.2: 142–68.

Childs, Brevard S. (1962), *Myth and Reality in the Old Testament*, London.

——(1979), *Introduction to the Old Testament as Scripture*, Philadelphia.

——(2001), *Isaiah*, Louisville.

Clark, W. Malcom (1971), "The Flood and the Structure of the Pre-Patriarchal History." *ZAW* 83: 184–211.

Clarke, Ernest G. (ed. and tr.) (1998), *Targum Pseudo-Jonathan: Deuteronomy*, Collegeville, Minn.

Clay, Jenny Strauss (2003), *Hesiod's Cosmos*, Cambridge.

Clines, David J. A. (1979), "The Significance of the 'Sons of God' Episode (Genesis 6:1–4) in the Context of the 'Primeval History' (Genesis 1–11)," *JSOT* 13: 33–46.

——(1994), "Theme in Genesis 1–11," in: R. S. Hess and D. T. Tsumura (eds.), *"I Studied Inscriptions from before the Flood." Ancient Near Eastern, Literary, and Linguistic Approaches to Genesis 1–11*, Winona Lake, Ind., 285–309.

Clines, David J. A. (ed.) (2007), *The Dictionary of Classical Hebrew*. Volume VI (ס–פ). Sheffield: Sheffield Phoenix, 2007.

Coats, George W. (1976), "Conquest Traditions in the Wilderness Theme," *JBL* 95.2: 177–90.

Cogan, Mordecai (2001), *1 Kings*, New York.

Cogan, Mordecai and Hayim Tadmor (1977), "Gyges and Ashurbanipal," *Or* 46: 65–85.

Cohen, Jeffrey J. (1999), *Of Giants: Sex, Monsters, and the Middle Ages*, Minneapolis.

Cohen, Mark E. (1993), *The Cultic Calendars of the Ancient Near East*, Bethesda.

Coldstream, John Nicolas (1976), "Hero-Cults in the Age of Homer," *JHSt* 96: 8–17.

——(2003), *Geometric Greece: 90–700 BC*, London.

Collins, John J. (2008), "The Sons of God and the Daughters of Men," in: M. Nissinen and R. Uro (eds.), *Sacred Marriages: The Divine-Human Sexual Metaphor from Sumer to Early Christianity*, Winona Lake, Ind., 259–74.

Collon, Dominique (1987), *First Impressions: Cylinder Seals in the Ancient Near East*, Chicago.

Conroy, Charles (1980), "Hebrew Epic: Historical Notes and Critical Reflections," *Biblica* 61: 1–30.

Considine, P. (1969), "The Theme of Divine Wrath in Ancient East Mediterranean Literature," *SMEA* 8: 85–159.

Cook, J.M. (1965), *The Greeks in Ionia and the East*, London.

Cooke, G. A. (1936), *A Critical and Exegetical Commentary on the Book of Ezekiel*, Edinburgh.

Coxon, Peter W. (1999a), "Gibborim גבורים," *DDD*, 345–46.

——(1999b), "Nephilim נפלים," *DDD*, 618–20.

Craigie, Peter (1975), "Helel, Athtar and Phaeton (Jes 14, 12–15)," *ZAW* 85: 223–25.

——(1976), *The Book of Deuteronomy*, Grand Rapids, Mich.

Cross, Frank M. (1968), "The Phoenician Inscription from Brazil: A Nineteenth-Century Forgery," *Or* 37: 437–60.

——(1973), *Canaanite Myth and Hebrew Epic: Essays in the History of the Religion of Israel*, Cambridge, Mass.

——(1974), "Prose and Poetry in the Mythic and Epic Texts from Ugarit," *HTR* 67.1: 1–15.

——(1983), "The Epic Traditions of Early Israel: Epic Narrative and the Reconstruction of Early Israelite Institutions," in: R. E. Friedman (ed.), *The Poet and the Historian: Essays in Literary and Historical Biblical Criticism*, Cambridge, Mass., 13–39.

——(1998), *From Epic to Canon: History and Literature in Ancient Israel*, Baltimore.

——(2003), "A Newly Published Inscription of the Persian Age from Byblos," in: F. M. Cross, *Leaves from an Epigrapher's Notebook: Collected Papers in Hebrew and West Semitic Paleography and Epigraphy*, Winona Lake, Ind., 282–85.

——(2009), "Telltale Remnants of Oral Epic in the Older Sources of the Tetrateuch: Double and Triple Proper Names in Early Hebrew Sources and in Homeric and Ugaritic Epic Poetry," in: J. David Schloen (ed.), *Exploring the Longue Durée: Essays in Honor of Lawrence E. Stager*, Winona Lake, Ind., 83–88.

Cross, Frank M., and Lawrence Stager (2006), "Cypro-Minoan Inscriptions Found in Ashkelon," *IEJ* 56.2: 129–59.

Crossley-Holland, Kevin (tr.) (1968), *Beowulf*, London.

Crowley, Janice L. (1989), *The Aegean and the East: An Investigation into the Transference of Artistic Motifs between the Aegean, Egypt, and the Near East in the Bronze Age*, Jonsered.

Currie, Bruno (2005), *Pindar and the Cult of Heroes*, Oxford.

Dafni, Evangelia (2006), "ΝΟΥΣ in der Septuaginta des Hiobbuches. Zur Frage nach der Rezeption der Homerepik in Hellenistischen Judentum," *JSJ* 37.1: 35–54.

Damon, Phillip and W. Wuellner (eds.) (1974), *The Cults of the Epic Heroes and the Evidence of Epic Poetry*, Berkeley.

Davidson, Olga M. (1994), *Poet and Hero in the Persian Book of Kings*, Ithaca.

——(2007), "Persian/Iranian Epic," *CAE*, 264–76.

Davies, Malcom (1989), *The Epic Cycle*, Bristol.

Davies, Malcom (ed.) (1988), *Epicorum Graecorum fragmenta*, Göttingen.

Davies, Philip R. (1992), *In Search of 'Ancient Israel,'* London.

——(2008), *Memories of Ancient Israel: An Introduction to Biblical History—Ancient and Modern*, Louisville.

Day, John (1985), *God's Conflict with the Dragon and the Sea: Echoes of a Canaanite Myth in the Old Testament*, Cambridge.

——(2002), *Yahweh and the Gods and Goddesses of Canaan*, Sheffield.

Day, Peggy (2002), "Ugaritic," in: J. Kaltner and S. L. McKenzie (eds.), *Beyond Babel: A Handbook for Biblical Hebrew and Related Languages*, Atlanta, 223–41.

Delcourt, Marie (1992), *Légendes et cultes de héros en Grèce*, 2nd ed., Paris.

Delcourt, Marie, and Robert L. Rankin (1965), "The Last Giants," *HR* 4.2: 209–42.

Der Manuelian, Peter (1994), *Living in the Past: Studies in Archaism of the Egyptian Twenty-Sixth Dynasty*, London.

De Vaux, Roland (1941), "Notes d'histoire et de topographie Transjordaniennes," *RB*: 16–47.

——(1997), *Ancient Israel: Its Life and Institutions*, tr. J. McHugh, Grand Rapids, Mich.

De Vries, Jan (1978), *Heroic Songs and Heroic Legend*, tr. B. J. Timmer, New York.

De Wette, Wilhelm Martin Leberecht (1822), *Lehrbuch der historisch kritischen Einleitung in die Bibel Alten und Neuen Testaments. 1. th., Lehrbuch der historisch kritischen Einleitung in die kanonischen und apokryphischen Bücher des Alten Testaments*, 2nd ed., Berlin.

Dexinger, Ferdinand (1966), *Sturz der Göttersöhne oder Engel vor der Sintflut? Versuch eines Neuverständnisses von Gen 6:2–4 unter Berücksichtigung der religionsvergleichenden und exegesegeschichtlichen Methode*, Vienna.

Dickie, Matthew W. (1978), "*Dike* as a Moral Term in Homer and Hesiod," *CP* 73.2: 91–101.

Dietler, Michael, and Carolina López-Ruiz (eds.) (2009), *Colonial Encounters in Ancient Iberia: Phoenician, Greek, and Indigenous Relations*, Chicago.

Dietrich, Manfred, Otto Loretz, and Joaquin Sanmartín (1976), "Die ugaritische Totengeister Rpu(m) und die biblischen Rephaim," *UF* 8: 45–52.

Doak, Brian R. (2011), "The Last of the Rephaim: Conquest and Cataclysm in the Heroic Ages of Ancient Israel," Ph.D. dissertation, Harvard University, Cambridge, Mass.

——(forthcoming), "Ezekiel's Topography of the (Un-)Heroic Dead in Ezek 32:17–32," *JBL*.

——(forthcoming), "The Fate and Power of Heroic Bones and the Politics of Bone Transfer in Ancient Israel and Greece," *HTR*.

Donlan, Walter (1985), "The Social Groups of Dark Age Greece," *CP* 80.4: 293–308.

Dörig, José, and Olof Gigon (1961), *Der Kampf der Götter und Titanen*, Olten.

Dothan, Moshe (1993), "Ethnicity and Archaeology: Some Observations on the Sea Peoples at Ashdod," in: A. Biran and J. Aviram (eds.), *Biblical Archaeology Today, 1990: Proceedings of the Second International Congress on Biblical Archaeology, Jerusalem, June – July 1990*, Jerusalem, 53–55.

Dowden, Ken (2001), "West on the East: Martin West's *East Face of Helicon* and Its Forerunners," *JHSt* 121: 167–75.

Drazin, Israel (1982), *Targum Onkelos to Deuteronomy*, New York.

—— (1998), *Targum Onkelos to Numbers*, New York.

Drews, Robert (1988), *The Coming of the Greeks: Conquests in the Aegean and the Near East*, Princeton.

—— (1989), "The 'Chariots of Iron' of Joshua and Judges," *JSOT* 45: 15–23.

Driver, Samuel R. (1890), *Notes on the Hebrew Text and the Topography of the Books of Samuel*, Winona Lake, Ind.

—— (1902), *A Critical and Exegetical Commentary on Deuteronomy*, Edinburgh.

Duchemin, J. (1980), "Contribution à l'histoire des mythes grecs. Les lutes primordiales dans l'Iliade à la lumière des sources proche-orientales," in: *Miscellanea di studi classici in onore di Eugenio Manni*, vol. 3, Rome, 837–79.

Duke, T. T. (1965), [Review: *Hellenosemitica: An Ethnic and Cultural Study of West Semitic Impact on Mycenaean Greece*, by Michael Astour], *CJ* 61.3: 131–36.

Dumézil, Georges (1986), *Mythe et Épopée* I–III, 2nd ed., Paris.

Dunbabin, Thomas J. (1979), *The Greeks and Their Eastern Neighbours. Studies in the Relations between Greece and the Countries of the Near East in the Eight and Seventh Centuries B.C.*, London.

Dundes, Alan (ed.) (1984), *Sacred Narrative: Readings in the Theory of Myth*, Berkeley.

Echols, Charles L. (2008), *"Tell Me, O Muse": The Song of Deborah (Judges 5) in the Light of Heroic Poetry*, New York.

—— (2007), "Heroes and Hero-Cults," in: D. Ogden (ed.), *A Companion to Greek Religion*, Malden, Mass., 100–14.

Edelstein, Gershon (1992), "Rephaim, Valley of," *ABD* V: 676–77.

Edwards, G. Patrick (1971), *The Language of Hesiod in its Traditional Context*, Oxford.

Ehrlich, Carl S. (1996), *The Philistines in Transition: A History from ca. 1000-730 B.C.E.*, Leiden.

Eichrodt, Walther (1970), *Ezekiel*, tr. C. Quin, Philadelphia.

Eisenstadt, Shmuel (1981), "Cultural Traditions and Political Dynamics: The Origin and Modes of Ideological Politics," *BJS* 32: 155–81.

—— (1982) "The Axial Age: The Emergence of Transcendental Visions and the Rise of Clerics." *AES* 23 (1982): 294–314.

—— (1986a), "Introduction: The Axial Age Breakthrough in Ancient Israel," in: S. Eisenstadt (ed.), *The Origins & Diversity of Axial Age Civilizations*, Albany, 127–34.

—— (1986b), "Introduction: the Axial Age Breakthroughs—Their Characteristics and Origins," in: S. Eisenstadt (ed.), *The Origins & Diversity of Axial Age Civilizations*, Albany, 1–25.

Eissfeldt, Otto (1939), *Ras Schamra und Sanchunjaton*, Halle.

——(1950), "Schwerterschlagene bei Hesekiel," in: H. H. Rowley (ed.), *Studies in Old Testament Prophecy Presented to Theodore H. Robinson by the Society for Old Testament Study on his Sixty-Fifth Birthday, August 9th, 1946*, Edinburgh, 73–81.

Ekroth, Gunnel (2002), *The Sacrificial Rituals of Greek Hero-Cults in the Archaic to the Early Hellenistic Periods*, Liége.

Eliade, Mircea (1959), *The Sacred and the Profane: The Nature of Religion*, tr. W. R. Trask, New York.

——(1996), *Patterns in Comparative Religion*, tr. R. Sheed, Lincoln.

Elliger, Karl (1935), "Die dreissig Helden Davids," *Palästinajahrbuch* 31: 29–75.

Emerton, John A. (1971), "The Riddle of Genesis XIV," *VT* 21.4: 403–39.

Ericson, Jr., Edward (1991), "The Sons of God in Paradise Lost and Paradise Regained," *MQ* 25: 79–89.

Eslinger, L. (1979), "A Contextual Identification of the *bene ha'elohim* and *benoth ha'adam* in Genesis 6:1–4," *JSOT* 13: 65–73.

Evans, Arthur J. (1901), "Mycenaean Tree and Pillar Cult and Its Mediterranean Relations," *JHSt* 21: 99–204.

Evans, C. D., W. H. Hallo, and J. B. White (eds.) (1980), *Scripture in Context: Essays on the Comparative Method*, Pittsburgh.

Evelyn-White, Hugh G. (1916), "The Iron Age in Hesiod," *CR* 30.3: 72.

Ewald, Heinrich (1864–1868), *Geschichte des Volkes Israel*, 3rd ed., Göttingen.

Fabry, Heiz-Josef, Frank-Lothar Hossfeld, and E.-M. Kindl (2003), "קהל *qāhāl*," *TDOT* XII: 546–61.

Falkner, Thomas M. (1989), "Slouching towards Boeotia: Age and Age-Grading in the Hesiodic Myth of the Five Races," *CA* 8.1: 42–60.

Fantalkin, Alexander and Oren Tal (2010), "Reassessing the Date of the Beginning of the Grey Series Transport Amphorae from Lesbos," *BABESCH* 85: 1–12.

Farnell, Lewis Richard (1911), *Greece and Babylon. A Comparative Sketch of Mesopotamian, Anatolian and Hellenic Religions*, Edinburgh.

——(1921), *Greek Hero Cults and Ideas of Immortality*, Oxford.

Farrar, W. (1867), "Aptitudes of Races," *TESL* 5: 115–26.

Farrell, Joseph (2007), "The Origins and Essence of Roman Epic," *CAE*, 417–28.

Fenno, Jonathan (2005), "'A Great Wave against the Stream': Water Imagery in Iliadic Battle Scenes," *AJP* 126.4: 475–504.

Ferwerda, Rein (1986), "Meaning of the Word σῶμα (Body) in the Axial Age," in: S. Eisenstadt (ed.), *The Origins & Diversity of Axial Age Civilizations*, Albany, 111–24.

Finkelberg, Margalit (2000), "The Cypria, the Iliad, and the Problem of Multiformity in Oral and Written Tradition," *CP* 95.1: 1–11.

——(2004), "The End of the Heroic Age in Homer, Hesiod and the Cycle," *OP* 3: 11–24.

——(2005), *Greeks and Pre-Greeks: Aegean Prehistory and Greek Heroic Tradition*, Cambridge.

Finkelstein, Israel (2003), "The Philistines and the Bible: A Late-Monarchic Perspective," *JSOT* 27: 131–67.

Finkelstein, J. J. (1966), "The Genealogy of the Hammurapi Dynasty," *JCS* 20: 95–118.

Fitzgerald, James L. (2004), "Mahābhārata," in: S. Mittal and E. Thursby (eds.), *The Hindu World*, New York, 52–74.

Flood, John L. (1967), "Theologi et Gigantes," *MLR* 62.4: 654–60.

Fontenrose, Joseph (1974), "Work, Justice, and Hesiod's Five Ages," *CP* 69.1: 1–16.

——(1980), *Python: A Study of the Delphic Myth and Its Origins*, Berkeley.

Forcey, Colin (1998), "Whatever Happened to the Heroes? Ancestral Cults and the Enigma of Romano-Celtic Temples," in: C. Forcey, J. Hawthorne and R. Witcher (eds.), *Theoretical Roman Archaeology Conference 97*, Oxford, 87–98.

Ford, James Nathan (1992), "The 'Living Rephaim' of Ugarit: Quick or Defunct?" *UF* 24: 73–101.

Foucart, Paul François (1918), *Le culte des héros chez les Grecs*, Paris.

Fowler, Mervyn D. (1982), "The Israelite *bāmāh*: A Question of Interpretation," *ZAW* 94.2: 203–13.

Fox, Michael V. (2000), *Proverbs 1–9*, New York.

Fox, Robin L. (2008), *Travelling Heroes: Greeks and their Myths in the Epic Age of Homer*, London.

Frame, D. (1978), *The Myth of Return in Early Greek Epic*, New Haven.

Franke, J. R. (ed.) (2005), *Ancient Christian Commentary on Scripture*, Old Testament, vol. IV, Downers Grove, Ill.

Frankenstein, Susan (1979), "The Phoenicians in the Far West: A Function of Neo-Assyrian Imperialism," in: M. T. Larsen (ed.), *Power and Propaganda. A Symposium in Ancient Empires*, Copenhagen, 263–94.

Frayne, Douglas (1993), *The Royal Inscriptions of Mesopotamia*, Early Periods, vol. 2, Sargonic and Gutian Periods (2334–2113 BC), Toronto.

Frazer, James G. (1919), *Folk-lore in the Old Testament: Studies in Comparative Religion*, 3 vols., London.

Freedman, David N., and C. Franke Hyland (1973), "Psalm 29: A Structural Analysis," *HTR* 66.2: 237–56.

Frymer-Kensky, Tikva (1983), "Pollution, Purification, and Purgation in Biblical Israel," in: C. L. Myers and M. O'Connor (eds.), *The Word of the Lord Shall Go Forth. Essays in Honor of David Noel Freedman in Celebration of His Sixtieth Birthday*, Winona Lake, Ind., 399–414.

Galbraith, Deane (2011), "Foreign to the Old Testament? An Anti-mythic Bias in the Interpretation of Numbers 13–14 and Some Disappearing Giants," presentation at the Society of Biblical Literature Annual Meeting, San Francisco.

——(forthcoming), "Giants in the Land of Israel," Ph.D. dissertation, University of Otago, Dunedin.

Galling, Kurt (1966), "Goliath und seine Rüstung," in: P. A. H. de Boer (eds.), *Volume de Congrès: Genève*, Leiden, 150–69.

Galter, Hannes D. (1984), "Die Zerstörung Babylons durch Sanherib," *SO* 55.5: 161–73.

García Martínez, Florentino (1992), "The Book of Giants," in: F. García Martínez, *Qumran and Apocalyptic: Studies in the Aramaic Texts from Qumran*, Leiden, 97–115.

García Martínez, Florentino, and Eibert J.C. Tigchelaar, eds. (1997, 1998), *The Dead Sea Scrolls*, 2 vols., Leiden.

Garelli, Paul (1975), "The Changing Facets of Conservative Mesopotamian Thought," *Daedalus* 104.2: 47–56.

Garfinkel, Yosef (2001), "Warrior Burial Customs in the Levant During the Early Second Millennium B.C," in: S. R. Wolff (ed.), *Studies in the Archaeology of Israel and Neighboring Lands in Memory of Douglas L. Esse*, Chicago, 143–61.

Garsiel, Moshe (2011), "David's Elite Warriors and Their Exploits in the Books of Samuel and Chronicles," *JHS* 11.5: 1–28.

Gaster, Theodor Herzl (1969), *Myth, Legend, and Custom in the Old Testament: A Comparative Study with Chapters from Sir James G. Frazer's Folklore in the Old Testament*, New York.

Gay, David (1995), "Milton's Samson and the Figure of the Old Testament Giant," *L&T* 9.4: 355–69.

Gayle, Monica (1994), *Myth and Poetry in Lucretius*, Cambridge.

Gehrig, Ulrich, and Hans Georg Niemeyer (1990), *Die Phönizier im Zeitalter Homers*, Mainz.

Gemes, Ken (2009), "Freud and Nietzsche on Sublimation," *JNS* 38: 38–59.

George, Andrew R. (ed.) (2003), *The Babylonian Gilgamesh Epic: Introduction, Critical Edition and Cuneiform Texts*, 2 vols., Oxford.

Gese, Hartmut (1973), "Der bewachte Lebensbaum und die Heroen," in: H. Gese and H. P. Rüger (eds.), *Wort und Geschichte: Festschrift für Karl Elliger zum 70. Geburtstag*, Zürich.

Gilan, Amir (2010), "Epic and History in Hittite Anatolia: In Search of a Local Hero," in: D. Konstan and K. A. Raaflaub (eds.), *Epic and History*, Malden, Mass., 51–65.

Ginsberg, Harold L. (1946), *The Legend of King Keret: A Canaanite Epic of the Bronze Age*, New Haven.

Gladstone, William W. (1869), *Juventus mundi: The Gods and Men of the Heroic Age*, London.

Glassner, Jean-Jacques (2004), *Mesopotamian Chronicles*, Atlanta.

Glosecki, Stephen O. (ed.) (2007), *Myth in Early Northwest Europe*, Tempe, Ariz.

Glueck, Nelson (1946), "Transjordan," *BA* 9.3: 45–61.

——(1970), *The Other Side of the Jordan*, Cambridge, Mass.

Gmirkin, Russell G. (2006), *Berossus and Genesis, Manetho and Exodus: Hellenistic Histories and the Date of the Pentateuch*, London.

Goff, Matthew (2009a), "Gilgamesh the Giant: The Qumran Book of Giants' Appropriation of Gilgamesh Motifs," *DSD* 16: 221–53.

——(2009b), "Subterranean Giants and Septuagint Proverbs: the 'Earth-Born' of LXX Proverbs," in: K. Dániel Dobos and M. Köszeghy (eds.), *With Wisdom as a Robe: Qumran and other Jewish Studies in Honour of Ida Frölich*, Sheffield, 146–56.

——(2010a), "Ben Sira and the Giants of the Land: A Note on Ben Sira 16:7," *JBL* 129.4: 645–55.

——(2010b), "Monstrous Appetites: Giants, Cannibalism, and Insatiable Eating," *JAJ* 1.1: 19–42.

——(forthcoming), *When Giants Walked the Earth*, Göttingen.

Good, Robert M. (1980), "Supplementary Remarks on the Ugaritic Funerary Text RS 34.126," *BASOR* 239: 41–42.

Gordon, Cyrus (1955), "Homer and Bible: The Origin and Character of East Mediterranean Literature," *HUCA* 26: 43–108.

——(1958), "Indo-European and Hebrew Epic," *EI* 5: 10–15.

——(1962), *The Common Background of Greek and Hebrew Civilizations*, New York.

——(1966a), *Evidence for the Minoan Language*, Ventnor, N.J.

——(1966b), *Ugarit and Minoan Crete: The Bearing of their Texts on the Origins of Western Culture*, New York.

——(1971), *Before Columbus: Links Between the Old World and Ancient America*, New York.

——(1997) "Father's Sons and Mother's Daughters: The Problem of Indo-European-Semitic Relationships," in: G. D. Young, M. W. Chavalas, and R. E. Averbeck (eds.), *Crossing Boundaries and Linking Horizons: Studies in Honor of Michael C. Astour on His 80th Birthday*, Bethesda, 271–78.

Gordon, Cyrus H., and Gary A. Rendsburg (1997), *The Bible and the Ancient Near East*, New York.

Gordon, Robert P. (2006), "The Ideological Foe: The Philistines in the Old Testament," in: R. P. Gordon, *Hebrew Bible and Ancient Versions*, Aldershat, UK, 157–68.

Goren, Yuval, H. Mommsen, I. Finkelstein, and N. Na'aman (2009), "A Provenance Study of the Gilgamesh Fragment from Megiddo," *Archaeometry* 51.5: 763–73.

Gothóni, René (2000), *Attitudes and Interpretations in Comparative Religion*, Helsinki.

Grabbe, Lester (2007), *Ancient Israel: What Do We Know and How Do We Know It?* London.

Graf, David F. (1992), "Dedan," *ABD* II: 121.

Graf, Fritz (1999), "Heros," *DDD*, 412–15.

Gray, John (1976), *I & II Kings*, Philadelphia.

Gray, George B. (1920), *A Critical and Exegetical Commentary on Numbers*, New York.

Green, William A. (1992), "Periodization in European and World History," *JWH* 3.1: 13–53.

——(1995), "Periodizing World History," *HT* 34.2: 99–111.

Greenberg, Moshe (1997), *Ezekiel 21-37*, New York.

Greenfield, Jonas C. (1967), [Review: *Evidence for the Minoan Language*, by C.H. Gordon], *JBL* 86.2: 241–44.

Greer, Margaret (2006), "Imperialism and Anthropophagy in Early Modern Spanish Tragedy: The Unthought Known," in: D. R. Castillo and M. Collini (eds.), *Reason and Its Others: Italy, Spain, and the New World*, Nashville, 279–95.

Gregory, Tobias (2006), *From Many Gods to One: Divine Action in Renaissance Epic*, Chicago.

Griffin, Jasper (1977), "The Epic Cycle and the Uniqueness of Homer," *JHSt* 97: 39–53.

Griffiths, J. Gwyn (1956), "Archaeology and Hesiod's Five Ages," *JHI* 17.1: 109–19.

——(1958), "Did Hesiod Invent the 'Golden Age'?" *JHI* 19.1: 91–93.

Grønbaek, Jakob H. (1957),"Kongens kultiske function i det forexilske Israel," *DTT* 20: 1–16.

——(1971), *Die Geschichte vom Aufstieg Davids (1. Sam. 15-2. Sam. 5). Tradition und Komposition*, Copenhagen.

Gruppe, Otto (1887), *Die griechischen Kulte und Mythen in ihren Beziehungen zu den orientalischen Religionen*, vol. 1, Einleitung, Leipzig.

——(1889a), "Aithiopenmythen," *Philologus* 47: 328–43.

——(1889b), "War Genesis 6:1–4 ursprünglich mit der Sintflut verbunden?" *ZAW* 9: 135–55.

Gulde, Stefanie U. (2007), *Der Tod als Herrscher in Ugarit und Israel*, Tübingen.

Gunkel, Hermann (1901), *Genesis: übersetzt und erklärt*, Göttingen.

——(1997, first published 1901), *Genesis*, tr. M. E. Biddle, Macon, Ga.

——(2006, first published 1895), *Creation and Chaos in the Primeval Era and the Eschaton: A Religio-Historical Study of Genesis 1 and Revelation 12*, tr. K. W. Whitney, Jr., Grand Rapids, Mich.

——(2009, first published 1903), *Israel and Babylon: The Babylonian Influence on Israelite Religion*, tr. E. S. B. and K. C. Hanson, Eugene, Or.

Gunn, David M. (1975), "Deutero-Isaiah and the Flood," *JBL* 94.4: 493–508.

Gunter, Ann C. (2009), *Greek Art and the Orient*, Cambridge.

Haas, Volkert (2000), "Death and the Afterlife in Hittite Thought," *CANE* III/IV: 2021–30.

Hack, Roy Kenneth (1929), "Homer and the Cult of Heroes," *TPAPA* 60: 57–74.

Hackett, Jo Ann (1980), *The Balaam Text from Deir 'Alla*, Chico, 1980.

Hägg, R. (ed.) (1999), *Ancient Greek Hero Cult: Proceedings of the Fifth International Seminar on Ancient Greek Cult, Organized by the Department of Classical Archaeology and Ancient History, Göteborg University, 21–23 April 1995*, Stockholm.

Hainsworth, John Bryan (1993), *The Iliad: A Commentary*, vol. 3 (books 9–12), Cambridge.

Hallo, William H. (1980), "Biblical History in Its Near Eastern Setting: The Contextual Approach," in: C. D. Evans, W. H. Hallo, and J. B. White (eds.), *Scripture in Context: Essays on the Comparative Method*, Pittsburgh, 1–26.

——(1992), "Royal Ancestor Worship in the Biblical World," in: M. Fishbane, E. Tov, and W. W. Fields (eds.), *Sha'arei Talmon: Studies in the Bible, Qumran, and the Ancient Near East Presented to Shemaryahu Talmon*, Winona Lake, Ind., 381–401.

Hallo, William H., James C. Moyer, and Leo G. Perdue (eds.) (1983), *Scripture in Context II: More Essays on the Comparative Method*, Winona Lake, Ind.

Hallote, Rachel S. (2001), *Death, Burial, and Afterlife in the Biblical World: How the Israelites and Their Neighbors Treated the Dead*, Chicago.

Halpern, Baruch (2001), *David's Secret Demons: Messiah, Murderer, Traitor, King*. Grand Rapids, Mich.

Hamilton, Malcolm B. (1995), *The Sociology of Religion: Theoretical and Comparative Perspectives*, London.

Hamilton, Victor P. (1990), *The Book of Genesis Chapters 1–17*, Grand Rapids, Mich.

Hammer, Reuven (tr.) (1986), *Sifre. A Tannaitic Commentary on the Book of Deuteronomy*, New Haven.

Hammond, Philip C. (1997), "Hebron," in: E. M. Meyers (ed.), *The Oxford Encyclopedia of Archaeology in the Near East*, Oxford, III: 13–14.

Hanson, Paul (1977), "Rebellion in Heaven, Azazel, and Euhemeristic Heroes in 1 Enoch 6–11," *JBL* 96.2: 195–233.

Hatto, A. T. (ed.) (1980–1989), *Traditions of Heroic Poetry*, 2 vols., London.

Hauer, Christian E. (1970), "Jerusalem, the Stronghold and Rephaim," *CBQ* 32: 571–78.

Haydon, A. Eustace (1922), "From Comparative Religion to History of Religions," *JR* 2.6: 577–87.

Healey, John F. (1978), "Ritual Text KTU 1.161—Translation and Notes," *UF* 10: 83–88.

——(1986), "The Ugaritic Dead: Some Live Issues," *UF* 18: 27–32.

——(1989), "The Last of the Rephaim," in: K. J. Cathcart and J. F. Healey (eds.), *Back to the Sources: Biblical and Near Eastern Studies in Honour of Dermot Ryan*, Dublin, 33–44.

Heiden, Bruce A. (2008), *Homer's Cosmic Fabrication: Choice and Design in the Iliad*, Oxford.

Heiser, Michael S. (2001), "The Mythological Provenance of Isa. XIV 12–15: A Reconsideration of the Ugaritic Material," *VT* 51.3: 354–69.

Heizer, Robert F. (1962), "The Background of Thomsen's Three-Age System," *TC* 3.3: 259–66.

Hendel, Ronald S. (1987a), *The Epic of the Patriarch: The Jacob Cycle and the Narrative Traditions of Canaan and Israel*, Atlanta.

——(1987b), "Of Demigods and the Deluge: Toward an Interpretation of Genesis 6:1–4," *JBL* 106: 13–26.

——(2004), "The Nephilim were on the Earth: Genesis 6:1–4 and its Ancient Near Eastern Context," in: C. Auffarth and L.T. Stuckenbruck (eds.), *The Fall of the Angels*, Leiden, 11–34.

——(2005), *Remembering Abraham: Culture, Memory, and History in the Hebrew Bible*, Oxford.

——(2009), "Biblical Views: Giants at Jericho," *BAR* 35.2, accessed online at http://basarchive.org, 23 December 2009.

Henrichs, Albert (1993), "The Tomb of Aias and the Prospect of Hero Cult in Sophokles," *CA* 12.2: 165–80.

Herder, Johann Gottfried (1825; first published 1782–1783), *Vom Geist der ebräischen Poesie; eine Anleitung für die Liebhaber derselben und der ältesten Geschichte des menschlichen Geistes*, Leipzig.

Herrmann, Hans-Volkmar (1959), *Omphalos*, Münster.

Hertzberg, Hans W. (1929), "Mizpa," *ZAW* 47: 161–96.

——(1964), *I & II Samuel*, London.

Hesiod (1902), *Hesiodi Carmina: accedit Homeri et Hesiodi certamen*, ed. A. Rzach, Lipsiae.

——(1967), *Fragmenta Hesiodea*, ed. R. Merkelbach and M. L. West, Oxford.

——(2006), *Theogony, Works and Days, Testimonia*, tr. G. W. Most, Cambridge, Mass.

——(2007), *The Shield, Catalogue of Women, and Other Fragments*, tr. G. W. Most Cambridge, Mass.

Hess, Richard S. (1992), "Nephilim," *ABD* IV: 1072–73.

——(1993), *Studies in the Personal Names of Genesis 1-11*, Neukirchen-Vluyn.

Hiller, Stefan (1983), "Possible Historical Reasons for the Rediscovery of the Mycenaean Past in the Age of Homer," in: R. Hägg (ed.), *The Greek Renaissance of the Eighth Century B.C.: Tradition and Innovation*, Stockholm, 9–15.

Hobbes, Thomas (1962, first published 1651), *Levaithan. Or the Matter, Forme and Power of a Commonwealth Ecclesiasticall and Civil*, ed. M. Oakenshot, selected and with an introduction by R. S. Peters, New York.

Hoffman, Gail L. (1997), *Imports and Immigrants: Near Eastern Contacts with Iron Age Crete*, Ann Arbor, Mich.

Hoffman, Yair (1999), "The Deuteronomistic Concept of the Herem," *ZAW* 111: 196–210.

Hoftijzer, J. and K. Jongeling (1995), *Dictionary of the North-West Semitic Inscriptions*, Part one ('-L), Leiden.

Honeyman, A. M. (1948), "The Evidence for Regnal Names among the Hebrews," *JBL* 67: 13–25.

Horsfall, Nicholas M. (1994), "The Prehistory of Latin Poetry: Some Problems of Method," *RF* 122: 50–75.

Horsfield, G., and L.H. Vincent (1932), "Une stele Égypto-Moabite au Balou'a," *RB* 41.3: 417–44.

Horwitz, William J. (1979), "The Significance of the Rephaim *rm.aby.btk. rpim*," *JNWSL* 7: 37–43.

Hossfeld, Frank-Lothar, and Erich Zenger (2005), *Psalms 2*, A Commentary on Psalms 51–100, tr. L. M. Maloney, Minneapolis.

Howard, Seymour (1996), "On Iconology, Intention, Imagos, and Myths of Meaning," *ArHist* 17.34: 83–94.

Hübner, Ulrich (1993), "Og von Baschan und sein Bett in Rabbat-Ammon (Deuteronomium 3,11)," *ZAW* 105: 86–92.

Huddlestun, John R. (2003), "Nahum, Nineveh, and the Nile: The Description of Thebes in Nahum 3:8–9," *JNES* 62.2: 97–110.

Huehnergard, John (2006), "On the Etymology of the Hebrew Relative šɛ-," in: S. E. Fassberg and A. Hurvitz (eds.), *Biblical Hebrew in Its Northwest Semitic Setting: Typological and Historical Perspectives*, Jerusalem, 103–26.

——(2008), "Outline of Ugaritic Grammar" (unpublished; Harvard University, Department of Near Eastern Languages and Civilizations), Cambridge, Mass.

Huggins, Ronald V. (1995), "Noah and the Giants: A Response to John C. Reeves," *JBL* 114.1: 103–10.

Hughes, Dennis D. (1991), *Human Sacrifice in Ancient Greece*, London.

Huizinga, Johan (1963), "A Definition of the Concept of History," in: R. Klibansky and H. J. Paton (eds.), *Philosophy and History: Essays Presented to Ernst Cassirer*, New York, 1–10.

Humbert, Paul (1960), "Démesure et chute dans l'Ancien Testament," in: *Meqqél shâqédh, La branche d>amandier: Hommage à Wilhelm Vischer*, Montpellier, 62–63

Hurvitz, Avi (1982), *A Linguistic Study of the Relationship Between the Priestly Source and the Book of Ezekiel: A New Approach to an Old Problem*, Paris.

Hutton, Jeremy (2007), "Isaiah 51:9–11 and the Rhetorical Appropriation and Subversion of Hostile Theologies," *JBL* 126.2: 271–303.

——(2009), *The Transjordanian Palimpsest: The Overwritten Texts of Personal Exile and Transformation in the Deuteronomistic History*, Berlin.

Huxley, George (1976), "Distinguishing Characteristics of Heroic Ages," *MR* 2.2: 3–12.

Ingham, Bruce (1993), "The '*Sālfah*' as a Narrative Genre," *AFS* 52.1: 5–32.

Jackson, David (2007), "Demonising Gilgamesh," in: J. Azize and N. Weeks (eds.), *Gilgamesh and the World of Assyria: Proceedings of the Conference Held at the Madelbaum House, The University of Sydney, 21-23 July 2004*, Leuvan, 107–14.

Jacobsen, Thorkild (1976), *Treasures of Darkness: A History of Mesopotamian Religion*, New Haven.

Jahnow, H. (1923), *Das hebräische Leichenlied im Rahmen der Völkerdichtung*, Giessen.

Jamison, Stephanie W. (1994), "Draupadî on the Walls of Troy: *Iliad* 3 from an Indic Perspective," *CA* 13: 5–16.

——(1997), "Penelope and the Pigs: Indic Perspectives on the *Odyssey*," *CA* 18: 227–72.

Japhet, Sarah (1993), *I & II Chronicles*, London.

Jaspers, Karl (1953), *The Origin and Goal of History*, tr. M. Bullock, New Haven.

Joffe, Alexander H. (2002), "The Rise of Secondary States in the Iron Age Levant," *JESHO* 45.4: 425–67.

Johnston, Philip (2002), *Shades of Sheol: Death and Afterlife in the Old Testament*, Downers Grove.

Jones, Nicholas F. (1984), "Work 'In Season,' and the Purpose of Hesiod's 'Works and Days'," *CJ* 79.4: 307–23.

de Jong, J. W. (1985), "The Over-Burdened Earth in India and Greece," *JAOS* 105.3: 397–400.

Joyce, Paul (2007), *Ezekiel: A Commentary*, New York.

Kahn, Charles H. (1994), *Anaximander and the Origins of Greek Cosmology*, 3rd ed., Indianapolis.

Kaldellis, A., and Carolina López-Ruiz (2009), "BNJ 790 – Philon of Byblos," in: I. Worthington (ed.), *Brill's New Jacoby (Fragments of Ancient Historians)*, Leiden.

Karageorghis, Vassos (1962), "A 'Homeric' Burial Discovered in a Royal Tomb of the 7th Century B.C.," *ILN* 240: 894–96.

——(1995), "J.N. Coldstream and the Archaeology of Cyprus," in: C. Morris (ed.), *Klados: Essays in Honour of J.N. Coldstream*, London, 9–12.

——(2006), "Homeric Cyprus," in: S. Deger-Jalkotzy and I. S. Lemos (eds.), *Ancient Greece: From the Mycenaean Palaces to the Age of Homer*, Edinburgh, 665–75.

Karge, Paul (1917), *Rephaim. Die vorgeschichtliche kulter Palästinas und Phöniziens. Archäologische und religionsgeschichtliche studien von dr. Paul Karge*, Paderborn.

Katz, Joshua T. (2005), [Review: *Troy and Homer*, by J. Latacz], *JAOS* 125.3: 422–25.

——(2007), "The Indo-European Context," *CAE*, 20–30.

Kay, Richard (2002), "Vitruvius and Dante's Giants," *DS* 120: 17–34.

Keel, Othmar (1975), "Kanaanäische Sühneriten auf ägyptischen Tempelreliefs," *VT* 25.2: 413–69.

Kellermann, Diether (1990), "Die Geschichte von David und Goliath im Lichte der Endokrinologie," *ZAW* 102: 344–57.

Kempinski, A. (1982), "*Talmaî*," in: B. Mazar (ed.), *Encyclopedia Biblica* (Hebrew), Jerusalem, VIII: 575–76.

Kikawada, Isaac M. (1975), "Literary Convention of the Primeval History," *AJBI* 1: 3–21.

Killebrew, Ann E. (2005), *Biblical Peoples and Ethnicity: An Archaeological Study of Egyptians, Canaanites, Philistines, and Early Israel, 1300–1100 B.C.E.*, Atlanta.

Kilmer, Anne Draffkorn (1972), "The Mesopotamian Concept of Overpopulation and Its Solution as Reflected in the Mythology," *Or* 41: 160–77.

——(1987), "The Mesopotamian Counterparts of the Biblical Něphîlîm," in: E. W. Conrad and E. G. Newing (eds.), *Essays and Poems in Honor of F. I. Andersen's Sixtieth Birthday*, Winona Lake, Ind., 39–43.

King, Philip, and Lawrence E. Stager (2001), *Life in Biblical Israel*, Louisville.

King, Philip (2007), "David Defeats Goliath," in: S. White Crawford, A. Ben-Tor (eds.), *Up to the Gates of Ekron: Essays on the Archaeology and History of the Eastern Mediterranean in Honor of Seymour Gitin*, Jerusalem, 350–57.

Kingsley, Bonnie M. (1979), "The Reclining Heroes of Taras and Their Cult," *CSCA* 12: 201–20.

Kirk, Geoffrey S. (1970), *Myth: Its Meaning and Functions in Ancient and Other Cultures*, Berkeley.

——(1972), "Greek Mythology: Some New Perspectives," *JHSt* 92: 74–85.

—— (1990), *The Iliad: A Commentary*, Volume II: books 5–8, Cambridge, U.K.

Kirk, Geoffrey S., John E. Raven, and Malcom Schofield (eds.) (1983), "The Extant Fragment of Anaximander," in: *The Presocratic Philosophers: A Critical History with a Selection of Texts*, Cambridge.

Kirwan, Richard (1810), "On the Origin of Polytheism, Idolatry, and Grecian Mythology," *TRIA* 11: 1–61.

Kitts, Margo (2008), "Funeral Sacrifices and Ritual Leitmotifs in Iliad 23," in: E. Stavrianopoulou, A. Michaels and C. Ambos (eds.), *Transformations in Sacrificial Practices: From Antiquity to Modern Times*, Berlin, 217–40.

Klein, Ernest (1987), *A Comprehensive Etymological Dictionary of the Hebrew Language for Readers of English*, Jerusalem.

Klein, Jacob (2000), "Shulgi of Ur: King of a Neo-Sumerian Empire," *CANE* I/II: 843–57.

Klein, Ralph W. (2006), *1 Chronicles*, Minneapolis.

Klengel-Brandt, Evelyn (1990), "Gab es ein Museum in der Hauptburg Nebukadnezars II. in Babylon?" *FB* 28: 41–46.

Kline, Meredith G. (1962), "Divine Kingship and Genesis 6:1–4," *WTJ* 24: 187–204.

Knohl, Israel (1995), *The Sanctuary of Silence: The Priestly Torah and the Holiness School*, Minneapolis.

——(2005), "Axial Transformations within Ancient Israelite Priesthood," in: J. P. Arnason, S. N. Eisenstadt, and B. Wittrock (eds.), *Axial Civilizations and World History*, Leiden, 201–24.

Knoppers, Gary N. (2003), *I Chronicles 1–9*, New York.

——(2004), *I Chronicles 10–29*, New York.

Koch, Klaus (1955), "Gibt es ein Vergeltungsdogma im Alten Testament," *ZTK*: 1–42.

Koenen, Ludwig (1994), "Greece, the Near East, and Egypt: Cyclic Destruction in Hesiod and the Catalogue of Women," *TAPA* 124: 1–34.

König, Eduard (1918), "Poesie und Prosa in der althebräischen Literatur abgegrenzt," *ZAW* 38: 23–53.

Kosmala, H. (1975), "גבר gābhar," *TDOT* II: 367–82.

Kozlovic, Anton K. (1949), "Constructing the Motherliness of Manoah's Wife in Cecil B. DeMille's Samson and Delilah (1949)," *WJ* 4.1: 1–20.

Kraeling, Emil G. (1922), "The Origin and Real Name of Nimrod," *AJSLL* 38.3: 214–20.

——(1947a), "The Earliest Hebrew Flood Story," *JBL* 66.3: 279–93.

——(1947b), "The Significance and Origin of Gen. 6:1–4," *JNES* 6.4: 193–208.

Kramer, Samuel Noah (1946), "Heroes of Sumer: A New Heroic Age in World History and Literature," *PAPS* 90.2: 120–30.

Kuhrt, Amélie (2000), "Ancient Mesopotamia in Classical Greek and Hellenistic Thought," *CANE* I/II: 55–66.

Kullmann, Wolfgang (1955), "Ein vorhomerisches Motiv im Iliasproömium," *Philologus* 99: 167–92.

——(1956), "Zur Διὸς βουλή des Iliasproömiums," *Philologus* 100: 132–33.

——(1992), *Homerische Motive: Beiträge zur Entstehung, Eigenart und Wirkung von Ilias und Odyssee*, ed. R.J. Müller, Stuttgart.

Kurtz, Johann H. (1857), *Die Ehen der Söhne Gottes mit den Töchtern der Menschen; eine theologische Untersuchung zur exegetischen, historischen, dogmatischen und praktischen Würdigung des biblischen Berichtes Genesis 6:1–4*, Berlin.

Kvanvig, Helge S. (2002), "Gen 6,1–4 as an Antediluvian Event," *SJOT* 16.1: 79–112.

Lambert, W. G. and A. R. Millard (1969), *Atra-Ḫasīs: the Babylonian story of the Flood*, with *The Sumerian Flood Story*, by M. Civil, Oxford.

Lambert, Yves (1999), "Religion in Modernity as a New Axial Age: Secularization or New Religious Forms?" *SR* 60.3: 303–33.

Lamberton, Robert (1988), *Hesiod*, New Haven.

——(2010), "Allegory," in: A. Grafton, G. W. Most, and S. Settis (eds.), *The Classical Tradition*, Cambridge, Mass., 34–41.

Landsberger, Benno (1965), *Brief eines Bischofs von Esagila an König Asarhaddon*, Amsterdam.

Lardinois, André (1998), "How the Days Fit the Works in Hesiod's 'Works and Days'," *AJP* 119.3: 319–336.

Larsen, Mogens Trolle (2000), "The 'Babel/Bible' Controversy and Its Aftermath," *CANE* I/II: 95–106.

Larson, Jennifer (1995), *Greek Heroine Cults*, Madison.

Latacz, Joachim (2004), *Troy and Homer: Towards a Solution of an Old Mystery*, tr. K. Windle and R. Ireland, Oxford.

Launderville, Dale (2007), *Spirit and Reason: The Embodied Character of Ezekiel's Symbolic Thinking*, Waco.

Law, Richard (1983), "The Heroic Ethos in John Dryden's Heroic Plays," *SEL* 23.3: 389–98.

Lazarus, William P. (2008), *Comparative Religion for Dummies*, Hoboken.

Lemardelé, Christophe (2010a), "Asiatic Lions *versus* Warriors: Archaic Motifs in Biblical Texts," *Semitica et Classica* 3: 223–25.

——(2010b), "Une gigantomachie dans la Genìse? Géants et héros dans les textes bibliques compilés," *RHR* 227.2: 155–74.

Lemche, Niels P. (1991), *The Canaanites and Their Land: The Tradition of the Canaanites*, Sheffield.

Lenormant, François (1899), *The Beginnings of History According to the Bible and the Traditions of Oriental Peoples*, New York, 1899.

Lenzi, Alan. "The Uruk List of Kings and Sages and the Late Mesopotamian Scholarship." *JANER* 8.2 (2008): 137–69.

Leveen, Adriane (2008), *Memory and Tradition in the Book of Numbers*, New York.

Levenson, Jon D. (1975), "Who Inserted the Book of the Torah?" *HTR* 68: 202–33.

——(1988), *Creation and the Persistence of Evil: The Jewish Drama of Divine Omnipotence*, San Francisco.

——(1993), *The Death and Resurrection of the Beloved Son: The Transformation of Child Sacrifice in Judaism and Christianity*, New Haven.

——(2006), *Resurrection and the Restoration of Israel: The Ultimate Victory of the God of Life*, New Haven.

Levin, Yigal (2002), "Nimrod the Mighty, King of Kish, King of Sumer and Akkad," *VT* 52.3: 350–66.

Levine, Baruch A. (1989), *Leviticus*, Philadelphia.

——(1993), *Numbers 1-20*, New York.

Levine, Baruch A. and J.M. de Tarragon (1984), "Dead Kings and Rephaim: The Patrons of the Ugaritic Dynasty," *JAOS* 104: 649–59.

Levinson, Bernard M. (1997), *Deuteronomy and the Hermeneutics of Legal Innovation,* Oxford.

——(2001), "The Reconceptualization of Kingship in Deuteronomy and the Deuteronomistic History's Transformation of Torah," *VT* 51.4: 511–34.

Lewis, Theodore J. (1989), *Cults of the Dead in Ancient Israel and Ugarit*, Atlanta.

——(1992), "Dead, Abode of the," *ABD* II: 101–05.

——(1997), "The Rapiuma," in: S. B. Parker (ed.), *Ugaritic Narrative Poetry*, Atlanta, 196–205.

L'Heureux, Conrad E. (1974), "The Ugaritic and Biblical Rephaim," *HTR* 67: 265–74.

——(1976), "The *yᵉlîdê hārāpāʼ*—A Cultic Association of Warriors," *BASOR* 221: 83–85.

——(1979), *Rank Among the Canaanite Gods: El, Baʻal, and the Repha'im*, Missoula.

Lichtenberger, Hermann (2004), "The Down-Throw of the Dragon in Revelation 12 and the Down-Fall of God's Enemy," in: C. Auffarth and L. T. Stuckenbruck (eds.), *The Fall of the Angels*, Leiden, 119–47.

Lincoln, Bruce (1997), *Theorizing Myth: Narrative, Ideology, and Scholarship*, Chicago.

Lindquist, Maria (2011), "King Og's Iron Bed," *CBQ* 73.3: 477–92.

Lipinski, Edward (1966), "Nimrod et Aššur," *RB* 73: 77–93.

——(1974), "'Anaq – Kiryat 'Arba' – Hébron et ses Sanctuaires Tribaux," *VT* 24.1: 41–55.

Liverani, Mario (1996), "The Bathwater and the Baby," in M. R. Lefkowitz and G. M. Rogers (eds.), *Black Athena Revisited*, Chapel Hill, 421–27.

Liwak, R. (2004), "רפאים," *TDOT* XIII: 602–14.

Lods, Adolphe (1906), *La croyance à la vie future et le culte des morts dans l'antiquité Israélite*, Paris.

López-Ruiz, Carolina (2010), *When the Gods Were Born: Greek Cosmogonies and the Near East*, Cambridge, Mass.

Loprieno, Antonio (ed.) (1996), *Ancient Egyptian Literature: History and Forms*, Leiden.

Lord, Albert B. (2000), *The Singer of Tales*, 2nd ed., S. Mitchell and G. Nagy (eds.), Cambridge, Mass.

Loretz, Oswald (1968), *Schöpfung und Mythos. Mensch und Welt nach den Anfangskapiteln der Genesis*, Stuttgart.

——(1978), "Vom kanaanäischen Totenkult zur jüdischen Patriarchen- und Elternverehrung: Historische und tiefenpsychologische Grundprobleme der Entstehung des biblischen Geschichtsbildes und der jüdischen Ethik," *JAR* 3: 149–204.

Louden, Bruce (2007) "The Gods in Epic, or the Divine Economy," *CAE*, 90–104.

——(2011), *Homer's Odyssey and the Near East*, Cambridge.

Louth, A., and M. Conti (eds.) (2001), *Ancient Christian Commentary on Scripture*, Old Testament, vol. I, Downers Grove, Ill.

Lowth, Robert (1839), *Lectures on the Sacred Poetry of the Hebrews*, tr. G. Gregory, 4th ed., London.

Luanois, Pierre-Emile, and Pierre Roy (1904), *Etudes biologiques sur les géants*. Paris.

Luckenbill, David D. (ed.) (1924), *The Annals of Sennacherib*, Chicago.

Lukács, Georg (1974), *The Theory of the Novel: A Historico-Philosophical Essay on the Forms of Great Epic Literature*, tr. A. Bostock, Cambridge, Mass.

Lundbom, Jack. R. (2004), *Jeremiah 37-52*, New York.

Machinist, Peter (1983a), "Assyria and Its Image in the First Isaiah," *JAOS* 103.4: 719–37.

——(1983b), "Rest and Violence in the Poem of Erra," *JAOS* 103.1: 221–26.

——(1986), "On Self-Consciousness in Mesopotamia," in: S. Eisenstadt (ed.), *The Origins & Diversity of Axial Age Civilizations*, Albany, 183–202.

——(1991), "The Question of Distinctiveness in Ancient Israel," in: F. Greenspahn (ed.), *Essential Papers on Israel and the Ancient Near East*, New York, 420–42.

——(1992), "Nimrod," *ABD* IV: 1116–18.

——(1994), "Outsiders or Insiders: The Biblical View of Emergent Israel and Its Contexts," in: L. J. Silberstein and R. L. Cohn (eds.), *The Other in Jewish Thought and History: Constructions of Jewish Culture and Identity*, New York, 35–60.

——(1997), "The Fall of Assyria in Comparative Perspective," in: S. Parpola and R. M. Whiting (eds.), *Assyria 1995: Proceedings of the 10th Anniversary Symposium of the Neo-Assyrian Text Corpus Project, Helsinki, September 7-11, 1995*, Helsinki, 179–95.

——(2000a), "Biblical Traditions: The Philistines and Israelite History," in: E. D. Oren (ed.), *The Sea Peoples and Their World: A Reassessment*, Philadelphia, 53–83.

——(2000b), "The Man Moses," *BR* 16.2, accessed online at http://basarchive.org, 22 March 2011.

——(2001), "Mesopotamia in Eric Voegelin's *Order and History*," Occasional Papers 26, *Eric-Voegelin-Archiv an der Ludwig-Maximilians-Universität München*, Munich, 1–54.

——(2003), "The Voice of the Historian in the Ancient Near Eastern and Mediterranean World," *Interpretation* 57.2: 117–37.

——(2006), "Kingship and Divinity in Imperial Assyria," in: G. Beckman and T. J. Lewis (eds.), *Text, Artifact, and Image. Revealing Ancient Israelite Religion*, Providence, 152–88.

——(2009), "The Road Not Taken. Wellhausen and Assyriology," in: G. Galil, M. Geller, and A. Millard (eds.), *Homeland and Exile. Biblical and Ancient Near Eastern Studies in Honour of Bustenay Oded*, Leiden, 469–531.

MacLaurin, E. C. B. (1965), "ANAK/᾿ΑΝΑΞ." *VT* 15.4: 468–74.

Maeir, Aren M., Stefan J. Wimmer, Alexander Zukerman, and Aaron Demsky (2008), "A Late Iron Age I/Early Iron Age II Old Canaanite Inscription from Tell eṣ-Ṣâfî/Gath, Israel: Paleography, Dating, and Historical-Cultural Significance," *BASOR* 351: 39–71.

Mainfort, Robert C. and Mary L. Kwas (2004), "The Bat Creek Stone Revisited: A Fraud Exposed," *AmAnt* 69.4: 761–69.

Maitland, Judith (1999), "Poseidon, Walls, and Narrative Complexity in the Homeric Iliad," *CQ* 49.1: 1–13.

Malamat, Abraham (1966), "The Ban in Mari and in the Bible," in: *Biblical Essays 1966, De Ou Testamentiese Werkgemeenskap in Suid-Afrika held at the University of Stellenbosch 26ᵗʰ-29ᵗʰ July 1966*, Potchefstroom, 40–49.

Malul, Maeir (1999), "Taboo חרם," *DDD*, 824–27.

Marbelstone, Howard (1996), "A 'Mediterranean Synthesis': Professor Cyrus H. Gordon's Contribution to the Classics," *BA* 59.1: 22–30.

Margalit, Baruch (1989), *The Ugaritic Poem of AQHT: Text, Translation, Commentary*, Berlin.

Marks, J. (2002), "The Junction Between the Kypria and the Iliad," *Phoenix* 56.1/2: 1–24.

Marks, Richard G. (1983), "Dangerous Hero: Rabbinic Attitudes Toward Legendary Warriors," *HUCA* 54: 181–94.

Martin, Richard P. (2007), "Epic as Genre," *CAE*, 9–20.

Matshushima, E. (1988), "Les Rituels du Mariage Divin dans les Documents Accadiens," *AcS* 10: 95–128.

Matthiae, P. (1979), "Princely Cemetery and Ancestors Cult at Ebla during the Middle Bronze II: A Proposal of Interpretation," *UF* 11: 563–69.

Mattingly, Gerald L. (1989), "Moabite Religion," in: A Dearman (ed.), *Studies in the Mesha Inscription and Moab*, Atlanta, 211–38.

——(1992a), "Anak," *ABD* I: 222.

——(1992b), "Emim," *ABD* II: 497.

Mayer, Kenneth (1996), "Helen and the ΔΙΟΣ ΒΟΥΛΗ," *AJP* 117.1: 1–15.

Mayes, A. D. H. (1979), *Deuteronomy*, London.

Mayor, Adrienne (2000), *The First Fossil Hunters: Paleontology in Greek and Roman Times*, Princeton.

Mazar, Benjamin (1963), "The Military Élite of King David," *VT* 13.3: 310–20.

——(1981), "The Early Israelite Settlement in the Hill Country," *BASOR* 241: 75–85.

McCarter, P. Kyle (1974), "The Early Diffusion of the Alphabet," *BA* 37.3: 54–68.

——(1975), *The Antiquity of the Greek Alphabet and the Early Phoenician Scripts*, Missoula, Mont.

——(1980), *I Samuel*, Garden City, N.Y.

——(1984), *II Samuel*, Garden City, N.Y.

——(2003a), "The Sarchophagus Inscription of 'Eshmun'azor, King of Sidon," *COS* II: 182–83.

——(2003b), "The Sarcophagus Inscription of Tabnit, King of Sidon," *COS* II: 181–82.

McCauley, Barbara (1999), "Heroes and Power: The Politics of Bone Transferral," in: R. Hägg (ed.), *Ancient Greek Hero Cult: Proceedings of the*

Fifth International Seminar on Ancient Greek Cult, Organized by the Department of Classical Archaeology and Ancient History, Göteborg University, 21-23 April 1995, Stockholm, 85–98.

McGregor, M.F. (1966), [Review: *Hellenosemitica: An Ethnic and Cultural Study of West Semitic Impact on Mycenaean Greece*, by M. Astour], *AHR* 71.2: 521–22.

McKeon, Richard (tr. and ed.) (1992), *Introduction to Aristotle*, New York.

McMillion, Phillip E. (1992), "Og," *ABD* V: 9.

Mendenhall, George E. (1962), "The Hebrew Conquest of Palestine," *BA* 25.3: 66–87.

Merkelbach, R. (1968), "Les Papyrus d'Hésiode et la géographie mythologique de la Grèce," *CE* 43: 133–55.

Meyer, Eduard (1913), *Geschichte des Altertums*, 3rd ed., 5 vols., Stuttgart.

Michalowski, Piotr (1993), "Memory and Deed: The Historiography of the Political Expansion of the Akkad State," in: M. Liverani (ed.), *Akkad: The First World Empire*, 69–90.

—— (1999), "Commemoration, Writing, and Genre in Ancient Mesopotamia," in: C. Shuttleworth Kraus (ed.), *The Limits of Historiography: Genre and Narrative in Ancient Historical Texts*, Leiden, 69–90.

—— (2003), "The Doors of the Past," in: A. Ben-Tor, I. Eph'al, and P. Machinist (eds.), *Festschrift for Hayim and Miriam Tadmor* (*ErIsr* 27), Jerusalem, 136–52.

—— (2005), "Mesopotamian Vistas on Axial Transformations," in: J. P. Arnason, S. N. Eisenstadt, and B. Wittrock (eds.), *Axial Civilizations and World History*, Leiden, 157–81.

Milgrom, Jacob (1990), *Numbers*, Philadelphia.

—— (2000), *Leviticus 17-22*, New York.

Milik, Józef T. (1976), *Books of Enoch: Aramaic Fragments of Qumrân Cave 4*, Oxford.

Millar, William R. (1976), *Isaiah 24-27 and the Origin of Apocalyptic*, Missoula.

Millard, Alan (1988), "King Og's Bed and Other Ancient Ironmongery," in: L. Eslinger and G. Taylor (eds.), *Ascribe to the Lord: Biblical & Other Studies in Memory of Peter C. Craigie*, Sheffield, 481–92.

—— "The Armor of Goliath," in: J. David Schloen (ed.), *Exploring the Longue Durée: Essays in Honor of Lawrence E. Stager*, Winona Lake, Ind., 337–43.

Miller, Patrick D. (2006), *The Divine Warrior in Early Israel*, Atlanta.

Milton, John (1968), *Paradise Lost & Paradise Regained*, ed. C. Ricks, New York.

—— (2003), *Samson Agonistes*, in: M. Y. Hughes (ed.), *John Milton: Complete Poems and Major Prose*, Indianapolis, 531–94.

Minton, William W. (1975), "The Frequency and Structuring of Traditional Formulas in Hesiod's *Theogony*," *HSCP* 79: 25–54.

Mirgeler, Albert (1958), *Hesiod; die Lehre von den fünf Weltaltern: Werke und Tage v. 106–201*, Düsseldorf.

Mobley, Gregory (1997), "The Wild Man in the Bible and the Ancient Near East," *JBL* 116.2: 217–33.

——(2005), *The Empty Men: The Heroic Tradition of Ancient Israel*, New York.

——(2006), "Glimpses of Heroic Saul," in: C. S. Ehrlich and M. C. White (eds.), Tübingen, 80–87.

Momigliano, Arnaldo (1957), "Perizonius, Niebuhr, and the Character of Early Roman Tradition," *JRS* 47: 104–14.

Mondi, Robert (1986), "Tradition and Innovation in the Hesiodic Titanomachy," *TAPA* 116: 25–48.

——(1990), "Greek and Near Eastern Mythology," in: L. Edmunds (ed.), *Approaches to Greek Myth*, Baltimore, 141–98.

Monroe, Lauren (2007), "Israelite, Moabite and Sabaean War-herem Traditions and the Forging of National Identity: Reconsidering the Sabaean Text RES 3945 in Light of Biblical and Moabite Evidence," *VT* 57: 318–341.

de Moor, Johannes C. (1976), "Rāpi'ūma – Rephaim," *ZAW* 88.3: 323–45.

Moore, Mary B. (1979), "Lydos and the Gigantomachy," *AJA* 83.1: 79–99.

——(1995), "The Central Group in the Gigantomachy of the Old Athena Temple on the Acropolis," *AJA* 99.4: 633–39.

Moran, William L. (1987), "Some Considerations of Form and Interpretation in *Atra-Ḫasis*," in: R. Rochberg-Halton (ed.), *Language, Literature, and History: Philological and Historical Studies Presented to Erica Reiner*, New Haven, 241–55.

Morris, Ian (1986), "The Use and Abuse of Homer," *CA* 5.1: 81–138.

——(2006), "The Collapse and Regeneration of Complex Societies in Greece, 1500–500 BC," in: G. M. Schwartz and J. J. Nichols (eds.), *After Collapse: The Regeneration of Complex Societies*, Tuscon, 72–84.

Motz, Lotte (1982), "Giants in Folklore and Mythology: A New Approach," *Folklore* 93.1: 70–84.

Mowinckel, Sigmund (1935), "Hat es ein israelitisches Nationalepos gegeben?" *ZAW* 53: 130–52.

——(1964), *Erwägungen zur Pentateuch Quellenfrage*, Oslo.

——(2004), *The Psalms in Israel's Worship*, tr. D. R. Ap-Thomas, with a foreword by J. L. Crenshaw, Grand Rapids, Mich.

Muellner, Leonard (1996), *The Anger of Achilles: Mēnis in Greek Epic*, Ithaca.

Muhly, James D. (1970), "Homer and the Phoenicians: The Relations Between Greece and the Near East in the Late Bronze and Early Iron Ages," *Berytus* 19: 19–64.

Murphy, Roland E. (2002), *The Tree of Life: An Exploration of Biblical Wisdom Literature*, Grand Rapids, Mich.

Mussies, Gerard (1999), "Giants γίγαντες," *DDD*, 343–45.

Myers, Jacob M. (1965a), *I Chronicles*, Garden City, N.Y.

——(1965b), *II Chronicles*, Garden City, N.Y.

Na'aman, Nadav (1981), "Hebron Was Built Seven Years before Zoan in Egypt (Numbers 13:22)," *VT* 31: 488–92.

——(2005a), "The Canaanites and Their Land," in: N. Na'aman, *Canaan in the Second Millennium B.C.E.*, Collected Essays, vol. 2, Winona Lake, Ind., 110–33.

——(2005b), "The 'Conquest of Canaan' in the Book of Joshua and in History," in: N. Na'aman, *Canaan in the Second Millennium B.C.E.*, Collected Essays, vol. 2, Winona Lake, Ind., 317–92.

Nabokov, Vladimir Vladimirovich (1973), *Strong Opinions*, New York.

Nagy, Gregory (1985), "Theognis and Megara: A Poet's Vision of his City," in: T. Figueira and G. Nagy (eds.), *Theognis of Megara: Poetry and the Polis*, Baltimore, 22-81.

——(1990a), *Greek Mythology and Poetics*, Ithaca.

——(1990b), *Pindar's Homer: The Lyric Possession of an Epic Past*, Baltimore.

——(1992), "Homeric Questions," *TAPA* 122: 17–60.

——(1995), "An Evolutionary Model for the Making of Homeric Poetry: Comparative Perspectives," in: J. B. Carter and S. P. Morris (eds.), *The Ages of Homer: A Tribute to Emily Townsend Vermeule*, Austin, 163–79.

——(1996), *Homeric Questions*, Austin.

——(1999a), "As the World Runs out of Breath: Metaphorical Perspectives on the Heavens and the Atmosphere in the Ancient World," in: J. Ker Conway, K. Keniston, and L. Marx (eds.), *Earth, Air, Fire, Water: Humanistic Studies of the Environment*, Amherst, 37–50.

——(1999b), *The Best of the Achaeans: Concepts of the Hero in Archaic Greek Poetry*, Baltimore.

——(2001), "The Sign of the Hero: A Prologue to the *Heroikos* of Philostratus," in: J. K. Berenson Maclean and E. B. Aitken (eds.), *Flavius Philostratus, Heroikos*, Atlanta, xv–xxxv.

——(2005), "An Apobatic Moment for Achilles as Athlete at the Festival of the Panathenaia," ΙΜΕΡΟΣ 5.1: 311–17.

——(2006), "The Epic Hero," 2nd edition (on-line version), http://chs.harvard.edu/publications/, Washington, DC.

——(2007), "The Epic Hero," *CAE*, 71–89.

——(2009a) "An Apobatic Moment for Achilles as Athlete at the Festival of the Panathenaia," (on-line version), http://chs.harvard.edu/publications, Washington, DC.

—— (2009b), *Homer the Preclassic* (on-line version), http://chs.harvard.edu/publications/, Washington, DC.

—— (2010), *Homer the Preclassic*, Berkeley.

—— (2012), "Signs of Hero Cult in Homeric Poetry," in F. Montanari, A. Rengakos, and C. Tsagalis (eds.), *Homeric Contexts: Neoanalysis and the Interpretation of Oral Poetry*, Berlin and Boston, 27–71.

Naveh, Joseph (1987), *Early History of the Alphabet: An Introduction to West Semitic Epigraphy and Palaeography*, Jerusalem.

Negbi, Ora (1992), "Early Phoenician Presence in the Mediterranean Islands: A Reappraisal," *AJA* 96.4: 599–615.

Neitzel, Heinz (1975), *Homer-Rezeption bei Hesiod: Interpretation ausgewählter Passagen*, Bonn.

Nelson, Richard D. (1997), *Joshua*, Louisville.

—— (2002), *Deuteronomy*, Louisville.

Nickelsburg, George W. (1977), "Apocalyptic and Myth in 1 Enoch 6–11," *JBL* 96.3: 383–405.

—— (2001), *1 Enoch 1*, Minneapolis.

Nickelsburg, George W., and James C. VanderKam (2004), *1 Enoch. A New Translation*, Minneapolis.

Niditch, Susan (1987), *A Prelude to Biblical Folklore: Underdogs and Tricksters*, Urbana, Ill.

—— (1993), *Folklore and the Hebrew Bible*, Minneapolis.

—— (1996), *Oral World and Written Word: Ancient Israelite Literature*, Louisville.

—— (2007), "The Challenge of Israelite Epic," *CAE*, 277–88.

—— (2008), *Judges*, Louisville.

—— (2010), "Epic and History in the Hebrew Bible: Definitions, 'Ethnic Genres,' and the Challenges of Cultural Identity in the Biblical Book of Judges," in: D. Konstan and K. A. Raaflaub (eds.), *Epic and History*, Malden, Mass., 86–102.

Niehr, Herbert (2002), "The Changed Status of the Dead in Yehud," in: R. Albertz and B. Becking (eds.), *Yahwism after the Exile. Perspectives on Israelite Religion in the Persian Era*, Leiden, 136–55.

Niemeyer, Hans Georg (1984), "Die Phönizier und die Mittelmeerwelt in Zeitalter Homers," *JRGZ* 31: 3–94.

Niemeyer, Hans Georg (ed.) (1982), *Phönizier im Westen: die Beiträge des Internationalen Symposiums über "Die phönizische Expansion im westlichen Mittelmeerraum" in Köln vom 24. bis 27. April 1979*, Mainz am Rhein.

Nietzsche, Friederich (2005), *The Use and Abuse of History (Vom Nutzen und Nachteil der Historie für das Leben)*, New York.

Nikolaev, Alexander S. (2004), "Die Etymologie von altgriechischem ὕβρις," *Glotta* 80: 211–30.

Nilsson, Martin P. (1967), *Geschichte der griechischen Religion* I.3, Munich.

Noegel, Scott B. (1998), "The Aegean Ogygos of Boeotia and the Biblical Og of Bashan: Reflections of the Same Myth," *ZAW* 110.3: 411–26.

——(2007), "Mesopotamian Epic," *CAE*, 233–45.

Nolan, Maura (2009), "Historicism After Historicism," in: E. Scala and S. Federico (eds.), *The Post-Historical Middle Ages*, New York, 63–86.

Nöldeke, Theodor (1869), *Untersuchungen zur Kritik des Alten Testaments*, Kiel.

Noth, Martin (1940–1941), "Num. 21 als Glied der 'Hexateuch'-Erzählung," *ZAW* 58: 161–89.

——(1968), *Numbers*, tr. J. D. Martin, London.

——(1981a), *The Deuteronomistic History*, tr. J. Doull, J. Barton, M. D. Rutter, and D. R. Ap-Thomas, Sheffield.

——(1981b), *A History of Pentateuchal Traditions*, tr. B. W. Anderson, Chico, CA.

Notopoulos, James A. (1960), "Homer, Hesiod and the Achaean Heritage of Oral Poetry," *Hesperia* 29.2: 177–97.

O'Connell, Robert H. (1988), "Isaiah XIV 4B–23: Ironic Reversal through Concentric Structure and Mythic Allusion," *VT* 38.4: 407–418.

Oden, Robert A. (1981), "Divine Aspirations in Atrahasis and Genesis 1–11," *ZAW* 93: 197–216.

O'Keefe, Katherine O'Brien (1991), "Heroic Values and Christian Ethics," in: M. Godden and M. Lapidge (eds.), *The Cambridge Companion to Old English Literature*, Cambridge, 107–25.

Olender, Maurice (1987), "The Indo-European Mirror: Monotheism and Polytheism," in: F. Schmidt (ed.), *The Inconceivable Polytheism: Studies in Religious Historiography*, New York, 327–75.

del Olmo Lete, G. (1999a), *Canaanite Religion According to the Liturgical Texts of Ugarit*, Bethesda.

——(1999b), "Og עוג," *DDD*, 638–40.

Olsen, Alexandra H. (1979), "The Heroic World: Icelandic Sagas and the Old-English 'Riming Poem'," *PCP* 14: 51–58.

Oppenheim, A. Leo (1975), "The Position of the Intellectual in Mesopotamian Society," *Daedalus* 104.2: 37–46.

Osborne, James F. (2011), "Mortuary Practice and the Bench Tomb: Structure and Practice in Iron Age Judah," *JNES* 70.1: 35–53.

Osborne, Robin (1998), *Archaic and Classical Greek Art*, Oxford.

Østerud, Svein (1976), "The Individuality of Hesiod," *Hermes* 104.1: 13–29.

Paden, William E. (2000), "Elements of a New Comparativism," in: K. C. Patton and B. C. Ray (eds.), *A Magic Still Dwells: Comparative Religion in the Postmodern Age*, Berkeley, 182–92.

Page, Denys Lionel (1959), *History and the Homeric Iliad*, Berkeley.

Pardee, Dennis (2005), "On Psalm 29: Structure and Meaning," in: P. W. Flint and P. D. Miller (eds.), *The Book of Psalms: Composition & Reception*, Leiden, 153–83.

——(2009), "A New Aramaic Inscription from Zincirli," *BASOR* 356: 51–71.

Parker, Simon B. (1989), *The Pre-Biblical Narrative Tradition: Essays on the Ugaritic Poems Keret and Aqhat*, Atlanta.

Parker, Simon B. (ed.) (1997), *Ugaritic Narrative Poetry*, Atlanta.

Parpola, Simo (1993), "The Assyrian Tree of Life: Tracing the Origins of Jewish Monotheism and Greek Philosophy," *JNES* 52: 161–208.

——(1998), "The Esoteric Meaning of the Name of Gilgamesh," in: J. Prosecký (ed.), *Intellectual Life of the Ancient Near East. Papers Presented at the 43rd Rencontre assyriologique internationale, Prague, July 1-5, 1996*, Prague, 315–29.

Paton, Lewis B. (1921), *Spiritism and the Cult of the Dead in Antiquity*, New York.

Patton, Kimberly C. and Benjamin C. Ray (eds.) (2000), *A Magic Still Dwells: Comparative Religion in the Postmodern Age*, Berkeley.

Pausanias (1913), *Description of Greece*, tr. J. G. Frazer, 6 vols., London.

Peabody, Berkley (1975), *The Winged Word: A Study in the Technique of Ancient Greek Oral Composition as Seen Principally Through Hesiod's Works and Days*, Albany.

Pearson, Brook W. (1999), "Resurrection and the Judgment of the Titans: ἡ γῆ τῶν ἀσεβῶν in LXX Isaiah 26.19," in: S. E. Porter, M. A. Hayes, and D. Tombs (eds.), *Resurrection*, Sheffield, 33–51.

Pedersen, David L. (1976), "The Yahwist on the Flood," *VT* 26.4: 438–46.

Pegg, Carole (1995), "Ritual, Religion and Magic in West Mongolian (Oirad) Heroic Epic," *BJE* 4: 77–99.

Penglase, Charles (1994), *Greek Myths and Mesopotamia: Parallels and Influence in the Homeric Hymns and Hesiod*, London.

Perkell, Christine (2008), "Reading the Laments of *Iliad* 24," in: A. Suter (ed.), *Lament: Studies in the Ancient Mediterranean and Beyond*, Oxford, 93–117.

Perlitt, Lothar (1994), "Riesen im Alten Testament: Ein literarisches Motiv im Wirkungsfelt des Deuteronomiums," in: L. Perlitt, *Deuteronomium-Studien*, Tübingen, 205–46.

Peters, Dorothy M. (2008), *Noah Traditions in the Dead Sea Scrolls: Conversations and Controversies of Antiquity*, Atlanta.

Petrakis, Vassilis P. (2006), "History versus the Homeric 'Iliad': A View from the Ionian Islands," *CW* 99.4: 371–96.

Pettinato, G. (1968), "Die Bestrafung des Menschengeschlechts durch die Sintflut," *Or* 37: 165–200.

Pfeiffer, Robert H., and William C. Pollard (1957), *The Hebrew Iliad: The History of the Rise of Israel Under Saul and David. Written during the reign of Solomon probably by the priest Ahimaaz*, New York.

Pfister, Friedrich (1909–1912), *Der Reliquienkult im Altertum*, Berlin.

Philo of Byblos (1981), *The Phoenician History*, ed. H. W. Attridge and R. A. Oden, Jr., Washington D.C.

Philostratus the Athenian (2001), *Flavius Philostratus, Heroicus*, tr. J. K. Berenson Maclean and E. B. Aitken, with a prologue by G. Nagy and an epilogue by H. Koester, Atlanta.

Pinnock, Frances (2001), "The Urban Landscape of Old Syrian Ebla," *JCS* 53 (2001): 13–33.

Pirenne-Delforge, Vinciane and Emilio Suárex de la Torre (eds.) (2000), *Héros et héroïnes dans les mythes et les cultes grecs: actes du Colloque organisé à l'Université de Valladolid du 26 au 29 mai 1999*, Liège.

Pistor, Erich (1932), *Griechenland und der Nahe Osten, mit einem Farbendruck und Illustrationen von Alfred Keller, 16 Photos und einem statistischen Schaubild*, Vienna.

Pitard, Wayne (1978), "The Ugaritic Funerary Text RS 34.126," *BASOR* 232: 65–75.

——(1987), "RS 34.126: Notes on the Text," *Maarav* 4: 75–86.

——(1992), "A New Edition of the 'Rāpi'ūma' Texts: KTU 1.20–22," *BASOR* 285: 33–77.

——(1994), "The 'Libation Installations' of the Tombs at Ugarit," *BA* 57: 20–37

Pliny the Elder (2005), *The Elder Pliny on the Human Animal: Natural History, Book 7*, tr. M. Beagon, Oxford.

Podbielski, Henry (1984), "Le mythe cosmogonique dans la Théogony," *LEC* 52: 207–16.

Pohlmann, Karl-Friedrich (2001), *Das Buch des Propheten Hesekiel (Ezechiel) Kapitel 20–48*, Göttingen.

Polak, Frank H. (2006), "Linguistic and Stylistic Aspects of Epic Formulae in Ancient Semitic Poetry and Biblical Narrative," in S. E. Fassberg and A. Hurvitz, *Biblical Hebrew in Its Northwest Semitic Setting: Typological and Historical Perspectives*, Jerusalem, 285–304.

Pope, Marvin (1964), [Review: *Before the Bible: The Common Background of Greek and Hebrew Civilisations*, by C. Gordon], *JBL* 83.1: 72–74, 76.

——(1994), "Notes on the Rephaim Texts from Ugarit," in M. S. Smith (ed.), *Probative Pontificating in Ugaritic and Biblical Literature: Collected Essays* [of Marvin Pope], Münster, 185–224.

Poplicha, Joseph (1929), "The Biblical Nimrod and the Kingdom of Eanna," *JAOS* 49: 303–17.

Popovic, Mladen (2006), "Physiognomic Knowledge in Qumran and Babylonian: Form, Interdisciplinarity, and Secrecy," *DSD* 13.2: 150–76.

Porter, Barbara N. (2002), "Beds, Sex, and Politics: The Return of Marduk's Bed to Babylon," in: S. Parpola and R. M. Whiting (eds.), *Sex and Gender in the Ancient Near East: Proceedings of the 47th Recontre Assyriologique Internationale, Helsinki, Jul 2-6, 2001*, Helsinki, 523–35.

Porter, Josias Leslie (1884), *The Giant Cities of Bashan, and Syria's Holy Places*, New York.

Powell, Barry B. (1989), "Why Was the Greek Alphabet Invented? The Epigraphical Evidence," *CA* 8.2: 321–50.

——(1991), *Homer and the Origins of the Greek Alphabet*, Cambridge.

——(2002), *Writing the Origins of Greek Literature*, Cambridge.

Price, Theodora Hadzisteliou (1973), "Hero-Cult and Homer," *ZAG* 22.2: 129–44.

Pritchard, James B. (ed.) (1969), *Ancient Near Eastern Texts Relating to the Old Testament*, 3rd ed., Princeton.

Propp, William H.C. (2006), *Exodus 19-40*, New York.

Provan, Ian, V. Philips Long, and Tremper Longman III (2003), *A Biblical History of Israel*, Louisville.

Purvis, J. D. (1968), [Review: *Hellenosemitica: An Ethnic and Cultural Study in West Semitic Impact on Mycenaean Greece*, by M. Astour], *JNES* 27.2: 154–55.

Querbach, Carl W. (1985), "Hesiod's Myth of the Four Races," *CJ* 81.1: 1–12.

Raaflaub, Kurt A. (2007), "Epic and History," *CAE*, 55–70.

Rabelais, François (1972), *The Histories of Gargantua and Pantagruel*, tr. J. M. Cohen, Harmondsworth.

Raglan, FitzRoy Richard Somerset 4th Baron (1956), *The Hero: A Study in Tradition, Myth, and Drama*, New York.

Rahlfs, Alfred (1979), *Septuaginta*, Stuttgart.

Rainey, Anson (1974), "The Ugaritic Texts in Ugaritica 5," *JAOS* 94: 184–94.

Rainey, Anson, and R. Steven Notley (2006), *The Sacred Bridge*, Jerusalem.

Rank, Otto (1990), "The Myth of the Birth of the Hero," in: *In Quest of the Hero*, Princeton, 3–86.

Redpath, Henry A. (1905), "Mythological Terms in the LXX," *AJT* 9.1: 34–45.

Reeves, John C. (1991), *Jewish Lore in Manichaean Cosmogony: Studies in the Book of Giants Traditions*, Cincinnati.

——(1993), "Utnapishtim in the Book of Giants?" *JBL* 112.1: 110–15.

Reeves, John D. (1966), "The Cause of the Trojan War: A Forgotten Myth Revived," *CJ* 61.5: 211–14.

Reichert, Hermann (2005), *Das Nibelungenlied. Text und Einführung*, Berlin.

Reimer, Andy M. (2000), "Rescuing the Fallen Angels: The Case of the Disappearing Angels at Qumran," *DSD* 7.3: 334–53.

Reuss, Eduard (1881), *Die Geschichte der Heiligen Schriften Alten Testaments*, Braunschweig.

Rilke, Rainer Maria (1989), *The Selected Poetry of Rainer Maria Rilke*, Bilingual Edition, ed. and tr. S. Mitchell, New York.

Riva, Corinna (2005), "The Culture of Urbanization in the Mediterranean *c*.800–600 BC," in: R. Osborne and B. Cunliffe (eds.), *Mediterranean Urbanization 800-600 BC*, Oxford, 203–32.

Roberts, J. J. M. (1991), *Nahum, Habakkuk, and Zephaniah*, Louisville.

——(2002), "Myth Versus History: Relaying the Comparative Foundations," in: J. J. M. Roberts, *The Bible and the Ancient Near East: Collected Essays of J.J.M. Roberts*, Winona Lake, Ind., 59–71.

Robinson, Fred C. (1991), "*Beowulf*," in: M. Godden and M. Lapidge (eds.), *The Cambridge Companion to Old English Literature*, Cambridge, 142–59.

Robinson, Theodore H. (1917), "Baal in Hellas," *CQ* 11.4: 201–11.

Rohde, Erwin (1950), *Psyche: The Cult of Souls and Belief in Immortality Among the Greeks*, tr. W. B. Hillis, London.

Röllig, Wolfgang (1995), "L'Alphabet," in: V. Klings (ed.), *La civilization phénicienne et punique. Manuel de recherché*, Leiden, 193–214.

Rollinger, Robert, and Christoph Ulf (eds.) (2004), *Griechische Archaik: Interne Entwicklungen-Externe Impulse*, Berlin.

Rollston, Christopher A. (2003), "The Rise of Monotheism in Ancient Israel: Biblical and Epigraphic Evidence," *SCJ* 6: 95–115.

Römer, Thomas (2006), *The So-Called Deuteronomistic History: A Sociological, Historical and Literary Introduction*, London.

Rosenmeyer, Thomas G. (1957), "Hesiod and Historiography," *Hermes* 85.3: 257–85.

Rouillard, Hedwige (1999), "Rephaim רפאים," *DDD*, 692–700.

Rowe, C. J. (1983), "'Archaic Thought' in Hesiod," *JHSt* 103: 124–35.

Ryan, Judith (2012), *The Novel After Theory*, New York.

Sarna, Nahum (1989), *Genesis*, Philadelphia.

Sass, Benjamin (1988), *The Genesis of the Alphabet and Its Development in the Second Millennium B.C.*, Wiesbaden.

Sasson, Jack M. (1994), "The 'Tower of Babel' as a Clue to the Redactional Structuring of the Primeval History (Genesis 1:1–11:9)," in: R. S. Hess and

D. T. Tsumura (eds.), *"I Studied Inscriptions from before the Flood." Ancient Near Eastern, Literary, and Linguistic Approaches to Genesis 1-11*, Winona Lake, Ind., 448–57.

——(2007), "Comparative Observations on the Near Eastern Epic Tradition," *CAE*, 215–32.

Sauer, James A. (1986), "Transjordan in the Bronze and Iron Ages: A Critique of Glueck's Synthesis," *BASOR* 263: 1–26.

Savage, Stephen H. (2010), "Jordan's Stonehenge," *NEA* 73.1: 32–46.

Sawyer, John F. (1983), "The Meaning of *barzel* in the Biblical Expressions 'Chariots of Iron,' 'Yoke of Iron,' etc," in: J. F. Sawyer and D. J. A. Clines (eds.), *Midian, Moab, and Edom: The History and Archaeology of Late Bronze and Iron Age Jordan and North-West Arabia*, Sheffield, 129–34.

Sayce, Archibald Henry (1892), "An Israelitish War in Edom: Hebrew Loanwords from Greek," *Ac* 42: 365–66.

——(1895), *Patriarchal Palestine*, London.

Scaife, Ross (1995), "The 'Kypria' and Its Early Reception," *CA* 14.1: 164–92.

Scammel, J. M. (1937), "The Races of the Eastern Mediterranean and Commerce Between the Aegean and the Euxine Seas in the Heroic Age," *CJ* 32.5: 281–95.

Schachermeyr, Fritz (1967), *Aegäis und Orient: die überseeischen Kulturbeziehungen von Kreta und Mykenai mit Ägypten, der Levante und Kleinasien unter besonderer Berücksichtigung des 2. Jahrtausends v. Chr. 233 Abbildunge auf 63 Tafeln*, Vienna.

Schaeffer-Forrer, C. F. A. (1978), "Épaves d'une bibliotèque d'Ugarit," *Ugaritica VII*, Paris, 399–405.

Scharbert, J. (1967), "Traditions- und Redaktionsgeschichte von Gen. 6:1-4," *BZ* 11: 66–78.

Schatz, Werner (1972), *Genesis 14: Eine Untersuchung*, Bern.

Schloen, J. David (2001), *The House of the Father as Fact and Symbol: Patrimonialism in Ugarit and the Ancient Near East*, Winona Lake, Ind.

Schmid, Hans H. (1974), *Altorientalische Welt in der alttestamentlichen Theologie*, Zurich.

——(1984), "Creation, Righteousness, and Salvation," in: B. W. Anderson (ed.), *Creation in the Old Testament*, Philadelphia, 102–17.

Schmidt, Brian B. (1996), *Israel's Beneficent Dead: Ancestor Cult and Necromancy in Ancient Israelite Religion and Tradition*, Winona Lake, Ind.

Schmitz, Christine, and Anja Bettenworth (eds.) (2009), *Menschen - Heros - Gott: Weltentwürfe und Lebensmodelle im Mythos der Vormoderne*, Stuttgart.

Schnell, R. F. (1962), "Anak, Anakim," *IDB* I: 123–24.

——(1971), "Rephaim," *IDB* IV: 35.

Scholz, Paul (1865), *Die Ehen der Söhne Gottes mit den Töchtern der Menschen. Eine exegetisch-kritische, historische und dogmatische Abhandlung über den Bericht Genesis 6:1-4*, Regensburg.

Schömbucher, Elisabeth (1999), "Death as the Beginning of a New Life: Hero-Worship Among a South Indian Fishing Caste," in: E. Schömbucher and C. Peter Zoller (eds.), *Ways of Dying: Death and its Meanings in South Asia*, New Delhi.

Schüle, Andreas (2009), "The Divine-Human Marriages (Genesis 6:1-4) and the Greek Framing of the Primeval History," *TZ* 65.2: 116–128.

Schwally, Friedrich (1892), *Das Leben nach dem Tode: nach den Vorstellungen des alten Israel und des Judentums einschliesslich des Volksglaubens im Zeitalter Christi, eine biblisch-theologische Untersuchung*, Giessen.

Schwartz, Benjamin (1975), "The Age of Transcendence," *Daedalus* 104.2: 1–7.

Scodel, Ruth (1982), "The Achaean Wall and the Myth of Destruction," *HSCP* 86: 33–50.

Scurlock, JoAnn (1990), "The Euphrates Flood and the Ashes of Nineveh (Diod. II 27.1–28.7)," *HZAG* 39.3: 382–84.

Sedley, David N. (2007), *Creationism and its Critics in Antiquity*, Berkeley.

Seemann, Otto (1869), *Die Götter und heroen, nebst einer Übersicht der Cultusstätten und Religionsgebräuche der Griechen; eine Vorschule der Kunstmythologie*, Leipzig.

Segal, Robert A. (1990), "Introduction: In Quest of the Hero," in: *In Quest of the Hero*, Princeton, vii–xli.

Segal, Robert A. (ed.) (1998), *The Myth and Ritual Theory. An Anthology*, Malden, Mass.

Sellschopp, Inez (1934), *Stilistische Untersuchungen zu Hesiod*, Ph.D. dissertation, Hamburg, 1934.

Seow, Choon-Leong (1989), *Myth, Drama, and the Politics of David's Dance*, Atlanta.

Shai, Itzhaq (2009), "Understanding Philistine Migration: City Names and Their Implications," *BASOR* 354: 15–27.

Shipp, R. Mark (2002), *Of Dead Kings and Dirges: Myth and Meaning in Isaiah 14:4b–21*, Leiden.

Sidhanta, Normal Kumar (1975), *The Heroic Age of India: A Comparative Study*, New Delhi.

Sievers, Eduard (1901), *Metrische Studien, I. Studien zur hebräischen Metrik. Erster Teil: Untersuchungen*, Leipzig.

Simkins, Ronald A. (1991), *Creator & Creation: Nature in the Worldview of Ancient Israel*, Peabody.

Singor, H. W. (1992), "The Achaean Wall and the Seven Gates of Thebes," *Hermes* 120.4: 401–11.

Sinos, Dale S. (1980), *Achilles, Patroklos, and the Meaning of Philos*, Innsbruck.

Skjærvø, P. O. (1995), "Iranian Epic and the Manichean Book of the Giants," Irano-Manichaica III, *AcOr* XLVIII 1–2: 187–223.

——(1998), "Eastern Iranian Epic Traditions I: Siyâvâs and Kunâla," in: J. Jasanoff, H. C. Melchert, and L. Oliver (eds.), *Mír curad: Studies in Honor of Calvert Watkins*, Innsbruck, 645–58.

Slatkin, Laura M. (2007), "Homer's *Odyssey*," *CAE*, 315–29.

Smith, John M. P., William H. Ward, and Julius A. Bewer (1911), *A Critical and Exegetical Commentary on Micah, Zephaniah, Nahum, Habbakuk, Obadiah and Joel*, New York.

Smith, Jonathan Z. (1982a), "In Comparison a Magic Dwells," in: J.Z. Smith, *Imagining Religion: From Babylon to Jonestown*, Chicago, 19–35.

——(1982b), "Fences and Neighbors: Some Contours of Early Judaism," in: J.Z. Smith, *Imagining Religion: From Babylon to Jonestown*, Chicago, 1–18.

——(2000a), "Acknowledgements: Morphology and History in Mircea Eliade's 'Patterns in Comparative Religion' (1949–1999), Part 1: The Work and Its Contexts," and "Part 2: The Texture of the Work," *HR* 39.4: 315–31, 332–51.

——(2000b), "The 'End' of Comparison: Redescription and Rectification," in: K. C. Patton and B. C. Ray (eds.), *A Magic Still Dwells: Comparative Religion in the Postmodern Age*, Berkeley, 237–41.

Smith, Jonathan Z. (ed.) (1995), "Comparative religion," in: *The HarperCollins Dictionary of Religion*, San Francisco, 276–79.

Smith, Mark S. (1992), "Rephaim," *ABD* V: 674–76.

——(2001), *The Origins of Biblical Monotheism: Israel's Polytheistic Background and the Ugaritic Texts*, Oxford.

——(2004), *The Memoirs of God: History, Memory, and the Experience of the Divine in Ancient Israel*, Minneapolis.

——(2008), *God in Translation: Cross-Cultural Recognition of Deities in the Biblical World*, Grand Rapids.

——(2009), "Warrior Culture in Ugaritic Literature," presentation at the Society of Biblical Literature Annual Meeting, New Orleans.

Smith, Mark S. and Elizabeth Bloch-Smith (1988), "Death and Afterlife in Ugarit and Israel," *JAOS* 108.2: 277–84.

Smith, Peter (1980), "History and the Individual in Hesiod's Myth of Five Races," *CW* 74.3: 145–63.

Smith, Suzanne (2011a), "The Gods of Epic: Polytheism and the Political Theology of Genre," unpublished paper.

——(2011b), "Partial Transcendence, Religious Pluralism, and the Question of Love," *HTR* 104: 1–32.

Smith-Christopher, Daniel L. (2002), *A Biblical Theology of Exile*, Minneapolis.

Snodgrass, Anthony M. (1971), *The Dark Age of Greece: An Archaeological Survey of the Eleventh to the Eighth Centuries BC*, Edinburgh.

——(1982), "Les origines de cult des héros dans la Grèce antique," in: G. Gnoli and J.-P. Vernant (eds.), *La mort, les morts dans les sociétés anciennes*, Cambridge, 89–105.

Soggin, J. Alberto (1972), *Joshua*, Philadelphia.

Solmsen, Friederich (1982), "The Earliest Stages in the History of Hesiod's Text," *HSCP* 86: 1–31.

——(1989), "The Two Near Eastern Sources of Hesiod," *Hermes* 117: 413–22.

Spalinger, Anthony J. (2002), *The Transformation of an Ancient Egyptian Narrative: P. Sallier III and the Battle of Kadesh*, Wiesbaden.

Spaulding, Jay (2007), *The Heroic Age in Sinnār*, Trenton, N.J.

Speiser, Ephraim A. (1964), *Genesis*, New York.

——(1994), "In Search of Nimrod," in: R. S. Hess and D. T. Tsumura (eds.), *"I Studied Inscriptions from before the Flood." Ancient Near Eastern, Literary, and Linguistic Approaches to Genesis 1-11*, Winona Lake, Ind., 270–77.

Speyer, Wolfgang (1988), "Heros," in: E. Dassmann, et al. (eds.), *Reallexikon für Antike und Christentum Sachwörterbuch zur Auseinandersetzung des Christentums mit der antiken Welt*, 24 vols., Stuttgart, XIV: 861–77.

Spronk, Klaus (1986), *Beatific Afterlife in Ancient Israel and in the Ancient Near East*, Kevelaer.

——(1999), "Travellers עברים," *DDD*, 876–77.

Stager, Lawrence E. (1985), "The Archaeology of the Family in Ancient Israel," *BASOR* 260: 1–35.

——(2006), "Biblical Philistines: A Hellenistic Literary Creation?" in: A. Maeir and P. de Miroschedji (eds.), *"I Will Speak the Riddles of Ancient Times." Archaeological and Historical Studies in Honor of Amihai Mazar on the Occasion of his Sixtieth Birthday*, Winona Lake, Ind., 375–84.

Starcky, Jean (1969), "Une inscription phénicienne de Byblos," *MMMD* 45: 259–73.

Steiner, Richard C., and C. F. Nims (1985), "Ashur-banipal and Shamash-shum-ukin: A Tale of Two Brothers from the Aramaic Text in Demotic Script," *RB* 92: 60–81.

Stephens, Walter (1989), *Giants in Those Days: Folklore, Ancient History, and Nationalism*, Lincoln.

Stern, Philip D. (1991), *The Biblical Herem: A Window on Israel's Religious Experience*, Atlanta.

Stewart, Susan (1984), *On Longing, Narratives of the Miniature, the Gigantic, the Souvenir, the Collection*, Baltimore.

Stone, Michael E. (1990), *Fourth Ezra*, Minneapolis.

Strathern, Alan (2009), "Karen Armstrong's Axial Age: Origins and Ethics," *HJ* 50.2: 293–309.

Stavrakopoulou, Francesca (2010), *Land of Our Fathers: The Roles of Ancestor Veneration in Biblical Land Claims*, London.

Strong, James, and John M'Clintock (1894), "Zamzummim," in: *Cyclopaedia of Biblical, Theological, and Ecclesiastical Literature*, 10 vols., New York, X: 1060.

Struble, Eudora J., and Virginia Rimmer Herrmann (2009), "An Eternal Feast at Sam'al: The New Iron Age Mortuary Stele from Zincirli in Context," *BASOR* 356: 15–49.

Stuckenbruck, Loren T. (1997), *The Book of Giants from Qumran: Texts, Translations and Commentary*, Tübingen.

——(2000), "The 'Angels' and 'Giants' of Genesis 6:1–4 in Second and Third Century BCE Jewish Interpretation: Reflections on the Posture of Early Apocalyptic Traditions," *DSD* 7.3: 354–77.

——(2004), "The Origins of Evil in Jewish Apocalyptic Tradition: The Interpretation of Genesis 6:1–4 in the Second and Third Centuries B.C.E.," in: C. Auffarth and L. T. Stuckenbruck (eds.), *The Fall of the Angels*, Leiden, 87–118.

Suerbaum, Werner (1999), *Vergils Aeneis: Epos zwischen Geschichte und Gegenewart*, Stuttgart.

Sukthankar, V. S., S. K. Belvalkar, and P. L. Vaidya (eds.) (1933–1966), *The Mahābhārata for the First Time Critically Edited*, Pune.

Sumner, W. A. (1968), "Israel's Encounter with Edom, Moab, Ammon, Sihon, and Og According to the Deuteronomist," *VT* 18.2: 216–28.

Tadmor, Hayim (1986), "Monarchy and the Elite in Assyria and Babylonia: The Question of Royal Accountability," in: S. Eisenstadt (ed.), *The Origins & Diversity of Axial Age Civilizations*, Albany, 203–24.

Talmon, Shemaryahu (1981), "Did There Exist a Biblical National Epic?" in: *Proceedings of the Seventh World Congress of Jewish Studies*, vol. 2, *Studies in the Bible and the Ancient Near East*, Jerusalem, 41–61.

——(1983), "Biblical repā'îm and Ugaritic rpu/i(m)," *HAR* 7: 235–49.

——(1991), "The 'Comparative Method' in Biblical Interpretation—Principles and Problems," in: F. Greenspahn (ed.), *Essential Papers on Israel and the Ancient Near East*, New York, 381–419.

Tandy, David, and Walter C. Neale (1996), *Hesiod's Works and Days*, A Translation and Commentary for the Social Sciences, Berkeley.

Teggart, Frederick J. (1947), "The Argument of Hesiod's Works and Days," *JHI* 8.1: 45–77.

Thompson, John A. (1980), *The Book of Jeremiah*, Grand Rapids.

Thompson, Paul B. (2005), "Sizing Things Up: Gigantism in Ancient Near Eastern Religious Imaginations," Ph.D. dissertation, University of Missouri-Kansas City.

——(2007), "Smiting Goliath: Giants as Monsters in the Ancient Near East," *GolJMR* 2.1: http://golemjournal.org/thomas%20ANE%20monsters.pdf.

——(2008), "The Riddle of Ishtar's Shoes: The Religious Significance of the Footprints at 'Ain Dara from a Comparative Perspective," *JRH* 32.3: 303–19.

Tidwell, N.L. (1979), "The Philistine Incursion into the Valley of Rephaim (2 Sam. vv. 17ff.)," in: J. A. Emerton (ed.), *Studies in the Historical Books of the Old Testament*, Leiden, 190–212.

Tigay, Jeffrey H. (1986), *You Shall Have No Other Gods: Israelite Religion in the Light of Hebrew Inscriptions*, Atlanta.

——(1996), *Deuteronomy*, Philadelphia.

Tinney, Steve (1995), "A New Look at Naram-Sin and the 'Great Rebellion'," *JCS* 47: 1–14.

van der Toorn, Karel (1991), "Funerary Rituals and Beatific Afterlife in Ugaritic Texts and in the Bible," *BibOr* 48: 80–101.

——(1996), *Family Religion in Babylonia, Syria, and Israel: Continuity and Change in the Forms of Religious Life*, Leiden.

van der Toorn, Karel, and Cees Houtman (1994), "David and the Ark," *JBL* 113.2: 209–31.

van der Toorn, Karel, and P. W. van der Horst (1990), "Nimrod before and after the Bible," *HTR* 83.1: 1–29.

Travis, William (1999), "Representing 'Christ as Giant' in Early Medieval Art," *ZK* 62.2: 167–89.

Trompf, G. W. (1979), *The Idea of Historical Recurrence in Western Thought: From Antiquity to the Reformation*, Berkeley.

Tropper, Josef (2008), *Kleines Wörterbuch des Ugaritischen*, Wiesbaden.

Tsagalis, Christos (2008), *The Oral Palimpsest: Exploring Intertextuality in the Homeric Epics*, Washington, D.C.

Tsagarakis, Odysseus (1969), "The Achaean Wall and the Homeric Question," *Hermes* 97.2: 129–35.

Tsumura, David T. (1994), "Genesis and Ancient Near Eastern Stories of Creation and Flood: An Introduction," in: R. S. Hess and D. T. Tsumura (eds.), *"I Studied Inscriptions from before the Flood." Ancient Near Eastern, Literary, and Linguistic Approaches to Genesis 1-11*, Winona Lake, Ind., 27–57.

Tucker, Aviezer (2001), "The Future of the Philosophy of Historiography," *HT* 40.1: 37–56.

Tylor, Edward B. (1920), *Primitive Culture*, 2 vols., London.

Uehlinger, Christoph (1999), "Nimrod נמרוד," *DDD*, 627–30.

Uffenheimer, Benjamin (1986), "Myth and Reality in Ancient Israel," in: S. Eisenstadt (ed.), *The Origins & Diversity of Axial Age Civilizations*, Albany, 135–68.

Ulf, Christoph (2003), *Der neue Streit um Troia: Eine Bilanz*, Munich.

Ungnad, Arthur (1923), *Gilgamesch-Epos und Odyssee*, Breslau.

Ussishkin, David (1993), *The Village of Silwan: The Necropolis from the Period of the Judean Kingdom*, tr. I. Pommerantz, Jerusalem.

Van Brock, Nadia (1959), "Substitution rituelle," *RHA* 65: 117–46.

Van De Mieroop, Marc (2004), "A Tale of Two Cities: Nineveh and Babylon," *Iraq* 66: 1–5.

VanderKam, James C. (1994), *The Dead Sea Scrolls Today*, Grand Rapids.

Vandiver, Elizabeth (1991), *Heroes in Herodotus: The Interaction of Myth and History*, Frankfurt am Main.

Van Seters, John (1972), "The Terms 'Amorite' and 'Hittite' in the Old Testament," *VT* 22.1: 64–81.

——(1997), *In Search of History: Historiography in the Ancient World and the Origins of Biblical History*, Winona Lake, Ind.

van Zyl, A. H. (1960), *The Moabites*, Leiden.

Veijola, Timo (2003), "King Og's Iron Bed (Deut 3:11): Once Again," in: P. W. Flint, et al. (eds.), *Studies in the Hebrew Bible, Qumran, and the Septuagint Presented to Eugene Ulrich*, Leiden, 60–76.

Verdenius, Willem Jacob (1985), *A Commentary on Hesiod: Works and Days, vv. 1–382*, Leiden.

Vermeule, Emily (1981), *Aspects of Death in Early Greek Art and Poetry*, Berkeley.

Vernant, Jean-Pierre (1976), "Grèce ancienne et étude comparée des religions," *ASSR* 41: 5–24.

——(1983), *Myth and Thought among the Greeks*, London.

Vian, Francis (1952), *La guerre des géants; le mythe avant l'époque hellénistique*, Paris.

——(1988), "Gigantes," *LIMC* IV: 191–270.

Vlaardingerbroeck, Menko (2004), "The Founding of Nineveh and Babylon in Greek Historiography," *Iraq* 66: 233–41.

Vlastos, Gregory (1947), "Equality and Justice in Early Greek Cosmologies," *CP* 42.3: 156–78.

Voegelin, Eric (1956), *Order and History*, vol. 1, Israel and Revelation, Baton Rouge.

——(2003), *The Theory of Governance and Other Miscellaneous Papers 1921–1938*, in: W. Petropulos and G. Weiss (eds.), tr. S. Bollans, et al., *The Collected Works of Eric Voegelin*, vol. 32, Columbia, Mo.

Von Rad, Gerhard (1966), *Deuteronomy*, tr. D. Barton, Philadelphia.

——(1972), *Genesis*, tr. J. H. Marks, Philadelphia.

——(1991), *Holy War in Ancient Israel*, tr. M. J. Dawn and J. H. Yoder, Grand Rapids, Mich.

Von Soden, Wolfram (1973), "Der Mensch bescheidet sich nicht. Überlegungen zu Schöpfungserzählungen in Babylonien und Israel," in: M. A. Beek, et al. (eds.), *Symbolae biblicae et mesopotamicae Francisco Mario Theodoro de Liagre Böhl Dedicatae*, Leiden, 349–59.

——(1985), *Akkadisches Handwörterbuch*, 3 vols., Wiesbaden.

Waardenburg, Jacques (1980), "Symbolic Aspects of Myth," in: A. M. Olson (ed.), *Myth, Symbol, and Reality*, Notre Dame, 41–68.

Walcot, Peter (1966), *Hesiod and the Near East*, Cardiff.

——(1969), "The Comparative Study of Ugaritic and Greek Literature," *UF* 1: 111–18.

——(1970), "The Comparative Study of Ugaritic and Greek Literature II," *UF* 2, 273–75.

——(1972), "The Comparative Study of Ugaritic and Greek Literature III," *UF* 4, 129–32.

Wallace, David Foster (1996), *Infinite Jest*, New York.

Waltke, Bruce K., and Michael O'Connor (1990), *An Introduction to Biblical Hebrew Syntax*, Winona Lake, Ind.

Wassner, Julius (1883), *De heroum apud Graecos cultu*, Kiliae.

Waterhouse, Helen (1996), "From Ithaca to the Odyssey," *ABSA* 99: 301–17.

Watrous, Livingston V. (1982), "The Sculptural Program of the Siphnian Treasury at Delphi," *AJA* 86.2: 159–72.

Webster, T. B. L. (1964), *From Mycenae to Homer*, 2nd ed., New York.

Weinfeld, Moshe (1972), *Deuteronomy and the Deuteronomic School*, Oxford.

——(1986), "The Protest Against Imperialism in Ancient Israelite Prophecy," in: S. Eisenstadt (ed.), *The Origins & Diversity of Axial Age Civilizations*, Albany, 169–82.

——(1991), *Deuteronomy 1–11*, New York.

——(1993), *The Promise of the Land: The Inheritance of the Land of Canaan by the Israelites*, Berkeley.

Weippert, Manfred (1971), *The Settlement of the Israelite Tribes in Palestine*, tr. J. D. Martin, London.

Wellhausen, Julius (1878), *Prolegomena to the History of Ancient Israel*, tr. J. S. Black and A. Menzies, Eugene, Or.

—— (1887), *Reste arabischen Heidentums,* Berlin.

—— (1927), *Prolegomena zur Geschichte Israels,* Berlin.

West, Martin L. (1971), *Early Greek Philosophy and the Orient,* Oxford.

—— (1985), *The Hesiodic Catalogue of Women: Its Nature, Structure, and Origins,* Oxford.

—— (1997a), *The East Face of Helicon: West Asiatic Elements in Greek Poetry and Myth,* Oxford.

—— (1997b), [Review: *Israel and Hellas,* by J. P. Brown], *CR* 47.1: 111–12.

—— (2000), "Ancient Near Eastern Myths in Classical Greek Religious Thought," *CANE* I/II: 33–42.

—— (2002), "'Eumelos': A Corinthian Epic Cycle?" *JHSt* 122: 109–33.

West, Martin L. (ed. and commentary) (1966), *Hesiod. Theogony,* Oxford.

—— (1978), *Hesiod. Works & Days,* Oxford.

West, Martin L. (ed. and tr.) (2003), *Greek Epic Fragments,* Cambridge, Mass.

West, R. H. (1952), "Milton's 'Giant Angels'," *MLN* 67.1: 21–23.

Westbrook, Raymond (2009), *Law from the Tigris to the Tiber: The Writings of Raymond Westbrook,* 2 vols., B. Wells and F. R. Magdalene (eds.), Winona Lake, Ind.

Westbrook, Raymond (ed.) (2003), *A History of Ancient Near Eastern Law,* 2 vols., Leiden.

Westenholz, Joan Goodnick (1983), "Heroes of Akkad," *JAOS* 103.1: 327–36.

Westermann, Claus (1984), *Genesis 1-11,* tr. J. J. Scullion, Minneapolis.

—— (1995), *Genesis 12-36,* tr. J. J. Scullion, Minneapolis.

White, David Gordon (2000), "The Scholar as Mythographer: Comparative Indo-European Myth and Postmodern Concerns," in: K. C. Patton and B. C. Ray (eds.), *A Magic Still Dwells: Comparative Religion in the Postmodern Age,* Berkeley, 47–54.

White, Stephen (2001), "Io's World: Intimations of Theodicy in Prometheus Bound," *JHSt* 121: 107–40.

Whitley, James (1988), "Early States and Hero Cults: A Re-Appraisal," *JHSt* 108: 173–82.

—— (1991), "Social Diversity in Dark Age Greece," *ABSA* 86: 341–65.

—— (1994), "The Monuments That Stood Before Marathon: Tomb Cult and Hero Cult in Archaic Attica," *AJA* 98.2: 213–30.

Wifall, Walter (1975), "Gen. 6:1–4—A Royal Davidic Myth?" *BTB* 5: 294–301.

Wilamowitz-Moellendorff, Ulrich v. (1928), *Hesiodos Erga,* Berlin.

Wildberger, Hans (1991), *Isaiah 1-12,* tr. T. H. Trapp, Minneapolis.

—— (1997), *Isaiah 13-27,* tr. T. H. Trapp, Minneapolis.

Willesen, Folker (1958a), "The Philistine Corps of the Scimitar from Gath," *JSS* 3.4: 327–35.

——(1958b), "The Yālīd in Hebrew Society," *ST* 12: 192–210.

Williams, Ronald J. (2007), *Williams' Hebrew Syntax*, 3rd ed., rev. and expanded by J. C. Beckman, Toronto.

Wilson, John R. (1986), "The Gilgamesh Epic and the Iliad," *EMC* 30.5: 25–41.

Winter, Irene (1995), "Homer's Phoenicians: History, Ethnography, or Literary Trope? [A Perspective on Early Orientalism]," in: J. B. Carter and S. P. Morris (eds.), *The Ages of Homer: A Tribute to Emily Townsend Vermeule*, Austin, 247–71.

——(1996), "Sex, Rhetoric, and the Public Monument: The Alluring Body of Naram-Sîn of Agade," in: N. Kampen (ed.), *Sexuality in Ancient Art: Near East, Egypt, Greece and Italy*, Cambirdge, 11–26.

——(2004), "The Conquest of Space in Time: Three Suns on the Victory Stele of Naram-Sin," in: J. G. Dercksen (ed.), *Assyria and Beyond: Studies Presented to Mogens Trolle Larsen*, Leiden, 607–28.

——(2010), *On Art in the Ancient Near East*, 2 vols., Leiden.

Winterson, Jeanette (1996), *Sexing the Cherry*, New York.

Wirth, Hermann (1921), *Homer und Babylon*, Freiburg.

Witte, Markus, and Stefan Alkier (eds.) (2003), *Die Griechen und der Vordere Orient: Beiträge zum Kultur- und Religionskontakt zwischen Griechenland und dem Vordere Orient im 1. Jahrtausend v. Chr.*, Fribourg.

Wolf, Eric R. (1967), "Understanding Civilizations: A Review Article," *CSSH* 9.4: 446–65.

Wolff, Hope Nash (1969), "Gilgamesh, Enkidu, and the Heroic Life," *JAOS* 89.2: 392–98.

Wolters, Al (1988), "Proverbs XXXI 10–31 as Heroic Hymn: A Form-Critical Analysis," *VT* 38.4: 446–57.

Wood, Christopher S. (2008), *Forgery, Replica, Fiction: Temporalities of German Renaissance Art*, Chicago.

Woodard, Roger D. (1997), *Greek Writing from Knossos to Homer: A Linguistic Interpretation of the Origin of the Greek Alphabet and the Continuity of Ancient Greek Literacy*, New York.

Wrenn, C. L. (1973), *Beowulf. With the Finnesburg Fragment*, 3rd ed. rev. W. F. Bolton. London.

Wright, George E. (1938), "Troglodytes and Giants in Palestine," *JBL* 57.3: 305–09.

Wright, Jacob L. (2011), "Making a Name for Oneself: Martial Valor, Heroic Death, and Procreation in the Hebrew Bible," *JSOT* 36.2: 131–61.

Wyatt, Nicholas (2005), "'Water, Water Everywhere…': Musings on the Aqueous Myths of the Near East," in: N. Wyatt, *The Mythic Mind: Essays on Cosmology and Religion in Ugaritic and Old Testament Literature*, London, 189–237.

——(2010), "A la Recherche de Rephaïm Perdus," in: N. Wyatt, *The Archaeology of Myth: Papers in Old Testament Tradition*, London, 69–95.

Yadin, Azzan (2004), "Goliath's Armor and Israelite Collective Memory," *VT* 54.3: 374–95.

Yadin, Yigael (1963), *The Art of Warfare in Biblical Lands, in the Light of Archaeological Study*, 2 vols., tr. M. Pearlman, New York.

——(1991), "'And Dan, Why Did He Remain in Ships?' (Judges 5:17)," in: F. Greenspahn (ed.), *Essential Papers on Israel and the Ancient Near East*, New York, 294–310.

Ziegler, Joseph (ed.) (1952), *Ezechiel*, Septuaginta, Vetus Testamentum Graecum, vol. 16 part 1, Göttingen.

Zimmerli, Walther (1983), *Ezekiel 2. A Commentary on the Book of the Prophet Ezekiel Chapters 25-48*, tr. J. D. Martin, Philadelphia.

Zorn, Jeffrey R. (2010), "Reconsidering Goliath: An Iron Age I Philistine Chariot Warrior," *BASOR* 360: 1–23.

Zuckermann, Bruce (2010), "Review of *The Invention of Hebrew*, by Seth Sanders," presentation at the Society of Biblical Literature Annual Meeting, Atlanta.

Index of Subjects

Index of Selected Ancient Sources